· LIfE ·
STYLE

·LIfE·

STYLE

YOUR SURROUNDINGS AND
HOW THEY AFFECT YOU

Edited by Dr. Peter Marsh

RD
PRESS

CONTRIBUTORS

VOLUME EDITOR

Dr Peter Marsh
Senior Lecturer in Psychology, Oxford Polytechnic, UK

DISTINGUISHED CONSULTANTS

Paul Oliver
Lecturer and writer on art and architecture, Woodstock, UK

Dr Harold M Proshansky
President, Graduate School and University Center, University of New York, USA

ADVISORY EDITORS

Psychology

Dr Roger Lamb
Research Officer and Tutor, Department of Experimental Psychology, University of Oxford, UK

Architecture

Ian Latham
Co-editor, *Architecture Today*, UK

KEY TO AUTHORS

AA **Alan Alcock**
Senior Lecturer in Architecture and Urban Design, School of Architecture, Oxford Polytechnic, UK

AC **Dr Arza Churchman**
Associate Professor, Faculty of Architecture and Town Planning, Technion-Israel Institute of Technology, Israel

BBB **Dr Barbara B Brown**
Assistant Professor of Family and Consumer Studies, University of Utah, USA

BM **Dr Byron Mikellides**
Senior Lecturer in Psychology Applied to Architecture, Architectural Psychology Laboratory and Colour Research Section, School of Architecture, Oxford Polytechnic, UK

CW **Professor Carol Werner**
Professor of Psychology, University of Utah, USA

CWd **Colin Ward**
Author, Suffolk, UK

DC **Professor David Canter**
Professor of Psychology, University of Surrey, UK

DS **Dr David Stuart**
Writer and garden designer, Dunbar, UK

IA **Professor Irwin Altman**
Distinguished Professor of Psychology and Professor of Family and Consumer Studies, University of Utah, USA

JFB **Jeff Bishop**
Environmental Consultant, Bishop Davison O'Rourke, Bristol, UK

JRB **Dr John Blunden**
Reader in Geography, The Open University, UK

KC **Karen Christensen**
Writer on environmental issues, London, UK

MF **Professor Marcus Felson**
Senior Research Associate, Social Science Research Institute, University of Southern California, Los Angeles, USA

MHB **Dr Michael H Banks**
MRC/ESRC Social and Applied Psychology Unit, Department of Psychology, University of Sheffield, UK

PBH **Paul B Harris**
Department of Psychology, University of Utah, USA

PLP **Dr Philip L Pearce**
Senior Lecturer in Psychology, Department of Behavioural Science, James Cook University, Townsville, Queensland, Australia

PM **Dr Peter Marsh**
Senior Lecturer in Psychology, Oxford Polytechnic, UK

RAM **Dr Roger A Mugford**
Animal Psychologist, Chertsey, UK

RF **Professor Robin Fox**
University Professor of Social Theory, Rutgers University, New Jersey, USA

RH **Dr Richard S Hayward**
Deputy Head, School of Architecture, Oxford Polytechnic, UK

RL **Dr Roger Lamb**
Research Officer and Tutor, Department of Experimental Psychology, University of Oxford, UK

RS **Dr Rachel Sebba**
Senior Lecturer, Faculty of Architecture and Town Planning, Technion-Israel Institute of Technology, Israel

SG **Dr Sue Glyptis**
Director of Studies, Recreation and Management Studies, Department of Physical Education and Sports Science, Loughborough University, UK

TP **Tom Porter**
Senior Lecturer in Graphics and Design, Oxford School of Architecture, Oxford Polytechnic, UK

TW **Teresa Wood**
Department of Psychology, Oxford Polytechnic, UK

ASSISTANT TO PETER MARSH
Kate Fox Kibby

PROJECT EDITOR
Sally Carpenter

TEXT

Assistant project editor
Joanne Lightfoot

Editors
Paul Barnett
Stephanie Boxall
Michael March
Pamela Mayo
Mary Melling
Wendy Neale
Justin Pearce
Vivienne Richardson

Indexer
Fiona Barr

Typesetting
Reina Foster-de Wit

PICTURES

Research coordinator
Thérèse Maitland

Research assistant
Nicola Whale

Researchers
Celia Dearing
Kathy Lockley
Linda Proud
Suzanne Williams

ART

Art editor
Chris Munday

Designer
Martin Anderson

Additional layout designer
Kevin Hinton

Artists
Martin Cox
Simon Driver
Mary Ann Le May

SERIES EDITOR
Stuart McCready

First published in Australia in 1990 by RD Press, a registered business name of Reader's Digest (Australia) Pty Limited (Inc. in NSW) 26-32 Waterloo Street, Surry Hills, NSW 2010

 Devised and produced by Andromeda Oxford Ltd Dorchester-on-Thames Oxford OX9 8JU, UK

Copyright © 1990
Andromeda Oxford Ltd

The National Library of Australia
Cataloguing-in-Publication data
Lifestyle: your surroundings and how they affect you, the complete illustrated guide.

Bibliography
Includes indexes.
ISBN 0 86438 105 0.

1. Environmental psychology. 2. Man – Influence of environment. 3. Human ecology.
I. Marsh, Peter
155.9'1

Originated by Scantrans, Singapore

Printed and bound in Spain by Graficas Velasco Torerias SA Madrid

CONTENTS

Introduction 6
Subject Guides 8
Preview Guides 12

PART 1

1 **The Home as Territory** *18*
2 **Needing a Home** *24*
3 **Choosing a Home** *32*
4 **Managing Privacy** *38*
5 **Personal Home Style** *46*
6 **Objects on Display** *56*
7 **Color in the Home** *60*
8 **The Effects of Light** *70*
9 **Touch, Sound and Smell** *74*
10 **Design for Leisure** *78*
11 **Eating and Entertaining** *84*
12 **Cars** *90*
13 **The Pets People Choose** *98*
14 **Garden Effects** *108*
15 **Living Together** *118*
16 **The Changing Home** *122*

17 **A Sense of Place** *132*
18 **Neighborhoods** *140*
19 **Out in the City** *148*
20 **Coping With Urban Life** *154*
21 **Scenes of Crime** *162*
22 **Country Living** *170*
23 **Color Outside the Home** *180*
24 **The Workplace** *190*
25 **Places for Learning** *202*
26 **Going Shopping** *210*
27 **Eating Out** *218*
28 **Vacationing** *226*
29 **Places for Recreation** *236*
30 **A Green Environment?** *244*

PART 2

Further Reading
and Sources 248
Acknowledgments 252
Index 254

THE KIND OF HOME we choose and the way in which we tailor it to suit our needs and personal characteristics is a public testament of our lifestyle. This is very evident in the case of the inhabitants of Beverly Hills, with their "designer" mansions, manicured lawns and the compulsory pools, jacuzzis, terraces and sundecks. It is equally true, however, of those of us who live in more modest row houses, city apartments, suburban dwellings or country cottages. A house, in itself, is not a home. A true sense of home, and the security that comes with it, is created by our expressive activity – our personal stamp.

Through our personal involvement we shape the immediate environments that we inhabit. Equally, our lives are influenced every minute of the day by the places in which we live, work and take our leisure. Those of us who live in cities or major urban areas cannot fail to be affected by the hustle and bustle that is an essential ingredient of these physical spaces. Some love it, others hate it, some tolerate it. But nobody is unaffected by it. Different, but equally powerful forces, shape the lives of those of us who live in rural environments. Here the pace of life may be slower – with less street crime and a more personal concern for neighbors. Some people, however, may feel restricted by the lack of facilities in the country, and the sense of peace, which many city-dwellers nostalgically yearn for, may turn out to be enervating.

Lifestyle examines the forces that shape our lives in both the immediate context of the home and the wider environments in which our homes are located. By understanding these influences we can not only deal more effectively with the pressures that derive from them; we can also turn them to our advantage. Rather than being passive victims of our physical surroundings, we can develop lifestyles that will enable us to relate to our environments in a much more fulfilling way.

We can see this process happening every day. A dull, anonymous house, in a row of identical buildings, is turned into a personal statement by its occupants. Perhaps it acquires a red door, window boxes with flowers and herbs and a brass mail box. Now it announces to the world that this is a home which somebody cares about very deeply and that it is inhabited by a person or family who rely on such involvement to establish their own sense of place. Inside the house lengthy discussions may have taken place concerning the precise color in which to paint the hall, or the style of sofa that would most suit the relatively cramped confines of the living room. The appearance of every wall, corner and decorative feature of this modest "nest" will be the result of the creative intentions of its occupants, and this investment of time and thought will, in turn, radically alter their lives. Impersonal spaces become personal territory, fulfilling one of the most basic of human drives. Without a sense of home "turf" we cannot function as truly social individuals. If we are to grow and develop personally, and establish satisfactory relationships, our basic territorial needs must be satisfied.

The first part of *Lifestyle* looks at territoriality in its many guises and examines the ways in which we can create an appropriate sense of place and home for ourselves. What are our needs for privacy, and how can these be satisfied while still giving us opportunities for social interaction? How can we use color and light to create the most appropriate settings for relaxation, stimulation, work or recreation? Why do we put objects on display? Why do we have pets? What is our car really for? How can we link our homes to the neighborhood through yards and gardens? Are communal housing schemes a realistic alternative to traditional homes?

These are not merely academic questions, although many of the contributors are leading figures in their disciplines. They are issues which directly affect the lives we all lead and which we need to understand if we are to make the most of our home life. It is often said that the family that plays together is the one that stays together. So how can we use leisure in the home more effectively to increase family bonds? By understanding the value of food sharing we might also come to see that mealtimes at home have more than a simple function of providing sustenance.

The second part of *Lifestyle* explores the ways in which we relate to our wider environments. As well as considering the problems of living in cities, with the associated levels of stress and crime, the contributors also emphasize the positive aspects that are there for the taking. How does a sense of neighborhood develop, and what part can we play in it? Can we improve our working environments? What should we look for in the places where our children are educated? How can we minimize environmental stress? What alternatives does the countryside offer us? And are problems of global pollution a matter for governments to deal with or can we, as individuals, contribute to their solution?

Lifestyle does not offer simple solutions to these problems. It does, however, open up opportunities for individual action and change through a fuller understanding of the ways in which we are influenced by our surroundings. If we can find one way of making our homes or offices more psychologically rewarding, if we can see one way of planning our lives to make greater use of the resources that exist in our neighborhoods, or if we walk down a familiar street with a heightened awareness of the shapes, textures and colors that surround us, then this book will have achieved its goal.

Peter Marsh

SUBJECT GUIDE TO PART 1
At Home

USE this alphabetical guide to find the main subjects in Part One, *At Home*. A single reference is given for each, indicating the page of its fullest treatment. For a guide to Part Two see page 10. For a wider reference to a subject and for a more extensive list of subjects, see the index at the end of the book.

Animals in domestic settings 98
Burglary 28
Cage birds 100
Car cults 96
Cars and personality 92
Cars and sex 94
Cars in your life 90
Cat companionship 104
Childhood home 26
Children and color 68
Children in a community 121
Choice in house moving 36
Co-housing 120

Collecting objects 58
Color for children 68
Color differences 61
Color in the home 60
Color and moods 66
Color and personality 66
Color schemes 67
Communal living 118
Communities and privacy 118
Company cars 92
Control and the home 24
Cooking for others 86
Coping with elderly relations 127
Creating an image with objects 57
Design for leisure 78
Diets 87
Displaying objects 56
Disruption in the home 28
Dog ownership 100
Driving at speed 95
Elderly people in a community 121

Electronic media in the home 22
Entertaining 84
Environmental noises 75
Environmentally friendly houses 129
Evocative smells 74
Façade signals 48
Family relations 41
Family rules and privacy 40
Fashions in food 87
Features of color 60
Food etiquette 88
Food rituals 84
Frequency of redecoration 50
Functions of the home 122
Gardening personality types 108
Gardening as therapy 112
Gardens 108
Gender and house design 122
Gifts 59
Group identity in home styles 54
Grouping of houses 35

Growing your own food 110

Home style 46

Home territory 18

Home-based activities 78

Homelessness 29

Homeliness 36

House selection 32

House styles 34

Houseplants 59

Housing an aging population 126

Hygiene and pets 107

Identity and the home 24

Identity and home style 46

Leisure and home design 78

Lighting and color schemes 64

Lighting and home decoration 70

Lighting effects 70

Location of your house 34

Mealtimes 89

Moods and color 66

Moving in 37

Moving house 32

Need for a home 24

Need for solitude 38

Openness in relationships 38

Organizing your personal space 45

Parenting and privacy needs 42

Personal style in the home 50

Personality and color 66

Pet ownership 98

Pet problems 104

Pets in the city 105

Pets and the environment 107

Privacy for children 42

Privacy needs 38

Psychological benefits of home 24

Psychological needs and pets 100

Public housing 33

Reasons for owning a dog 102

Relocation 31

Responses to noise 75

Rooms and color 61

Rooms for different purposes 80

Satisfaction from your garden 113

Self-expression and your garden 108

Sensual stimuli and the home 74

Signaling intentions 43

Smell and the environment 74

Socializing in the garden 114

Sound and the environment 74

Satisfaction from your garden 113

Tactile sensations 77

Taste and color 66

Technology and the home 123

Territorial aggression on the road 94

Territorial behavior 18

Territorial revolutions 20

Textures 77

Touch and the environment 74

Traditional home styles 54

Uniqueness of home 21

What possessions mean 56

Working from home 124

USE this alphabetical guide to find the main subjects in Part Two, *The Wider Environment*. A single reference is given for each, indicating the page of its fullest treatment. For a guide to Part One see page 8. For a wider reference to a subject and for a more extensive list of subjects, see the index at the end of the book.

Activities and places 136
Airconditioning 194
Alternative agriculture 178
Alternative schools 208
Ambience 142
Anonymity in the city 159
Associations with localities 135
Attitudes to country life 177
Attitudes to neighborhood 147
Business entertaining 224
Car pollution 245
Caring about neighborhoods 146
Children in the country 172
Children's learning places 202
Cities and crime prevention 168
City apathy 158
City life 154
City personalities 155
Classroom environments 205
Color for buildings 180
Color and culture 184
Color in the workplace 188
Community education 209
Community health services 175

Community life 143
Community life in rural areas 172
Commuters in the country 171
Conservation 244
Consumer research 210
Consumers and environment 244
Contact with nature 244
Control of our environment 159
Control of personal space 197
Crime and personal territory 166
Crime prevention 164
Crowding patterns 242
Customer psychology 216
Dating and eating out 223
Desk arrangement 199
Dining out 218
Discovering the city 152
Displays in shops 217
Distance and shared space 196
Drinking habits 224
Eating in a restaurant 218
Eating and role playing 218
Education and school design 203
Environmental protection 244
Factory design 201
Family farming 178
Family holidays 231
Farming population 171
Flexible architecture 198
Foreign food 220
Friendship in the city 159
Global pollution 245

Greenhouse effect 244
Group holidays 232
Holidays 226
Homes vulnerable to crime 163
Identity and locality 139
Learning environments 202
Leisure activities and age 137
Leisure environments 238
Lighting at work 195
Living in the country 170
Location of your office 196
Loneliness in the city 159
Mental maps of the city 150
Natural resources and leisure 240
Neighborhood planning 144
Neighborhoods 140
Noise in the city 156
Noise levels at work 193
Office design 190
Open-plan school design 205
Personal space at work 190
Places with special meaning 132
Planning vacations 230
Pollution in the city 156
Privacy at work 192
Privacy versus security 167
Restaurant decor 222
Rules of a place 137
Rural employment 176
Rural life 170
Rural public services 174
Scenes of crime 162

School design 206

School size and education 204

Self-discovery and holidays 227

Self-service shopping 210

Sense of place 132

Settings that breed crime 168

Shops and neighborhoods 214

Shopping habits 210

Shopping and personal contact 212

Sick Building Syndrome 194

Significant places 132

Souvenirs 235

Sport participation 238

Stress in the city 154

Stress of holidays 228

Teenagers in the country 173

Tourism and the environment 234

Traditional associations of color 184

Traveling for new experiences 232

Urban landscapes 150

Urban planning 160

Urban recreation 242

Urban stress 158

Victims of crime 162

Visual cues in the city 148

Vulnerability to crime 162

Wall decorations 187

Waste control 244

Working environments 200

Working with new technology 193

Workplace and job satisfaction 190

Workplace and temperature 196

11

Every family's home is their castle. When we are at home, a complex system of **territorial** rights, fortifies us against the outside world. We exercise more control over our lives at home than anywhere else.

TURN TO PAGE **18**

The **objects** in your house tell your personal story. Ornaments, paintings, books and furniture – what do they reveal about your personality and values? What social status do they claim on your behalf?

TURN TO PAGE **56**

Our **need for a home** is crucial to every stage of our development. The family home provides children with the experiences that shape them into adults. Later, their own home fulfills their need to express their personality.

TURN TO PAGE **24**

Understanding how **color** works in the home can change your approach to decoration. How does the color of a room affect its shape, size and atmosphere? Do the colors around you have any influence on your mood?

TURN TO PAGE **60**

What do we really mean by a "home"? How much freedom of **choice** do we really have when looking for somewhere new to live? Our decisions are affected by many factors, and we are not always aware of them.

TURN TO PAGE **32**

Lighting creates the mood in your home. Lights have a marked effect on your color scheme. Often, we do not take enough care to match lighting to the function of the room. Changing lights can transform your home.

TURN TO PAGE **70**

Managing **privacy** effectively is crucial to your relationships with others. Does the organization of your home allow you the privacy you need? How well do you read the signals of other family members when they need privacy?

TURN TO PAGE **38**

All of our **senses** contribute to our feeling of being at home. Touch, sound and even smell are important when we are looking for somewhere to live. We use them to personalize our environment in diverse and subtle ways.

TURN TO PAGE **74**

12

How does your home express your **identity**? Homes announce who we are and what we are like. Façades are a public face that we turn toward the world. Indoors, we reveal our personalities in detail.

TURN TO PAGE **46**

The home is by far our most important **leisure** facility. We spend most of our time there, and three-quarters of our leisure activities are home-based. Most homes have an unused potential to serve our leisure needs better.

TURN TO PAGE **78**

*What we **eat**, how and where are mainly questions of social ritual, not nutrition. Meals are a fundamental form of sharing. How we entertain guests is crucial to their impression of how much they matter to us.*

TURN TO PAGE **84**

*What does your style of **gardening** reveal about you? It is one of your most public vehicles of self-expression. It tells people not only how you feel about your neighborhood but also how you feel about yourself.*

TURN TO PAGE **108**

*Why does your **car** matter so much? The family car and its garage dominate the fronts of our houses. We spend as much on cars as we invest in our homes. For many people, it would be less expensive to use a taxi.*

TURN TO PAGE **90**

*Would a **"co-housing"** lifestyle appeal to you? Provided that privacy needs are met, the rewards of living with other people include fun, variety, emotional support and a kinder set of demands on the environment.*

TURN TO PAGE **118**

*Do we choose the **pets** we keep in our homes, or do they choose us? The animals we have domesticated as household pets developed social lives in the wild that already suited them to be willing companions of human beings.*

TURN TO PAGE **98**

*Technological and social **changes**, as well as changing time of life, affect your personal home style. New trends in family life have affected house design. We now have the option of buying low-maintenance, low-energy homes.*

TURN TO PAGE **122**

13

PREVIEW GUIDE TO PART 2
The Wider Environment

Places that make up the environment we notice and care about have special meanings for us. The parts of the world around us that make an impression on us stir associations with places and things we have already experienced.

TURN TO PAGE **132**

Do you long for a home in the **country**? Your image of the good life might be out of date. Commuters are moving in and farmers are moving out. What is happening to the rural idyll? Is life in the country really for you?

TURN TO PAGE **170**

Your choice of **neighborhood** may reflect aspects of your personality. Why is it that only some people identify strongly with their neighborhoods? Do we mold neighborhoods, or do they mold us?

TURN TO PAGE **140**

Color is all around you. Do you like what you see? Would you like to see more? The more we take part in **coloring our environment**, the better we feel. Color gives us identity and a sense of place.

TURN TO PAGE **180**

What are the signals that enable us to read the **city**? How do we react to the fact that everywhere is beginning to look like everywhere else? When we move from place to place we use subconscious techniques to find our way.

TURN TO PAGE **148**

Did you have a good day at the office? If you do not feel happy in your **workplace**, your company may not be making the most of your potential. Employees who like their environment enjoy greater job satisfaction.

TURN TO PAGE **190**

Are you exhilarated or stressed by **city life**? Crowding, pollution and noise cause mental and physical stress. How should we cope with stressors like these? What can planners do to minimize them in the future?

TURN TO PAGE **154**

What does it matter where a child is taught? The most important variable in **education** is the teacher's skill, but the physical environment can help to make it easier for teachers to teach and for students to learn.

TURN TO PAGE **202**

How vulnerable is your neighborhood to **crime**? Do the roads provide easy access and escape for housebreakers? Are your neighbors at home during the day? Can they clearly see and hear what is going on?

TURN TO PAGE **162**

The places where you **shop** can shape your behavior and affect your lifestyle. Are you being unconsciously manipulated by well-planned stores and shopping centers? Or are you exercising your own choice?

TURN TO PAGE **210**

Are you **dining out** tonight? Do you do so often? Why do people choose to dress up and leave their home comforts to go out in possibly inclement weather for a meal that may be no better than they could prepare themselves?

TURN TO PAGE **218**

We get out of the house for 40 percent of our leisure. Where we go and how well we like it depend in part on available facilities and the success of their design. The environment both suffers and benefits from **outdoor leisure.**

TURN TO PAGE **236**

What is the right **vacation** spot for you? The choice of places to go is immense, but we often overlook sound basic principles when deciding between them. Have you tried to match your destination with your expectations?

TURN TO PAGE **226**

Your present **lifestyle** could pose a threat to the quality of your life. How does the way you live now affect the natural environment? What can you do to make a more positive contribution to sustaining a healthy planet?

TURN TO PAGE **244**

1

AT HOME

PART ONE

The Home as Territory

OUR HOME is our patch, our territory. Both physically and psychologically distinct from the outside world and the homes of other people, it is uniquely meaningful to us. In our home we expect to exercise the kind of control that we do not have at the workplace or in our wider environment.

An itinerant gunslinger in a famous Western once described home as "where I hang my hat," but for most of us who live settled lives it is more than just bricks and mortar or a place to live. Our home may stand alongside or even be adjoined to neighboring homes, but symbolically it divides the world into what is ours and what lies beyond. It gives us territorial rights over part of our environment.

This does not, however, mean that we need behave as if we were only concerned with ourselves. Human territorial behavior is more than a matter of fulfilling our immediate personal needs; it also entails a recognition of other people's right to exist and provides us with realistic expectations about the degree of control we can exercise both in the home and away from it. For example, someone who expects to be served first at the dinner table in their own home would probably be content nevertheless to wait their turn along with the other clients in a restaurant. An understanding of what is and is not acceptable outside the home is important in maintaining social cohesiveness.

Controlling our territory

Territorial behavior in human beings is complex. It involves people's relationships both with their environment and with other people. A hermit who erects a "keep out" sign on his land and chases away intruders is behaving territorially, as are a married couple who assiduously observe the "his" and "hers" embroidered on their bath towels and would never venture to hang up their clothes in their partner's closet rather than their own.

▶ **Putting down roots** might be one way of describing making a home. But not in the case of this tree house which had to be moved because the land in which the tree was growing changed hands. John Kendall Thurston, with permission from the farmer who leased the land, lived and received his mail at Root 1, Tree 1, Branford, Florida, for four years but when the farmer died, the new landowner wanted him to leave.

Only among humans are social systems complex enough to cope with divisions of territorial rights such as those agreed by a landlord and a tenant. Territorial rights are not simply a matter of ownership — you would ordinarily not expect to have to cope with a landlord who let himself into your apartment without an invitation, who intruded on your privacy, or expected to be consulted about who your guests will be.

As your primary territory, your home is probably the place where you have more decision-making power than anywhere else.

Every family's home is their castle ■ When we are at home, a complex system of territorial rights fortifies us against the outside world ■ We exercise more control over our lives at home than anywhere else.

Essentially, territorial behavior is about control within an area – who is exercising it, in what way and how that message is being communicated. Control can take many forms and operate at many levels – from minimal to total. A couple renting a one-room apartment will generally exercise joint – if not necessarily equal – control over how they use their living space, or the relationship may soon founder. However, if they fail to keep up with the rent payments, the landlords may demonstrate the legal control they have over the territory by evicting them. If you habitually park on the street outside your house, and your neighbors acknowledge your right to do so, you are exercising control over that space. Territorial control by custom and practice – whether parking the car, or always using the same cue at the local pool hall – can be as inhibiting as legal boundaries to would-be transgressors.

Clearly, we have more territorial control in some of the places we spend our time than in others. How great that control is will depend on a number of factors, such as our status at work (if we are a top manager we will probably have plenty of say in allocating places and spaces to our subordinates), our social position (if we are wealthy and a partygoer, one of the best tables at our favorite night spot might be permanently reserved for us), and cultural or ethnic traditions (such as the greater deference to age that is found in many nonWestern cultures).

Primary and secondary territories

As the place where we usually spend the most time, and to which we normally feel most attached, the home is our primary territory. There, it is we – and our own family – who decide how we behave, who we will admit, what color the walls will be, what sort of food we eat, and generally how we will live our lives. Any arguments between children over play areas in the home will be resolved within the family.

Secondary territories are those that we regularly lay claim to outside the home, either as an individual or as one of a group. They might include, for instance, your office desk or places in neighborhood bars that you frequent with your friends. These shared environments, which exist between the privacy of the home and the purely public domain, have less clearly defined rules of permissible behavior and are potentially more open to conflict over territorial control.

Local services, parks and roads are all examples of public territories. Here, your behavior is governed by social and cultural norms and by constraints that you, as a member of the public, accept as appropriate and reasonable. For instance, people generally respect the fact that public libraries are open only between certain hours and that users should not run about or make a noise inside them. Furthermore, we acknowledge that if we wanted to change the opening hours, complain about conditions in the library or protest about its being sold to a property developer, we would have to make representations to the controlling authorities and the ultimate decision would be theirs.

▲ **Be my guest**. An important distinction between our territorial behavior and that of animals is that we invite outsiders onto our territory. Nevertheless, it is important to us that the proper relationship between guest and host is observed.

TERRITORIAL REVOLUTIONS

■ *Unlike the rest of the animal kingdom, humans developed a form of social organization in which individual survival depended not on the scattering of the species across the land so that each had enough to live on, but on their coming together in numbers to use the land intensively. Even in the early days of the hunter-gatherers, when in our search for food and the building of shelters we differed little from animals, our territorial behavior was unique in that we admitted guests to our homes.*

With the agricultural revolution, we began to water and work the land, forming larger social groups and permanent settlements. For the first time, we began, through our labor, to invest in our territory rather than just drawing resources from it. We built strong, solid houses and erected boundaries to indicate who was entitled to extract food from which area. Through irrigation and cultivation of the land we could look beyond the immediate to the future and, freed from the worries of day-to-day survival, we developed culturally, promoting the growth of the arts and sciences.

The industrial revolution severed many people's link with the land and the rural community, herding them into urban factories and turning them into wage-earners. Within the towns, population densities increased as mass production by machinery replaced handicrafts and cottage industry. The division of labor and the separation of the home from the workplace drastically changed territorial behavior, compartmentalizing our lives and creating the impersonal relations found in today's big cities. The information revolution of the late 20th century that began with the microcomputer may yet prove to be no less a milestone in human development than the earlier revolutions, and may have just as strong an impact on our territorial behavior.

In general, when we move through the home range – from primary to secondary to public territories – our behavior may undergo changes. As the size of the territory, or the social group that uses it, increases, so the cohesiveness of the group may tend to decline along with our attachment to it – whether by kinship, friendship or other emotional ties. At the same time, our control over the territory is reduced as more constraints are imposed from outside to ensure that our behavior will not encroach on the rights of others. Social and legal restrictions in the public domain replace the unspoken understandings and tacit agreements that govern relations within the family, between friends and among smaller groups.

Even at the public level, however, there is a broad consensus based on social convention and shared moral values as to what constitutes acceptable behavior. This is a vital part of the territorial mechanism that enables us to coexist with others in our modern, densely populated societies. Although it sometimes breaks down, as, for example, in the case of gangs of youths who behave in an antisocial way, society would soon collapse into chaos without it.

Every home is unique

Despite the social values that you or your family may have in common with many other people, your home will have certain characteristics that make it distinctive. In the first place, it is the most basic primary territory – we are unlikely to have others (such as a store or private office) where we have maximum control. We admit or refuse entry to the home as it suits us, unlike a store, which is open to the gen-eral public at certain times and where refusal of service or admission would be exceptional. (Even the stately homes of Britain that are open to the public but still inhabited by their owners have private quarters that are permanently closed off and inaccessible to visitors.)

Against the background of the modern city, the home is arguably more important today that it has ever been. Although we rely heavily on contact with the outside world for our livelihood and the provision of basic services such as health and education, the home is an essential sanctuary for the family. Unlike a small village community, where everybody knows everybody else, in the city, wherever you go – on the subway to and from work, in the supermarket, at the sports stadium – you come into contact with thousands of strangers. Every day, we are forced to share time and space with people with whom we may have little in common beyond our situation, some of whom are culturally different from us and may not even speak the same language. Not surprisingly, the quality of relationships in the city is a source of concern to social scientists, law-enforcement agencies and others.

The feeling of alienation from a world that, individually, we can do little to influence, makes our need for a home, where we do have control and the opportunity to take initiatives of our own, vital to our psychological well-being. Indeed, while many of the activities that take place in the home – washing, cooking and so on – might be done better and possibly less expensively outside it, we continue to perform them at home because there we can control how, when or even whether we do them.

The control that we have in the home takes many forms. It

▶ **Marking out your territory with color.** *The people who live in these canalside houses in Italy have chosen a striking way of delineating their territorial boundaries. The exterior decor of each of these properties sends a clear message – here is a distinct place, where a distinct occupant exercises rights of possession, and expresses more freely than anywhere else in the world a distinct personality.*

implies security – physical as well as psychological. It also provides continuity: you have your own routine at home and are less likely to be surprised or upset by what happens there. It can offer comfort: you are free to put your feet up or open a bottle of wine without worrying about what outsiders might say or think. It provides opportunities for freedom of expression – whether the freedom to speak Spanish, bring up your children in a particular faith or try your hand at home decorating – and is in many ways a statement of your personality and character. Finally it provides a sense of belonging, being in the company of people who are near and dear to you and who value you for yourself, not because you are a customer or are in a position to promote them.

Whereas the home was once primarily a shelter from the physical climate and from wild animals, it has become a shelter from the excesses of the social and cultural climate and from other people. Its purpose is not only to keep us warm and safe, but also to protect our personalities, values and beliefs. Although cultural and social norms affect what we do in the home, our behavior there is usually less inhibited than outside, where we are under social scrutiny and our role and status impose obligations and responsibilities on us. (The obvious exceptions to this are adolescents who feel constrained by parental rules in the home but can express themselves more freely in public places such as discotheques where they can meet their friends, smoke, drink and dance to loud music without incurring the disapproval of their parents.)

Electronic intruders

Over the course of human history, our direct economic dependence on the land has decreased, and our dependence on social institutions has increased. Settlements have become more crowded together and communications have improved immensely.

As a result of improved communications technology, the relationship between home territory and the outside world has been changing. In particular, the need to have personal contact with people outside the home, at work and elsewhere in the course of our everyday lives, has been reduced. Yet, while we are still free to decide on who we will physically admit to our homes, this area of control – for better or worse – is being electronically eroded.

Over the years, the inventions of the telephone, radio and television have provided communication links between the outside world and an increasing number of homes, sometimes bringing uninvited or unwelcome information across the threshold. The latest addition to our electrical and electronic hardware – the personal computer – has the potential to change our lives more dramatically. Futurists say that by

▲ **Electronic technology – a Trojan Horse?** *A family in France, with their backs to the traditional focal point of the home – the fireplace – are captivated by a television program. The radios, television sets and telephones that we install in our homes can undermine our control. Parents may find it difficult to regulate what children see on the television screen. The telephone may be an unwelcome intruder summoning us from what we are doing. Answering machines may help to replace some of our control by screening us from the outside world.*

the 21st century, using computer telecommunication links, not only will we be able to do our shopping and banking without leaving the home, we will even be able to have a medical checkup from a distance.

Instead of contact – however perfunctory – with actual people in the outside world, we will increasingly be interacting with them by means of telecommunications. For the elderly and infirm, and for those who have difficulty leaving the house, this may be a very welcome development. Children might benefit from having a wider choice of information made available to them, especially if they are raised in an atmosphere of strict conformity in which freedom of expression is denied them. For others too, it can have obvious advantages – for example, saving time and energy by removing the need to go to the supermarket or to work. It may also offer valuable educational opportunities for people of all ages.

On the other hand, the computer may be a dangerous intruder on our territory. Already it is often said that children grow up more quickly today than they used to because of their early exposure to sex and violence on television. A home-computer link with the outside world will provide access to a much wider range of, often unauthorized, information, which must increase the danger of exposure to undesirable influences. (For instance, in France even drug-peddlers and prostitutes have been known to advertise on local area networks.) The implication is that the home is losing one of its most central functions as a primary territory – protection of the young.

The advantages of electronic media to adults are similarly double-edged and attitudes toward them are often ambivalent. Telephone answering machines, designed to improve communication by receiving calls in our absence – and presumably installed for that purpose – are increasingly being used by their owners to ward off callers or avoid interruption even when they are at home. Personal telefax machines, serving a similar purpose, are also becoming more popular. Both provide opportunities for what might be seen by some people as territorial behavior at its most defensive, or by others as an effective means of preserving territorial integrity.

Electronic communication can, to some extent, protect us from much of the stressful, superficial contact with people that hectic city life requires, removing our dependence on our immediate surroundings and instead creating a network of relations based on electronic representations of people. However, the long-term implications of these developments for the future of the home, for the quality of our relationships with other people, and for our territorial behavior in general are still unclear. **AC, RS**

23

◀ **Taking possession of a territory**. *When new people move into a new house, they make haste to mark it as their own. Only when they begin to put their possessions on view does the new space start to feel like home. Personal objects are important territorial markers because they reflect an internal world of thoughts, feelings and memories. By representing us in this way they give us a sense of control over our surroundings and make that control clear to other people (see Ch6).*

Needing a Home

A HOME in Western society, normally suggests a very permanent building, perhaps the house you own or a rented apartment. To people of other cultures it might imply a grass hut, a boat or a tent. But in most cultures home is more than just the place where we live. What makes us attach so much importance to our living space that losing or leaving it can be a devastating experience? What are the psychological benefits of having a home?

Why is your home important?

Even if you do not live in a home that you would describe as tidy or well-organized, you know at least, for the most part, what is going on there. Compared with our knowledge of other places that we come into contact with in our lives, at home we are the experts. Often, we know the layout so well that we could probably get around blindfolded if we had to. We know who is likely to be there at any time, and what they will be doing – watching their favorite television show, perhaps, or preparing the evening meal. Also we usually know where we expect to find things – the toothpaste, the detergent or yesterday's newspaper. The home gives us a sense of control and order.

This order and predictability is reinforced by the way we give different functions to the different parts of the home. For example, unless you lived in a one-room apartment, you would not expect to cook in the bedroom or to find anyone else doing so. Unlike the world outside, which is often stressful and chaotic, the home offers familiar routines, comfort and relaxation. Not for nothing do we try to put our guests at ease by inviting them to "Make yourself at home."

We are not forced to invite anyone into our home if we do not want to – our sense of order is partly the result of a feeling that, in contrast to the outside world, we can control what goes on at home. If you want to rearrange the furniture

or teach yourself to play a musical instrument, you can. Home is both the place where we can choose what we do, unrestricted by external constraints, and our personal refuge, the place where we feel most secure.

Identity, control and connection

It is because of these feelings of control, comfort and security that we usually identify more closely with home than with anywhere else. Indeed, it initially helps to shape our identity and later becomes what is in many ways an expression of that identity. During the first few years of a child's life, the home represents most of the known world.

WHY DO YOU NEED A HOME?

■ "Home" is a difficult word to define but we all understand what it means. We know from our own experience or we recognize what it means to others.

"Home" is about everything that concerns us and our family and the relationships that take place there. There are countless things – both physical and psychological – that might mean "home" to you and help to make your home unique.

■ The psychological importance of the home. There are four functions of the home that are vital to our mental well-being: order, control, identity and connection.

To make sense of our lives we all need some kind of order in them. Home is normally the place where we can most easily achieve this.

◆ In the familiar surroundings of the home we are confident and in control. When we step outside our front door, we know that we must take our chances along with everyone else.

◆ Home is home because it is home to us. It is part of us, and without it our identity would be incomplete.

◆ Home is our base, our connection with family and neighbors.

■ The physical importance of the home. Physically, our homes provide us with shelter from the elements and a degree of comfort that perhaps we don't get anywhere else. But these are also vital to our psychological well-being. It is very difficult to separate the physical and psychological importance of home.

▲ At home in the ice. Even the temporary home of a nomad, such as this igloo, is more than just a shelter. Our homes express our identity – for example, through the way they reflect the traditions of our culture. In our homes, we are in control – we know where everything is, who is likely to be there, and the sort of things they might be doing.

Our need for a home is crucial to every stage of our development ■ The family home provides children with the experiences that shape them into adults ■ Later, their own home fulfills their need to express their personality ■ The home gives us a sense of order, control and identity that is vital to our well-being.

It is the place where we learn to walk, talk, explore and coexist with other people. And just as the relationships we enjoy with our family at this early stage are an important influence on what kind of people we become in the future, so too is our home environment.

Moreover, it is in the home that we first learn, through play, to exert control over our lives; this serves as a grounding for our experiences in the outside world. In later life, when we acquire our own home, we tend to change it in ways that reflect our personality. In other words, we want our home to be the way that we want it to be because it is ours and because it is the environment in which we feel most free to express ourselves (see *Ch 5*). We might, for instance, choose to display prominently a painting that we particularly like by hanging it in the living room above the fireplace.

Teenagers, too, though they may have little say in how their parents run the house, often jealously guard what they see as their right to decorate their own room, adorning their walls with pictures of their favorite film stars or pop idols. Likewise, students living on the college campus may put up political posters in their rooms or reproductions of their favorite paintings. Even prisoners sharing cramped living conditions with other inmates in a cell often have photographs of their relatives, or a picture calendar, on the wall above their bunk to personalize their living space.

Furthermore, wall decoration can reinforce the sense of connection that we feel with the environment and with the people we associate with it. The home usually provides the setting in which our most intimate relationships, and our interaction with family and friends, take place. As a result, it becomes linked in our minds with the people we feel emotionally attached to. Most homes display symbols of these connections, whether a wedding photograph, chil-

◄ **Through the eyes of a child** *the world may be almost entirely encompassed by her home. It is where we have our first experiences and where we first learn how to manage our lives and live with other people. The childhood home helps to shape our personalities. When we have our own home, it becomes a place in which we express the personalities that have taken shape.*

WHEN A HOUSE IS NOT A HOME

"This is the true nature of home – it is the place of peace, the shelter, not only from all injury, but from all terror, doubt and division. In so far as it is not this, it is not home; so far as the anxieties of the outer life penetrate into it and the...unloved, or hostile society of the outer world is allowed...to cross the threshold, it ceases to be home; it is then only a part of the outer world which you have roofed over, and lighted a fire in."

JOHN RUSKIN (1819-1900)

dren's artwork on the walls or photographs from last year's holiday. Because of these close emotional ties, home is where we feel we have our roots, the place we always return to because of our strong sense of attachment to it. It is our past and present and represents our hopes and aspirations for the future.

What is home?

Inevitably, our attitudes toward the home do not remain fixed. Circumstances in the home change and our idea of what "home" is also changes. Sometimes changes recur; at other times they are of the once-and-for-all kind. What brings them about are our changing needs. A new baby, for instance, because it needs constant care and attention, will not only cause the routines of family members to alter, it may change the home physically, for example if the study is converted into a nursery. Home and family routines will continue to change as the child grows older. After the children have left home, parents once again have more time and space to themselves and might decide to reconvert the old nursery or playroom to a study.

However, running in parallel with these changes are daily routines in the home that may alter little over many years. Most obviously, these cyclical patterns of behavior include waking in the morning, showering, breakfasting, leaving for work and so on.

Holiday celebrations are a good example of activities that can involve both permanent and cyclical changes within the

▶ **A place for relationships**. *Home is where we make our most important connections with other people – children bond with their parents and siblings and couples make a life together. It is the place where we invite friends and kin, to show them that they matter to us.*

26

EXPLORING YOUR CHILDHOOD HOME

■ *One way to appreciate the home in all its richness and complexity is to try to think back and recall how you experienced it as a child.*

■ *Close your eyes and imagine you are walking around the outside of the house, viewing it from all angles. Now, enter through the front door and make a mind's eye tour of the house, looking in every room and absorbing as much detail as you can. This will give you the overall feel of the place and* *may rekindle old memories associated with some of the rooms. If so, think hard about what happened there before resuming the tour, and see if it triggers further recollections.*

I REMEMBER MY PARENTS' ROOM

It had wallpaper with blue-birds on branches. Big windows let in the sun in the morning. At the foot of the bed was a cedar chest that smelled of mothballs inside...

Sometimes my sister and I would play here, though we were not supposed to.

When I had a nightmare, I would go to my parents' room and climb into the middle of the bed between them. I felt warm and safe there.

■ *When you have finished examining every room and explored your reminiscences to the full, write down as much as you can remember. Include not only descriptions of the rooms,* *but also anything that sprang to mind while you were thinking about them.*

■ *When you examine your record, you will see that it includes not only physical descriptions of your childhood surroundings, but also information about family relationships. As these relationships change over time, you may even find that if you repeat the exercise, you will evoke a whole new series of memories about your childhood home.*

home. Christmas festivities, for instance, are cyclical because they involve certain patterns of behavior that recur on a yearly basis. For many of us Christmas would not be the same without the usual round of visits to and by relatives and friends, exchanging presents and, in most homes, putting up decorations. Moreover, every Christmas, the festive activities are likely to focus on the same parts of the home – usually the living room, with the decorated tree and the presents, as well as easy chairs to relax in, and the dining room, where the family can sit down to enjoy a traditional Christmas dinner. Yet even our holiday periods are made up of events that are unique. In this sense, no two Christmases are alike. Perhaps the children no longer believe in Santa Claus as they did last year, or perhaps they are now living away from home and will be among the visitors, or are abroad and cannot visit.

Just as our ideas about home may change over the years no single aspect can be singled out to define comprehensively what home is. When we think of Christmas, we think of the setting – the rooms with their decorations; we think of the people – our own family, relatives and friends who were present; and we think of the period over which it all happened – when we bought the tree, when we opened the presents. Indeed, many of these aspects are so interrelated in our minds that it is difficult to imagine one without the others. Similarly, it is the decor, the people, what they do and when, that are all important in summing up what we mean by "home."

▲ **Home for Christmas**. *Traditionally, this is a time for bringing the family together, and for many people it sums up what home is all about. The home at* *Christmas time is special – we decorate the house, exchange presents, visit with friends and relatives. Each Christmas is also different from the last –* *family circumstances may change, or feelings or beliefs. Christmas may be as difficult to define for every one of us as home is.*

27

Disruption in the home

Because the home is so central to our lives, we depend on it for our physical and psychological well-being. To lose our home, or even to suffer some violation of it, robs it of some of its meaning and is often a deeply disturbing experience. Indeed, some people never fully recover from it or regain the confidence to believe in the home as they did before.

In law, burglary is a crime against property, and the victim is a victim largely of material loss. In fact, the psychological distress that we feel when the home has been violated often far outweighs any grief over the value of the stolen property. The thought that someone has intruded into your personal space can change the whole meaning of "home" so that it will never feel the same again. It destroys – at least temporarily – the sense of control that you feel you exercise there. Most obviously, the right to admit or refuse entry has been flouted, making us feel vulnerable and perhaps overanxious about the possibility of the same thing happening again. Burglary is an attack on our sense of self, because the home is our personal territory. Some of the items stolen, or – if the house is ransacked – willfully destroyed, may not be worth much as hard cash, but they may be uniquely valuable to us in sentimental terms – a brooch that belonged to Grandmother or a family photograph, for example.

Among the emotions that are commonly felt by burglary victims are anger, fear, sadness and shock. Very often, how upset the victim is – and how far their sense of security has been shaken – corresponds to the physical upset caused by the break-in. If it was violent, with the burglar causing damage in many of the rooms, the effect on the victim is generally worse. Likewise, people whose losses are primarily material rather than personal generally recover from the

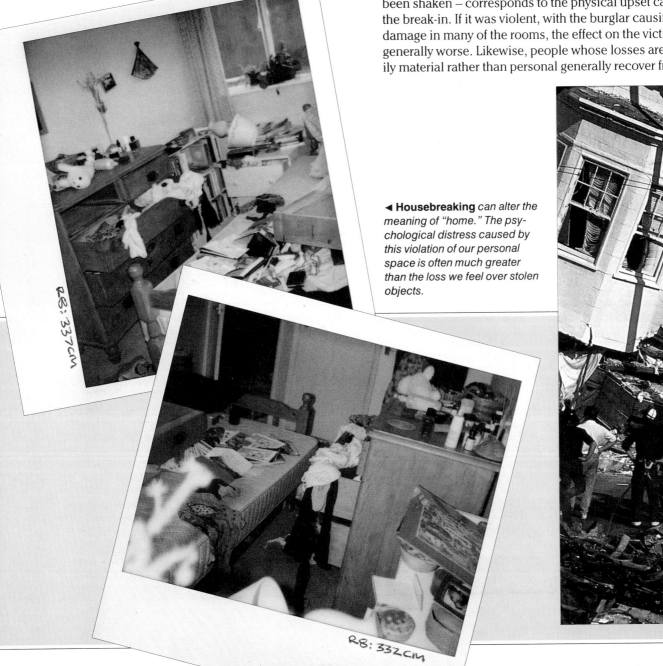

◄ **Housebreaking** *can alter the meaning of "home." The psychological distress caused by this violation of our personal space is often much greater than the loss we feel over stolen objects.*

experience more quickly. Some burglary victims have helped themselves to overcome the crisis by seeking out and talking to others who have suffered similarly. Some respond by installing sophisticated alarm systems. Some do both and yet for many months – or even longer – they are unable to come to terms with what has happened to them.

The trauma of being homeless

Every year, as a result of floods, earthquakes, fires, hurricanes and other disasters, thousands of people around the world find themselves homeless. Very often, the tragedy is made worse by death and injury or the threat of disease. Those who survive are left numb and in a state of shock, psychologically devastated by the disappearance of their home and perhaps of family members who once shared that home with them.

Even if the casualties are few, and immediate steps are taken to provide temporary shelter for the victims, the disruption not only to the home, but also to the neighborhood,

29

◄ **Sudden homelessness.** *Even more devastating than burglary is the loss of your home through a natural disaster like the San Francisco earthquake in 1989 LEFT or the subsidence that threatens to swallow up this mobile home ABOVE. Survivors experience the psychological trauma of losing their home and possibly loved ones too. Grief can still be felt years after the event as well as guilt over having survived. But those who manage to put the event behind them, or even derive some psychological strength from it, show fewer physical and psychological symptoms of stress.*

can affect people deeply. In the aftermath of one disaster, 4,000 flood victims who had seen their own homes washed away were randomly assigned to mobile homes. They experienced disorientation and demoralization that compounded their sense of loss. Families were split up, people from different towns found themselves living near one another, while former neighbors were no longer easily accessible. Consequently, friendships were severed and people tended to become indifferent toward one another, because they had lost their sense of belonging to a community.

Urban homelessness

Homelessness is a social problem that affects not only the developing world but also the wealthier countries of the West. In almost every major city squatter settlements have grown up among poor people compelled to eke out a living and build their makeshift homes from a variety of discarded waste materials. Often, with no running water or sewerage, and with scant protection from the oppressive heat or the

cold, such living conditions are both psychologically and physically destructive.

Some local government authorities have responded to the plight of the homeless by acquiring land for them and providing basic services. Others are less sympathetic, either doing nothing or even bringing in the police to drive them off the land.

Low wages, rising house prices and cutbacks in government subsidies and welfare provision have been blamed for the increase in the numbers of homeless. Whereas formerly most of the residents of the shelters for the homeless were single elderly men, today they are increasingly women and families with children. In the United States families now account for 30 percent of homeless people and in some cities the figure is as high as 50 percent.

Another 30 percent of the homeless in the United States are mental patients who have been discharged from institutions that have been closed or reduced in capacity to save public money. More often, however, homelessness is the cause, not the consequence, of mental disorder. The romantic idea of the "urban nomad" is a fiction – very few people are homeless by choice.

Attempts to assist homeless people in New York City by allowing them to acquire the deeds to abandoned buildings have met with some success. With the support of the government, the church and voluntary labor, they have sometimes been able, by hard work, to turn uninhabitable housing into desirable homes. As a result of this, they are often more satisfied with, and take more pride in, the homes they have worked hard to put together than the residents of government-subsidized housing.

▲ **Tent City interior**. *Even in a squatter settlement, a sense of "home" can be created with personal objects – photographs, mirrors, ornaments (see Ch 6). People are rarely homeless by choice but even if they are forced to relocate, they are likely to be happier in surroundings they have put something of themselves into.*

Coping with homelessness

The survivors of a fire that destroyed their homes and claimed lives described the experience in terms such as "devastating," "a nightmare," "traumatic," "heartbreaking," "tragic." Indeed, some people still feel considerable grief years after such an event, as well as guilt at having survived and a sense of hopelessness.

Others, however, somehow manage to put the incident behind them and perhaps even to derive some psychological or other benefit from the experience. As a result of the help given by friends or relatives when they were recovering from their ordeal, they might, for instance, have learned to value those relationships more. They might feel that their character has been strengthened by coping with adversity, so that they are no longer so upset by minor problems. They might have improved their own self-esteem by realizing how well they coped in stressful circumstances. Whichever is the case, given the right incentives and sufficient human support, people who succeed in extracting something positive from the experience exhibit fewer physical and psychological symptoms of stress in the aftermath.

Voluntary and involuntary relocation

Forced relocation under any circumstances has been shown to be a painful experience. So-called blighted areas have often been targets of redevelopment. In the name of modernization, whole neighborhoods have been demolished to make way for office blocks, sports centers or even new freeway systems.

Even if the displaced residents receive help in finding alternative housing, and manage to move along with their former neighbors, they can rarely recreate the old neighborhood or its atmosphere entirely. Some residents who had been forcibly relocated in this way reported a sense of loss as long as seven years afterward. Although their housing was adequate – and in many cases better than it had been before – they still felt that they had been deprived of their real homes, which to them had fond associations with the physical and social environments of their old neighborhoods. Recent studies of these problems have recommended that planning authorities take more account of social relationships and try to transfer people to an environment that can be adapted to their lifestyle, rather than expect them to adapt to the new environment.

In contrast to forced resettlement, relocating by choice can be an exciting prospect. Moving to a bigger home or to a quieter neighborhood, or because we have got a new job, usually has a positive effect on us. Moreover, because we are in control of our situation, we can look forward to meeting new people and exploring the new environment with confidence and optimism. However, though we may be happier once we are resettled, organizing the move and all the attendant procedures is reckoned to be a highly stressful experience. **BBB, PBH, CW, IA**

◄ **Homeless by choice.** *The West Berliners who opted to camp out by the Berlin Wall – before it was breached in 1989 – did so in pursuit of a cause they felt more strongly about than the comforts of home. Moving one's home can be stressful under any circumstances, but when we exercise choice over where we live we are likely to feel more confident and optimistic.*

THE SOCIAL VALUE OF HOME

■ *The Egyptian Nubians experienced the disruptiveness of relocation after their traditional homes along the Nile had been destroyed by the lake created by the Aswan Dam. Although the government provided new housing that was modern and physically sound, it did not meet the people's social needs.*

Whereas the traditional homes had "mastabas" – bench-like seating areas – near the front door, where residents would daily sit and talk to the neighbors, the new homes had none. Children were forced to play in the dirt, and adults who wanted to maintain social ties had to sit on the ground or on temporary stools. In the original villages, extended families lived in distinct homes in large kin-based compounds. Neighbors were close and enjoyed good relationships that had been built up over many generations. In the new villages, homes were built on long, straight streets and families were assigned to them, not by kin group or their hamlet of origin, but by family size. This caused the complete fragmentation of previous family and social relationships.

Privacy was also a problem in the new homes. The old dwellings had been carefully constructed to prevent neighbors from looking inside each other's homes, but the new homes had front doors and windows that allowed visual access. The homes also lacked the Nubians' traditional painted decorations, which many of the residents added soon after moving in. In fact, many home-owners made major modifications to their government-provided houses. Some even went so far as to build a new dwelling outside the town.

The Nubians' experience shows how people can cope with unsuitable environments, but, at the same time, it highlights the importance of homes for social relationships and a sense of identity.

Choosing a Home

WHAT DO WE mean when we use the expression "choosing a home"? The question might seem obvious, yet most of us do not choose *homes*. Instead, we choose houses or apartments and then make homes out of them. In many ways, we treat houses as short-term commodities, like cars or refrigerators. Furthermore, to some extent our notions of choice are illusory. When we look around for a new home our options are obviously narrowed by factors such as our income. But other, less immediately apparent, factors also play a part, among them our job, social aspirations and our past experiences of homes. In addition, of course, there are the sales pressures put on us by real estate agents.

A house or a home?

For some people, choosing a house is really no more important than choosing a new car. A successful young executive, for example, in order to continue rising in his or her career, may need to move jobs, and hence house, every few years. For such a person the choice is dictated almost entirely by the requirement that it will be readily resalable. Research has consistently shown that such people almost entirely ignore their home-making aspirations until they reach a career plateau. If they redecorate their house, it is with the aim of making it more attractive to potential purchasers. They do not make any alterations or additions, they only rarely "personalize" the house, and usually they do not become involved in neighborhood social life. In other words, they have no homes – only dwelling-places.

This approach can be contrasted with that of, for example, a Malawi household keen to build afresh in order to accommodate new family members. Their choice of location will be affected by strong traditions concerning valued sites, social hierarchies and spiritual connections. The building process will likewise be rooted in tradition. So the new house will become a home – a full part of their lives – long before it has actually been finished. In fact, it may *never* be finished, each subsequent generation contributing to its growth and change.

What do we really want?

One way of finding out what people want in a home is to ask people who are preparing to buy or commission a house which aspects would most appeal to them. There has

"FORCED" MOVES AND "CHOICE" MOVES

■ *There seems to be a split between those who move because they have to and those who move through choice. A typical "forced" move is job-related; a typical "choice" move occurs on retirement.*

There are also moves that some of us would describe as "forced" and others as "choice." An example of this hybrid would be a move linked to job promotion: the physical distance may not be far but the social distance may be considerable. To some people this is something they have to do: a "forced" move. To others it is a welcome bonus and therefore regarded as a "choice," even though they may have little option if they want promotion.

"Forced" movers often feel rushed and less able to explore alternatives. "Choice" movers, however, may well be faced with more choices than they would wish, so that they are forced to think in novel ways about how to live.

▲ **Building a new house,** or buying from an earlier occupant, the process of choosing a home is usually a joint one, but husbands and wives almost always contribute to the choice from different perspectives. Husbands usually consider criteria related to the cost of the property, such as its size and location; wives ensure that factors such as suitability for children and practicality of housekeeping also influence the decision.

What do we really mean by a "home"? ■ *How much freedom of choice do we really have when looking for somewhere new to live?* ■ *Our decisions are affected by many factors, and we are not always aware of them.*

been much research done along these lines, but the results are not very helpful in terms of predicting people's choices. First, people are inhibited by their own preconceptions: what they think they are likely to get and what they have experienced in the past. Second, a pressing urgency – for example, homelessness – may make them select something quite different from their stated preferences. Finally, people's preferences, when analyzed statistically, show that what they say they want often differs from what they choose.

There are several possible explanations for this last discrepancy. The people may, in effect, have had no choice at all: they needed to find a new home quickly in the right area and at the right price. Or perhaps their aspirations were simply unrealistic: it is easy enough to say that you would like a large conservatory, but quite another matter when you are faced with the prospect of paying for it. Advertising or marketing strategies can change people's ideas of what they want. There may also be deadline pressures on people that preclude proper discussion; a curious factor in this respect

is that it is often people who seem to have the greatest ability to choose what they want (for financial or other reasons) who afterward claim that they had no choice at all.

For all of these reasons – and more – there is little relation between people's stated likes (and dislikes) and their eventual choice. Unfortunately, in many countries the provision of public housing is based on analyses of what people say they would like. The matter is further confused by architects, planners and politicians who produce decrees about what they think the rest of us "need" or "ought to have." There is considerable evidence that people often dislike public housing largely because they feel it has been imposed on them. Around the world, there have been a number of extremely successful private housing schemes based on intensive "user involvement" and prior research. In fact, some of these schemes look much like public housing, so clearly the element of choice has great importance. However, the same approach has produced many housing schemes that people strongly dislike. In this context the typical private developer's claim that "We know what people really want so that is what we give them" becomes difficult to defend.

33

◆ Is the home weatherproof and solidly constructed as well as being visually striking?

◆ How near is it to my work, public transport, shopping and other facilities?

◆ Do I want a harbor view if it means tolerating damp air and possibly noise?

◆ Will the striking design prevent me from adding my own personal touches?

◆ Will the unusual look go out of fashion, making my purchase a bad investment?

■ **Complex questions**, *often with contradictory answers, face the buyer of any home. Offered one of these apartments, for example, what considerations about family, work, style and the practicalities of everyday living would your final decision have to resolve?*

The importance of location

Studies suggest that the two fundamental aspects to house selection, the location and the house itself, are often surprisingly unconnected. Some people will talk of choosing their dream house regardless of its surroundings, while others will gladly admit to buying a house they barely like simply because it is in the right area.

One man, when asked how he chose his house, took out a map and immediately dismissed a startling 95 percent of the area shown, saying, "I couldn't possibly live there!" The areas concerned were scarcely known to him, but he had a set of very strong assumptions – perhaps stereotypes – about "the wrong side of the tracks." Similar assumptions are deeply embedded in almost all societies – not just in Western ones – and can have a major influence on house choice. Research has so far failed to explain the origin of these assumptions, but they appear to be related to a wish for certainty and control: the desire to be able to "map" and "place" people gives rise to a need to be able to rank and classify areas. We judge areas according to negative factors such as perceptions of density, vandalism, noise and racial mix, and positive ones like: spaciousness, standard of amenities, greenery and cleanliness. True or false, these judgments are based on a wish to be among people like ourselves or, preferably, one step above ourselves on the social ladder. In general, wider social aspirations have replaced commitment to values passed down from parents.

Of course, there are other, more practical, considerations. These include transport and access to schools, our workplace, the countryside, theaters and so on. Nevertheless, the situation is not nearly as simple as it was a century ago. As a result of increased mobility, for example, many people can now choose to live in places that are desirable – perhaps because they are high-status areas – even if they are not close to these amenities.

Exterior styles

Many people seem to regard the outside of a house much as they would a set of clothes: selected to make the right impact on the right people and to be in fashion (rarely ahead of it). And, as with clothes, fashion in houses runs in cycles – although very different ones. For example, house-styles of different past eras come and go in present-day fashions. However, it is still important to some people that the house does not *look* old; in fact, one research team coined the description "traditional modern."

It seems that some people will always buy new houses, looking on old ones as they might regard secondhand clothes – somehow soiled. Yet they want the old style, so that they have all the status benefits of owning the genuine article but all the management, maintenance and resale-value benefits of a new property. Other people refuse to buy new houses, arguing that they have no character or history, or may not be as solidly built as older houses.

As fashion and style are so important, houses built perhaps a decade ago tend to be marginalized: not for another few decades will their style become popular again. So, rather like cars, houses are either resold fairly quickly or kept for a long time. A big difference between houses and cars is that many people make often quite dramatic changes to their not-so-new house, hoping to push its value up toward that of a new but less well-equipped property.

WHEN A FAMILY MAN RECEIVES PROMOTION	"Should I change my job so that we can stay in our current home?"	"Must move" Start looking quickly	Initial selection of possible areas	Wife and children would prefer to stay put?	Weekend tour; seeking information to select specific areas
	▲	▲	▲		▲
THE BASICS OF CHOICE	Family recently settled into area, schools and so on	Relocation with promotion prospects	Done at a distance (stereotyped assumptions likely)		Husband cannot go midw colleagues and friends of advice; real estate agen indicate prices

■ Not all families have the same reasons for moving to a new home, and neither do they have the same criteria of choice. The flowchart shows how two typical, but very dissimilar, families might go through the decision process.

	Newfound freedom; enjoy traveling together so might as well make a sort of holiday out of it		Near the sea, perhaps, or near family and friends; deciding on the right sorts of areas		Perhaps one partner concentrates on houses' "character," the other on their ease of maintenance for reasons of age, increased importance of closeness to ameniti
	▼		▼		▼
A RETIRED COUPLE MAKE THEIR CHOICE	"Let's move" "Let's stay put" "We can look anywhere"	"Let's stay near where we are"	Look "anywhere"; "Where?"	Focusing:	"An old house?" "A new house?"

How houses should be grouped

The arrangement and grouping of houses can have major effects on our choice. The relative importance of these varies from culture to culture though it is possible to make some generalizations. Density is one factor. We do not like too many houses or people (especially children) cramped together – although in many Latin and Latin American cultures, people strongly prefer a high density. We like a degree of social mixture, but not too much, and certainly not a mixture of owned and rented dwellings. Detached houses have the highest social status, followed by duplexes (semi-detached houses), row houses and finally apartments. (In areas like France and Scandinavia, however, city apartments are often still seen as highly desirable.)

Other concerns relate to new developments. The detailed arrangement and grouping of the houses on a site do not seem to affect people very much, although there is a strong preference for a feeling of spaciousness. This is common to all societies, although other factors may take priority. Then there is the size of the development: if there are more than about 25 houses we are less likely to want to live there. There is now a strong prejudice against large developments, especially in previously green spaces. (In third-world countries the converse can be true: because urban living is widely regarded as desirable, a large development may be preferred.) Between and within cultures the desirability, use and value of a garden vary. If buyers want a well-stocked garden, this can cause problems because new houses cannot have mature gardens. Some market analysts, however, suggest that prestocked and easily maintained gardens may boost the sales of new houses.

Personalized interiors

The inside of a house usually comes last in the process of choosing a home, and it is at the final stage in our decision-making process that pressure to purchase becomes most intense. This does not mean that we ignore our original preferences; merely that our assessments at this stage are made quickly. Our final choice depends on whether or not the houses we have focused on in our chosen area show any significant range of different interiors, and whether or not a house has the potential to be personalized and so become a home.

In 1986 a study of house buying in Milton Keynes, England, threw light on both these factors. First, despite the remarkable variation in external design and layout, there was generally very little variation in internal design. Second, architects have to strike a balance in the extent to which

e makes midweek visits to areas	More precise selection of areas	Select newly built houses	Further visits; working toward list of possible houses	Shortlist
▲	▲	▲	▲	▲
Need to see schools, real estate agents and so on	Quite precise areas; would you prefer isolated splendor as in this Arizona home ABOVE or somewhere closer to shopping or to your children's school?	Probably need to move again soon; no time to do home improvements; easier to compare new houses in different areas (also to compare them with those in current area)	Man (usually) more concerned for status location, woman (usually) for amenities, both for schools; specific houses selected for style, space and cost; minimal input (as ever) from children	Pressure from work prices rising rapidly; most importantly, will the chosen house increase in value?

s going up, so want uy something less pensive and give us cash to children	Weigh up the merits of older and modern houses	Decide new houses are badly built and that this is more important than the advantages they might have	The criteria of both partners are weighed up against each other	Reconsider whether a move is necessary at all	Grandchildren on the way, children need money sooner rather than later, and so on
▼	▼	▼	▼	▼	▼

| "Let's stay in this area?" | Focus on a few old houses | Focus on a few new houses | "Stop!" Settle for an older house | Produce a shortlist | "We're not sure..."? | CHOOSE – Now is the time |

they design houses. If they impose too uniform a pattern, people feel that there is little point in trying to personalize a home because they will never be able to "defeat" the original design. On the other hand, many people do not wish their house to be so individual that it does not fit in with all the others.

Another factor is whether or not people feel willing or able to personalize a house. For those of us who enjoy altering our homes, regarding it as an important leisure pursuit, a house that seems to require major changes is a positive attraction. Those who see the task of home improvement as a painful chore, however, will seek a house where little or no alteration is required.

Several basic factors affect our choice: the number of bedrooms, for example. There are also more individual considerations: we might need somewhere to put the grand piano. The small but often important details that will affect our daily life tend to be ignored at this stage: child safety around the windows, the number of electrical outlets, the suitability of the rooms for the furniture we already possess, and so on. We are much more likely to concentrate on how the house "feels" and how quickly our decision must be made.

The "feel" of the house – however hard to quantify or analyze – should not be dismissed as unimportant. A great number of subtle factors convey "homeliness" when we are looking at places we might live. These vary between different cultures, times and individuals. Somehow we know if a house has this quality but we cannot define exactly why; it is even more difficult to pinpoint reasons why, for us, a particular house lacks it.

Who makes the final decision?

As so many moves are job-related, the pressure to decide may be on the family's major income earner, still often the man. (Even if the woman earns more than the man, his job may be regarded as more important than hers because of longer-term considerations – such as whether she will leave her job to have children.) Traditionally, the woman's role in the final choice usually comes later, when details of specific houses are being considered. She may be directly involved earlier if the criteria of choice are connected with the children – size of house or garden, proximity to good schools and so on. Such choices are made not with but on behalf of the children – in fact, it is quite rare for the views of the children to be taken into account at all.

▲ **A blank canvas** *on which to paint your own personal picture of a living space. Few househunters look for a distinctive interior. Getting the right look inside is a task they save for after their move – when they* *will have their own possessions to personalize their home (see Chs 5, 6). A distinctive exterior is often a priority before purchase, however, as owners are likely to make few changes other than repainting.*

▶ **Personalization or quick resale?** *Some buyers seek homes that require minimum redecoration – others look for houses with room for improvement, either to personalize their home or to increase its value.*

Although much research contradicts the popular assumption that women are central to decision-making, property developers attempt to change this situation, because other studies have shown that women are more likely than men to be influenced by advertising. It is here that one can find some emphasis on children but, almost always, the aim is merely to reach women through focusing on child-related concerns.

How free is our choice?

Most of us change a new home in some way – at the very least, we furnish it. Major internal and external changes are less frequent but still reasonably common. In fact it is often only through these alterations that our house becomes our home. Does it matter then if the property market fails to provide exactly what each of us wants when in any case we are sure to alter what we buy, according to our own needs?

For most people in Western societies the choice of a house and the making of a home, while affected by our aspirations, are influenced at all levels by the operations of the housing market. This has been described as the "commodification" of housing – the "home" is regarded as a product little different from a car or a camera. The effect may be to force us, as individuals, to subjugate our deeply felt needs and aspirations regarding "home" to the priorities of producers whose major concerns are not with us but with profits.

But the operations of the housing market may also be seen as having a positive effect. It could be argued that it is only because of market forces that people in developed countries can live in houses which in size and opulence exceed the wildest dreams of most people from the rest of the world.

Many developers like to assume that potential purchasers are "empty vessels" whose views can be redirected to favor whatever novelty is likely to be profitable at the time. So, within the professional circles involved in housing development, market research – what little there is of it – is focused far more on how to persuade people to buy than on asking people what they want.

Perhaps it is foolish for us to expect that the large-scale production of houses will ever provide us with a selection of ready made homes. After all, our home is what *we* make it. Nevertheless we could at least demand that the choice of houses on offer depend more on our wants than on the preconceptions and economic priorities of building contractors. **JFB**

HOW OFTEN WE MOVE

■ *Figures from the 1960s showed that in the United States people moved home, on average, every seven years. By the end of the 1980s people were moving almost every eight months. This average is remarkable; after all, some people never move at all.*

Before and in the early years of marriage, moves are likely to occur fairly frequently (perhaps for job reasons). When children arrive a "family home" may be established – perhaps two in quick succession, if the first proves unsatisfactory. There is then a longer period of stability. The departure of the children may trigger the next move, with perhaps another on retirement: in both cases, the reasons may be a mixture of choice and

economy. Often there is then a final move: this may be a trading-down to more modest accommodation which is easier for elderly people to maintain.

Changing lifestyles are complicating all these patterns: marital breakdown occurs more frequently, many couples defer having children, children often leave earlier and, in any case, a rising proportion of people never marry.

▶ **Decision made.** *Moving in is the culmination of a lengthy process of choice which researchers have listed among the stressful life events. Moving highlights tensions between profound but unexpressed feelings about our roots, family and status. This means that even after resolving your doubts about finding the right property, affording the price and completing formalities, you may face weeks of strain as you adjust to new surroundings.*

Managing Privacy

A NEIGHBOR who interpreted an unlocked door as an invitation to walk into your house and ask you probing questions about your personal life would be unwelcome. There is an unwritten rule that says we should not enter another person's house uninvited and such an obvious breach of this social etiquette would be considered odd and unnatural. Inside the home too we usually communicate our desire for privacy or sociability without explicitly stating our needs. We do this partly through the way we plan and use our home territory.

"I want to be alone"

It is through our relationships with other people that we establish our own identity and our individuality. But as well as putting ourselves forward and being open to contact with others we also need to hold back at times. In this way, we regulate our privacy, that is, the "openness" or "closedness" of how we interact with others.

Some people are more open by nature – they tend to be gregarious and often extroverted in their speech and behavior. Others are habitually quieter, more reserved and sometimes shy in the presence of company. But, whichever type of person we are, we all at some time need to be able to withdraw and be alone – whether to reflect, ponder life's mysteries, relive a moment's sadness or just enjoy the silence. Being in control of how closed or open we are in our relationships is important to our well-being. Uninvited openness or intimacy can embarrass us and cause a feeling of crowding; unrequited attempts at intimacy can make us feel lonely and rejected. Either way, continual failure to achieve a blend between togetherness and privacy can be a frustrating, and even stressful, experience.

Privacy in the home

Good privacy management – achieving the right blend of openness and privacy – is important, above all, in the home. Too little social interaction can impair family cohesion (as indeed can too much where children may have too little time alone, in the longer term). Sharing each other's company in the family some of the time and at other times being apart is good for both the family as a unit and for its individual members.

Without even realizing what we are doing, we regulate our use of space in the home to achieve the privacy we need. Naturally, if you want to be alone, perhaps to write a letter, you will go to a part of the house where you are less likely to be disturbed, such as your bedroom. This is a signal to others that, unless they have a good reason for doing so, they should not seek you out or interrupt you. Having finished your letter, you may desire company again and

▲ **A private entrance to a private home.** *One of the most important ways we have of managing privacy is to mark clearly which places are public territory and which are private (see Ch1). Even though this door is open, we would not feel comfortable about simply walking in. Without a large sign clearly labeling it as a government office, a store or restaurant, people will almost always feel they need an invitation to go through a doorway.*

38

THE PRIVACY REGULATION EQUATION

■ *If you are stuck on a crowded subway train, you can lower your eyes to avoid looking directly at the person standing next to you, retreat into a book, think about something more pleasant or just be consoled by the fact that you will soon be out of it. Feeling crowded in your own home is more of a problem. You cannot ignore members of the family as you can strangers, or so easily withdraw from them if they will not let you. Moreover, unless your home is very large, there is often nowhere else to run to. The experience of being unable to close yourself off in your home imposes a far greater psychological strain on* *you than being caught up in the hustle and bustle of the city.*

In this case, too much openness can cause distress but too much closedness can be equally distressing. Ideally, we would always expect to attain our desired degree of openness or closedness in our relations with others. That way, we would never feel intruded on or feel that our ambitions had been thwarted by others, as may happen when the openness achieved exceeds what we desire. Equally, we would never feel left out of things or spurned, as we may do if we seek more openness than we manage to achieve.

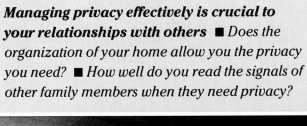

Managing privacy effectively is crucial to your relationships with others ■ *Does the organization of your home allow you the privacy you need?* ■ *How well do you read the signals of other family members when they need privacy?*

HOW MUCH PRIVACY IS RIGHT FOR YOU?

TOO MUCH
You feel lonely
- because of how others behave: they are not taking enough interest in you.
- because of how you behave: you are not communicating to others.

TOO LITTLE
You feel embarrassed
- because of how others behave: they are crowding you, intruding upon you.
- because of how you behave: you sense that you need to be less open.

JUST RIGHT
- *Solitude* – when you want and have a high degree of privacy for yourself alone.
- *Superficial contact* with others may be all that you want.
- *Sociability* – you feel relaxed and somewhat open with other people – you may need privacy for the group you are with – eg no neighbors eavesdropping as you chat with friends.
- *Intimacy* – you feel especially open and unguarded with someone, and want them to be unguarded with you – privacy from outsiders is essential.

 ▲ A private moment *may simply be a minute or two to be alone with your thoughts. Privacy can also mean freedom – freedom from observation, or the freedom to do something, not necessarily unobserved but without interference or interruption from others, for example, reading a book or newspaper in a crowded restaurant. Even though we often need privacy for the two of us or the three of us, solitude is also an important part of privacy and has little to do with loneliness.*

return to the living room or to another more sociable part of the house.

Our need for privacy in the home is not the same all the time, but is constantly changing. Often it ebbs and flows in a way that depends as much on the desires of others as on the surroundings. Without this give and take, the home would be in danger of becoming a permanent battleground. Suppose, for instance, you feel the need to discuss something urgently with your partner who happens to be engrossed in a television program; or, you might be watching your favorite show at the same time as your small son expects you to help him with his arithmetic. Are you going to give up your own needs to fall in with someone else's or are you determined to impose yours on them come what

may? Do you, resignedly, settle down next to your partner to watch television after perhaps unsuccessfully starting to say your piece and possibly being ignored, or do you get hurt and angry at their apparent indifference, march over to the television set and switch it off to command their attention? Clearly, following the second course of action might easily provoke confrontation.

Family rules

Most families evolve rules to cover certain potential flashpoint situations. If one member of the family wants to listen to music on the stereo while another is watching television in the same room, a rule that involves a reasonable compromise in the use of shared space will normally be

▼ **A father's accessibility** *to his children is usually less than a mother's and this can sometimes create distance, weakening the father-child bond. In many families children are less free to interrupt or intrude upon him than upon their mother. By creating situations in which there is a sense of closeness – for example, allowing his children into the bath, a father can help to reassure them of the special status they have in his world.*

▲ **Privacy for a mother** *from her small children is often less than a father's because of their special dependence on her but the parent's need to assert a separate identity of her own is an important one. It can be served by allowing children the privacy they need in order to develop independence and* *self-confidence. For example, children who are not accustomed to parental intervention in their quarrels are less likely to interrupt a conversation between parents with demands for arbitration.*

observed by the family. The television might perhaps take precedence until the mid-evening news broadcast is over, but after that anyone who wants to play records may do so. Similarly, a would-be conflict between children over the use of a room for entertaining their friends might easily be avoided by each child having first refusal on certain days of the week.

A predictable use of space by family members can reinforce a family's cohesiveness. Because of their implied long-term commitment, married couples may be more territorial in their use of shared space such as bedrooms, bathrooms, closets, dressers and dining-room tables than couples who are simply living together. Some married couples tend, for instance, to keep their toothbrush in the same place and to use the same half of the closet. This helps to ensure that one partner's belongings do not prevent the other from finding theirs and so heads off a potential source of conflict.

Privacy inside and outside the family

Privacy management is pervasive and ongoing; not only does it occur within the nuclear family but it is also important in relating to other kin. You might, for instance, generally prefer to spend Christmas at home with your own family, but feel obliged to visit your parents or in-laws because it is the season for doing so and it is expected of you. On the one hand, you do not want to spend too much time with them because that would intrude on the privacy and intimacy of your own family's Christmas; on the other,

you must be careful not to spend too little time with either set of in-laws or you risk causing offense, and possibly jealousy, which might then have the effect of weakening ties within the extended family.

Family relations – and indeed social relations generally – are complex and many-sided and we regulate the boundaries of privacy accordingly. For instance, a person may desire a high degree of intimacy with their partner, and perhaps to a lesser extent with their children, but would probably avoid this amount of intimacy with their in-laws.

Openness and total honesty has sometimes been advocated as the goal of our family relationships, to be achieved by shared interests, spending more time together and sharing our feelings through self-disclosure. But this is impossible to attain and is indeed undesirable. In fact, parents who are able to spend some time alone, away from children and spouse, are often more content as parents. Moreover, most married couples feel the need to arrange their lives so that they have some time apart, either physically by leaving the house, going to an empty room, or psychologically by withdrawing behind a newspaper.

▲ **Family relationships and social expectations.** *These grandparents obviously enjoy having their grandchildren in bed with them but might not feel the same way about the neighbors' children. Privacy expectations can be greatly influenced by the seasons. Christmas is a time for the* *family and tends to be more private than Thanksgiving or Halloween. When we celebrate national holidays, we do not usually confine ourselves to family, but Mother's and Father's Days are more private, focusing on the relationship between parents and their children.*

PRIVACY IN EXOTIC SETTINGS

■ *Are there any societies in which people manage without privacy? At first glance, some may seem to be like this but anthropologists usually find privacy-regulation systems at work behind the scenes.*

■ *The Mehinacu, a small tribe of Brazilian Indians, have a lifestyle which, on the surface, appears to be totally open. Not only do they live in small villages with all the homes clustered together around a central plaza, but the thatched walls of their huts offer no soundproofing. Moreover, several families live under the same roof, and the activities of each family member are easily visible and within earshot of the others.*

However, families do not intrude on one another's territory or enter one another's homes uninvited. Asking personal questions or gossiping about other people's misdemeanors is socially unacceptable, and lying to avoid breaking someone's confidence is perfectly permissible.

Outside the home, life in the *village is very public, secret tracks beyond the village lead to secluded places where people can be alone. Indeed, it is not uncommon for whole families to move away from the village and live somewhere else for long periods.*

■ *Families of the BaMuti, a pygmy tribe of Zaire, can also escape the close-knit life of the encampment to live alone as a family. To achieve greater privacy within the community, pygmies may rearrange and repair their huts, moving the front door to face away from the huts of other families and, in the event of a serious dispute with a neighbor, erecting a fence between them.*

■ *Villagers living on the Woleia atoll, a tiny South Pacific island, have found other ways of offsetting their close-community living and satisfying their privacy needs. They have a strict division of labor between men and women who are also separated from one another during the day by means of different pathways.*

Children need privacy too

Observing children's needs for privacy is also important if we are to maintain harmony and cohesiveness in our families. Furthermore, since small children spend most of their time at home, it is there that they gain their first experience of the privacy management that will be needed when they venture further afield.

To some extent, children learn about privacy and how to achieve it by experiencing the privacy of others, usually their parents. As a young child we might have been told, for example, "I have work to do, I don't want to be disturbed." As children grow up, they learn to recognize behavior that indicates a desire for privacy, such as withdrawal to another room, without needing to be told. At the same time, the child's own privacy needs are developing.

Very young children have no private space, though some establish their own personal space by resisting close or prolonged physical contact more than others. Children

entering or in adolescence will often deny activities such as cigarette smoking when confronted. This is partly because they want to avoid disapproval or punishment, but also because they feel that they should not have to justify their behavior to their parents. Indeed, telling a lie is considered by some experts to be a developmental milestone in a child's life because it sets limits on what children are prepared to let their parents know about them.

As children mature physically, and become more sexually aware, they also close bathroom and bedroom doors behind them more often and expect others to knock before entering. One study found that around 70 percent of sisters knock on their brothers' doors, while about 50 percent of brothers knock on their sisters' doors. The corresponding figures for children with same-sex siblings are very much lower. This behavior may be in part culturally influenced, reflecting other examples of the segregation of the sexes in society. Styles of parenting, including such things as atti-

▲ **Retreating outdoors for privacy,** *a little girl has found a secluded spot to be alone with her book. We first learn about privacy from our parents when* *they both exercise their own and allow us ours. Children learning to recognize behavior that indicates a desire for privacy are also developing* *skills that will enable them to manage their own. Parents who are strong disciplinarians may inhibit this process by demanding total openness from their* *children, for example, insisting they keep their bedroom doors open while they are playing.*

tudes to nudity, also influence children's privacy needs, while obviously the amount of space available is an important factor – children living in bigger houses with fewer family members usually manage to satisfy their need for privacy more easily.

All families face problems of privacy management and all have ways of attaining a blend of openness and closedness that work with varying degrees of success. Some families rely on a fairly formal regime in which members' roles are strictly defined, and everyone respects closed doors and acknowledges the rights of others to solitary pastimes. Others operate a more relaxed, open system in which activities and space are more often shared.

In most homes, the table at mealtime is a symbol of family openness and togetherness. Parents and children sit round the table, sometimes in set places arranged according to age and status. Because they are close together they can all easily look at one another and converse, though the manner and topics of conversation may vary from the formal to the familiar according to the family's cultural background, the strictness of the household and so on.

Signaling our intentions

While conversation may be the norm over a meal, we would not expect to be able to talk so freely to someone who, after dinner, curls up in their favorite chair to read a book (even if they are in the family room where everyone else is chatting away happily). Although being in a particular room can indicate your intentions and expectations of openness or closedness – intimacy at the one extreme and solitude at the other – items of furniture and the way that you use them can send out important signals. Even outside the home and in the company of strangers, chairs that face each other encourage their occupants to strike up a conversation, whereas chairs strung out in a line do not. Similarly, choosing a center seat at a long table in a library tells others that you want it all to yourself, whereas sitting at a corner of the table suggests a willingness to share.

All the time, whether or not we are aware of it, we are sending out messages about our desire for openness or closedness. If someone knows you very well, the signals you emit through eye contact, gestures and other body language may be more obvious to them than to a stranger. They can, for example, use their experience of how outgoing or reserved you are normally as a standard of comparison for your present behavior. But even a stranger can discern a lot about you just by looking at you, and by observing how you are dressed and how you use the space provided by the furnishings and the surroundings. Smiling, touching and moving closer are all signs indicating a desire for greater openness, while leaning back, looking away

43

■ **Signaling the need for privacy.** LEFT *It is easy to recognize that someone working with her back to the room does not want to be disturbed.* RIGHT *If grandfather retires to a greenhouse that has seating for precisely one to watch television, smoke his pipe, and sip his tea, he is indicating clearly that he would like to be alone. The need for privacy is not always signaled so explicitly, however, and often we have to judge whether the time is right* *to involve another member of the family in our own concerns. Does their withdrawn look mean that they should have a chance to rest and relax before talking? Can the matter in hand wait? Is there someone in the room who makes them feel less free to say what they think? If their reactions confuse you, it may be useful to discuss later what each of you was privately thinking at the time.*

and, of course, leaving, all indicate a desire to keep your distance.

In addition, they know whether the occasion is formal or more relaxed and can see whether or not you are observing social conventions in your behavior and speech. They can tell whether you are being polite or rude, and probably identify your accent, for example, as regional or well-educated. If you speak in the present tense, using the first person and naming the people you refer to, you show a desire for openness; if you use more impersonal constructions in your conversation it indicates a guardedness and reserve on your part.

Marking out our territory

Not surprisingly, we most often feel off our guard and at ease in our own homes. The home is our territory and the place where, most of all, we feel in control of our environment and how we use it. Being able to admit callers or refuse them entry makes our home seem like a secure haven.

From the outside, the home sends out conflicting signals that show the complexity of our territorial tendencies. On the one hand, we may have a "Welcome" mat at the front door, but this is addressed only to friends and relatives and possibly neighbors. The burglar-alarm sticker in the front window is clearly a "keep out" message to anyone who might seek to enter uninvited. Likewise, a display of Christmas decorations might show religious leanings and our willingness to enter into the spirit of the season of goodwill, but it is not to be interpreted as a blanket invitation to callers, while a well tended flower-bed is not only the sign of a keen gardener – it also tells others that you care and warns neighbors not to let their dogs stray onto your patch.

Inside the home some territories are more central than others. We may invite guests into the living room or front room, but we still retain control of the situation: we offer them a drink, or not, as we choose. The room for entertaining is usually downstairs, at the front of the house, and is easily reached from the front door. Rooms toward the back of the house and those upstairs are more private – bedrooms generally being the most private in Western cultures – and visitors do not enter them without being invited (with the obvious exception of the bathroom, after asking permission).

Exceptions to these norms are generally cultural or idiosyncratic. For example, in one survey researchers discovered a couple who divided their home into distinct

PRIVACY IN CRAMPED QUARTERS

■ *How do people achieve privacy when there are limited opportunities to get away from each other? Submarine crews who live in cramped conditions, sometimes for months on end, have nowhere to escape to. They achieve solitude through psychological withdrawal, for example, by listening to music on personal stereos, reading or watching movies. They also divide up the small space so that each has his own territory to retreat to, and avoid too much openness by restricting conversation to unemotional, noncontroversial subjects. Although the men work together, they display the greatest social cohesiveness at mealtimes, which become important events in their own right and often last twice as long as in family homes.*

▶ **Screening in a Japanese home**. *In Japan a densely packed population must accommodate itself to small homes in which privacy is difficult. At night family may place their sleeping mats (futons) close together on the floor in one room. Until recently the practice was to use partitions in place of walls. These partitions could be moved at will, so that the same small area could be used for many different purposes over the course of a day.*

Here a mother helps her son learn computing, while the screen behind separates them from other activities. More common now are one- or two-room apartments with fixed walls, which makes privacy virtually impossible. The lack of sexual privacy has given rise to highly popular "love hotels."

areas: the upstairs was the wife's domain, which was considered to be more formal and higher in status than the downstairs to which the husband was permanently relegated. Some, often lower-income, households keep the front room as a formal area for special occasions, protecting the furniture, lamps and rugs with a plastic covering. Even when families live in extremely cramped settings, they will often opt to restrict their use of space in order to preserve cultural traditions regarding the appropriate use of space within the home.

Organizing our personal space

People who have their homes built to their own specifications usually make privacy a central factor in how their space is organized – sometimes without realizing it. Often they instruct the architect to produce open-plan designs for rooms intended for daytime and household activities, with closed rooms for more personal uses, such as sleeping. Typically, the parents' bedroom is the most private and the adolescent's workroom the most exposed.

Architects are increasingly turning their attention to meeting the psychological as well as the practical needs of occupants. For example, a single parent working from home in a one-room studio apartment might increase the available space and meet some of their own and their child's privacy needs by means of a split-level design. Indeed, some families who are not short of space have also occasionally found that this kind of arrangement works well. A couple who wanted to be together and be able to share a view from the same window while the one did paper work undisturbed but did not inhibit the other, found the ideal architectural solution in a raised office, shaped like an open box, and situated in the middle of the main living area. The fact that both partners could see each other and enjoy the same outside scenery preserved the feeling of intimacy between them, while the physical separation of the office from the rest of the room allowed them both to carry on with their activities uninterrupted and without fear of encroaching on each other's privacy. **BBB, PBH, CW, IA**

45

■ **Creating private places in the home.** *Here are two very different strategies for achieving privacy within the home. Extending into the outdoors* ABOVE *a semi-enclosed deck has been built away from the house, offering a space where people might go to be alone with their thoughts, or a book, or to have a private conversation. The cozy arrangement in this corner* LEFT *creates a place where people are likely to be left alone because other people will sense an atmosphere of intimacy.*

Personal Home Style

HOMES come in all shapes and sizes, all colors and styles. If you compare homes in Europe with homes in Africa and the Far East or homes in Scotland with those in Düsseldorf, the differences are immediately clear. Although building codes or limited finances may restrict what we do to our homes, the interiors and exteriors typically express our personal tastes and values.

In most neighborhoods there is considerable variety in the way people treat the outside of their homes. Some are neat and well-maintained, some are stylish, some are neglected, some are dull and uninteresting. The gardens may be landscaped, unkempt, full of flowers or nothing more than a parking space. In urban areas the variety is generally less marked, but even here some homes have window boxes, while others have no exterior decoration at all. The similarities are probably due to the fact that the occupiers belong to the same social or cultural group. All groups share certain customs and tastes and the type of

decoration you choose reflects not only your individual characteristics but the inbuilt habits, traditions and norms of your group. It may also reflect your social status.

The need for an identity

Many researchers believe that we all need to know who we are and how we fit in with the rest of our society – a clear sense of self is essential to our psychological well-being. Often, when people move between cultures or change social position they maintain certain traditions simply because these are part of their identity, and these traditions

▲ **Symbols of wealth** *express a sense of achievement in the boxer who proclaimed himself "The Greatest" when he was at the height of his career. Expensively elegant furniture and fittings create the setting in which Mohammed Ali daily takes his breakfast.*

▶ **Uniquely personal sur-roundings** *express her creative flair, an essential ingredient in Susan Colyer's sense of identity. A fabric designer by profession, she has made for herself a home that serves to remind her, and inform anyone who visits her, of the talents that are such a crucial part of her*

makeup. Flooring, wallpaper, tablecloth, even the decora-tions on pottery, all announce that this woman's life has a special connection with pat-terns in two dimensions. One of the most common uses we make of interior decoration is to convey positive information about ourselves.

Inside and out, our homes announce who we are and what we are like ■ *Façades are a public face that we turn toward the world* ■ *Indoors, we reveal our personalities in detail* ■ *Our homes reinforce our sense of identity and help others to know how to behave appropriately with us.*

may reveal themselves in the way they decorate their homes and in their taste for colors, ornaments and furnishings.

One person can have many identities: some are based around the family, others come from our position in society or at work and some are a result of our personal likes and dislikes. We can express all the sides of our personality through our choice of home and the way that we look after, decorate and use it. For example, a woman may be an accountant, an accomplished pianist, a wife and mother: evidence of all these identities will be present in the way certain parts of her home are arranged. Some aspects of the style will reflect the fact that she is a professional businesswoman, while her musical talents may be expressed by a piano, music and perhaps photographs or framed awards. Other aspects will be a compromise between her personal preference and the needs of her family.

FAÇADE SIGNALS – WHAT HOUSES SAY

► An impression of a human face returning our gaze *through eyes that we know are really only windows – seems to be the explanation why we sometimes have an uncanny impulse to attribute to houses personalities of their own. This cottage is in Cornwall in England. Chiefly, however, it is to householders that we will attribute the personalities that façades convey. When you have the right to decide what a house will look like, you show something of yourself in the decisions you make.*

■ "I have a taste for fantasy" *seems to be the message delivered opulently ABOVE by this bizarre architectural extravaganza in Beverly Hills, California, and more modestly, RIGHT in a suburban house in Arizona, mainly by means of an out-of-the-ordinary gardening style. This first impression will be carried with us if we go inside – and it will color our interpretations of what we see and hear*

◄ Self-congratulatory displays *of prowess were painted on tepees by Indians, and hunting trophies were mounted over doorways by settlers, in the old days. This set of moose antlers survives on a cabin in Alaska. Picture stories about the occupant are a common sight on the mud walls of houses in many other remote corners of the world. City-dwellers are more private, displaying their certificates and trophies indoors.*

► Saying it with flowers. *"Gardening is not for me" announces a Phoenix, Arizona, architect, through this plywood cut-out display RIGHT in front of his home. A family in Germany FAR RIGHT asserts that in spite of the austerity of the design styles that have inspired the architecture of their home, they value a soft, vegetative and colorful environment.*

Personality clashes

Other people may be an important influence on the way you arrange your home – its style probably reflects the presence of every member of the household. If you have young children, you will have to balance your own ideas about decoration and furnishing with practical considera-tions such as the fact that children are untidy. If your partner loves Victorian decor and you prefer a more austere style, one or both of you will have to compromise. One solution would be to divide the house so that each partner's taste and requirements are catered to in different rooms.

The community you live in can also affect your home

HOW OFTEN DO YOU REDECORATE?

■ We pay more attention to the decoration of our home as we get older.

20-30 years *On average the under-thirties redecorate their living rooms every two years and their bedrooms every four years. This is a time of excitement and experiment when they are trying to find their own style, and when people also have a lot of energy.*

30-50 *People in their thirties usually spend less time on* the house. They are more concerned with practicalities and less experimental. For many, this period coincides with raising a family, and having children in the house means that personal taste often has to come second.

50-60 *By the time they are in their fifties most people only redecorate their living room and bedroom once every seven years.*

60+ *Many people over 60 redecorate as often as people in their forties. They have less energy but a great deal more time. They also tend to be more adventurous than some younger couples in their choice of style.*

■ *Your occupation may also be reflected in how often and in what way you furnish and redecorate your home. As a general rule, manual workers redecorate most frequently. They redecorate their living rooms* every two years and bedrooms every three years. White-collar workers redecorate about half as often.

One reason for this may be that manual workers usually live in smaller homes where limited space causes more wear and tear on paintwork and carpets.

Different social groups may use different materials in building and decorating a home, and the differences can stem from both taste and income. The status professions – doctors, lawyers, bankers – usually avoid artificial materials such as synthetic stone or plastic wood effect finishes. Simple, unpainted surfaces are more suitable for those who have expensive possessions to display.

People on lower incomes may choose patterned wallpapers and carpets, often in synthetic fabrics to make their home look more luxurious.

YOUR PERSONAL STYLE: A CHECKLIST

■ *What does your home say about you? Think of the outside of your home:*
◆ *In what ways does it reflect your personality?*
◆ *Does it tell people that you are open to contact or are there clues that you prefer to be left alone?*
◆ *Does it convey any other information about you – your membership of a group or some purely personal characteristic?*
◆ *How do you balance the desire to express your individuality with the need to show that you are part of the community?*

style. Although most of us like to express ourselves as individuals, we may at the same time want to fit in with our immediate group, whether it is a social group or the local residential community. Sometimes, however, our desire to be part of the community conflicts with our personal identity. The easiest way to express both individual and group identities is to adopt the communal way of doing things but put our personal stamp on them. If you live in a street where everyone paints their front door a bright color and you would prefer a plain glass door, you could break away from the tradition of the street. Alternatively, you could compromise by having a door that is mainly glass but with a painted

surround. The uniformity of a community can occasionally be suffocating and some people deliberately introduce an unconventional element into the style of their home in an attempt to express their own identity.

What kind of person lives here?

Because the style of a home is the result of a mixture of influences, it can be difficult to make accurate assessments of your neighbors' personalities or lifestyles just from the appearance of their house. Even though people do express themselves through the way they fix up their home, it is sometimes difficult to decode the signals accurately. For

■ **Bathroom personality.**
Slow, leisurely baths are not in the style of this extroverted New Yorker. He has created an energetic mood that will probably have him quickly out of the tub and on to the next part of his daily routine. BELOW *Bathroom decoration has become an exercise in heritage preservation in this home in the Dordogne region of France. Here too, part of what is desired from surroundings is that they should be interesting.*

51

■ *Now move to the inside of your home:*
◆ *What does it show about your likes and dislikes?*
◆ *What would you like to change?*
◆ *Are there some aspects of style that are not a true reflection of you?*
◆ *If so, who or what do they reflect – the community, other members of your family, a stage you have outgrown?*
◆ *How do you balance your own style preferences with those of your partner and family?*

example, if one of your neighbors displayed a large orna-mental flamingo in their window, how would you know whether they were being stylish or humorous? The flamingo alone would not be sufficient evidence to make a judgment about their personality.

False clues can also come from other factors such as whether someone has hired a decorator to design the interior of their house or what the current trend is in home decorating. If the house has been decorated by an interior designer, the taste it reveals may not be the owners' at all, but the designer's. In the 1960s and 70s, the fashion was to strip pine and expose the wood, but the latest advice from the home decor magazines is "Don't strip it, paint it." Con-formity to trends says more about when we live than the sort of people we are. Different climates will also affect the style of furnishing – there is less need for bright interiors and warm carpets and curtains when you live in a hot, sunny climate.

The situation is further complicated by the fact that we project ourselves in different ways in different parts of the house. Public and private areas often give out conflicting messages. A living room may be tastefully arranged with *objets d'art* but this does not necessarily mean that the occupants are art lovers. You would probably need to see the rest of the house and visit it often to deduce more about their personalities.

Outward signs and inner meaning

Despite these conflicting signals it is possible to draw some general conclusions about people from the appear-ance of their homes. You probably use your home to express your values, attitudes, aspirations and activities, revealing something about the social and cultural group you belong to, and about your status within that group. The way you arrange things may not say much about your personality but it will reflect your lifestyle; and the style will change if your lifestyle changes.

Some people use the outside of their home to convey information about themselves. They may put up a plate with their name and details of their qualifications or profession; they may give their homes names that reflect an important event in their lives or their reasons for buying the house. Summer homes are often given names that capture the spirit of the place – "Hanson's Hideaway," "Robinson's Roost." The British often call their house after a favorite holiday place – "Marbella," "Helvellyn" – or even combine family names into the name of the house. The Plains Indians of North America used to paint decorations on their tepees that symbolized important skills and events connected with the occupants; and it was common for Egyptian Nubians to illustrate the fronts of their houses with illustrations depic-ting important life events, such as a trip to Mecca or time spent working away from the village.

52

▶ **Open to the world or closed?** *One resident of this street in Bradford, England, keeps her net curtains drawn – an obvious strategy for privacy, since nothing separates her window from passers by – but her neighbor displays objects on the sill, with curtains pulled back – practically an invitation to look inside. Relationships studies find that people who have lived all their lives in many traditionally working-class neighborhoods in England treat the home as a much more private place than more mobile newcomers do; only relatives are invited in, while friends are seen mainly at work, in pubs and while shopping.*

The outside of the house may not reflect what is inside, however. It is not always possible to adapt the architectural style of the building to our own taste and a Victorian exterior may conceal a 2001 interior. The inside of the house tells you a great deal more about how the family lives. People with young children often put all breakables above a certain height; busy working couples are more likely to have uncluttered kitchens; older people often have unusually warm homes; people who work at home have functional rooms. If the house is large enough, then different members of the family will be able to express their own style in their own room.

It is important to remember, though, that we look at other people's decor through the filter of our own cultural traditions and personality traits. This is why it is easier to make factual judgments than judgments about character. If you see a sign saying "Beware of the dog" on someone's gate, then it is fairly safe to assume that they have a dog. But if you are not a particularly neat person you are likely to consider someone who keeps their home tidy as a *very* tidy person. They may, actually, be no more tidy than most people. Generally, Western societies do not use garish colors in home decoration, but the fact that someone from India paints their house red and yellow does not mean that they have bad taste; it is simply that tastes vary from culture to culture as well as from person to person.

The personal touch

One way of forming a basic impression of a person is to look at the objects they display in their home (see *Ch 6*). People with absorbing or creative hobbies or an interest in sport usually display examples of their work and trophies. Keen gardeners may reveal themselves through thriving indoor plants; artistic people will probably display their own sculptures or drawings; a fisherman may have a mounted fish on his wall. Decorating our home with these personal touches is an indication that we feel attached to the place. Research among students has shown that the way in which they decorate their own room relates to whether or not they remain in college. At the University of Utah, students who stayed at college had decorated more with items associated with the university, whereas those who dropped out had decorated with objects and scenes from their past life.

Sometimes people use this kind of decoration to make a statement about their personal values. Many college students put up posters, badges or stickers that express religious or moral values, such as their attitude toward drugs or their commitment to civil rights.

Other people can guess a great deal about us just from the way we arrange our living rooms. In one study, strangers were shown photographs of various living rooms and were asked to speculate about the personality traits of the inhabitants. Their predictions about whether people were adventurous, interesting, efficient, self-disciplined, emotional, warm or relaxed were surprisingly accurate.

▲ **Alternative styles within the home.** *Having separate rooms for different members of the family is something that serves much more complex needs than mere privacy. When each person in the house has an area of it to call their own and stamp with their own personality, this helps them to feel that they matter in the home and that the home matters to them.*

Keeping in season

Decoration can be symbolic as well as personal. Research in the United States suggests that the decorations we put up at holiday periods like Christmas and Halloween are more likely to be an expression of our desire to be part of the community than an indication of personal characteristics. Public celebrations give everyone the opportunity to express solidarity with their community or nation. Even if you think Christmas is overrated or you do not support the government, you are more likely than not to join in to some degree.

Residents in one housing block were surveyed twice – in the summer and at Christmas – about their lifestyles, friendships and religious affiliations. In the summer the way they cared for and maintained their homes was due mostly to their personal circumstances. The ones who had a well-kept house and garden were people with no children, retired people, long-term residents and those who owned their own home. However, at Christmas, people who made their homes look festive were those who expressed strong liking for their neighbors or the Christmas tradition.

The kind of decorations we put up also tell others something about us. People who put up Halloween decorations, for example, are more likely to know their neighbors well because these particular decorations are an invitation to others to act in a playful way and a sign that the normal conventions of social life have been discarded for a short time. Another indication that people know their neighbors well is the positioning of decorations, particularly at Christmas. Decorations placed near the door may be put there to encourage neighbors to come and visit.

Group identity

People from similar groups decorate their homes in similar styles, though details may vary between groups, regions and countries. The newly restored city streets in many Western countries show clear evidence of a mixture of groups in the variety of house styles. In one study, prosperous, middle-class people had moved into a previously working-class area, and the style of the houses in the area gradually changed. The smart doors with brass fixtures or the demolition truck in front of the house were not the only signs. Windows revealed a great deal. Older working-class residents may have had lace or net curtains at the front windows to keep the rooms private, whereas the newcomers often left their windows without curtains or put up fashionable venetian blinds and festoon drapes that were almost always left open. The interiors of the houses were also radically altered. The older residents preferred to keep distinct rooms in the house, thereby separating activities such as entertaining, cooking and eating. The new residents very often knocked down as many internal walls as possible to create a single, larger living space.

When people are expressing a uniform identity, external features of decoration tend to become more uniform. In the Basque region of south-west France all houses must be built in a local style and must have their exterior paintwork in dark red or green – the traditional Basque colors.

Making a personal statement

Although common decorating features can express a communal and social identity, it is the positioning of the features that gives a home its individuality. Many suburban

◀ **A design that identifies vigorously with tradition** *is pursued in this modern Sardinian home. The more limited technology of past eras gave earlier generations than ours less scope for expressing themselves through the shapes and styles of the buildings they lived in – walls were thick, irregular and cool in hot countries, and cottages were densely thatched in wet countries, because these were practical solutions to practical problems. Choosing such styles today is way of saying that you want to associate yourself with a certain time or region.*

homes have large picture windows facing the street through which passers-by can see into a living room. But the residents' personal style comes from the way they arrange this room, the furniture they choose to put in it and the colors they use (see *Ch 7*). Other cultures show this combination of solidarity and individuality in similar ways. They may express their group identity through common religious and cultural symbols, or display objects and symbols that show their individual accomplishments.

In many cases, the style we choose for the decoration of our home shows not only the kind of lifestyle we have but also the lifestyle we would like to have. Our home may not be in the ideal position, it may not be the style of architecture we really like, but we can modify it to reflect our aspirations. You can create the illusion of country living by choosing natural woods and stone and farmhouse furniture. You can imagine you live in the Mediterranean by using terracotta, glazed tiles, pure colors like white, yellow and green and by arranging a table and chairs under the trees outside. You can even turn a ranch house into a high-tech home with chrome, spotlights and industrial-style heating units. Our home is our primary territory, the place where we feel most secure and able to be ourselves, and as such it is a measure of who and what we are. **CW, BBB, PBH, IA**

▲ **"I am part of this neighborhood"** *proclaims house after house in the Haight Ashbury district of San Francisco. Although modifications such as double garages have crept in with time, and although a house here and there still uses psy-* *chedelic colors, reminiscent of the hippie era of the 1960s (of which Haight Ashbury was at the center), residents today tend to emphasize the unity of style in their neighborhood's 1890s architecture. This unified style still contains ample scope* *for proclaiming that each building is individual, containing a household with a unique personality, doubtless something that the original occupants similarly valued.*

Objects on Display

A FRENCH radio program invites its listeners to play detective by letting someone wander round a complete stranger's house, then asking them to describe that person and guess what sort of life they lead. The only information they have is the arrangement of the house and the objects in it. In everyday life we consciously or unconsciously invite visitors to play this game in our own homes. We use our possessions to communicate something to others about ourselves. Some objects have a personal message – they say something about our personality; others have a social message – they say something about our culture and our status.

For many people, objects are a link between the past and the future as they are rich in associations with other places or people. In a recent fire in a historic house the fire fighters were instructed to save all the artifacts before even attempting to put out the fire. It was considered that the objects were of more value than the architecture. The house could be rebuilt but the things were irreplacable, as they carried with them traces of the people who had owned and cherished them.

Extensions of ourselves

Many studies have shown that when people lose their possessions after theft or disaster or when they are put into institutions, they suffer a traumatic sense of loss. People who have been burgled may also feel a sense of violation, just as if they had been physically assaulted. Why does the fate of our possessions have such a profound bearing on our feelings? One psychologist has suggested that possessions which are part of our daily activity, or which evoke special memories, are so important to our personal world that they become in effect a part of ourselves.

The objects we own do not just reflect our present lifestyle, they also prompt memories of past experiences or of associations with people. When people describe their important possessions they often indicate that the object has a certain significance – "That was my grandmother's," "We bought that on our honeymoon." As heirlooms, these objects will extend a family's sense of group identity. If you live in a multiethnic society, traditional objects can also help to reinforce your cultural identity. Immigrants and

---

LET YOUR HOME TELL ITS STORY

■ *Imagine you are visiting your home as a complete stranger. Try to look at the things in your home as the stranger would see them, constructing an image of yourself from what you see in each room.*

Ask yourself questions about the objects around you.

◆ *What kinds of things does this person display and how do they vary from room to room?*
◆ *What significance would you think the objects have for their owner?*
◆ *What do the books tell you about the person's tastes and interests?*

◆ *Are the pictures and ornaments a mixture of styles or do they look like collections?*
◆ *What kinds of relationships do the photographs of people tell you of?*
◆ *Are the furnishings in one controlled style or a mixture of styles?*

◆ *How many of the objects look as if they are just for show; how many as if they are for practical reasons only; how many for both?*

Do you think the stranger got an accurate picture, or one of you as you would like to be seen?

56

■ **Picture preferences**. *A small minority of people give esthetic appreciation as the main reason for hanging a picture on their wall – LEFT Walter Annenberg, former American Ambassador to Britain, and his wife Leonore cherish for its beauty "The Irises" by Claude Monet. Usually, identification with the scene, or a relationship with the artist, is more important – children's drawings, may cover more wall space than professionally created images. Another influence is identification with the person portrayed – RIGHT Curtis Sharpe Jr displays the portrait of himself that he commissioned after winning a million-dollar lottery.*

The objects in your house tell your personal story ■ *Ornaments, paintings, books and furniture – what do they reveal about your personality and values?* ■ *What social status do they claim on your behalf?*

people who have lived for some time in other countries often display objects from their previous homeland as a reminder of its way of life.

Objects for the image-conscious

But our possessions do more than reassure us about who we are and remind us of times past – often we choose our possessions so as to project a particular image to others (in some cases this may be an image which we find desirable even if it is not an entirely accurate portrayal of what we are really like.) Someone who is active in sports, for example, will want to show off trophies and photographs, parents display their children's handicrafts, musical people have musical instruments and people who pride themselves on their artistic taste collect paintings and *objets d'art*. In this way, material possessions are a kind of second skin, an integral part of the image we present to others. We empha-

size objects that reflect the side of ourselves we think is most important.

Men traditionally prefer objects to do with action – cars, stereos, sports equipment and trophies. Women often choose more contemplative objects like sculpture, ornaments, textiles, plants and photographs.

What we collect and display varies from person to person, room to room, and group to group. You might have collections of rare and valuable antiques or functional objects that contribute to visual style, or objects that show status and wealth. Books can be a sign of intellectual taste and accomplishment. You can see instantly from someone's bookshelves if they are a doctor, linguist, lawyer or artist; if they like gardening, travel, photography or steam trains. Books embody ideals and express values in a more direct way than any other type of possession. Coffee-table books, in fact, are specifically designed to be displayed rather than read. These are glossy, expensive and usually on currently fashionable topics.

The same principle applies to furniture. While it is func-

▲ **Pursuing a lost era**. Though not born until the early 1960s, Jim Burgess probably has more 1950s odds and ends in his home than any genuine household of that decade ever had. Few of these objects make

claims to artistic merit – many are simply everyday clutter of the time – but they put him in contact with a way of life that fascinates him. The things that accumulate around a person – whether haphazardly or

through conscious design – help to stimulate moods and ways of thinking that make particular sense to the person.

CREATING AN IMAGE

■ *Status used to be measured by whether or not we owned individually produced items made from expensive and rare materials. Nowadays, when so much is mass-produced, the mere fact that we own an object is no longer enough. Only the right brand carries the desired status.*

Design has, to some extent, taken the place of craft in determining the value of an object. It employs a subtle language of its own. Black metal finishes, for example, often signify "serious" and "professional," pastel shades may indicate a more frivolous function. Design is a manufacturer's most important means of differentiating their product from that of a competing firm. Think of the hundreds of makes of car that fulfill an identical function but which are distinguished from one another only by design.

The image-building process depends on change. Every year sees new designs become cult objects, and last year's begin to look dated. A cult object has to convince buyers that it belongs to the age and that it conveys status to the owner – function is of secondary importance.

tional, style is a major determinant of what we choose. Furniture can be used to reinforce our image and we are able to choose from a wide range of styles. A padded black leather chair conveys a message of taste linked to status, whereas antiques show our appreciation of the craftmanship of previous centuries.

Velvet drapes and Persian carpets give a note of grandeur, while a stripped-pine dresser suggests natural, country-style living. However, even if our lifestyle or aspirations change, we may still keep some of our old furniture and the combination of our old and new tastes will add to the picture of who we are.

Why are pictures and ornaments important?

We often expect pictures and ornaments to reflect some sort of esthetic appreciation, but very often these, too, have quite a different role.

In a survey of homes in Chicago, only 16 percent of people said the attraction of their pictures was their esthetic qualities, and only 10 percent said the pictures were displayed for fashionable or stylistic reasons. Why then do we have pictures on our walls? The main reason given was that the pictures had memories or associations to do with other people. They were done by children, grandchildren or friends, or reminded their owners of a holiday.

◀ **An obsession with color.** *When the home is a workplace – as it is for Kaffe Fasset, a designer of knitwear and needlework patterns – work objects become part of the household decor. Fasset's first advice to anyone trying to create a rewarding effect with these materials is to use as many colors as possible.*

▼ **An obsession with Barbie and Ken.** *When collecting takes over your life, collections can take over your home.*

58

THE COLLECTORS

■ *Serious collectors devote their whole house or at least whole rooms to the display of their treasures.*

A trait of the compulsive collector is that they "have to have" something. If they see an object that would complement their collection they will stop at nothing to acquire it.

One couple collected so much Victoriana that they had to go into the business of selling off what they could not fit into

their house. Another couple restored their home entirely with shop fittings and shopping memorabilia of the 19th century.

Once you start to collect something it can change your life. One woman who bought a couple of plates from an antique dealer became so fascinated by them that she eventually made a new career in ceramics research.

Art is one of the few areas where social class makes a difference to why and what people own. Upper-middle-class families are much more likely to have pictures than lower-middle-class ones, and this is not a question of money but of the perceived status the objects have. Lower-middle-class families prefer to show off their purchasing power through expensive cameras, stereos and gadgets than through artistic objects such as paintings or ornaments.

Three-dimensional art objects displayed in the home often have ethnic or religious associations. Catholics display statues of saints, Jewish families may have a seven-branched candlestick, Hindus have statues of gods and goddesses.

Ornaments are sometimes prizes or trophies for some achievement at work or in a sport, sometimes the relics of a childhood hobby. In relatively few cases is artistic or esthetic merit the only reason for displaying an object.

Living sculptures

An essential decorative feature in most homes is the houseplant. In Victorian Britain they were popular because they symbolized the country's extensive empire – every home had its exotic aspidistra or rubber plant. These days they are sometimes a symbol of an ecological consciousness. For some people they are a substitute garden, for others merely a design feature. Plants can be evidence of the emotions and personality of those who have them. We tend to think that a house full of plants is cared for and that the owner is in touch with nature. Plants are also one of the most popular gifts as they have a rather neutral function – they do not usually offend our taste, they fit in with most styles and an extra plant will always be welcomed by someone who already owns one.

Plants do not communicate strong messages about status or wealth unless they happen to be a particularly exotic or rare specimen. Generally when people want objects as status symbols, they use objects such as stereos, televisions, lighting systems – anything that is updated frequently.

State-of-the-art technology can be a style object as well as a status symbol. Some people buy the latest, most expensive equipment to emphasize their purchasing power; they are not necessarily genuinely interested in music or lighting. Where the stereo is located in a house can be significant. If someone puts an elaborate, expensive sound system in the most public room in the house, it is possible that this is for display rather than listening. If, however, they hide it away in a private room or study, this is a strong ground for judging that they really do enjoy high quality sound.

Though people still define themselves by what they produce – dress designer, baker, artist – in today's consumer society, our acquired possessions also say a great deal about who we are. Every object in our home represents one facet of our identity.

59

▶ **The ideal gift** may be a houseplant – there is always room for one more in most homes, they do not usually offend anyone's taste, and they fit in with most styles. Gifts often go wrong because they contradict the image that the recipient wants to project, but a houseplant does not usually say enough about status to undermine social prestige, and it is the way the recipient uses the plant that will say the most about their personality and values. Here, lighting and a variety of leaf textures and colors has created an illuminated living sculpture in the bathroom.

Color in the Home

THE COLORS we use in the decoration of our homes reflect changes in fashion and contemporary design. They also say a lot about *us*. We use color to express ourselves, to make statements about the way we see ourselves, the way we feel and what we like. The color of a room can have a direct influence on our mood, efficiency and general well-being. But how do you know which color will be suitable for a particular room or will create the right atmosphere? Is it just a matter of choosing your favorite color, or is there more to it than that?

Seeing color

Color depends on direct and reflected light. In low light levels, such as moonlight, objects appear to have no color at all and in some artificial lights colors will change completely. To some extent, our experience compensates for any distortion caused by filters or effects of lighting. Because we learn to connect certain objects with color, we usually project back from our mind the color associated with that object whenever we see it – grass is green, blood is red, oranges are orange.

Other factors can influence the quality of a color and the effect it creates. The colors we use in our homes rarely consist of pure hues. A pure (or saturated) color has had no other pigment added to it, and the purer the color, the more intense it appears. The effect of a color on your surroundings will depend partly on whether it is a pure color or a mixture – saturated or unsaturated.

Different colors for different rooms

Your choice of color for a particular room may be dictated by having to coordinate existing furnishings such as carpet or tiles, or by practical considerations like wanting a color that does not show the dirt. However, our choices are most often made for psychological, rather than purely functional, reasons – we want colors that are right for us as individuals and for the kind of life we lead.

Moreover, although we are likely to choose colors because we like them, we would not necessarily use our favorite colors randomly throughout our home. Most people like to control access to various parts of their homes, reserving some places for the immediate family and others for visitors (see *Ch 4*). One way to make this distinction clear is by a subtle use of color. Think about your own

UNDERSTANDING COLOR

■ *Words are often inadequate when it comes to describing colors. This is not surprising when you realize that a particular red that you are having trouble describing is only one of over 35,000 colors that people can distinguish.*

Names given to household paint colors such as "Muffin" and "Avocado" are often confusing because, not only will the colors, together with our understanding of the colors, of muffins and avocados vary, but, often, different paint manufacturers will use the same names to describe quite different colors.

If we can assess and describe the appearance of colors more precisely we will be better able to choose colors that will produce the effect we want. To do this we need to understand what color is.

Each color that we experi- *ence embodies three attributes: hue, brightness, and saturation. "Hue" represents the redness, greenness, blueness and yellowness of a color, while "brightness" (or "value") represents the brightness and darkness of a color. It is the modification of a color by the addition of black or white.*

"Saturation" or "chroma" represents the chromatic strength of a color – such as the difference between a fire-engine red and a soft pink. Saturation refers to the density of the pigment: a pure saturated color has had no gray mixed with it. **TP**

▶ **The color sphere**, *here exploded to create a flat diagram of color relationships. The equatorial region is a color wheel, with saturated (full-strength) hues arranged in rainbow sequence. Moving* *toward the north pole, the color bands are brightened by the addition of white. Toward the south pole they are darkened by the addition of black.*

Understanding how color works in the home can change your approach to decoration
■ *How does the color of a room affect its shape, size and atmosphere?* ■ *Can the colors around you alter your mood?* ■ *What do the colors you choose say about your personality?* ■ *Why is green a relaxing color?*

home. Which rooms are decorated in the most intense colors?

You will probably find that they are those to which few other people have access – your bedroom or study, for example. You will probably have used more muted colors on large areas, such as walls and carpets, in the living room, kitchen and bathroom – all rooms that are freely available to visitors. In these "public" rooms, and in rooms that may have to serve more than one purpose, intense, pure colors

are likely to be used in smaller quantities and on smaller areas – such as rugs and cushions. There are, of course, exceptions to this, especially when the choice of color is in keeping with the function of the room. Bold colors stimulate conversation and may be useful in a room used primarily for entertaining. Kitchens are often painted in colors connected with food, such as green, red and brown. Blue kitchens are quite rare – perhaps because we do not connect the color blue with things to eat.

On the other hand, bathrooms are often blue – or pink. Research indicates that people associate pink more with cleanliness and blue (or green) with relaxation. So, if you see your bathroom purely in terms of hygiene, choose a pink color scheme. But if you like to retire to your bathroom to unwind, it would be better to choose blue or green.

■ **Private colors**. *Many people tend to use neutral colors in the more public areas of their homes and are often more personal or more adventurous in their choice of colors for private rooms.* ABOVE LEFT *The* predominance of pale blue, and the small, unobtrusive patterns on the fabrics and wallpaper, create a relaxing atmosphere: this bedroom is a place to unwind after a busy day. ABOVE RIGHT *Red and pink have erotic* connotations, making this bedroom more exciting and sensual. The luxuriant blinds and the bold shapes of the bedcover enhance the stimulating effect.

Equator

S

SEEING RED!

■ *To recognize differences between colors requires no experience and no learning – it is one of the few truly innate human responses.*

We react involuntarily to color. If you look at brilliant reflected light on a warm color such as red, for example, a chain reaction occurs.

First, your muscular tension increases, and your body tends to lean toward the bright light and vivid color. Your respiration and heart rate speed up and your blood pressure rises.

Finally, there is an increase in your brain activity that is strong enough to be electrically recorded. Dim light and a cool color, such as blue, can have the opposite effect: your muscles relax, your respiration and heart rate slow down and your blood pressure drops. You may well fall asleep.

Red objects often seem closer and larger than others because the natural focal point of reflected red light lies behind the retina in the front of our field of vision.

Getting the temperature right

Our impression that some hues are warm and others are cold is very strong. In an experiment in Norway, people were put in blue or red rooms of exactly the same temperature. Those in the blue rooms tended to set their thermostat four degrees higher than those in the red rooms.

However, another study – this one in Japan – found that people judged the degree of warmth in a room not just by the color itself, but also by its lightness and saturation. For example dark green, which is intense but not bright, is considered warmer than light orange which is bright without being intense.

As a rule, the colors that we consider to be warm are oranges, reds and shades of brown. Cool colors are generally shades of green and blue. But many colors can be made warmer by adding a little yellow or red, or cooler by adding a little blue, blue-green or white.

The warmth of a color also depends on whether it is seen next to another warm color or a cool color and what the texture of the object is.

The ability to manipulate color can be very important if you are trying to achieve the right psychological effect in a particular room. You may want to make a private living room cozy and intimate, and a functional kitchen cool and businesslike. By using color carefully, you can enhance or counteract the qualities of a room. A large room with many windows will feel less chilly and unwelcoming, for example, if you use warm colors on the walls, but if the same room is to be used as a workroom you may choose to bring out its airiness by painting it in light shades.

Weighing up a color

Colors are not only seen as warm or cold; they also appear to have different weights. A number of psychological studies have shown that if two identical boxes are painted red and green respectively, people will judge the red one to be heavier than the green one. Other experiments have shown that the brightness of color also affects our judgment of weight – a box painted bright yellow would probably be judged the lightest of all. In general, objects painted in pure, cold, light colors seem physically lighter than those painted in warm, dark, earthy colors. Red also has an influence on the apparent weight of other colors so that something painted yellow and red would appear heavier than if it were painted yellow and green. To complicate matters still further, even a light color appears heavier if it is a mixture of pigments than if it is a pure color.

How can you put this to work in your own home? If dark colors make a surface seem heavy, while light colors make it seem to weigh less, try to use dark shades in rooms where you want to create a serious atmosphere, such as a study or a library. Dark colors can also make flimsy screens or partitions seem more solid. This can be important if you live in crowded surroundings and want to feel private. We usually

▲ **The relationship between color and heaviness.** *Dark walls and window frames make this study seem substantial. This encourages a serious atmosphere in keeping with the function of the room – it is a place for solitary concentration. Lighter walls are generally more appropriate in rooms used for informal social occasions.*

■ **Harnessing the effect of white.** ABOVE *If a room lacks strong points of visual interest, extensive use of white can be unstimulating.* RIGHT *Here, however, white walls help to emphasize the room's focal point, an unusual window upon a world of sharply contrasting greens. The effect is both stimulating and comfortable.*

paint ceilings in white or some other light color because we do not want to feel that there is a great weight hanging over our head – dark colors on low ceilings can be unsettling and oppressive.

Seeing things in a different light

When you are planning a color scheme in order to create a particular atmosphere you should remember that our perception of color varies according to the light conditions (see *Ch 8*), and that different kinds of light have their own effect depending on the time of day and the aspect of the room. Direct sunlight makes colors fade to whitish tones, while sunset turns yellow to orange and blue to purple.

Artificial lighting in the home is usually electric light or, occasionally, candlelight, both of which produce a yellow light that makes warm colors look brighter. But it also tends to suppress colder colors, so that they appear duller. If you are only going to use a room at a certain time of day, then it makes sense to choose colors that combine to the best effect with its light source and its aspect. A room that faces south could successfully be painted in cool colors if you are using it during the day but, if you also want to entertain

friends there in the evening, the same cool colors will turn an uninviting gray under electric lighting and will not seem welcoming.

Color and complexity

The effects of color can be modified even further by the degree of complexity in a room. A combination of intense colors in an otherwise plain room could provide just enough stimulus and interest for social activities or even for working. A room containing highly complex decorative or structural features, however, needs no further complication. Strong colors here might be highly unsettling – shapes, colors and patterns would clash for attention and prevent any sense of harmony. Such a room would be particularly unsuitable for quiet or meditative pursuits. Complex visual

64

> ▶ **Different shades of red?** *In choosing a particular color we need to bear in mind other colors that will be used next to it. The same shade of red is used in all these boxes but it appears different in each one. It is most dominant against a background of green and least obvious when used with dark pink – a shade of red itself.*

SPECIAL EFFECTS AND ILLUSIONS

■ *You will get along better with the people you live with if you feel comfortable with your surroundings. Color is the vital element in design that brings shape to life. You can create a great many optical illusions with color and there is no need to put up with a room that infuriates you because it is the wrong shape, makes you feel claustrophobic or has too much space.*

If a room makes you feel cramped, you can change its apparent size by using light colors on the walls and ceiling. Dark hues appear to advance toward you, so if you spend a lot of time alone in a vast, high-ceilinged room, paint it in dark, warm colors. Dark colors on the ceiling lower the apparent height and these colors on the walls will draw in the dimensions of the room and make it more intimate.

A poorly-lit room can be irritating if you are reading or doing close work: you can reflect more light by painting some areas white. In a room with little or no daylight you can give the illusion of sunlight by using warm, light colors.

◀ **Disturbing effects.** *Black changes our perception of boundaries and can make us feel insecure. The black paneling of this living room seems to be advancing ominously toward us.*

▶ **Our reactions to colors** *are influenced by pattern and texture. The highly patterned surfaces in this room and the amount of detail in the large paintings could result in an overstimulating atmosphere. But this potentially irritating effect is offset by the use of colors that blend attractively and by the unifying Indian theme.*

stimuli can be highly disturbing and if you are aiming to produce the ideal setting to suit your mood, personality and lifestyle, you should try to establish a balance between arousing or restful colors and levels of sameness and variation. In a room that has to serve several functions it is especially unwise to use dominant colors or decoration. A suitable setting for a party may be quite inappropriate if you want to hold a meeting of parents and teachers from your children's school. If your room has plain, featureless walls and you want to add a note of excitement, you can introduce small quantities of bold color and pattern into furnishings and upholstery. Conversely, if the room has odd angles, a sloping ceiling or an ugly patterned carpet that you cannot afford to replace, you can create a calmer atmosphere and play down these features by painting the walls in plain, light colors.

One color affects another

The effect of a color is always modified by other colors, especially those next to it, partly due to the reflectivity of colored surfaces. This obviously has implications for our choice of colors in our homes. For example, complementary colors (see p60) in proximity can produce a sense of tension – red is most dominant against green, blue against orange, black against white.

This stimulating effect may produce the excitement we want but in large quantities the clash of complementaries can be tiring. But it is not only complementary colors that affect each other. For example, a bright yellow cushion may look elegant on a gray sofa but exotic on an orange one. Some colors work well alone or in certain combinations but look dull or dirty when seen next to other colors. Yellowish greens, in particular, turn some shades of blue to purple. You may have considered this combination for a cool, sophisticated living room but the actual effect could be far from what you had imagined.

Just as colors seem to be warmer or colder depending on the warmth of the color they are next to, light colors always look brighter if they are seen against a dark background, and dark hues always look more dramatic against a white background than against a color. If your home is your refuge from a monotonous or repetitive job, perhaps you should create an exciting, stimulating atmosphere in at least one of your rooms by the imaginative application of color.

Does color influence our moods?

We often talk about someone being in a black mood, feeling blue, seeing red or going green with envy. Expressing moods in terms of color is one thing, but can differently colored surroundings alter or affect the way we are feeling? We associate green with restfulness, blue with peaceful settings and yellow or red with energy and exitement.

In a study carried out in the United States two identical lectures were given in differently colored rooms – one green and one blue. People listening to the lecture in the blue room found it dull and thought it lasted beyond the 20 minutes taken to deliver it. Those in the red room found it much more interesting and felt that it was over too soon.

However, other studies have called into question the relationship between color and mood. The strength and brightness of a color may in fact make more difference than the color itself – a strong green is as exciting as a strong red. If you think of where you go to relax in your own home, the chances are it will be a room with very little bright color. It is important, then, to select the right intensity of color for a room when you want it to stimulate a particular mood. Yellow, for example, can have different associations and effects. A bright yellow often symbolizes lightness and happiness, but yellow is also traditionally the color of cowardice and, in France, the color associated with cuckolds. Clinical psychologists have noticed that people contemplating suicide are often drawn to yellow: Vincent van Gogh, for example, went through a distinctly yellow period just before he killed himself.

It might be a mistake to try to surround a depressed friend or partner with bright color since the contrast between the color and their mood could well make them even more miserable. When we are feeling low we often feel more comfortable with peaceful, unstimulating colors.

Color and personality

If you go into almost any home you will find a somewhat similar pattern of color variation, public rooms being painted in neutral colors and private rooms in more intense colors. Nevertheless, the actual colors chosen will reflect the personalities of the occupants, especially in the most private rooms.

People are sometimes divided into those who like warm colors and those who prefer cool colors. Preference for warm colors is said to indicate a responsive, open person-

COLOR AND TASTE

■ *Our attitudes to color in home decoration change often – sometimes dramatically. The colors considered harmonious by one generation may be quickly judged as discordant and tasteless by another. These cycles in color closely linked preference to movements in art and design which in turn, are influenced by technological innovation.*

For example, the taste for white interiors in the 1930s (made possible by the development of a nonyellowing titanium dioxide paint) quickly became less popular during World War II. Later, the 1950s saw the emergence of vividly colored

wallpapers, laminates and paints in pinks, oranges and turquoises. These used the newly developed dyes and pigments to react against a wartime drabness and transformed the home into a Hollywood filmset. However, this "brash" color was superseded in the early 1960s with a taste for black and white and subdued interiors which paralleled interest in outer space, Op Art and the black miniskirt. By the mid-1960s this, in turn, had given way to coordinated colors in the home: this interest in color themes corresponded with ethnic clothes and psychedelic visions of inner space. The new

▲ **Green is nature's neutral** and for most of us it has associations with fresh leaves and grass. Although emerald green can be exciting, many greens are calming. The backstage areas of television studios and

theaters are known as "green rooms" – even though they are often blue or cream – because of the traditional use of green to keep guests and actors calm before they go on stage or in front of the cameras.

dyes developed in the 1960s brought primary hues into the 1970s to pick out the elements of hi-tech interiors. The 1980s added white to color to begin a fascination for muted hues and the ensuing pastel craze (reminiscent of the 1940s) permeated all facets of design. By the end of the decade pastels gave way to an interest in the "organic

hues." These are the moss greens and terra cotta browns of the environmentally friendly interiors of the 1990s.

In reacting to and replacing one trend with another, we extend our appreciation of the world of color and our experience of our environment is continuously refreshed. **TP**

ality – someone who is emotional and feels strongly about things. A preference for cool colors, on the other hand, is said to mean that you are more detached, less adaptable and rather reserved. But there are many exceptions to these generalizations.

If you are an extroverted, outgoing person you probably have a lot of red or yellow in your home. Extroverts feel relaxed in rooms that contain substantial amounts of strong, bright color. They tend to need more arousing environments than introverts. Introverted people feel more at home with subdued, earthy colors than with primaries.

Color preference may also be related to other personality traits. Research has found that people with a strong drive to succeed, especially in managerial or financial careers, tend to prefer somber browns and blues containing a lot of gray. They avoid bright yellows, pale blues and pastel shades. Idealistic people are happy to have a lot of white in their homes, offset with areas of deep blue or purple. Very self-conscious people – those who are concerned about what other people think of them – often use rather washed-out colors in their home environment.

But we do not exercise our personal preference in a vacuum. Our likes and dislikes are also influenced by fashion and by background. Take a look round your own home. What do the colors you see there reveal about *your* personality? **PM**

► **Color preference is not just a matter of personality**. *Many factors are involved in determining which colors we like and which colors we choose to have in our homes. Your reaction to a color may well depend on past experience. If you associate a particular shade of blue with a place where you like to go on holiday you may find yourself working the color into your decor.*

67

CHOOSING A COLOR SCHEME

■ *What do you do if you love red, your partner hates it and your children want an orange bathroom?*

Colors in the home have to be tolerated by the whole family as well as being right for the room they are used in.

When you come to deciding on a color scheme it is helpful to draw up a checklist of questions:
◆ *How big is the room?*
◆ *Does the room get a lot of daylight or is it mostly dark?*
◆ *What sort of artificial light is there?*
◆ *What is the room going to be used for?*

◆ *Will the room be used mostly during the day or at night?*
◆ *Who is going to use the room most? How old are they?*
◆ *How long will each of these people use the room?*
◆ *What existing colors will remain – carpet/tiles/curtains?*

◆ *What sort of colors do various members of the household like?*
◆ *What atmosphere do you want the room to have?*

Once you have thought about these questions – with the help of this chapter – you can make

a considered choice of the best way to use color in your rooms, bearing in mind the different effects colors have in different situations.

SHOWING YOUR TRUE COLORS

■ *There are thousands of paint shades available for use in the home. With so much choice it should be easy to pick just the right shade to suit your mood, the function of the room and the type of the building. Unfortunately, however, color charts cannot show you how a color will work in practice when it is seen with other colors, in a dark corner, under fluorescent light or as a background to your furniture. It is not enough to know that red makes things look bigger or that green is relaxing: it is the type of red or green – or any other color – that counts. You have to consider, for example, whether it is a pure or mixed color, a pale shade or a bright one.*

The first thing to do when deciding on a color scheme is to look at where you live. Is it a high-rise apartment, a country cottage, a mansion, a log cabin or a suburban villa? Does it have a period feel that you want to enhance or do you prefer a contemporary, hi-tech interior? Secondly, consider what you do in each room and who uses it. You may have your own workroom, an all-purpose living/dining/entertaining room, a family bathroom, a galley kitchen. Do you live alone or will you have to take into account the taste of a partner or other family members? Think about how much time you spend at home: if you are there all day you may need more variety than someone who experiences several environments during the day. How much space do you have? If you feel cramped in a small house or studio apartment, you will need to make the space feel bigger. Finally, do not forget your own preferences. If you like purple, find somewhere you can use it effectively.

A SPECTRUM OF COLORS

The effect of any color in the home is influenced by factors such as light, texture and the proximity of other colors. However, it is possible to generalize about the effects a particular color tends to have.

■ **Reds** *start with pale pink and intensify to pure red. Pale pink is warm and pleasing; it combines well with greens. As pinks turn to reds, they become more stimulating. Pure red is seldom used in large quantities*

COLOR FOR CHILDREN

■ *Children usually have quite definite ideas about color, and the choice of color for their rooms is just as important as for any other room in the house. Wherever possible, try to incorporate your child's preferences so that they feel happy in their room. We all need time away from other people to enjoy our own tastes and interests. Try to make your child's special place as inviting as possible.*

A color plan for a child's room might look something like this:
◆ **Birth-2 years** *Even newborn babies are capable of perceiving color. Choose soft, warm colors such as mixtures of pinks and greens in opaque tints to avoid tiring reflections.*
◆ **2-4 years** *Toddlers and young children are attracted to bright colors, so choose multicolored, primary hues.*

◆ **6-12 years** *Use a neutral background so that a variety of shapes, pictures and images can be pinned up to stimulate the child's imagination.*

◆ **Teenagers** *Let teenagers choose their own colors and express their developing taste – even if it is purple walls and an orange ceiling!*

in the home. On ceilings it produces a disturbing and heavy effect. It makes walls advance and reduces the sense of space. Red can be used to accentuate detail and attract attention but it needs to be used with care. Pinks and reds reflect light that is flattering to the skin and complexion, so they are good colors for a room used for social gatherings – when people look healthy, they feel better.

■ **Orange** is a warm, stimulating, cheerful color that is strongly associated with the taste of the fruit. It is a good choice for kitchens but could be overarousing if used on the ceiling. It gives walls a warm and luminous appearance. If you like bright orange, it can produce a jovial effect and, in the northern hemisphere, is very successful in north or east-facing rooms. But it is not one of the most popular colors and some people find it irritating. You may find shades of orange – ginger, apricot and burnt orange easier to cope with.

■ Pure **yellow** is said to be our least favorite color. Yellow highlights can be cheering, but yellow can have an irritating effect when used on walls. Yellow is the lightest of the primary colors and it reflects more light as it pales into primrose. Lemon yellow makes ceilings look light.

■ Pale **green** is thought to be the most restful of all colors, although pure green, like pure red, can be cheerful and stimulating. Green ceilings can feel protective, but the reflected light produces unattractive effects on the skin. On walls dark bluish-green gives a secure feeling and works well in places where concentration is required.

■ Dark **blue**, like dark green, yellow and red, will bring things closer. It can seem oppressive, especially on the ceiling. Dark blue is a good color for floors, however, and gives them a substantial quality. Pale blues are cool and calming. Pale blue walls and ceilings tend to recede, increasing the sense of spaciousness. But since pale blue reflects a pale light onto the skin, it could make you look pale and washed-out. Blue on its own can look rather bleak in entrance halls or other rooms that do not get much direct daylight. It is hardly ever

used in kitchens – it has no natural connection with food and can look harsh under fluorescent lighting.

■ The paler **shades** of purple – lavender and violet – are soft and calming. Purple itself is rarely used in homes, except in small quantities to accentuate something or add a colorful note. In large quantities it can disturb your ability to focus your eyes.

■ There are many shades of **brown** – from reddish browns and yellowish browns to almost black. Dark browns can have a very depressing effect when used on ceilings but they suggest stability when used on the floor. There was a fashion for brown bathrooms in the 1970s but it is not generally a suitable color for rooms that need good illumination. Brown at its most neutral – beige – is probably one of the most common colors found in the home.

■ When **black** pales to gray it is a neutral, calming and slightly hard color. It is important that the exact shade of gray used is compatible with other colors in the room. Pure black is usually confined to woodwork or detail and can produce very odd effects if used in any quantity: rooms painted black would seem to have no boundaries.

■ **White**, on the other hand, is possibly the most overused color in modern home decoration. It is often used on ceilings so that we do not notice the height of a room. It is also used on walls, either to create more reflected light or to increase the apparent size of the room. White is a neutral color. It can appear clean and crisp and is suitable for rooms where hygiene is important, such as bathrooms and kitchens. One of the qualities of white is its reflectivity (see Ch 8). It can therefore be useful, for example, in a small room with little natural light. However clear, crisp and elegant, large amounts of white can look harsh and glaring in some lights and may cause quite severe eye strain if not relieved by some other color. Black and white together can create a dramatic, modern, sophisticated effect but they are very difficult to keep looking good – the slightest scuff or finger-mark makes them look dirty.

The Effects of Light

YOU CAN create a dramatically different effect in any room – without even redecorating or moving the furniture – just by altering the way you illuminate it. Very few interiors need only one level of light – variations in lighting indicate that particular rooms are used for a particular purpose. A kitchen, for example, should be bright enough to make you want to cook in it, and a living room should welcome you with a feeling of warmth. We do not use lighting just to increase the visibility of an area; it also affects the appearance of colors and textures. It can make spaces seem larger, smaller, inviting, functional, or intimate. Knowing how light works is essential to creating the right effect in a room.

Seeing colors in a different light

Traditionally, artists have always preferred to paint their canvases in daylight. This preference is the basis of the conventional image of artists painting in a garret. In the northern hemisphere artists usually prefer to work in a studio against north light – an orientation that provides a balanced and more constant illumination in which to judge hues and their combination. Sunlight, depending on its direction and upon atmospheric conditions, can dramatically alter our impression of colors and colored surfaces. For example, colors seen on a gray and cloudy day are quite different from the same colors seen in brilliant sunshine. It is the constantly fluctuating nature of light that accounts for the elusiveness of color.

Domestic lighting and home decoration

Another important factor concerns the development of artificial lighting which began with the glow of candles and oil lamps. Safe, cheap and universally available electric

◆ A floodlight points upwards from floor level, creating an interesting visual feature and gently illuminating the room with the light reflected off the wall.

◆ The shades of these table lamps stop the light from shining into your eyes, but lets it reflect off the walls and ceiling. The translucent cloth allows a muted light for general illumination.

◀ Walls, floors and ceilings influence the level of light in a room. This is why people often paint their ceilings white – to make their rooms seem brighter. But it is in fact reflection from floors that helps a room most to benefit from natural light, since the floor is where most of it falls. The pale varnished wooden floor of this Japanese home reflects the light better than dark wood can, illuminating the whole room naturally and warmly.

▲ Lighting divides a room unobtrusively for the two functions it is to serve during the evening's entertaining – a pendant lamp encircles the dining area in a pool of soft light while the seating area is marked out

Lighting creates the mood in your home
■ *Lights have a marked effect on your color scheme* ■ *Often, we do not take enough care to match lighting to the function of the room* ■ *Changing lights can transform your home.*

lighting has altered the way we use our homes and also the way we decorate them. Interest in home decoration began to increase with the development of the kerosene lamp in the 1820s. The Victorians, and later the Edwardians, started to match the lighting of their homes with their lifestyles, moving from elaborate fittings to subdued, tasteful lighting. The effect of each lamp was carefully considered and lighting became a part of every decorating scheme.

As the amount of light given off by individual lamps increased, so too did the function of the lamps. People could afford to have some lighting just for effect rather than for illumination. Lamps and fittings became decorative objects in their own right and began to take the place of more traditional ornaments in the home. Prior to the 20th century it had been the function of ornamental fittings to reflect light, and the traditional role of crystal, china and gilt had been to replace the sparkle and vitality lost when daylight faded from a room. Whereas today we use mirrors to increase the sense of space, these used to be positioned so

by lamps, each of which casts light on a small area only, creating a sense of intimacy which is enhanced by the generally subdued level of lighting.

◆ This unusual lamp forms an ornamental centerpiece for the dining area. It casts most of its light on the table setting and food, and also casts a softer light to enable diners to see one another.

HOW EFFECTIVE IS YOUR LIGHTING?

■ *Consider the effects of the lights in your rooms. Is a spotlight spoiling the effect by conflicting with something more important? Are people being made uncomfortable by glare from a badly placed light source? If you are using indirect lighting, do other important surfaces seem dimly lit in comparison to walls and ceilings?*

Here is a quick checklist of lighting effects to help you give the right feel to every room in your home:

◆ *Spotlights throw objects into relief and are useful for highlighting decorative features such as pictures or houseplants.*
◆ *Fluorescent lights tend to flatten objects and are unflattering to the complexion.*
◆ *Light flooding down a wall makes a room seem larger and low lights make a room more intimate.*
◆ *Ceiling lights can lack warmth and often cast shadows on work surfaces.*
◆ *Light coming from more than one source, whether natural or artificial, can have a subtle and interesting effect.*
◆ *Natural light can be filtered through thin curtains and slatted blinds to give a calm, diffused light.*

71

as to increase the illumination of a room by means of reflected light.

Up until the invention of gaslight at the beginning of the 20th century, the lighted wicks of wax and oil lamps were the only means of extending daylight hours and, indeed, an ability to work beyond dusk. However, gaslight could effectively extend people's waking hours. Although producing a harsh contrast within homes and workrooms, gas mantles, quickly followed by the electric light bulb, functioned as efficient "artificial suns."

The widespread use of electric lighting in the 1940s also brought new attitudes to interior decoration and these, together with an unprecedented increase in industrial wages, laid the foundation of a do-it-yourself boom in home decoration. Rooms which had once remained gloomy and dirty from the soot of oil lamps, open fires and kerosene stoves were transformed into brightly painted and, often, gaudily colored spaces with the dust-free atmosphere provided by central heating. For example, by the late 1940s the kitchen – up until that period often the most depressing room in the home – suddenly became a more clinical but colorful workroom that was also a pleasant place to spend leisure time in.

The transformation of the kitchen, where color was now applied to *show* the dirt rather than hide it, reflected a revolution in the interiors of suburban factories. Here, electric light had not only extended hours into night-shift work but had also exposed the grime that had been invisible in gaslight.

Artificial lighting greatly extends the way we can use our home. Rooms can be employed at any time for more or less any function, and hitherto unusable spaces with no natural light can be transformed into bathrooms, kitchens, studies and bedrooms. However, as with sunlight, electric light sources in use today vary dramatically in their color-rendering properties. Compare, for instance, the effect of a color seen in the yellowish-orange light of the common tungsten filament lamp with the effect created by the same color when seen in the blue-greenish light of a fluorescent tube, or compare the insipid appearance of objects under a sodium discharge street light with the ghostly white impression created by the tungsten halogen beam from the headlight of a car.

Color constancy

Though we instinctively recognize these differences, we rarely apply them. This is due to an interesting aspect of our normal everyday experience of color: our association of a

CREATING DIFFERENT EFFECTS

■ Lighting does not just help us to see better– it can also add variety and sparkle and prevent a room appearing dull. In the past, people used gilded mirrors to create pinpoints of light in a room but the most common method these days is to highlight certain areas or features with spotlights. Our response to light depends on how well we see, our age, the climate, where we work and what we are doing. One person may consider a room gloomy, while another finds it relaxing. It is therefore very difficult to be sure we are creating the same effect in a room for everyone who experiences it. As a general rule, however, most rooms need two lighting schemes – one for daylight and one for artificial light. They will be quite different from each other in character and each will produce different effects. This ability of light to alter an interior can be useful if you live in a small or open-plan home where there are few distinctions between living areas. It can be a welcome change to vary the feel of parts of the room or the house.

■ **Lighting dual-purpose rooms**. In a room that has to be used for more than one function, it is all the more important to have a choice of lighting to suit each particular use. In a multipurpose kitchen/dining-room, for example, you can create a focus. Other lights in the room can be reduced to a subdued level so as to camouflage the other functions of the room. It is important the people are comfortable when they are eating and you may want to create an atmosphere of cozy intimacy. The kinds of lighting for this purpose are pendant lights, wall lights with dimmer switches and candles. When using either candles or pendant lights, it is important to ensure that you do not ruin the effect by having the light glaring in your guests' eyes. Candlelight should be above eye-level and pendant lights should not be shining directly onto your face.

THE RIGHT LIGHT FOR THE JOB

■ Most rooms benefit from a mixture of lighting so that different moods and uses can be catered for. You need a bright light for specific activities such as writing a letter, but if you are relaxing, listening to music or talking to friends you will probably be more comfortable with a soft background light.

Reading and writing
Reading lights should shine down on the page and they are best used in conjunction with some soft background light to cut down the glare of the light on the page. Older people need much more light than younger ones to do the same activity.

Washing up and cooking
Light above the sink ensures that the whole work area is illuminated. A central ceiling light will cast shadows over work surfaces around the edge of the room. "Warm white" fluorescent lights help to make food look appetizing.

Makeup and shaving
Strong light is best for the tasks. The best place for li is on either side of the mirr that they shine on your fa rather than on the glass. A above the mirror is unflatte because it casts shadows the face.

hue with an object can retain its identity under a wide range of lighting conditions. This phenomenon, called "color constancy," means that, for example, we will accept an orange as "orange-colored," even when its color impression is modified slightly by different light sources. When color judgments are critical, we do recognize these subtle nuances. This can happen if we want to buy a new suit – we often take it toward the shop window and away from the electric light source – to make an accurate judgment of its color. By doing this we are recognizing, like the artist who chooses natural light to illuminate a canvas, that color is best judged in daylight.

This awareness is rarely applied when making color selections for the home, however, though the fact that different light sources can play visual tricks with color is important. Sometimes, a hue or a combination of hues chosen in the light of fluorescent lamps in a store look wrong when placed in tungsten illumination. When we are making decisions about colors, then, we should take account of the way that electric lighting can change colors, as well as the effects of the direction of sunlight. Obviously, the simplest method of doing this is to test a trial sample of a color in its intended setting.

Recently, an important innovation has reached the paint section of the supermarket. This is the lighting booth, which up until now was found only in design technology laboratories and in the showrooms of major lighting companies. This device allows the customer to accurately predict a color scheme at the flick of a switch. This chance to see the effect of various types of electric light on a large sample of color before purchasing the paint is a major breakthrough in home decoration. **TP**

73

▲ **A decorative object** in itself, this art nouveau table lamp does not add much to the level of illumination in the room, nor does it highlight any other object. As an example of period design sought after by collectors, the lamp becomes a focus of attention on its own, in much the same way as a painting or a sculpture would in other homes.

Watching television
Watching television with all the lights off can strain your eyes as the glare of the screen contrasts harshly with a dark room. The most comfortable light is a lamp or down-lighters that illuminate the floor without interfering with the screen.

▲ **Functional chic** is the message of this room's decor, including a lamp which, while clearly a designer product, could hardly be less obtrusive. Its purpose is to illuminate the statue, making it into a focal point of the room's design. The lamp is a descendent of the classic Anglepoise design conceived in the 1930s as a utilitarian means of lighting doctors' consulting rooms. It was soon adopted by homeowners – and by furniture designers.

Touch, Sound and Smell

WHEN WE DISCUSS our environment, as with much in human society, we tend to assume the dominance of visual aspects: "What does it look like?" we usually ask. We do however have five senses (some would say more), so what can we say about the relevance of smell, touch, hearing and taste to our experience of the environment?

Many of our ideas and feelings emerge from the deep psychological links between touch and vision, events and taste or smells and loved people and places. We have all experienced the sensation of having a memory triggered by a sound, a touch or a smell. A tune on the radio may call up a memory of childhood Sunday dinners so vividly that we can almost taste roast lamb and see the family sitting around the dining table.

How are smells evocative?

Human beings, unlike most other animals, make only limited use of pheromones – the almost imperceptible chemical indicators given out by animals, unique to each individual and often used to structure group and sexual affinities. And yet smells can evoke images in a subtle way. A certain pipe tobacco may recall a loved grandparent, the smell of a tweed jacket a favorite uncle, or a silk scarf an unhappy childhood association. Most people will recall particular houses they know where it is not any single object but the house itself that has a distinct and unique smell – they lend their personal smell to familiar objects (the favorite blanket that many young children carry around with them, for example), and also to their bed and bedroom as a whole.

Most houses are occupied by more than one person and hence have several smells. Do we perhaps "synchronize" our personal smells? Some overall house smells merely originate from household objects such as a large book collection or houseplants. Pets can also give a house a distinctive smell.

There are different cultural attitudes to smell in general and smells in particular. Mediterranean societies are "contact cultures" for which smell is important. What bearing does this have on house design? Writers have suggested that the traditional central courtyard house is an important element in filtering the contact between intimate private spaces and the hustle and bustle of the public street. Perhaps scented plants contribute to this filtering process.

In some Anglo-Saxon societies a lack of smell is considered essential and an antiseptic cleanliness is striven

AT HOME WITH YOUR SENSES

◆ *Our furnishings are normally planned for comfort, but how often are we aware of the precise feeling of a favorite chair or of a living room carpet?*

◆ *When you are not playing music, listen for other sounds – ones so familiar that we are often unaware of them: the crackling of a fire, or the wind in the trees outside.*

◆ *Sometimes, odors that we might not normally consider pleasant are a part of the distinctive smell of our homes – as any dogowner knows.*

74

HOUSE-SMELL

■ *Some people will never buy a new house; others will never buy an old one. Why is this? They will usually provide objective reasons for their preference but behind these logical explanations may well be some concern for the way houses smell. Not perhaps the smell of*

◀ **The distinctive sounds, smells and textures** *of our homes are often so familiar that they go unnoticed, yet these senses make a unique contribution to the way we perceive our most familiar territory. We may include sensual stimuli by choice, such as flowers to make a room smell pleasant. But equally often sensual stimuli contribute to our perception of home without having been put there deliberately.*

All of our senses contribute to our feeling of being at home ■ Touch, sound and smell influence our choice of home ■ We use them to personalize our environment in diverse and subtle ways.

for. These communities are ones that tend to avoid close physical contact. Here, houses are designed to contain smells – for example, by the separation of zones through the use of lobbies, and until recent years, the separation of the kitchen from other rooms. Modern technology has given us perfumed cleaning agents, air extractors which have made us more willing to use the kitchen as a social space, and so on.

Attitudes to food smells in the house are a good single example. Inviting people to dinner is regarded as an important social activity, but smelling food in preparation is almost a taboo, and house planning, use of doors and devices such as stove hoods all conspire to ensure that we do not smell anything being prepared or cooking. By comparison, among Afro-Caribbean groups in the United States, the intermingling of all sorts of cooking smells is given a positive value.

Although we have only limited control over our sense of smell or hearing we can control or create the domestic environment that produces the kind of smells and sounds we like. In India, for example, banister rails are often made of cedar so that hands touching the wood can raise the scent in the air.

drying plaster in a new house, but the lack of any personal human smell may deter some from buying it. By the same token, perhaps some people who never buy old houses would, if pressed, admit that this is due to a feeling that they cannot reoccupy space

stamped with someone else's smell. Are similar perceptions at play in considering "damp" smells in houses – each of which might be valued differently by someone in Sweden or someone in Samoa? Research has not yet provided evidence to answer such questions.

RESPONDING TO NOISE

■ People have very different views of the value of environmental noises. There is a whole medley of anecdotal examples of people who have moved to a country house to escape the noise of the city and have found themselves severely discomfited by hearing cows moving up their road or a farmer plowing at dawn. Similarly, those who have moved from the country to a town house regularly express concern about traffic noises early in the

morning – even though the actual noise level may be less than that of the cows and tractors they left behind. For some people the sounds a house itself makes may be comforting – the familiar squeak of the third stair or the rattle of the window panes in the wind – or they may feel frightened by them. The sound of rain on a corrugated roof in houses in warm countries may evoke a sense of well-being perhaps associated with relief from

Acceptable and unacceptable sound

We cannot always control the sounds we do not like but our attitudes to sound differ depending on where the sounds come from. Research has shown that people are most bothered by a particular noise if they regard it as coming from "next door," less bothered if it comes from "outside" and least bothered if they think it is from someone in their household. In Japan, partly because of earthquakes, houses used to be very flimsily built and, for economy of space, often very close together. One response to this was to ensure that most households indulged in selected activities

drought that rain may bring, but others may find the sound intrusive. Someone living in a thatched cottage may dislike the lack of sound and feel out of touch with the elements, whereas another's reaction may be of snug insulation against any assault on the ears.

▲ **Bringing outdoor sounds inside.** American architect Frank Lloyd Wright designed the house 'Fallingwater' at Bear Run, Pennsylvania, to make thorough use of the site's potential. By positioning the house over a small waterfall he allowed the noise of the torrent to permeate the entire house.

75

at the same time. You could hardly be bothered by intruding noise if everybody was making the same noise as you at the same time.

This can be contrasted with the increasingly diversified society of the West – in which each member of a household reserves the right to create their own sounds (notably music) – and the resulting demands that this is placing on house design, construction, and even housing estate layout. A more extreme example can be found in the street culture of West Indian society, where, as with smell, the intermingling of different sounds is actually regarded as essential. Both the size and the noise levels of radios might even be seen as an assertion of personal space or group territory. These differing Asian and Afro-Caribbean attitudes to smell and noise frequently pose a problem for many managers of rented housing.

In some societies, certain noises are acceptable but not others, and room layouts and details may respond to this. These perceptual differences are as yet unrelated to scientific notions of the ear's ability to tune in to certain frequencies and will often reflect the society's concepts of the individual and the group. If one group is perceived as dominant, then any noise by any member of that group may be acceptable while softer noises from elsewhere are not tolerated. In Western societies people are now far more individualized. Music is personal but it should not transfer to others, so it is banished to distant rooms where possible, or at least to rooms which may be insulated by thick carpeting, soft furnishing and heavy curtains.

Some sounds are deliberately used in house furnishings to provide pleasant and comforting noises. The tick of a grandfather clock, a jangling mobile placed in a breezy spot, or a creaky rocking chair are, to most people, positive sounds. Sounds can provide security and the feeling that

76

you are not alone. In the 1960s in Britain an organization existed to promote timber-frame houses at a time when most new housing was being built outside urban areas. In an extremely clever way this organization managed to turn the sound insulation problems of timber houses to their advantage by insisting that town-dwellers in the country needed to hear as much as possible so that they did not feel cut off.

Feeling our way

Unlike our sense of hearing and smell we can, if we choose, limit our tactile experiences extensively. Nevertheless, there are three important ways in which we can observe the relevance of touch in our relationship with the environment.

First, observing children once again shows us how we use touch to tune in to our environment. Tactile experiences

▲ **A child's awareness** of the multitude of tactile sensations that surround us normally far surpasses that of adults. Our early lives are spent absorbing information about the world, and by the time we reach adulthood we know without having to think about it which objects are hard, which are soft, which are pleasant to touch, which are likely to cause pain. This young girl is more acutely aware than her parents would be of the wool of the carpet under her feet, the fur of her teddy bear, the textured wallpaper, the smoothly varnished banister.

CLOSE YOUR EYES

■ Does your home fulfill all your senses in the way you would like? You may be being guided by sight alone. Go through your house room by room and carry out this experiment. Close your eyes. Smell, then listen, then touch your surroundings – the walls, doors and the furniture around you. Did you discover anything you particularly liked or did not like: the curve of a balustrade; the clicking of a radiator; the pattern of the door paneling; the smell of wet dog hairs; or perhaps the slippery texture of an armchair fabric? You may not have recognized why you never liked a room until you realized that the fragrance of the floor polish reminded you of a place where you spent an unhappy time.

Once you divorce yourself from the dominant visual impact of your living environment you could find that there are ways you would like to improve in such a way as to satisfy not only your sense of sight, but all the senses through which you perceive the world.

are very important to them: very young children in any culture explore a room as much by touch as by any other sense. But in Western societies, parents quickly attempt to steer children away from touching either people or things in unfamiliar settings. There is now a great burgeoning of psychosocial group processes which attempt to recover for us the joy of tactile experience.

In the less developed societies, it is an essential skill of adult life literally to "get in touch" with the environment – many initiation and social development rites demand some direct engagement with the local area. Despite the apparent availability of free space in much of Africa, the dense groupings of houses in villages are often aimed at bringing people together, and despite easily available building resources, house layouts often ensure an almost continual element of touching between people. In some societies such as the Aborigine, Maori, Navajo and Inuit the very language tends to be more "physical" – there is considerable intermingling between "people" words and "place" words around issues of direct, tactile experience.

Touch and memory

A second way of approaching touch is by thinking of the ways in which we invoke the memory of touch but not the reality. For example, the slats of white picket fences do not have rounded tops but pointed tops. When we look at them we seem to feel the sharp sensation of the pointed tops on our fingers and we receive the message that the space is being defended against intruders. We have based our sensation on an association with the defensive wooden palisades of bygone fortifications. So too with the use of cobbles. The rounded texture may be uncomfortable under the feet but they suggest a more leisurely, elegant age of

coach and horses and we think of them as warmer than, say, stone slabs.

Thus designers and architects can select certain materials which, by their tactile promise have the effect of making a place seem either welcoming or forbidding. We do not have to touch to feel such responses. In fact one of the resistances to modern architecture's approach to houses has focused on what people judge to be the inappropriate materials – not so much visually as in assumed tactile qualities. Concrete is the best-known example but many people also respond negatively to the "coldness" of high-tech metal or ceramic tiling. Brick, though, despite its actual roughness, is perceived as "softer" than concrete, and timber is universally described as "warm." The feel of the furniture you choose reflects your lifestyle as much as its appearance does.

Again, some qualities can be seen differently by different cultures. Under the heat of an Indian sun the very "coldness" of tiling is appreciated, the same aspect which makes it less popular in cooler climes. Today heating and air-conditioning iron out the differences in the impact that materials have on us, but perceptions of "cold" and "warm" still stay stubbornly with us.

Third, we often describe surfaces in terms of their texture – calling them hard, rough, knobbly and so on – which relate to textural properties, even when we are talking about how they look rather than how they feel. We also translate human character traits into physical terms when, for example, we describe someone as "abrasive" or "compliant," even "slippery." It is through considering touch more than any other sense that we can realize the interconnected way in which all the senses work to reinforce and complement our full experience of our environment. **JFB**

77

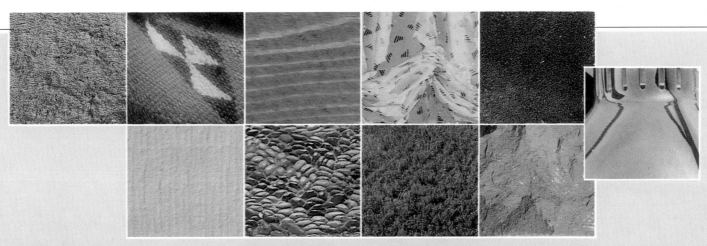

■ **Keeping in touch with textures**. *Whenever we look at a material that has a distinctive texture we are reminded, whether consciously or unconsciously, of how that material feels to the touch and what* associations it has for us. Thick, soft carpets give a feeling of luxury, while hand-woven rugs or the use of rough-sawn wood suggest a rustic lifestyle. Drapes made out of a light fabric give a delicate touch to a room, while velvet is still soft but heavier and consequently more imposing. Stone and concrete, cold and rough, are to be used judiciously in interior design as they can be depressing if they dominate a room.

Design for Leisure

SOME OF US have as many as eight hours of leisure a day and, of that, two-thirds is likely to be spent at home. How rewarding our leisure is, then, will partly depend on how pleasant it is to be at home and whether or not our surroundings invite a happy use of spare time. This in turn depends on how effectively we plan and use the home.

Although most people spend a certain amount of their spare time elsewhere, there are many advantages to pursuing interests at home. Home-based activities are often more convenient; we do not need to make any special arrangements or plan them in advance. Also, if you live with other people, companionship – one of the most important

aspects of leisure – is guaranteed. Our homes can accommodate all kinds of leisure, however – from sociable to solitary. For most of us, an entirely solitary leisure life would be lonely and unfulfilling but, on the other hand, we all need to be alone at times. The way we arrange our homes can also help us create a balanced life style involving both solitary and social pastimes.

Making the most of your space

Our activities at home are defined partly by the space available. Finding or making space for hobbies and children's play is a common problem and such activities gen-

▲ **Designed for a natural effect**, this family's pool serves several other leisure functions in addition to swimming. It makes a visually attractive and well-shaded place just to sit. The pond's wild vegetation attracts birds, frogs, dragonflies and other wildlife, enhancing the children's opportunity to observe nature closely. At first sight this feature looks unplanned, but it makes a more versatile use of the available space than a conventional swimming pool could have done.

The home is by far our most important leisure facility ■ *We spend most of our free time there* ■ *Three-quarters of our leisure activities are home-based* ■ *Most homes have an unused potential to serve our leisure needs better.*

erally have to co-exist with others, and with the demands of other family members.

With some thought and care, however, we can probably do a lot better than we realize. In many cases, the leisure potential of our homes has been taken into consideration in their design, and it is only our good management that is needed to make the best use of that space.

Some parts of the home are more fully used than others. In Great Britain, for example, evidence shows that most households concentrate their activities into two or three rooms, even when there is space available to spread out more evenly.

Living rooms and kitchens each accommodate over a quarter of home-based activity, and bedrooms around a fifth, but other rooms are used much less. We tend to show a strong sense of concentration and convention. Although modern comforts and multiple ownership of leisure equip-

▲ **A spotless blue pool** *surrounded by concrete is an almost universal design feature of these Californian suburban homes, ideal for outdoor entertaining but not very adventurous.*

▶ **Opulent elegance** *at the Hearst Castle in San Simeon, California. The design of this pool reflects the original owner's intentions – it was built to impress, with no expense spared. For all its grandeur, the overall effect is lifeless and unwelcoming, worlds away from the natural look.*

▶ **A new leisure space awaits discovery** *in the attics of many homes. There is no rule that says an upstairs room must be a bedroom. In this home in Rotterdam, Holland, designed from the outset for upstairs living, white walls smooth out awkward angles and reflect a maximum of the natural light that has been amply provided.*

▶ **Using a bedroom as leisure space** *is usually something that children and adolescents do. When adult guests visit the home, the living room becomes adult territory, while younger people may regularly entertain themselves and their friends upstairs, even when there is a recreation room in the basement. This bedroom reflects its double function – what is a bed by night is covered with cushions to provide seating by day.*

▶ **A large kitchen** *is often the home's most-used gathering place, where family members can pursue their own activities without feeling isolated. The kitchen table is a natural magnet for someone looking for a place to sit and do something, and there is room enough for a busy mother to tolerate the presence of children who have gravitated to her.*

ment such as television sets mean that many rooms are fully usable for leisure, there are few signs of individuals dispersing away from the central living space to do independent activities in independent places.

We could make more effective use of the space available by thinking about what we need – what suits us – rather than sticking to conventional patterns like the dining room for eating, the bedroom for sleeping, and so on.

There is a considerable underuse of bedrooms for example. Main bedrooms tend to be used for sleeping and for little else. Of other bedrooms, less than 40 percent are ever used for sleeping at all – their most common usage is for storage.

The typical daily cycle of bedroom use – even in homes where living rooms and kitchens are cramped – leaves space unoccupied for most of the day. There is some use of children's bedrooms for play, and in the largest houses some modest use of spare bedrooms as hobbies rooms, studies, music rooms or home gymnasia. These, though, are the exceptions – we see bedrooms much more readily in terms of storage space than activity space.

Gardens fulfill a mixture of roles, both productive and esthetic. The garden itself, of course, is a major object of leisure interest for those who enjoy gardening. But it can provide a setting for many other leisure activities, acting as an open air living room, dining room, playroom and barbecue area, and, regardless of size, as an impromptu football pitch and tennis court.

Throughout the house, space can be made more usable and more attractive by considering carefully your needs for storage. Storage requirements always exceed expectations, and often exceed the money and space available.

Open shelving systems are not ideal since they gather dust easily, but they are affordable, adaptable, and can usu-ally be bought in separate units that link together to build a system.

Storage capacity can be enhanced by making maximum use of vertical space, not only by the use of stackable systems, but also – especially in workshops and studies – by means of pegboards and hooks.

Maximizing the potential of each room

By ensuring that particular types of rooms have certain key qualities, we can make them more suitable and more attractive as places for spending our leisure time.

Living rooms, for example are the principal rooms for relaxation, family togetherness and social activities. If a living room is to meet these demands, it will help if chairs face a suitable focal point such as a fireplace, television, plant or picture, and allow people sitting in them to see and talk to each other easily.

Neutral wall coverings and colors will help to create a relaxed atmosphere, though colorful fabrics, curtains, cushions, plants or flowers are useful to add brightness and interest. Lighting should be flexible to allow you to vary levels of brightness, with independent lighting for specific areas and for features you wish to highlight.

COMPILING A LEISURE INVENTORY

■ *Consider each room in your house and make as full a list as possible of all the activities you use them for – noting how often each activity takes place, at what times of day, for how long, who takes part, and whether there are other things going on in the same room at the same time. Is the room well suited to the activity? If so, why? If not, note the reasons why. Is it, for example, lack of space (or too much space); lack of privacy; conflicting activities going on together; too hot or too cold; too dimly, too brightly, or too harshly lit? Is the activity too noisy or too dirty for the space used? The clattering of a type-writer, the reverberance of a budding drummer, the spattering of clay, and the splashing of paint, motor oil, or home brew are perhaps extreme examples, but there can be many misfits of activity to space. Think about how such problems can be prevented by relocating activities to different places, or by rearranging rooms. Take stock of underused spaces and underused times of day. Think of the opportunities as well as the constraints of space. Creative thinking about what could be done in particular spaces can spark off new leisure interests.*

MAKING THE MOST OF YOUR BEDROOM

■ *How do you think of your bedroom? Is it merely space for sleep or is it a a meeting-place of family and friends and pets; the center of the household?*

Thomas Jefferson designed his bedroom as two rooms, a study and a dressing room, separated by his four-poster. He could get out of one side of the bed to work or think in his study, the other to prepare for the day. On the whole, however, main bedrooms tend to be used for sleeping and for little else. Of other bedrooms, less than 40 percent are ever used for sleeping at all. Their most common usage is for storage. The typical daily cycle of

bedroom use – even in homes where living rooms and kitchens are cramped – leaves space unoccupied in the day.

Look at your bedroom and think about whether it could be used in other ways. Children's bedrooms, for instance, can be used for play. Keeping floor space free gives small children room to move their toys around. In large houses it may well be possible to use spare bedrooms as hobbies rooms, studies, music rooms or home gymnasia. But an exercise enthusiast with a large sleeping area and high ceilings could fix rings from the ceiling for their daily workout or put Swedish

wall bars against the bedroom wall. If you keep a diary as a hobby, you could have a useful desk in a recess to do your writing, and a shelf of books in another recess.

A working couple with a three-roomed studio apartment would need to use each room for several different purposes.

Their bedroom might be an extension of the sitting room, which could in turn be an extension of the kitchen.

Similarly, by breaking the rules governing which space is for what use, you can create extra space for your leisure activities.

In a dining room the atmosphere to be created will depend on whether the dominant use is for family meals or for entertaining guests. For family meals a bright and sunny air is appropriate, whereas for dinner parties a more subtle and cozy feel created with darker walls and multipoint lighting is more effective. Lighting systems can help make your room adaptable to both types of use by means of dimmer switches and height-adjustable pendant lighting over the dining table.

Bedrooms offer almost infinite flexibility in choice of design, furnishings and fittings. More than anywhere else in the house, as private rooms they can be tailored entirely to the tastes of the people who use them. If they are to be used additionally for leisure activities (for example, teenagers listening to music), there will be implications for furnishing as well as for decor: adequate storage space, such as desk space, storage, shelving and surfaces, can turn the most modest of bedrooms into a self-contained, independent activity space.

Studies need careful siting, away from the distraction of general family activities. Equally, if writing involves using a typewriter, the clatter should not intrude on other family members. If a separate study is not available, bedrooms can usually be adapted for dual use.

This involves a higher level of heating than usual, and an undistracting decor. It is probably a good idea to separate functions of study and sleeping as much as possible both physically, in terms of furnishings (group the desk, bookshelves and storage together along one wall), and aesthetically, by the use of independent lighting for the different areas.

Finally garages can generally be used additionally as workshops and as places to accommodate noisy or dirty leisure activities such as woodwork and metalwork. Normal levels of insulation, heating and lighting will probably need to be improved.

Most garages offer surplus space at the rear even when cars are inside, and this could be used for a workbench, with storage racks on the wall behind and suspended from the ceiling. If the area is to be used frequently, easier access can be provided by installing an additional door to the garage, in the side wall at the workshop end.

Creating the right setting

Light and heat play a crucial role in maximizing the potential of your home as a personal leisure center, because they help to make your surroundings more pleasant, relaxing or practical. In the typical Victorian home, with only one good lamp in the parlor, reading was often aloud to the whole family. Only at the end of the 1880s, with the coming

WHERE IS YOUR TELEVISION SET?

■ *Television is the greatest consumer of home leisure, taking up 10 percent of home-based activities, the most time after eating, cleaning and sleeping. How we watch it and where it is can be either a source of pleasure or a source of conflict.*

Some people have their television sets on all the time. For them it provides a comforting background noise while they are carrying out tasks, and prevents them from feeling isolated.

If this is your lifestyle you will have the set wherever it is you spend the most time. If you see watching television as an indulgence you may like to have it in the bedroom so that you can relax and feel decadent as you watch.

If parents find that their children rarely sit down at the table with them for a meal because their favorite programs

are on at mealtimes, they could put the television set in the dining-room, or wherever they eat. This may mean the death of family conversation, however.

Families often evolve rules to solve the problems that may arise from conflicting desires.

For example, television can be watched until 8 o'clock. After that, the stereo may be played. This sort of rule is necessary if space is limited and the stereo and television set need to be in the same room. Another source of conflict arises when different

people want to watch different programs. Families may solve this by having more than one television set, going to a friend's house to watch, taking turns or giving in to a democratic vote.

82

of the first practical incandescent gas mantle, was there enough light throughout the room for individuals to read for themselves. Later still, of course, electricity brought effective lighting to all parts of the home and, increasingly, the flexibility to create decorative effects far beyond the merely functional.

Diffuse lighting, spreading light evenly, upward, sideways and down, creates the general mood for a room. With the use of simple dimmer switches a room can be changed from a brightly lit, practical setting to a much more cozy and intimate one. In any case, good lighting is essential to virtually all leisure activities. Where possible, work surfaces should be placed near windows to make the best use of natural daylight but preferably at right angles to the window, to avoid glare.

Though it may lack the cheerful glow of a real fire, central heating brings to all parts of the home the warmth that is crucial to basic comfort, making rooms far more usable throughout the whole year. Heating requirements vary according to activity, with sedentary pastimes clearly needing the most warmth. The degree of physical activity that a leisure activity involves, however, is not the only criterion. Some hobbies generate heat directly for example from irons, blow-torches and stoves. **SG**

FOR LEISURE WE MAINLY STAY AT HOME

▶ We spend about 60 percent of our leisure time at home. About 75 percent of the leisure activities that the average person can think of are home-based.

At home   Away

Where we spend our leisure time

At home   Away

Where we pursue leisure activities

▲ **A room's finest leisure asset** might lie outside its windows. Here, design for leisure provides accordingly. Picture windows frame a view that is the focus of the room's decor. Fabrics pick up the colors of the sea, and unpainted wood, wicker and pottery contribute to the outdoor look.

Eating and Entertaining

SINCE our survival depends on consuming food it might be expected that we should be concerned solely with the nutritional benefits of what we eat. But eating is also a form of recreation – nutrition is only one among many factors we bear in mind when we choose what to eat and when to eat it. In fact, our eating habits reflect our lifestyle in the same way as what we wear or how we decorate our houses.

Why do we share food?

As well as being a necessity, eating is a highly social activity. Food is frequently shared, and we arrange to eat with other people at our home or theirs, or in restaurants. Because food is basic to survival, giving or providing food is a way of expressing love right from the time a baby is fed by its mother. Parents may even deny themselves food if their children do not have enough to eat. Because eating is often a shared activity, we have evolved various rituals about food – about what we eat, and how, when and where we should eat it.

Eating together as a family is not only convivial but can also be a way of strengthening family bonds. If conversation over the dinner table is encouraged, problems can be aired and resolved. Sitting round the table together to share food provides the chance for family members to seek advice, share their successes and failures, or recount anecdotes and events. Often, mealtimes may be the only time that a family is together and some parents have strict rules about all the family being present for at least some meals during the week. These circumstances, however, can also create stress.

Eating and sexuality are closely linked. They are linked by the limbic system of the brain which controls emotional activity and motivation. Both food and sex are sensual so it is not surprising that the puritan and the ascetic will tend to

84

A PLACE FOR EATING

■ Most of us do not eat all our meals in the dining room. The very fact that we call it the dining room and not the eating room is significant since it is often reserved for ceremonial meals – those involving extended families on special occasions, older relatives, in-laws and important guests to be honored. Unless it doubles as a study or library, it is frequently the most underused room in the house.

Despite the modern trend for more informal dining, recent surveys have shown that an overwhelming majority of home buyers request a dining room. When asked what purpose they

needed it for, they frequently replied "To entertain the boss and his wife." Since this would be likely to happen at best only once a year, however, there must be something deeper than mere practicality behind our desire for dining rooms. For some people this room is more an indication of ambitions and hopes than a functioning part of the home.

■ The idea of having a dining room separate from the kitchen originated among the wealthy classes, who found it both a practical and pleasant option to isolate their eating experience from the noisy and smelly pro-

cess that produced it. In many cases this meant that food had to travel long distances from the kitchen to the banqueting hall. As with so many customs, the ambitious middle class imitated this practice, albeit on a smaller scale. Their dining rooms were usually dignified and elegant rooms with luxurious curtains and ornate dining furniture. Silver platters sparkled under elaborate chandeliers. The set-

ting was appropriate for a display of the finest glass, cutlery and china and was, above all, a formal place where people took food seriously.

■ In the more egalitarian climate of the late 1950s and 1960s many people turned against the tradition of the separate dining room. In those two decades and beyond, the fashion was to knock down the walls that

What we eat, how and where are mainly questions of social ritual, not nutrition
- Meals are a fundamental form of sharing
- Entertaining guests is crucial to their impression of how much they matter to us.

◄ **Open-plan dining room**. *Changing fashions have meant that in many homes the dining room is replaced by the kitchen or an open-plan area for eating. Jane Asher's dining room opens onto the kitchen behind her and the living room to one side. Even though this room has all the elegance of a formal dining-room, the open plan lends it an air of fashionable informality.*

▼ **Eating outdoors**. *This group has taken informality a step further by having a meal al fresco. Sharing simple food with family and friends in the open air is possibly the most relaxing way of eating, perhaps because we associate it with warm weather and holiday time.*

85

separated the kitchen and dining room. This became a popular trend and influenced architects to design eating areas in open-plan living spaces rather than dining rooms.

This in turn influenced eating styles so that informal buffets became a more popular way of dining than having dinner parties. Lighting, needed both to cook and eat by, became brighter and more revealing, furniture more practical and versatile. The kitchen table, for instance, provided both a surface for preparing the food and somewhere to eat it. Importantly, the kitchen became a focal point for designers. The fitted kitchen, to which many people aspire, is no longer hidden from visitors' eyes and therefore must be not only practical but attractive as well.

In the 1980s there was a swing back to more formal dining, but while the dining room has made a comeback, other rooms continue to be used as eating places, particularly those rooms where there is a television set.

"TV dinners" may well be eaten in solitude on a stack-away table. They are not an occasion for social intercourse or formal manners.

refrain from the pleasures of both, and that the hedonist will embrace them.

When a relationship starts to get serious there comes a time when an important ceremonial meal is likely to be taken with the family of one member of the couple. A meal is used as a bridge marking the importance of the event, as an ice breaker and a demonstration of the family's good will. The prospective mate joins the family at its most familial: eating the family meal. He or she can be scrutin-ized in this setting. Manners, speech and behavior can be assessed. In turn, the guest can see prospective in-laws close up in a setting which both offers information and lub-ricates the difficult mechanisms of social interaction.

Cooking for other people

Entertainment organized around food has long been part of a tradition of hospitality used mainly to impress strangers. Even such modest gestures as making tea or coffee for visitors are a way of demonstrating thoughtfulness and care.

Since rich food has little to do with the satisfaction of physiological needs, we tend to save our special foods for sharing. Few of us would eat caviar or foie gras alone without a vague feeling of guilt – it is food meant to be shared, and often to be shared with those we wish to impress. To feed someone is one of the most direct and intimate ways of conveying something of ourselves to someone else. We like to show that we care about someone by giving them the best food we can. And as guests we would probably take offense if we felt we were being served inferior food – especially if we knew that our hosts enter-tained other people more lavishly.

While entertaining is just as subject to fashion as clothes or furniture, the essence of entertaining is still a display of

86

▲ **Taking trouble over preparation** *of food is some-thing we do for guests to indicate that they are special to us. The food laid out in this kitchen is simple but the people providing it have taken great pains to present it in an attractive and appetizing way. Finishing touches are important – tasting the soup and arranging flowers for the table show that you care enough to pay attention to detail.*

► **Flowers that look good enough to eat** *turn a simple meal into a feast for the senses. The roses, carnations, pot pourris, lavender, and vine leaves not only make an impressive display, but have also been used to flavor and scent the food. Roses, in parti-cular, have been valued for centuries, not only for their fra-grance and beauty, but also for their culinary uses.*

concern and effort for the welfare of our guests. Despite the enormous popularity of frozen and convenience food and of ready-made take-out meals, we seldom serve these to guests. Hand-prepared meals show that we are willing to expend some thought and effort on pleasing our guests. Nowadays they can be made in advance with the help of food processors and microwave ovens. But while complicated dishes are impressive, the quality, style and flair of a simple goulash or curry is likely to be just as critically appraised and warmly appreciated. The content is less expensive, but the message remains the same, "You are important guests and so we have taken the time and the trouble on your behalf."

Food and fashion

If our desire for food were governed solely by the body's need for fuel, we would be satisfied with a rough diet of small game, roots and berries, as human beings were for several million years. Pills could even be synthesized to give us virtually all we need. But rapid changes in food fashions prove the idea that nutrition is our first priority to be a myth. As different foods were gradually introduced into the West, eating habits changed. At first foreign foods such as spices were a privilege of the rich, but these tastes were soon copied. Once foods became plentiful and varied, personal taste and fashion took over.

With growing public awareness of the importance of healthy eating, fashionable food is often erroneously described as healthy. The benefits of nouvelle cuisine, for example, are doubtful. And while some recommended foods, such as those included in a high-fiber diet may indeed have lower levels of fat, cholesterol or sugar, they are just as often popular because they are fashionable. Like clothes, then, the food we eat can indicate how up-to-date we are. When cheeseburgers were shown to produce enzymes that might inhibit cancer, many food faddists were dismayed, since the cheeseburger was not a fashionable food. Just as the fashion industry thrives on change, so too do food suppliers. The vast food industry can only survive if people's tastes are constantly encouraged to change. The tremendous number of books and television programs on the subject of food encourage us all to keep up with the latest trend.

There is also the modern obsession with diets. Previously people dieted only for health reasons; diets were rarely to do with weight for its own sake. Now dieters are mainly concerned with weight reduction, and calorie-controlled diets are a major part of the food-fashion industry. In fact, the only way to lose weight permanently is to eat less. If any one diet were foolproof, there would not be so many and we

87

▲ **Family celebrations are often informal**. *With family, you do not need to go to such elaborate lengths to show them how much you care for them, because they already know.*

But even simple food in modest surroundings can convey the message that your guests are important to you. This Finnish family has chosen the cozy atmosphere of the kitchen to

celebrate a homecoming but makes it into a special occasion with candles and wine.

would not be faced with the announcement of a new and infallible one virtually every week.

Peasant food can also be fashionable. Meals like chili con carne, huevos rancheros and pancakes are reminiscent of the Old West; equally romanticized is the Cajun cooking of the Louisiana French. The popularity of these foods may be partly a result of the rediscovery of ethnic roots and partly a form of reverse snobbery. But the food industry demands novelty and is quick to foster any new desire for traditional regional foods. One example of this is New American cuisine – a homely cooking style and yet another food trend.

Culture-bound eating habits

Publishers often find that their cookery range is their most lucrative, and cookbooks of all nations now crowd the bookstore shelves. While a lot of this can be attributed to a genuine pleasure in new tastes, there is also an aura of sophistication surrounding the food expert. If you want to develop refined tastes, you may have to learn to like caviar, artichokes, snails, and asparagus, and to scorn hamburgers, french fries and other less exotic foods. But what we eat and also how we eat are still strongly influenced by nationality, religion, social class and race.

The order in which we eat our foods is highly ritualistic. In Western countries, soup, fish, meat, then dessert is the standard order of courses. If we were to start a meal with cheese, then dessert, and go backward through to the soup, we would probably find it highly unappetizing, because it is so unfamiliar. However, there are a few notable variations in the way food is served. The French, for example, eat salad after the main dish, while many Americans eat it before and both of these groups are disgusted by the English habit of putting salads and meat on the same plate.

In Western countries, the table is arranged with a separate place setting for each person, while in the East it is more common to serve all the food at once, often in communal dishes from which the diners eat directly, sampling widely of different items.

Each culture lays down right and wrong ways to eat, and not knowing how to eat properly is universally a sign of outsider status – the intricacies of the Japanese tea ceremony, for example, are familiar only to those who have known it all their lives. Proper eating includes the kind of food used, and the way it is prepared, served and eaten.

Food etiquette also varies from culture to culture. Shoveling food into the mouth with a fork would be seen as the height of indelicacy by some people; the absence of forks as the height of barbarity by others. Ever since Catherine de Medici brought these indispensable tools for managing noodles from northern Italy to France in the 16th century,

◄ **Cooking outdoors** is an event, not an ordinary domestic duty, and as in many other special rituals concerned with food – such as carving meat at the table – some families still accord the role of honor to the man. Social customs are changing but it is still mainly women, whether or not they are employed, who perform the routine tasks like shopping for food, planning meals and preparing and serving them.

SITTING AT A TABLE

■ When you next set the table for a meal, bear in mind that how people interact with one another can depend on where they are sitting.

At a rectangular-shaped table, sitting side by side is unpopular if you want to talk as well as eat. The most popular choice for conversing is facing across the width of the table. On the other hand, if you need to cooperate with a partner – pull crackers at Christmas, or help serve the main course – you will probably choose to sit next to each other.

If a table is round, it is possible to sit next to someone and converse easily because you are sitting at an angle. As with the rectangular table competitors will tend to sit opposite one another. If you are entertaining newlyweds, however, you would probably put them side by side, as this is the most intimate seating arrangement. And you could make someone feel important by seating him or her at the head of a rectangular table.

When you arrange furniture to entertain in the living room after a meal, remember that there are limits to comfortable conversation. Although people in conversation will normally prefer to sit across from one another, if the gap is too large they will instead choose to sit side by side on a sofa, even if they are strangers. If two sofas are placed about a meter (3.5ft) apart people are likely to sit on different sofas. But if the sofas are farther apart, they will probably choose to sit side by side, as this is beyond the limit for comfortable conversation. In the smaller rooms of private houses, however, conversational distance may be longer because the size creates a sense of intimacy.

▶ **Circular or rectangular seating** – which is best? At a circular table, guests **1** and **4** do not have to sit as far apart as they do at a rectangular table of comparable size – it is easier for them to converse. At the rectangular table, pairs such as **1** and **2** – and especially **5** and **6** – run a greater risk of excluding others if they turn to each other to speak. Unlike **2** and **3**, or **5** and **6**, at the rectangular table no one at the circular table is paired more intimately with their neighbor than anyone else is.

88

the use of fingers in the West has been socially unacceptable, except for bread, fruit and cheese. It took the elaborate dining habits of the wealthy classes to establish the use of multiple forks, as well as knives, spoons and glasses.

What time should you eat?

There is little nutritional sense to the way we time our eating. Some dieticians recommend a heavy protein meal in the morning, a light lunch and a heavier carbohydrate meal such as pasta in the evening while others advise that the evening meal be a light one. When we eat our meals reveals both class and cultural differences. In hot countries the main meal is at midday, followed by a siesta. In Norway the evening meal is early, between four and five.

Changes in our lifestyles in different periods of history have influenced the timing and size of our meals. When lunch became an important meal to the business community, dinner was pushed back into the evening making supper superfluous. Now, with many families having both partners at work, there are further changes. The woman is no longer at home during the day to prepare a large evening meal, so in some families the tendency is to take a substantial lunch at work or at school and have a light meal at night to fit in with the family's activities. **RF**

▲ **Solving the problem of entertaining a large party,** *this hostess has seated her guests at a number of small tables. Keeping the number of people at a table below 10 or 12 ensures that diners can sustain a single conversation in which everyone feels included. When a larger group breaks into two subgroups, the person sitting in the middle of a long table can easily be left out of both, turning their attention from one to the other, always as a fringe participant.*

Cars

WHEN ASKED why we have a car, most of us would give fairly conventional, practical reasons: to go to work, to take the children to school, to be able to shop at the hypermarket; or we might stress the extra freedom it offers us to get away at weekends or visit a downtown theater. As to our choice of car, we would probably mention its reliability, performance, roominess, comfort, cost and so on. But a car is much more than a functional object. It is, above all, a statement about ourselves – about our self-image, our social status and our aspirations – and an extension of our territory, often guarded as jealously as our own home.

Does your car overshadow your home?

The car is not only an extension of the home, it can also become its territorial competitor. The increase in the number of privately owned cars, and the dominant part they play in our lives, has transformed not only our wider surroundings, but the home itself.

Before the mid-1930s the garage was usually a crude shed or outbuilding – detached from the house, out of sight, and often little better than the stable it replaced. In houses built after 1935, the garage moved to the front of the plot, reflecting the changing status of the car, as a more universal expression of taste and affluence. Later homes were designed so that the garage was a part of the house itself, affecting its interior layout. As a consequence, the front porch, opening onto a central hallway, became a less prominent feature, while the garage took over as the primary entrance to the kitchen. This change, which particularly

▲ **Usurping the place of the home in our hearts.**
Since the mid-1930s, the architecture of the family home has been adapted to reflect the special importance of the car as a key family possession and a central element in the family's public image. Now garages and car ports dominate the fronts of houses. In earlier days the garage was at the back, often in a converted stable.

▶ **At home away from home.**
Cars are mobile personal territory, and this probably does more than anything else to explain why we prefer them to public transport. Other factors play their part – for example, the convenience of being able to set out on a trip when you like, or the fact that you do not have to worry about making connections – but a main part of the appeal of traveling by car is that you feel a greater sense of freedom, possession and control of the space you occupy than you do on a bus or in a passenger plane.

Why does your car matter so much? ■ *We allow the family car and its garage to dominate the fronts of our houses* ■ *Over a lifetime, we spend as much on cars – which depreciate in value – as we invest in our homes – which usually appreciate in value*.

affected suburban houses in the United States, made almost as much of an impact on the lifestyles of the occupants as the new-found mobility that came with the car.

Houses built in Britain and western Europe during the 1950s often devoted the whole of the ground floor to the garage and small utility rooms – a pattern that is still common today. Seen from the outside, the large expanse of garage frontage dwarfed the front door, suggesting that easy access is more important for the car than for the inhabitants.

Architects such as Le Corbusier took this "motorcentric" approach to the extreme, designing houses where owners could drive straight in. The Villa Stein in France, with its bright red rectangular garage door, is testimony to his idea that a house should be a "machine for living in." Similar approaches are apparent in designs by American architects. Lovelace, for example, built very expensive houses whose only point of access was through a centrally placed garage.

Viewed objectively, there is something absurd in house designs which set aside the largest room not for family recreation, nor for meals or sleeping, but to shelter a robust piece of machinery. Admittedly, finding a parking space for

your car on the street may be difficult, and there are attendant risks of vandalism, theft and possibly rust. However, housing a car under the same roof as ourselves, where it takes up valuable space, goes far beyond the need to solve these problems. It underlines the almost irrational sense of attachment we feel for our cars and the special relationship we have with them. It is as if we want to include the car as a family member and are prepared to make sacrifices for it.

Do you express yourself through your car?

The private car is both a mobile indicator of our monthly salary check and, more subtly, of our values. Market research findings indicate that distinct categories of lifestyle are allied to particular makes and models of car. Americans who drive big American cars are usually very different from those in the same income bracket who prefer European cars. A Cadillac is often a sign of someone of fairly humble origin who has "made it" and wants to tell the world. The BMW driver is arguably doing the same thing, but is also claiming to be a person of taste and sophistication – one who eats sushi rather than steak with lobster.

The difference between "old" and "new" money is also reflected in the choice of car in other countries. In Britain, both a Rolls Royce and a Bentley have the same body shell, but they communicate different messages. The Rolls has become a symbol of newly acquired wealth, while the Bentley makes a more muted statement of the self-assurance that comes only from affluence extending back many generations.

At the other end of the car market, the messages are no less easy to decode. Skoda, Lada and other economy-class East European cars have a strongly negative image – which is why they are the butt of jokes.

Does your car reveal your personality?

When asked to distinguish between types of drivers and the cars they associated with them, respondents in a British survey identified "young," "trendy" and "aggressive" drivers most closely with sporty models and "conservative," "family-oriented," "middle-aged" drivers with Volvo station wagons. They drew a second major distinction between "warm and friendly," "ordinary" people, with whom they associated the small Citroen Deux Chevaux imported from France, and owners of big cars such as the Rover, whom they saw as more likely to be "professional, successful and status conscious."

Findings such as these suggest that when we buy a car we – consciously or otherwise – choose a model that in some way reflects our personality. In fact, it is not only car models that can be identified with individual traits, but more general characteristics such as shape. Researchers in the United States have discovered that long hoods, for example, especially square ones, are popular with "macho" types and suggest arrogance.

A long hood with a short trunk, however, will generally signify an older driver's car. To project an image of sophistication combined with youth, you should choose a car with a low body height and a long, rounded hood. A Porsche fits the bill perfectly.

If you are not at all image-conscious, but just want to be

COMPANY CARS

■ *The company car is a good illustration of how cars fix and reinforce our position in life. Many lines are predominantly fleet-owned, and up to 70 percent of cars of some makes are sold to companies rather than to private individuals. The apparently meaningless letters and numbers that are often associated with company cars – such as L, GL or 381, 521, 861 – often define precisely where you are in the corporate hierarchy. As you move up the ladder, the numbers and letters change. Electric windows, air conditioning, car telephones and other accessories add* precision to this whole scaling process. When someone from another company draws up in your parking lot, you can immediately note their importance by the car they drive and behave toward them accordingly.

▲ **At the top of the company hierarchy,** *an executive car needs to be exceptional if it is to signal distinction more strongly than all the ranks beneath.*

seen as a nice, unaffected person, you should opt for a car such as a secondhand VW Beetle, with a short, rounded hood, high body and short trunk. If you prefer something a little tougher looking, then select one of the middle-range Detroit products with its squarer hood.

Cars such as the Beetle, Deux Chevaux and the aging Morris Minor have achieved almost cult status among their owners. They are often looked after with a loving care that seems inappropriate for an inanimate object. Psychologists have explained this behavior by the "Bambi" effect – the nurturing instinct triggered by the car's "cuddly" appearance, which suggests the rounded forehead, fattish body and large eyes typically found in newborn animals and humans.

AN IMPRACTICAL FORM OF TRANSPORTATION

■ To run at all, the family car needs specially built roads. These are expensive. They scar the countryside and the inner city LEFT, destroying people's homes and changing the character of local communities irrevocably. Even then, its average speed in town is little more than that of a pony and trap. These cars RIGHT making their way down Lombard Street in San Francisco, are progressing at a rate that a fast pedestrian could easily beat.

Viewed solely as a means of transportation whose aim is to enable people to travel where they want whenever they want, cars are surprisingly impractical. Big enough to carry five or more people, they often contain only the driver. Moreover, not everyone can afford a car – it is the most costly item you are likely to buy after your home – and it has an average life expectancy of only about five years. It is noisy, emits poisonous fumes and regularly collides with other vehicles and pedestrians, causing hundreds of thousands of deaths.

So why do we bother with cars? The answer is that they are deeply symbolic – a point that has been brilliantly exploited by car manufacturers' advertisements ever since Henry Ford's Model Ts first rolled off the production line. Beneath all the sales talk about brake horsepower, drag coefficients, acceleration and fuel consumption, car advertise- ments appeal to our sense of identity, to the way we do or would like to see ourselves – wealthy, sporty or a hit with the opposite sex. We are what we drive and we judge others accordingly.

Retreating to a mobile home ground

As well as expressing our personality, a car symbolizes our freedom. When we are at the wheel we feel we are in control, much as in the same way as when we are at home. It is our turf – our "living room on wheels," as an advertisement for the 1949 Ford once expressed it.

Indeed, the style, fabrics and colors of car interiors match those that are current in home decorations. This helps us to feel that when we back out of our driveway, we are not so much leaving home as taking a piece of it with us. By contrast, when you use public transport you share alien territory with others. Even in the comfort of a first-class lounge of an airliner we have to go where we are taken and cannot choose all our traveling companions.

This distinction is vitally important to agoraphobics. They fear the environment outside the home and can find even the thought of traveling by bus or train a terrifying prospect. However, they are often quite at ease in their own car out on the freeway, even driving long distances away from home.

Territorial aggression on the road

It is because we regard our car as our territory that we can sometimes become so aggressive in defending it. The car provides a protective position from which we can make threatening signals in relative safety. The amount of raw hostility exchanged between drivers of both sexes is far greater than between pedestrians. We typically apologize to people who bump into us on the street, acknowledging some responsibility for the collision. In our cars, however, we are very different. To defend our territorial integrity some of us shout and gesticulate in a way that would ordinarily be thought of as most uncharacteristic.

The territory to which we lay claim includes, of course, not only our car but also a stretch of road in front and behind us. Rear-window stickers warning "Keep your distance" or ruder versions of the same message are more than just precautionary measures.

CARS AND SEX

■ From the time of the Model T Ford, cars have been cloaked in sexual symbolism and have provided opportunities for covert liaisons. They have been described as vehicles of sexual emancipation by some, and of promiscuity by others. The writer John Steinbeck remarked that, during the early part of the 20th century, "Most of the babies of the period were conceived in Model T Fords and not a few were born in them."

In the 1920s, when car ownership in the United States was becoming quite commonplace, a judge denounced the automobile as a "house of prostitution on wheels." About two-thirds of the girls who appeared before him charged with "sexual crimes" had, he complained, committed them in cars. The International Reform Society even tried to frame legislation forbidding "the use of the motor car for immoral purposes." It has been suggested that Henry Ford's redesigning of the seats of the Model T was in response to these criticisms. Today, even with apartments and hotel rooms more easily available, making love in a car has lost none of its appeal.

THE DRIVE-IN

■ Among the clearest expressions of the car as a cultural phenomenon, not just a mode of transport, are the drive-in movie and drive-in restaurant. People do not patronize drive-ins because they are more convenient. They go because they like to sit in their cars, even when stationary, watching the film or eating their meal on their own territory. There, they feel free to behave as they do in their own home. They can talk, smoke, eat, kick off their shoes, make love or go to sleep, as they choose.

The drive-in movie began modestly in New Jersey in the late 1930s. Very quickly, it spread to other states, finding particular favor in the Sun Belt, with a climate allowing open-air screening throughout the year.

Today, there are nearly 3,000 drive-in theaters in the United States, including some that can accommodate 3,000 cars. When in-car heaters were provided along with the in-car speakers dangling from flexible cords at each parking space, drive-in movie theaters became very popular in colder climates such as Canada, but have not taken hold in countries where space is limited. The first drive-in church was begun by the Californian preacher Robert Schuller in the 1950s. Delivering his sermons from a converted drive-in movie theater, he quickly built up a regular congregation and today enjoys millionaire status.

Indeed, while "tailgating" – driving too close to the car ahead – is clearly dangerous, the behavior of the driver in front is often more so. Quite sane and sober people will talk proudly about how they dabbed the brake pedal and watched the swerving, screeching reaction to the brake lights by the driver behind.

Some drivers even resort to physical violence in such situations. In Houston, Texas, a few years ago an unfortunate who suffered brake failure and touched the truck in front was killed when the truck driver later pulled alongside him and shot him. The investigating police officer, to whom such behavior clearly came as no surprise, commented dryly "There's just a lot of unfriendly driving going on."

We can also become very aggressive when a car violates our territory by cutting in front of us. This most often happens when an overtaking car needs to return to our lane quickly (possibly because there is someone roaring up behind them flashing madly for them to move out of the way). To prevent cars from doing so, drivers will often close up the gap between themselves and the car in front, with potentially fatal consequences.

To preserve our territoriality we do things that can directly lead to the death or injury of other people – and usually we get away with it.

Car drivers are no more tolerant of other nonmotorized road users. "You toucha my car, I smasha your face" is one of the more lurid rear-window messages warning off tailgaiters. If you ride a bicycle in traffic, however, you should perhaps take the warning literally. When cyclists stopped at traffic lights steady themselves – as some do – by harmlessly resting their hand on the roof of the car next to them, it can increase the adrenalin level of the driver in an astonishing way. Some drivers have been known to chase the offending bicycle. **PM**

THE APPEAL OF SPEED

■ Driving is not always the fastest way to travel. Studies show, for example, that it actually takes longer to commute by car than it does to use public transport. Almost every car available, however, is capable of speeds that go well beyond our actual needs and well beyond what is safe and legal. Manufacturers have found that people do not want a car unless it is capable of speeds at which it will very seldom, if ever, be driven. What is the appeal of knowing that you can go so fast?

Traveling at speed produces rapid changes to our senses and our emotions. As our bodies accelerate, nerves in the muscles react instantly, sending messages along the spinal cord and increasing arousal throughout the body. For some people the resulting emotional state translates into fear. Others experience a thrill, finding the sharply tingling sensation intensely pleasurable.

In performance cars, acceleration forces can be particularly strong. Throughout your body, the bones and muscles are jerked back, distorting and flattening the face and stomach. Your balance is also affected because of the displacement of the liquid in the semi-circular canals of the ear. All this, in turn, causes the internal organs to react, adding to the agitation triggered by the nerves in the muscles. As the speed increases, the excitement of acceleration gives way to perceptual distortions. The brain can no longer cope with the rapidly changing signals coming from the eyes. Normally, we can take in information within an arc of about 160 degrees, but at high speeds this arc reduces considerably. Things to the side become a meaningless blur as the brain concentrates on what it really needs to know.

Our sense of thrill is heightened by our awareness of risk. We all seek to maintain a degree of risk somewhere between total safety and total danger. Whereas we avoid actions that put our lives in jeopardy, we soon tire of situations that are completely safe. We aim for a balance that keeps our level of arousal comfortably high but avoids the heart-stopping sensations of uncontrolled fear. And even when we do not take the option of speed, knowing that it is there makes us feel less limited. Driving within a reasonable margin of safety is more satisfying when it reflects our judgment than when it reflects our not being capable of anything else.

CAR CULTS AND CAR ACCESSORIES

■ Just as we choose a home and then re-decorate to put our own stamp on it, so we often attune the messages that our car communicates to accord more closely with our personality. Car accessories have become a multimillion-dollar business, catering for almost every automotive whim. They include not only the means to improve speed and performance, but also the scoops, dams, spoilers, special steering wheels, custom paints, wheel disks and other bolt-on devices that add a touch of fantasy to the most ordinary family saloon. For the wealthier among us, personalized number plates may appeal.

Some of the car-accessory market's best customers are teenage boys who have inherited the family sedan and want to distance themselves from its middle-aged, staid image. However, car decoration is by no means confined to the young. Nodding dogs, furry dice, ski racks, seat covers, stickers and decals all testify to the variety of tastes found among car owners of all ages.

Not surprisingly, it is usually the standard, mass-produced car that receives most decoration – you rarely see a Ferrari with added "go-fast" stripes. It is as if the manufacturer of the basic design cannot satisfy drivers' needs to show off their individuality. Embellishing your car, how-

ever, can sometimes be motivated as much by a desire to establish a collective identity as to express your own. In this way the car becomes a kind of uniform, affiliating you to a specific culture or interest.

At the extreme are the hot-rod and custom car cults. Having originated on the West Coast of the United States, they quickly spread to Europe, with a strong following in Sweden. These enthusiasts modify their cars so much that an outsider would have difficulty in determining the original source. The process of modification, however, is governed by strict rules. You cannot simply chop up a car and put it back together in any form you like – not, at least, if you want to be accepted within the subculture. You must use the right wheels and seats, reduce the car's height, or increase it, according to specific criteria, and use only approved paints and styling.

In the everyday world, drivers express group allegiance by attaching stickers and badges to their cars. Voluntary associations, sports clubs, political parties, religious orders and professional associations are among the numerous organizations that receive free advertising in this way. Most significantly, these and other adornments are evidence that, however useful a car may be, for many people it is primarily a vehicle for expression.

■ **Personalized license plates** are used in California to say the sorts of things about yourself that you would when meeting people for the first time – for example, what your name is, or, as here, that you are enthusiastic about water sports. Among well-known personalities, Telly Savalas has TELLY2, while Ernest Borgnine's plates show BORG9. In Britain, the Princess Royal has 1ANN on her horse box. In Hong Kong, the sought-after plates carry numbers that the Chinese traditionally regard as lucky.

◄ **Four-wheel drive vehicles** are the focus of several car-recreation cults. Worldwide, four-wheel drive vehicles are available mainly for their practical advantages to farmers and other people doing a job that requires them to get through rugged off-road terrain. Here, however, sporting town dwellers meet for a weekend of competitive mud slogging.

■ **Period fantasies** *fuel many of today's car cults – here a 1959 Cadillac Fleetwood proudly raises the 1.6m (5ft 4in) long fins that stun devotees of 1950s car design. During that decade designers of almost all American makes of car were fascinated by the shape of the jet-powered aircraft that had recently appeared in their skies.*

■ **Embellishment** *helps a car owner to feel a sense of individual distinction that goes beyond that bestowed by the car itself. Paintwork decoration, for example, is a frequent addition when the vehicle is a common make RIGHT, widely owned and currently manufactured. When the car is an antique LEFT extra decoration is more unusual.*

The Pets People Choose

IF YOUR house was on fire and you only had one chance to go inside and retrieve your most precious possessions, your pet would probably be one of them. The love and care we lavish on our animal companions shows that we rank them almost as highly as members of our immediate family. Like these, a pet has needs which we take into consideration when choosing where to live and how to organize our daily routine.

Why do we share our house with animals? Deep down in the psyche of a citydweller you may find a farmer and, even deeper, a huntergatherer – we seek animal companionship as much as our ancestors did. However, the animals we choose have to fit in with our present-day homes and lifestyle.

Universal favorites – the dog and cat

During our evolution we could have adopted and genetically modified many different animal species to keep as companions. We have, however, given pride of place to just two – the dog and cat. Why not foxes and polecats? The wolf and North African wildcat simply met our needs better than all the others. One of our most basic requirements of an animal that shares our home is that it should toilet with care and not indoors. Both dog and cat instinctively toilet outside their home area to the edge of their territories.

The wolf particularly appealed to man because he could relate to it easily – they had much in common. The basic unit of primitive man's society was the family and beyond that, a tribe of related individuals. In a wolf pack, one male-female pair dominates a group of about 20 related

■ **Matching your pets to your lifestyle** *can mean stretching your imagination beyond cats and dogs.* ABOVE RIGHT *A lizard lover appears unperturbed at having to accommodate his pets in his daily routine, despite the bemusement of passersby.* ABOVE FAR RIGHT *If you can bear the havoc, why not allow a pet squirrel to adapt your home environment to its own needs?* FAR RIGHT *A tiger at the wheel could signify the ultimate refusal to keep ordinary pets.* RIGHT *Count Basie's boxer is more conventional yet with its mixture of sprightliness and dignity it seems completely in tune with this owner and his home.*

Do we choose the pets we keep in our homes, or do they choose us? ■ *The animals we have domesticated as household pets developed social lives in the wild that already suited them to be willing companions of human beings.*

individuals. Both tribe and pack had their social hierarchy. Man and wolf both hunted animals larger than themselves by perfecting the art of teamwork. They even ate the same food, being omnivorous with carnivorous tendencies. The behavior of the wolf was easy for man to understand because it resembled his own. It signaled dominance or

subordinance with eye contact, body and tail postures and like man, could "smile." Both use this gesture of submission and appeasement to redirect aggression.

The clinching factor in the wolfdog's favor was its ability to become attached to man. We help a new puppy to bond with us emotionally in the first weeks of its life by handling and feeding it and encouraging it to follow us about. We become its pack leader and ensure that the fully grown dog will be our faithful companion.

Our relation with the cat, though, looks like an attraction of opposites. Although cats often live in colonies in urban areas, in nature they are usually solitary. Females defend their territory against all but a passing male seeking a mate. They hunt alone and their vocal, body and chemical language is unlike ours. They do not, like dogs, make gestures of appeasement that we easily recognize, nor are they capable of the subtleties of eye contact dogs engage in. If your kitten or cat does not bond with you, it will revert to being wild more quickly than a dog. But it is the cat's very self-sufficiency that make it a desirable pet for many people.

Other animals we live with

Keeping horses and ponies means adapting many aspects of your lifestyle to suit these animals. You need 0.5-2 acres of grazing, depending on the animal and time to exercise and groom your mount daily. Donkeys are cheaper as they need less grazing and no shoeing. They also get most of their exercise in their field but still need your company every day to stop them fretting and developing bad habits.

Rodents make rewarding pets, needing only minimal care. You can keep them indoors as they smell very little, but rabbits are best in an open run outside as their urine smells of ammonia. Gerbils, being desert-dwellers, urinate little and produce dry feces so are virtually odor-free. You

THE LURE OF THE EXOTIC

■ *If you are interested in natural history, you may find it rewarding to study and possibly breed from a species you have seen in nature programs in your own home: exotic species, loosely defined as those wild species which have not been traditionally domesticated or genetically modified by man. Captive-bred exotics are more expensive (a hand-reared Macaw can cost around $3,000) but make better pets beside allowing their wild-caught cousins to stay in the* *habitat where they belong. Captive-bred parrots, having bonded emotionally with humans at a tender age, enjoy your company instead of being stressed by it, are more responsive and live longer. Macaws and cockatoos appeal because of their wonderful colors. If you want a bird that will talk easily, the African gray parrot is for you. If you want to breed birds, cockatiels are a good choice.*

can also study them more easily, since unlike most rodents they are active by day and for this reason they are now a favorite classroom pet in many schools. Children love handling small furry animals like these and develop a sense of responsibility through looking after them.

Budgerigars and canaries are our favorite indoor cage birds. Both need company, either of other birds or humans. You can teach a cock budgie to talk, and you can train both sexes to perch on your shoulder as you work about the house. Cock canaries are ideal songbirds.

What do our pets do for us?

Whatever pet you have, you probably rely on it emotionally more than you do on most humans you know. In times of stress, you may turn to it for relief or refuge – it helps meet psychological needs. All pets are of great emotional importance to children, the elderly and other vulnerable groups. The presence of these silent psychotherapists in sheltered accommodation for old people, psychiatric institutions and prisons brings very positive benefits to the inmates. Elderly people living alone feel needed by their pets who depend on them for food, care and exercise. Having a pet to look after gives them the necessary incentive to look after themselves which often means they live longer.

The health of dog-owners also benefits from the daily ritual of walking their pet and from the energetic games they play together. As we grow older, we tend to laugh and play less but dogs help to rejuvenate us.

People who have suffered from heart attacks always make a better recovery if they have a dog or cat. Stroking and talking to it helps to keep their blood pressure low.

▲ **A docile rabbit** *seems an ideal living toy, but its daytime gentleness comes from being half asleep. The real nature of these nocturnal pets is best seen after most children have gone to bed.*

▶ **Raising children and keeping dogs** *are simultaneous pursuits for many families. During the child-rearing years a couple is likely to look for a house with a yard and ample recreational space, and mothers frequently give up full-time work in order to spend time in the home – such circumstances favor dogownership. Most dogs make ideal companions for children too, sharing the same degree of unchanneled energy – and often seeming remarkably tolerant of the indignities of being a plaything.*

Living in a dog's world

Worldwide we keep about half a billion dogs as pets. Approximately 35-50 million belong to households in the United States. In Europe, France has about 9 million and Britain about 6 million. Interestingly, only 2.5 million live in Germany, while on a per capita basis many more live in neighboring Holland. This is because more Germans are apartment-dwellers and do not have gardens. They are also probably more concerned with hygiene and tidiness than many other countries.

For economic and cultural reasons, dog ownership in Mediterranean and Eastern European countries is lower than in northwestern Europe. That distinction is rapidly blurring, however, as economic prosperity establishes itself there. In Eastern Europe, meat allowances have been too meager to leave much for pet carnivores. Dogs are popular in Hungary, the most liberal and prosperous of the Comecon countries and residents in all the large Eastern European cities certainly want to keep pets just as in the West. With the introduction of political and economic reforms, it is only a matter of time before they follow the Hungarian trend. Peasants and farm cooperative workers live and work among animals so their working dog is, in reality, also an animal companion.

In Japan in the 1950s, it was unusual and conspicuously Western to have a dog, but now it is normal. The Japanese used to be accused of neglecting and ill-treating their dogs but their attitudes to them have changed over the last 40 years. Japan used to import fashionable Western breeds like poodles and old English sheepdogs which were expensive

because of their status value. Because it is a crowded country, though, with small homes usually without gardens and poorly insulated against noise, small dogs are now favored. In most countries, the number of dogs is increasing as the human population increases.

The right dog for you

Where you live will influence your choice of animal, and different people want different things from their dogs. It is, therefore, a good idea to talk to a veterinarian before you finally decide which dog to have. Perhaps you want a guard dog to protect you. In some countries, there has been a dramatic increase in the popularity of large guarding breeds such as the German Shepherd, Doberman and Rottweiler.

In 1940, Rottweilers were rare but today there are around 200,000 of them in Britain alone. Reports of their attacks on people and even young children, however, will have turned many people against them.

Dogowners are less likely to have their homes burgled. It has been proved that it is the dog's bark rather than the physical threat that is most effective in keeping burglars away. Terriers and Shetland sheepdogs are particularly good as watchdogs. Some insurance companies will reduce your household policy premiums if you own any sort of dog.

Status-seekers will want a dog with a kennel club certificate showing five or more generations of ancestors. Perhaps they will show their animal and breed from it. Others, however, are only too aware that when the dog's appearance is of such importance, its health, disposition and working ability often suffer in consequence. Selective breeding can produce defects such as retinal disease and blindness (collies, shelties), cataract (Afghans), hip dysplasia (most large breeds) and behavioral faults. Cocker spaniels are prone to aggression when they see themselves as "pack-leader" and attack their owner. In the bulldog, features such as the large head and narrow hips have been refined to such an extent that this breed suffers from breathing problems, undershot jaws, ingrowing teeth and can seldom give birth without a cesarian section.

The dictates of canine fashion even demand that some breeds have their tails docked and ears clipped, but if you want your dog to respond to you with all its expressive capabilities you will leave its tail and ears as nature intended.

There are other competitive outlets for dogs that test their mental and physical ability. Obedience competitions are popular in northern European countries. Agility competitions, where small fast breeds such as Border collies negotiate a complicated assault course alongside their owner, are popular in the UK. Dogs are naturally competitive and you can train them to work in teams. Husky and malamute owners like to go sledging; greyhound and whipper owners go racing and bloodhound owners go scenttrailing.

If all you want is a healthy and affectionate companion, a mongrel could be just right. They are physically and

◄ **Bred for hunting**, *these hounds have been genetically selected to produce characteristics that are useful in the field: boundless energy, an aggressive temperament, and resilience. It is precisely these traits that make them unsuitable as housepets – unless you want your home to look and sound as if a hunting pack has just passed through it, it is better to stay with the breeds of dog that are intended to be kept indoors.*

► **Do you look like your dog?** *It is almost certainly a fallacy that we come to resemble our pets, but certain likenesses cannot be denied.* RIGHT *Maybe tall, blonde sophisticated people are drawn to tall, blonde sophisticated dogs such as Afghans which form a telling accessory to this owner's public image.* FAR RIGHT *Or if your appearance marks you as fussy and oldfashioned, it may well be that you will choose a dog like a Pekinese, similar in temperament – and in appearance – to yourself.* ABOVE RIGHT *Alternatively, it may be a matter of bearing rather than physical appearance – this couple are every bit as sleek and confident as their Samoyed.*

SALESDOGS

■ Advertising can have a marked effect upon popularity of dog breeds. In the United States, Spuds McKenzie is a star because he helps sell beer in alluring female company. Spuds is a Bull Terrier and this breed was probably chosen because the campaign was aimed at young, working-class males who could identify with his physical qualities. As a side effect of the campaign, Bull Terrier puppies now command a high price in the United States and unfortunately are bought by many unable to understand or control this demanding breed. Similarly in Britain, labrador puppies are pictured unrolling a soft brand of toilet paper, an Old English Sheep Dog markets paint, a Basset Hound shoes and so on.

psychologically sounder than pedigree dogs, so will cost you less in vet's bills. You can establish intense emotional bonding with a mongrel who will really pine while you are away. Like pedigrees, they come in all sizes, so there is bound to be one to suit you.

Your personal fitness is an important factor. Large energetic breeds like Irish setters and Afghans need a 5-7 mile walk every day, so you may prefer to take your bicycle along. Bulldogs and St Bernards, on the other hand, cannot walk great distances, so will suit a less athletic owner. The smallest breeds of dog, such as Yorkshire terriers and Pekineses get most of their exercise running about within the confines of your home so only need a short walk of a few hundred yards.

103

Cat appeal

Cats are on the increase everywhere and outnumber dogs in some countries, even though many people claim to dislike them. The Japanese, who have not traditionally favored cats as pets, are rapidly changing their minds because cats are so easily suited to the typically small Japanese homes.

If you lead a busy life and are often out, a cat is an ideal pet. Many people say that cats become attached to places rather than to people, and a catflap will allow your pet to come and go as it pleases. It will not object to being alone and will not demand exercise. Cats are fastidiously clean, usually quiet and, being smaller than most dogs, they are cheaper to feed. All cats are good with young children, too. But you cannot manipulate a cat as you can a dog – it will do what *it* wants, not what you want and any attempt you make to punish it for undesirable behavior is likely to have entirely the wrong effect. What do you get in return for satisfying your cat's needs for food, warmth and play? The pleasure of observing the many subtle nuances of its language and behavior – your cat will probably have the upper paw over your dog as well as over you.

Pedigree cats are as prone to the physical defects of inbreeding as dogs. Blue-eyed white Angoras are often deaf and Persians have such short noses that sometimes their tear ducts disappear and their eyes run. The Ragdoll, a relative newcomer, goes so limp when picked up that it is easily injured by careless handling.

If you own a show cat or even a crossbred with an attractive coat, you may well be the target of cat thieves and will need to take precautions to stop your animal roaming if you let it out.

You need patience with longhaired varieties, as they can be fussy eaters, and with Burmese and Siamese which are very mischievous. Siamese are also loudly talkative and could disturb your neighbors.

The problems of having a pet

Pets both define and restrict your lifestyle. Dog-owners prefer houses in suburbia or rural areas because they have gardens. If they live in an apartment, it must have a park nearby, and in cities dogowners may congregate in the expensive accommodation around parks.

Most pet owners must make do with a less than perfect house and garden. Your carpets, furniture and clothes will get covered in dog hair and cat fur and it can even appear in the food you cook. Some people are allergic to this and suffer asthmalike attacks when dogs or cats are present. Your windows will be smeared inside with nosemarks where the animals look out and cats will cover them outside with pawmarks as they scratch to come in. The toys of both dogs and cats lurk in unlikely places to trip you up and all those sticks and deflated footballs your dog has brought home from walks do little to improve the look of your front porch. Cats need to scratch at rough surfaces to keep their claws down, so your chair legs and mats may suffer. Both

► **As a companion to an elderly person** cats cannot be bettered. They do not need to be taken for walks, can live happily in a small apartment, and feeding them need not exceed a pensioner's budget. Moreover, there are proven medical benefits to owning a pet: petowners have shown a significantly higher rate of recovery after heartattacks than nonpetowners. The reason is that actions such as stroking a dog or cat, or watching fish swimming in a tank, are relaxing and cause a reduction in blood pressure.

dogs and cats carry fleas which could bite you if you do not control them with pesticide. Young puppies and kittens are bound to have "accidents" while you are housetraining them and old animals are vulnerable to such problems as well. Rodents and budgerigars, when out for exercise, toilet randomly and may gnaw your furniture. Owning a parrot or a cockatoo means living where its shrieks will not annoy the neighbors. Also, as with a dog, your lifestyle must allow you to be with your bird as much as possible. The destructiveness of a bored parrot knows no bounds and some can even chew through chainlink fencing.

In the garden, if you have tortoises, you will need to net your flower beds. If you have dogs, cocking males scorch the dwarf conifers and urinating bitches leave burn rings on the lawn. Your pet can also dictate your choice of car. How can a Great Dane stretch out comfortably in anything other than a large station wagon? If you have a trailer for your pony you will need a car powerful enough to pull it. Special design innovations such as rear grills, safety harnesses and ventilators make certain cars attractive to mobile dog-owners.

Vacations are a problem. Despite the improvements in kennel management, dog-owners often feel guilty about putting their pets in kennels and prefer either to hire a homesitter or take them along. One factor restraining dog-owning Americans and Europeans from visiting the UK, Australia or New Zealand is their strict six-month quarantine laws, which also deter dog-owning nationals of those countries from vacationing overseas.

Urban planning for pets

A neighborhood with parks and footpaths give a dog ample room for exercise. In many cities, however, development has swallowed open spaces and left little for public

105

■ **Cats as children's pets** *may find themselves playing diverse roles, though given the cat's individualistic temperament this is more likely to depend on the whims of the animal rather than on the needs of the owner.* ABOVE LEFT *It is rare enough for a cat to accompany its owner on a walk – but when it does it will never be content to trot at your heels.* LEFT *Of all breeds of cat, it is the Siamese that becomes most closely attached to its owner and – often vocally – demands constant attention when other cats would be content to walk alone.*

■ **More than 90 percent of pet cats** have no pedigree. However, some cat owners are cat "fanciers" and it matters to them that their animal belongs to a recognized breed and is registered with a cat fanciers association. Of the hundreds of breeds and varieties registered the most popular are:

1 Persian (Pedigree Longhair)
2 Siamese
3 Himalayan
4 Abyssinian
5 Burmese
6 Shorthair (with minor variations from country to country)
7 Maine Coon
8 Birman
9 Cornish Rex
10 Manx

recreation. We criticize postwar planners for replacing two-story housing with highrise apartments, but this freed large areas of communal space. These are better for exercising dogs than letting them out alone in pocket-handkerchief-sized back yards. On walks your dog wants space, your company and the company of other dogs, all of which are guaranteed in parks.

The current housing trend favors lowrise dwellings with open-plan landscaping. In many developments, you cannot have fences or only low ones which make the area unsuitable for dogs. One answer is a buried electric cable which will give a shock to any dog trying to cross it. Many behavioral experts and animal societies, however, reject this solution as cruel. Although open-plan developments have scenic advantages petowners tend to avoid them.

In certain countries many apartments and condominiums restrict petownership, but in the United States a congressional decree prohibits such restrictions being imposed in publicly subsidized housing. Many pet bans are total, even when there is no reason why apartment-dwellers should not keep cats or small species of animal that cause no nuisance to others. Public authorities would do better to forbid

DOGGED WITH PROBLEMS

◄ **The desire for distinction** has led breeders to create varieties which tend further and further away from the dog as nature intended it to be, with inhumane results. The Shar Pei has been selectively bred to become grotesquely wrinkled, a feature which makes painful infections almost inevitable for those dogs. Other breeds that have developed flat faces, such as the Pekinese, often suffer breathing difficulties.

◄ **Fouled sidewalks** cause many citydwellers to dislike dogs, but for dogs which live in apartments there is no alternative to marking out their territory on the daily walk round the block. Signs like this one in Paris request that dogs be taught to use the gutter.

◄ **Walking the dog** is a major undertaking if you live in a built-up area and have to weave your way through traffic and pedestrians. The services of a professional dogwalker provide an easy way out for the owner even if the walker's job has its fair share of stress.

certain kinds of antisocial pet behavior in apartments and make the owners of quiet and inoffensive pets more welcome.

Pets and the environment

You may have had doubts about whether it is right to feed our companion animals while people in the third world go hungry. The international petfood industry argues that prepared dog and catfood utilizes byproducts from food production which are unfit for human consumption and would otherwise be wasted. Also, by encouraging farmers to produce meat for dogs and cats today, we are constructing a buffer against worldwide famine tomorrow. Pets can be a food bank for people. In impoverished societies, famine has driven people to eat dogs and other pets.

Hygiene is an important issue. Dog feces are distasteful if owners allow them to be deposited upon walkways and in parks. People can occasionally catch diseases from contact with dog feces. In most American and many European cities, scoop laws now require people to clear up after their dogs. Parks often provide special devices at their gates, but your hand inside a plastic bag does the job just as well. Scoop laws and public information campaigns will do much to make public recreation areas safer and more enjoyable.

Pets can cause a nuisance in other ways, too. Neighbors often complain about dogs barking or howling when left alone, or cats toileting on their lawns and killing pet birds, fish and mice. If your pet does have antisocial habits, try consulting an animal behavior therapist. This is now an established branch of veterinary practice and a few simple behavior modification techniques may solve your problem more humanely than by having your pet destroyed. Greyhounds, which can chase and kill small dogs and cats, are not dangerous if you fit them with muzzles.

We need our pets emotionally and we are keeping more of them. The best way of meeting their needs and protecting the environment is by encouraging the positive provision of facilities for petowners in urban areas. Veterinarians, therapists, training clubs and boarding facilities all help us to manage our pets in a responsible way. **RAM**

FUTURE TRENDS IN PETOWNING

■ *The traditional concept of home as a place where children live is changing. Today's couples often postpone child-rearing to a later age or decide not to have children at all. The single extended family household of western society has given way over the past 50-100 years to a large number of much smaller units. More people live alone or just with their partner and for many of them the ideal way of making their house, apartment, trailer or narrowboat into a home is to add a pet.*

All recent changes in our lifestyle favor cats RIGHT as they can play quite happily in a small home.

The indications are that we are learning to appreciate cats more. As with dogs, companionability is important, so sociable breeds like the Burmese and Siamese might become favorites although because of their cost they will never outnumber the ordinary crossbred.

Many women, who used to stay at home minding children and pets, now want to go out to work. It is unkind to leave dogs alone for long periods so employers could increase their

workforce by offering animal-care facilities along with child-care ones. Flexible hours and dog creches would mean more contented owners and pets.

In future we will want smaller dogs to fit our smaller homes and to keep feeding costs down. This has the negative effect that breeders are already trying to reduce the size of breeds by breeding from the

runt of the litter – this could aggravate the genetic weaknesses of dogs like toy poodles and schnauzers. Now that we are aware of the harmful effects of inbreeding, geneticists should bear ethical issues in mind. Working breeds – sheepdogs and hunting dogs for example – that we have transformed into pets will have to be made more companion-

able as their herding, tracking and hunting skills are of little relevance in an urban or suburban environment. Committed vegetarians may abandon pet carnivores for rodents or even herbivores like llamas and goats if they have the facilities for keeping them.

Environmental concerns may lead to restrictions on the import of birds, primate and reptiles captured in other countries. This would encourage captive breeding and with more captive-bred exotics on the market, their price would become more accessible to fanciers. We would not be depriving the countries that exported them of income if, as tourists, we visit the areas where they grant these species protection. Our awareness of the importance of habitat in conservation could lead to a revival of the Victorian vivarium. This can consist of any combination of plants and animals in an aquarium, aviary or reptile house. You can extend this concept by managing your own garden to encourage birds, bees, butterflies and other wildlife to visit it or make their homes there.

107

Garden Effects

GARDENING, for many of us, is not simply an occasional activity but an absorbing interest – and not only in the suburbs and the country. People who live in apartments in the city, may hunt eagerly for land or allotments to create their own "green space."

One reason why gardening is such a popular leisure pursuit is that it can satisfy some of our basic psychological needs, such as to relax and reduce stress, or to be creative. Some people look upon gardening as a way of getting back to nature, by growing their own food, for example. From another point of view, gardening can enrich our social lives if we mix with others who share the same interest, perhaps by joining gardening societies.

Saying it with flowers

The way you look after the area around your house reflects something of your social status, not so much in the actual plants you choose, as in the way the lawns and gardens are laid out and looked after. Many people feel that their property should live up to their position in society in

WHAT IS YOUR GARDENING PERSONALITY?

■ *The lawns and gardens around your house can say a great deal about your character and your lifestyle. The way you use your space and what you choose to grow can all be indicators of the kind of person you are. Do one or more of the following categories apply to you?*
1 **Controlled**. *You have well-clipped lawns and hedges, neat paths, formal bedding*

schemes and well-hoed borders. Nothing is allowed to get out of hand. You probably prefer predictability and regularity in other aspects of your life as well.
2 **Natural**. *Your garden is the opposite of a controlled garden. It is crammed with vegetation but low on design. Nothing is pruned and everything is encouraged to grow to its*

natural shape. The rest of your life is probably also an adventure.
3 **Visual**. *You are a visual gardener if your primary concern is how the garden looks. Visual gardeners are most likely to want to adapt their garden design to their lifestyle. Romantics fill the garden with climbers and shrub roses; those with more formal tastes choose*

What does your style of gardening reveal about you? ■ *It is one of your most public vehicles of self-expression* ■ *It tells people how you feel about your neighborhood and how you feel about yourself.*

the same way as their car does. But this interest in outdoor image is nothing new. Books about modern lifestyle first began to appear in the early years of the 19th century in Europe and North America as a result of the prosperity brought about by the industrial revolution. New home-owners were unsure about the best way of proclaiming who and what they were.

Books such as John Claudius Loudon's *The Villa Gardener* were designed for this new class – people who had rapidly become prosperous and were able to afford one of the new suburban villas in a fresh plot of ground but who had not been brought up in the social class to which they now belonged. Gardens in front of their houses became an important badge of newly-acquired wealth and status for many people.

Books on gardening proliferated, with their readership extending beyond the modest suburban house to larger,

stone urns and uncluttered, geometrical schemes.
4 Organic. Health is important and you use natural products as much as possible. Your garden is filled with compost-fed beds of fruit and vege-tables; water barrels catch rainwater and a compost heap takes all the refuse.
5 Botanical. *You take a scien-tific interest in the plants you*

grow – you probably know the botanical names for most of them. Some of the plants are rare and they are a talking point with interested visitors.
6 Recreational. *For some homeowners, flowers and vegetables come a poor second to barbecues, swim-ming pools, swings, tennis nets and parking space.*

more gracious residences. Social status was not the only issue, as people were coming to love gardening for more spiritual and esthetic reasons – a garden was a place of harmonious color, intoxicating scents and pleasant views.

Growing your own produce

Gardening may provide additional satisfaction by providing food. Even though the easy availability of fruit and vegetables in stores makes it no longer necessary for most of us to grow our own supplies, the pleasure of tending the crop and the feeling of being at least partly self-sufficient is enough reason for many gardeners to plant a vegetable garden or fruit trees on their property.

Another, ever increasing, group of people grow their own food because they are concerned about the many pesticides and fungicides that are used on commercially grown crops.

If you grow something yourself you have more control over what you eat because you can be sure of what has gone into its production. In this respect gardening has acquired an essential place in 20th-century culture, as it complements our developing ecological awareness.

Feeding the senses

Gardens provide not only visual pleasure, but food for all the senses. When you are planning, you can combine the colors, textures, shapes and scents of various flowers and plants to create complementary effects.

Color is a matter of individual preference and its effects will vary according to the way plants are grouped. If you want a riot of constantly changing color you will have to work mostly with flowering plants. If you prefer softer backdrops or dark dramatic effects you will probably use foliage plants or evergreens.

Many gardeners like to experiment with themes of color – white and silver, yellow and green, all blue. There are endless possibilities for expressing your own ideas about color.

There are also many "rules" about what to do and what not to do with color in the garden but the important thing is to satisfy yourself. Colors, alone or in combinations, may affect our mood (see *Ch 7*). It may lift your spirits, for example, to see a blaze of yellow, scarlet, purple and orange flowers together, and in this case it is probably worth ignoring the advice of the experts.

An eye for shape and form

The eye is also attracted by differences in shape and form. Careful choice of shapes can create different effects outside just as it can inside the home. Plants can be sculptural as well as colorful; borders can be circular, square, oblong or in a horizontal line.

Some shrubs and trees reveal almost architectural forms when bare of their leaves in winter and thus provide interest in an otherwise bleak landscape. We can also create variety with changes of level. It all depends on what you want from what you see. You may need a restful, unchallenging vista to relax you after a busy day; you may yearn for hillsides when you live in the middle of a flat, featureless suburb. Once you have discovered what your needs are, you can choose features to reflect them.

◄ **Beauty and utility can go together**. *You might not think of using vegetables for visual effect, but they allow scope for creative choice of color and texture and for imaginative plot design. Here, two-tone paving stones complete the pattern, as well as providing convenient access to the plants for weeding and thinning. This vegetable bed is part of a unique formal kitchen garden at Barnsley House in Gloucestershire, England.*

THE FORMAL GARDEN

■ Until the 18th century almost all gardens were formal, making extensive use of topiary (trees clipped into shapes), geometric paths, fountains and mazes, such as these RIGHT in the 16th-century "Love Garden" at Château Villandry near Tours in France.

Why were formal gardens so popular? Classical rules of art and architecture were highly respected, but perhaps the real reason is to be found in the basic question of why we make gardens at all. We like to create an atmosphere that contrasts with our natural surroundings. The development of natural, landscaped gardening in the 18th century came about largely because the countryside had been tamed by farming and was, itself, no longer really wild. Formal gardening in

North America persisted long into the 18th century – the wilderness remained untamed and the garden was used to keep it at bay. Gardens at Gunston Hall, Stratford and Williamsburg all displayed the familiar clipped "greens," straight hedges, alleys and

paths edged with box, of Tudor and Stuart gardens in England.

Formality does not necessarily involve looking to the past, however – it is also perfectly suited to futuristic garden design. Essential ingredients are paths and focal points that create a visual

framework. You can add topiary (if you have suitable trees to clip), sculpture, rocks, whatever suits your house and lifestyle. If you cannot wait for your yew trees to grow, put a bay tree in a terracotta pot for an instant formal effect.

THE ECOLOGICAL GARDEN

■ The ecological garden is a new trend in garden style that reflects the current concern with environmental issues. Conservation of wild flowers, wildlife and the ozone layer is part of many people's gardening policy. The simplest of gardens can have natural areas where wild flowers are encouraged and where the use of pesticides and fungicides are banned. The ecological garden often needs little maintenance, it can look immensely attractive and it will bring into the garden a wide variety of wildlife such as butterflies, dragonflies, frogs, toads, birds, and mammals such as hedgehogs.

WILD FLOWERS
◆ never take plants from the wild, always use ripe seed from seedpods.
◆ plant only native, or near-native species.
◆ choose plants that thrive in your type of soil – natural

meadows tend to do best on impoverished soils because these restrict the growth of vigorous grasses.
◆ if you have a waterlogged area, create your own watermeadow with plants such as marsh marigold.

DIGGING PONDS
◆ dig a pond to attract insects such as dragonflies, and amphibians such as frogs, toads and newts.
◆ make a shallow corner in the pond so that birds can come to drink and bathe.

GROWING HEDGES
◆ use native species to encourage wildlife.
◆ mix species in clumps for variety, interest and a more natural result.
◆ plant in the autumn using nine plants per meter (3ft) in staggered rows and protect the young plants from rabbits or other nibbling animals.

The sounds and scents of the garden

Scent is also a matter of personal preference. The particular scent of a flower or a fruit can evoke long-forgotten memories of a garden you played in as a child or of an idyllic holiday. Many plants, even nonflowering varieties, have fragrances that can enhance the pleasure of the garden. Some give off a scent only in sunshine and recall the aromatic air of the Mediterranean, while others develop after the rain. Night-scented stocks, wallflowers and jasmine are at their most fragrant in the evening. A scented garden is particularly pleasing for blind or visually handicapped people who can derive great pleasure from smelling the subtle or intense perfumes of the plants.

A garden also has its own special sounds and you can do a number of things to create them. Water provides a soothing noise that brings a feeling of tranquillity. This can be especially beneficial if you live in a city. You can plant trees so that the wind rustles the leaves. Planting branching trees and shrubs with berries is a way of tempting as many songbirds to your garden as possible.

Creativity and therapy

The creative combination of color, scent and sound is the key to successful outdoor homekeeping. The design may take many years to complete but the components provide a constantly changing and evolving picture. One major attraction of gardening is that it brings us into contact with living organisms and natural cycles.

This may explain why so many gardeners become obsessive about their interest. Methods of clinical treatment have even been designed around gardening. For example, horticultural therapy has been used to help handicapped people. One survey of gardeners found that 60 percent described their main source of satisfaction as "peacefulness and tranquillity."

Also, your garden constantly needs care. You cannot go away for a weekend at the height of summer without making provision for someone else to take over as provider. If you nurture and protect your plants all year round, they repay your attention. Gardening offers a low-key, undemanding yet dependent relationship that can be very satisfying and

USING FLOWERS AND HERBS

■ *The use of garden plants has the status of folklore in many countries. Herbs have many more uses than merely adding flavor to cooked dishes, and flowers grown chiefly for decoration can be utilized in surprising ways.*

Roses, *keenly cultivated for their beauty and their scent, have been recommended as a salad ingredient – mix in some rose petals with the usual salad greens, and use rose vinegar in the dressing. Rose vinegar is made by packing the petals into a glass jar, covering them with vinegar and leaving them in a sunny place for two weeks. The leaves of many other herbs can be used in the same way: basil, tarragon and lavender are particularly good.*

Lavender *can also be used to make an aromatic sugar – just leave a few flowers in the sugar shaker for a day or two and serve with fruit or dessert. Rose petals and lavender are essential ingredients for a sweetly scented pot pourri.*

Nasturtiums, *grown for their bright orange flowers, are also delectable in salads – the circular leaves and fleshy stems have a surprisingly peppery*

tang. The seeds which you can gather after the flowers have withered can also be used in salads, or to flavor dishes.

Certain types of **geraniums** *have delicately scented leaves that can be used imaginatively in salads and desserts.*

One of the simplest uses for many herbs is in herbal teas, which are refreshing without the harmful side-effects of caffeine. **Mint, thyme, rosemary** *and* **fennel** *are among the plants that can be used in this way. Mint tea is said to aid digestion,*

and an infusion of fennel seeds, left to cool, makes a soothing lotion for eye irritations.

With its yellow flowers and lacy leaves, fennel is a decorative garden plant, as is **thyme,** *which produces a delicate purple flower. The bulbous stem of* **Florence fennel** *can also be cooked and served as a vegetable.*

Sage, *in addition to its traditional affinity with onions, combines well with cheese and cream cheese, but its most startling use is in a hair tonic – pour a liter of boiling water onto a mixture of one tablespoon each of tea leaves and dried sage, and simmer it for two hours. Rubbing it into your scalp regularly will darken your hair, getting rid of gray.*

Many garden herbs yield less or die off completely during the colder months, so you may want to dry your own herbs to keep yourself supplied throughout the winter. Cut whole stems from your herb plants and hang bunches of them in a dry, well ventilated place. They will lend their fragrance to the room, and the more aromatic species such as **sweet basil** *will keep flying insects away.*

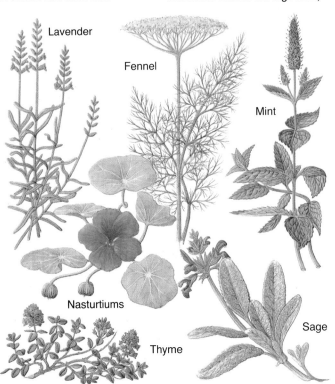

Lavender

Fennel

Mint

Nasturtiums

Thyme

Sage

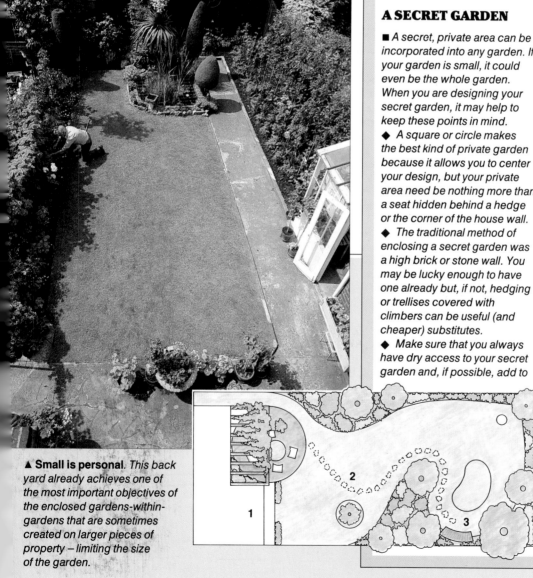

relaxing. People who are on their own or who are in unfulfilling relationships can derive great emotional support from gardening. The act of nurturing a plant provides an outlet for caring urges that might be repressed and frustrated in our daily lives.

Recreating the Garden of Eden

The emotional pleasure of gardening has, in some cultures, been extended to include a spiritual satisfaction. The earliest known word for garden is "Paradise." In many religions, particularly those of the Middle East, the scenes of early primal bliss and innocence are set in a garden – Eden or Ilam.

The myths of ancient Persia were also centered on gardens and ancient garden plans were based on the supposed original garden and world layout. This plan would have a central mount with a single tree, such as a date, quince or apple – the Tree of Life. Sometimes there would be a snake twined round its stem and four stems issued from its roots, dividing the garden into four quarters. The plan usually included outer fortified walls with a gateway facing each of the four compass directions.

Although for most of us the religious aspect of the garden is no longer important, we still combine many of the same elements in our own gardens. We have walls for protection and privacy (see box), water for irrigation and trees for fruit and shade.

A SECRET GARDEN

■ A secret, private area can be incorporated into any garden. If your garden is small, it could even be the whole garden. When you are designing your secret garden, it may help to keep these points in mind.

◆ A square or circle makes the best kind of private garden because it allows you to center your design, but your private area need be nothing more than a seat hidden behind a hedge or the corner of the house wall.

◆ The traditional method of enclosing a secret garden was a high brick or stone wall. You may be lucky enough to have one already but, if not, hedging or trellises covered with climbers can be useful (and cheaper) substitutes.

◆ Make sure that you always have dry access to your secret garden and, if possible, add to the sense of privacy by constructing a path that leads in a roundabout route rather than one that goes straight there.

◆ An enclosed area of garden is ideal for developing a theme based on herbs, color, water or a style quite different from the rest of your garden. The private part of a functional family garden, for example, could be designed with formal topiary and a sundial or as a romantic arbor.

◆ Permanent seating is another essential. You will want to spend time in your secret garden; you may want to get there unobserved. Whatever the reason, you do not want to have to carry your seat on every visit. Choose seating that you find comfortable and that is weatherproof as well as suiting the style of the garden.

113

▲ **Small is personal.** *This back yard already achieves one of the most important objectives of the enclosed gardens-within-gardens that are sometimes created on larger pieces of property – limiting the size of the garden.*

1 The garden is secluded, cannot be seen from the house, or from the neighbor's house.
2 The path to the garden is indirect, adding to the secluded effect.
3 There is permanent, sheltered seating, with a focal point in view.

Retreating to the garden

A great attraction of going outside can be a place there to escape to, a place to be private and unobserved. Even in areas that are not densely populated, people still create enclosed gardens so that they can shut out the world. Some enclosed gardens are extensions of the home itself: from medieval cloisters to today's conservatories, verandas and sun-rooms – all are outdoor rooms that have been carefully integrated into the home.

The whole of your outdoor space or just a part of it might form an oasis of tranquillity – somewhere to relax and forget the stresses of daily life. In crowded urban and suburban environments gardens may be a valuable buffer of privacy between neighboring houses.

Our own private space, however small, is essential to our well-being (see *Ch 4*), and for large families, going outside can be a much-needed escape from the pressures of limited space within the house.

A place to socialize

Not everyone is looking for a place of retreat from society, however. Often what is needed is a setting for leisure interests and other activities – an open-air living room, dining room or play room, or a barbecue area. Outdoors may also provide an overspill area for household chores, such as drying washing and bathing pets. We like to invite our friends to see the roses. We hold social functions outside whenever the weather permits. In many countries where the climate permits it, guests spend most of their time there, hardly entering the house at all.

Sometimes neighborhoods are open-plan with no visible fences or hedges between properties. Far from being places to hide away from the world, gardens and lawns are used as places from which to observe what is going on and who is passing by, and so they provide a means of increasing social contact that can be particularly beneficial to people who live alone. With an open plan, going outside allows you

---

WHAT DO YOU WANT FROM YOUR PROPERTY?

■ *The property on which you live should suit your lifestyle. You may have to work at it to make it fit in. When planning, make a checklist of essentials. For example:*

◆ *Do you want an outdoor retreat from the stress of daily life?*

◆ *Do you need privacy?*

◆ *Do you want to grow your own food? If you do, how much?*

◆ *Do you want a play area for children?*

◆ *Do you want to restrict access by pets or children to particular areas?*

◆ *Will the outdoors be used for social functions and entertaining?*

◆ *Is it important to you to be able to enjoy your lawns and gardens from inside the house?*

◆ *Do you need a greenhouse?*

◆ *Do you want your gardens to fit in with the style and period of your house?*

◆ *Are you a keen gardener or do you want to do the minimum?*

◆ *Is your property's size more important than its style?*

◆ *Do you want to recreate a natural or wild environment rather than a conventional, cultivated one?*

◆ *It is rare to find a homeowner whose needs are genuinely simple. What are your requirements, and how can you plan a garden that fulfills them within the available space?*

◀ **The social lives of children** benefit when parents create outdoor settings that playmates can enjoy. Especially in cities, parents are increasingly reluctant to allow children to explore their environment unsupervised or arrange solely between themselves who they will play with and where. As compensation, children need the world close to the back door to be made as interesting as possible.

to be seen by neighbors and offers an excuse for a conversation about your flowers, if nothing else. Children can also benefit from having an outdoor place to play – it is somewhere safe for them to play with their friends where they can enjoy games and fresh air. When families move to a new area, having an outdoor area to invite people to can help children to make new friends quickly.

Sharing your interest

Joining garden societies is a good way to make friends and get involved with the community. People with a shared interest in plants get together, have discussions, compete and exchange information. There are often organized talks and visits to exhibitions, horticultural shows and well-known gardens. The increased mobility, companionship and stimulation offered by one of these societies can greatly enhance our emotional well-being and quality of life. And there is sometimes a commercial as well as a social benefit

to be gained. Many societies are able to buy essential garden supplies in bulk so that their members can obtain small amounts at a low cost.

Satisfying the territorial need

Gardening is not always a gentle pursuit. Flower shows and societies often encourage intense rivalry between gardeners. For some people, however, the gardening aspect of the patch of land around the house is of little importance – what it represents is territory. The massive formal gardens of Versailles in Paris, for example, were created as much to give an impression of power and wealth as for any esthetic or horticultural reasons.

The amount of land your own house sits on is probably crucial in determining its value. Neighbors frequently come to blows or are taken to court over seemingly trivial boundary disputes. We have a very strong desire to own and control our own space, however small our plot may be (see *Ch1*), and we may become angry if a neighbor's fence intrudes into our garden, or if one of their trees overhangs our lawn. **DS**

▲ **Brightening up a window** *or a balcony may be the only gardening opportunity for an apartment dweller, but it offers a potentially rewarding outlet for design judgment and a green thumb.*

▶ **Indoor and outdoor home-life** *combine their attractions in a well-managed conservatory. Sheltering its human and its green occupants from wind, rain and cold, it provides long seasons for relaxing in garden-like surroundings.*

115

ORIENTAL GARDENS

BONSAI GARDENING

■ The Japanese word "bonsai" means a plant in a tray or container. The Chinese have been growing plants in containers for over a thousand years. According to the principles of Taoist philosophy all natural phenomena have magical properties. If we produce these natural phenomena in miniature we are able to focus on the magical properties and thereby obtain for ourselves some of their powers. The greater the reduction in size, the higher the concentration of magic.

The art of Bonsai in Japan dates from the 14th century and draws much of its philosophy from Zen Buddhism. Zen lays stress on self-discipline and contemplation and the Japanese approach to all gardening, including bonsai, is that art is studied not only for art's sake but also for spiritual enlightenment. Bonsai aims not to reproduce nature but to symbolize it and encapsulate its essential qualities. The slow growth and nurturing of the bonsai is a kind of medication and the gardener develops a oneness with nature as he tends and contemplates his plants.

► **Reflections in water** are a favorite element in the design of a Japanese garden. This one in Singapore was created as a friendship gesture by Japan.

■ Western interest in oriental gardens is not new. Design ideas have gone back and forth between East and West since the 17th century, when plants began to be imported directly. Even earlier, in the time of Marco Polo, there had been an exchange of ideas between the two cultures. The Eastern tradition was centered on China, an ancient gardening culture that was largely concerned with nature and the symbolism of garden elements. This symbolism was based on the worship of springs, rivers, mountains and rocks. The Chinese believed that great spirits inhabited all these sacred locations and in their gardens they tried to duplicate the most important sites. The gardens became symbolic landscapes and places of meditation, varying in scale with the wealth of the owner.

Oriental houses usually consisted of a series of buildings or pavilions contained within a compound, which allowed the garden to flow between them. This fluid effect made a great impression on early Western travelers whose own houses tended to be single dwellings surrounded by formal gardens. The integration of house and garden in the East seemed to them to justify their own desire to break away from controlled, enclosed gardens in favor of the new "landscaped" garden.

THE JAPANESE STYLE

China not only influenced the design of Western gardens; as the dominant cultural power in the East, it naturally also had a profound influence on its neighbors, especially Japan. The stylization of Chinese garden design was formalized in Japan and became a series of rigid rules and specifications for gardening. Although the resulting gardens were often fine works of art, the strict constraints also produced a lifeless effect. However, with the rise of Confucianism and the Zen influence in Japan there arose a new clear and flowing style. The number of elements in the design of gardens was vastly reduced and the aim was always to give a feeling of serene, changeless space. Unlike the earlier style of gardening, this new style was also adaptable to quite small spaces, often no more than a courtyard.

These gardens were the embodiment of tranquillity and were much admired in the

MOORISH GARDENS

■ Spain has many fine examples of courtyard gardens, such as this one LEFT at the Palacio de los Marques de Viana in Cordoba, that reflect Spain's occupation centuries ago by Moors from Muslim North Africa.

In Muslim houses attention is turned inward to the center of family life – the courtyard. The Arab word for "home" comes from the same root as the word for "peace." In a city the courtyard is an essential haven of seclusion and safety. The courtyard is entered through an arch; it is paved with patterned tiles and softened with flowering vines, herbs, palms or fruit trees; and of course, a fountain. In the Arab world, fountains conjure up images of a cool oasis – a symbolic refuge from the parched deserts outside the city.

Water is the symbol of a Moorish garden. Sometimes it is a fountain bubbling up through the floor into geometric guttering, like those reserved for the royal palaces of Morocco. Sometimes it is a rectangular pool surrounded by colonnades, like the one in the Alhambra Palace in Granada. Along with water go shade and intricate design. The whole is combined to create an atmosphere of simple esthetic tranquillity.

West. The design of the traditional Japanese garden is imbued with religious symbolism and philosophy – a landscape in its own right where the gardener is part of nature. It is restrained, often extremely formal, and at one and the same time natural and artificial. The simplicity of a Japanese garden is exceptionally sophisticated. Each stone, each tree, even the pattern in the raked gravel, has a meaning. The gardens have a sculptural and architectural quality and a minimalism that is very attractive to contemporary Western society. They provide a stark contrast to the luxuriant or cottage-garden styles that are so prevalent and are perhaps more in tune with modern architecture and interior

design. However, the ideals of simplicity and the quality of materials in the temple gardens of the city of Kyoto are not just another superficial garden style. Every element in their design has a very precise spiritual purpose and without its deeper significance the garden is merely a stage set.

However much we are fascinated by the design of the "dry" gardens of Japan, we should not forget that many of our most popular flowers also came from the East. Chrysanthemums, peonies, camellias, hostas, hemerocallis, rhododendrons, clematis are but a few of the once exotic but now commonly grown plants in everyone's garden.

Living Together

THE SHAPE of many neighborhoods and living spaces has been determined by a way of life which has all but vanished. The nuclear family – consisting of a male breadwinner, a female homemaker, and two to four children – is no longer the norm. In some countries the percentage of families able to afford their own home is falling, and homelessness is becoming more common as rental prices fall.

The assumption that each home will have one member of the family at home each day to cook the meals, wash the clothes and care for children is at odds with the way we actually live. The average American family has both parents at work, and the fastest growing family group is the single-parent family. Women often find that they have to cope with their day job in addition to running the home.

Even for those families in which a father goes out to work and a mother stays home each day, the nuclear family household may not always be the best arrangement. Some of the difficulties and stresses in our lives are the result of patterns which simply do not suit us. Research suggests that the nuclear family is not by itself a viable social form. It is too small to provide the support and the variety of contacts that human beings need. Full-time homemakers may suffer from social deprivation because there are simply not enough other adults around. Is there any alternative? In fact, a more extended style of household continues to be an option. It is one that is actively pursued by groups of people who adopt shared housing schemes.

Problems of the nuclear family home

Single family suburban dwellings have been the norm since World War II when returning soldiers took up civilian employment and women who had worked through the war in munitions factories became suburban housewives. Mass production methods and a booming economy required the kind of mass consumption which individual dwellings made possible. Increased car ownership and social mobility meant that local communities were valued less than they had been in the past.

As housewives, women were responsible for cooking, cleaning and child care, but unlike farm wives and women in most traditional cultures, they made no direct economic

▲ **Meeting on common ground,** graduate students enjoy the sun on a shared patio. Co-housing schemes create for themselves much the same sense of community combined with privacy that university married student quarters achieve. In a co-housing scheme, however, there is usually a much wider age distribution, and sense of being permanently at home in shared surroundings.

▶ **Separate but connected households** in this street are brought closer together socially by the fact that all of the residents go to the same spot to collect their mail. Their clustered mailboxes also make lower demands on the postal delivery services, including reduced demand on fuel for starting and stopping delivery vehicles and driving from one mailbox to another. Communities that want to be closer and to reduce their demands on the environment through efficient use of resources share many other facilities.

PRIVACY IN A HOUSING COMMUNITY

■ One of the main reservations people have about joining, or founding, a co-housing community is that they are afraid of losing their privacy or personal space.

The degree to which members of a community live together varies a great deal. While you may hate the idea of meeting other people on the way to the bathroom in the morning, you might love having people around during the evening to go to a movie with, or for a leisurely brunch on Sunday morning.

Most communities recognize that individual family groups, and couples, need private realms. This separate territory is essential to maintaining their life as a family, or as two adults. Creating separate children's realms can help create a healthy balance of togetherness and privacy, and while children will go in and out of the couple's area, it is not their territory and will remain to some extent inviolate.

In the same way, living together in an extended group of 10 or 12 adults should not prevent each person having time and space to be alone. Even couples may want to have separate but connecting rooms, remembering that we need both solitude and community.

Would a "co-housing" lifestyle appeal to you? ■ *Provided that privacy needs are met, the rewards of living with other people include fun, variety, emotional support and a kinder set of demands on the environment.*

contribution to the family. Children, too, have been losing their economic role, a trend which began with public schooling in the 1800s. Furthermore, in the modern city children's leisure activities have been curtailed by increasing traffic and a loss of personal security.

On a practical level, the nuclear family has various disadvantages. Each home has to have a full range of domestic appliances – washing machine, dishwasher, vacuum cleaner and so on – whether the household consists of two people or 10. Meals need to be prepared for the family group, even though cooking for larger numbers is more efficient and less expensive.

In addition, there has been a breakdown in social support networks. An awareness of this has led some people to a reassessment, and perhaps to radical changes in the way they organize their homes, work and daily lives. While a degree of solitude is a human need, the difficulties we face in making friends and developing supportive relationships outside the family are often underestimated.

Varieties of communal living

In the past (and in many cultures today), a single home would contain a mixed group of parents, children, hired hands, grandparents and other relations, and lodgers. This arrangement often provided practical help with child care and domestic tasks, and a flexible social support network. Relationships within the nuclear family become strained in part because the bonds are too tight. When one relationship goes through a difficult period there may not always be a variety of other people to turn to.

It is unlikely that we will go back to the extended family system, but many people are looking for new housing arrangements which will satisfy their practical and social needs. In the 1960s, communal living meant freedom and "doing your own thing," and there were few rules or restrictions. Drugs and sexual experimentation were common, and links with mainstream society were rejected. Today, many communities seeking an alternative to the nuclear family home have found that clear organization of practical and financial matters are essential to long-term stability. The communities which have survived the 1970s tend to be those that are not based on an extreme ideology or a single

leader. Some form of communal living can solve many of the problems that plague young parents: finding suitable child care, and providing children with the freedom and companionship they need for their own development, for example. Although children do need to be supervised and protected from danger, they do not require the constant attention of adults. In fact, studies suggest that their emotional development depends at least as much on early relationships with other children as it does on their relationship with their mother.

In a communal house, single people and couples will have their own room or suite of rooms. Children may live with their parents, or in a separate children's wing. All facilities – kitchen, laundry and bathrooms – are used in common. The most striking advantage of this kind of housing is a financial one. A large house is likely to cost less per square foot than a small one, and overhead expenses are shared.

Some communities eat together only occasionally, while for others a meal together each evening is a time for sharing ideas, exchanging stories and discussing plans for the house. The rewarding aspects of community living include the variety of intellects and the different senses of humor. Because of this variety, life in a community can be more interesting and more fun.

Communal living with this degree of sharing is unlikely to suit everyone. Group decision-making can be frustrating if even minor decisions may have to go through half a dozen committees. Practical organization can be difficult. Common areas can become utilitarian in decor, and pets, children and even houseplants can be points of conflict.

Sharing resources Danish-style

"Co-housing" is a term that has been coined to describe a Danish system of shared housing. Under this system, each family, couple or single person still has their own home, but a jointly-owned building holds a communal kitchen, a laundry room and other facilities.

Communities organized on this model can afford to buy well-made, commercial quality appliances, and to have a variety of facilities. One communal house in Britain maintains a pottery, a darkroom, a workshop and separate rooms for table tennis, pool and television (with video machine and cable television). Outdoors, there are extensive greenhouses and a volleyball court.

Communal living does require greater flexibility than living alone or in a nuclear family home. It offers greater stimulation, however – both from other residents and from their friends. There will always be someone around for a chess game or tennis, and many people find that the

DESIGNING A COMMUNITY

■ *Co-housing communities can be set up as purpose-built villages or in converted houses. Either way, it is important to balance easy access to facilities with adequate privacy for each of the resident families. In the plan shown RIGHT the back doors of converted houses in an older inner-city neighborhood open into a central area of shared facilities. Communal life here provides residents with luxuries they might not otherwise be able to afford – a swimming pool, for example. Children in particular stand to benefit – a specially designed play area will encourage them*

to socialize. FAR RIGHT A common house can help to increase cooperation between residents of all ages. Communal facilities for doing laundry, cooking and watching television cut the costs of

living. The basement is divided into three separate sections. Adjoining television rooms for adults and children in the first section lessen the burden on parents to supervise their children. The ground-floor sections

are joined by glass partitions and designed for maximum sociability. Residents can eat here or in their own house. Also joined, the upstairs caters to more creative pursuits – reading, writing or sewing.

Road
Common house
Barbecue Patio
Swimming pool
Sports area
Playground
Shed
Work-shop
Vegetables
Lawns/Gardens
Street refuse collection
Street parking

company of other adults can take the pressure off marital and parent-child relationships.

While many residents of communities travel to ordinary jobs, others find the expanded and varied lifestyle in the community exactly right for locally based work. Some communities survive on the money brought in from residential workshops, and others run stores or farm jointly-owned land. A group of adults can do many things which would be difficult or impossible for a couple on their own: generating electricity or tending an extensive vegetable garden or running a day-care center.

Setting up a housing community

If you are thinking of joining or starting a co-housing unit or other form of community, you will need to work out the details carefully in advance. It might be possible to share your present home, or simply rent out a couple of rooms, while you make decisions about the sort of system which would suit you and your family.

Decisions about money and responsibility must be spelled out clearly, and legal help will probably be necessary to decide about the formalities of joining and leaving the association or group.

Informal communities can be created by friends who buy adjacent properties, and you can keep your friends informed of any plans to sell, so that you can extend your community network within your own street. There should always be common space for shared functions: for example, cooking, gardening and child care, as well as play areas for children. Common areas could be built between the homes, walls could be knocked through, or, alternatively, rooms could be added.

Living together in flexible co-housing provides an ideal environment for everyone who is unhappy with the isolation and impracticality of our present housing systems. **KC**

Sewing room / Living room / Toilet / Bathroom / Guest room / Guest room / Toilet / Library/Computer room / Meeting room / Children's play room / Games room / Common room / Entrance / Kitchen / Dining/Meeting room / TV room / Children's TV room / Store-room / Dark-room / Laundry / Furnaces / Freezers

INCLUDING OLD PEOPLE IN A COMMUNITY

■ *Every society creates special social links between people of similar ages, and such links are beneficial – we have more in common with people of our own age and we find it easier to exchange emotional support with them.*

However, contact between the generations is also beneficial and it can easily be lost when children play only with children of their own age, college students live in dormitories in student-oriented towns, young married couples buy homes in suburban areas with other young couples, and the elderly live in retirement communities.

Maturity and a sense of perspective are qualities that the elderly can offer to the rest of the community. The Western attitude toward older people, who in other societies are venerated for their wisdom, is often one of disregard and disrespect. Many old people are forced to live in tiny, miserable rooms in the back of run-down hotels, because there are no decent small houses compatible with a reduced income and reduced mobility.

Living in a co-housing community with a mixture of age groups can enable retired people to maintain their own homes for many years – with the knowledge that other people are nearby in times of trouble. They can be independent, without being isolated.

Many elderly people have the free time to help with child care, and children need to have friends who are at different stages of life. In most societies in the past, the elderly helped to instruct and protect the young children, and the children in turn acted as eyes, ears, hands and feet for older people.

RAISING CHILDREN IN A COMMUNITY

■ *There are many advantages to raising children within tightly knit communities, whether traditional villages or modern communal housing units. While the extremes of communal child rearing – as practiced, for example, on Israeli kibbutzim – is one which psychologists would reject today; living in some kind of extended family may benefit both parents and children. One reason for this is that communities offer casual* support to parents, as well as an environment in which children can be left to fend for themselves more easily. When there are many children, a daycare center can be set up. Some researchers suggest that every neighborhood should have a "children's home," where a couple or other workers live and where children can be left for a few hours, for regular daily care, or even overnight.

The Changing Home

IN RECENT YEARS our homes have had to fulfill new functions in order to keep pace with rapidly changing lifestyles. With many single-parent families, and more women in paid employment, old social patterns are breaking down, and in many cases the traditional family home is no longer appropriate. For an increasing number of people home is a place for working, as well as a place for eating, sleeping and relaxing. Also, because people are living longer, home design more often has to cater to the needs of the elderly. How will future homes accommodate these changes and what can we do in the meantime to adapt our existing homes to their new roles?

The architecture of gender

According to experts, much of our present housing reinforces old-fashioned values. Many of our homes were built at a time when, almost invariably, it was the men who went out to work to earn the money, while the women stayed at home to look after the children. Home was a place where a man could relax and spend time with the family, far removed from work both physically and psychologically, while the woman put in long hours of unpaid housework feeding the family and generally taking care of their needs.

As a result of the changes that have taken place in the position of women over the past two decades, however, the traditional architecture of the home often no longer reflects the social reality or satisfies current demands. Some women are totally independent and live on their own. Others may have a husband or partner but also follow a career which takes them out of the house, so that in the home they expect a more equal division of labor. Cooking, child care and cleaning are now often shared activities that are carried out

▲ **Technological change** creates new possibilities in home design. Here, for example, is the rotating home. Built on a platform complete with electric motor, this is the ideal residence for anyone who enjoys a change of scene. Depending on the weather, the occasion or simply your mood, you can adjust the house so that it faces in any direction. The glass and metal construction allows for maximum light and gives the house a high-tech appearance. And mobility is not its only advantage. The house is also portable – measuring about 130 square meters (1399 square feet) it can be packed away and reconstructed elsewhere. So, if you want to move, you can take your home with you.

Technological and social changes, as well as changing time of life, affect your personal home style ■ *New trends in family life have affected the design of rooms* ■ *As we grow older, we may want a smaller, more manageable place to live* ■ *We now have the option of buying low-maintenance, low-energy homes.*

THE CHANGING KITCHEN

■ *The traditional kitchen was often an austere workshop situated at the back of a house, away from the main living areas. There, the woman of the house was expected to prepare the family's meals, in surroundings designed to maximize efficiency on the principles of a factory production line. Stove, sink, refrigerator and worktops were all arranged to enable her to accomplish her task in as few steps as possible. Members of the family who might want to go in for a chat or help with the cleaning would be put off by the cramped surroundings, while the presence of children in the kitchen was considered to be a hazard. Even helping with the cooking was difficult for someone who did not know the kitchen intimately, as everything was arranged in tightly spaced storage areas closed off by cabinet doors.*

Modern kitchens are larger, and often have seating arrangements and eating areas or a bar to make them more sociable. Mini televisions that fit on worktops or purpose-built undercabinet radios also help to reduce the workshop atmosphere. Inventions such as the microwave oven, by making

cooking safer and easier, have further contributed to changing the kitchen into a room for the whole family. Today's television commercials show young boys in the kitchen, unsupervised, happily making cakes in a microwave oven, something that would probably not have been possible with conventional cooking. A growing fascination for the food of other cultures, reflected in the many specialist cookery books now available, has further encouraged an interest in cooking. The preparation of exotic Turkish, Thai or Mexican dishes for a forthcoming dinner party can be fun for the whole family.

in inappropriately old-fashioned surroundings. The old-style kitchen, for instance, was a small room designed to enable a woman to prepare her family's meals uninterrupted and with a minimum of fuss. Kitchens have now become more sociable places, however, with modern designs allowing space for both parents and children. Many new homes also have a family room for recreation or play, as well as – but distinct from – the more formal, traditional living room used for entertaining. Home entertainments such as hi-fi music systems and video-cassette recorders have provided further opportunities for a family to share common interests and enjoy social occasions together.

Furthermore, planners have suggested ways for us to have more social contact with our neighbors. You might, for instance, turn the backyard of all the houses on your block into communal areas for gardening, child-minding or just mixing socially. At the same time, you can make your home look more welcoming by reducing the size of the front yard and fitting larger windows to overlook the street.

Future technological innovation might even more dramatically change some of our attitudes toward the home and who should do what in it. For example, any arguments over whose responsibility it is to do the cleaning or the laundry might be resolved by having a home that cleans itself. At the press of a switch, the floors would flood with water while your clothes could be cleaned periodically by closets that do double duty as washing machines.

123

▶ **Social change** *creates new demands on home design. For example, because families today often share domestic chores, the kitchen is a room that everyone can enjoy using. With a breakfast bar, large work surfaces and an attractive decor it looks back to the traditional farmhouse kitchen that provided a social center for the household.*

THE CHANGING OFFICE AT HOME

■ One effect of new technology on human potential is the way that workers are no longer bound to the physical location of the organization that employs them – so called "teleworking."

The immediate benefit to the employee is increased flexibility in work schedules, together with reduced time and costs since they no longer have to commute. Furthermore, it broadens the work opportunities of groups such as the disabled. To the organization, advantages include savings in office rents and related overheads, plus the possibility that they may have a more productive and satisfied workforce.

On the other hand, doubts have been expressed about the resulting social isolation in the home, especially of female teleworkers for whom one reason for working is a desire to be part of a social network out-side the home. Working from a computer at home may also place tacit demands on employees to work outside normal office hours, perhaps to the detriment of their families, although, once freed from the need to commute, the home-worker should, in fact, have more time to spend on nonwork activities.

▼ **Making your home your workplace** can save you time, money and energy. The downside is that you have nowhere to go to escape the office.

■ **Fitting everything in** in the bedroom. LEFT An increased health consciousness has encouraged many people to equip their homes with exercise facilities (see Ch10). You may feel more inclined to work at fitness if everything you need is close at hand. RIGHT As more toys that help with learning are produced, children's bedrooms become learning centers. It is a challenge, in the increasingly affluent home, to find room for possessions. Many get tucked away in inaccessible corners and are never used.

The home as workplace

Just as traditional distinctions between gender roles have been eroded to some extent by changes of attitude in society, greater independence on the part of women and increased job opportunities, so the separation of home and workplace is now being called into question. Thanks to the technology of the microcomputer many professional office jobs can now be done in the comfort of your own home. Domestic "workstations," as they are called, would seem to have much to recommend them. In the first place, they eliminate the problems of commuting: no need to dress up, no stressful traffic jams or fighting for a parking space (or alternatively being almost crushed to death on the subway train), no delays in crowded restaurants or lining up outside sandwich bars at lunchtime. Society too might benefit from less pollution and fewer rush-hour accidents, caused by fewer cars on the roads, and possibly even happier children who can spend more time with their parents.

If you examine the working conditions and employment prospects of the homeworker, however, the picture is less rosy. Very often, to gain promotion in a firm you have to cultivate a face-to-face relationship with your boss, which would put homeworkers at a disadvantage. Moreover, homeworkers are not usually on a company payroll, but are treated as self-employed, and so enjoy none of the benefits such as paid sick leave or holiday entitlement that are due to full-time staff members. Isolated from fellow workers, and with no trade union representation, they are also more vulnerable to exploitation by firms who see them as a cheap source of labor. The working environment too may not provide sufficient motivation, as it lacks the stimulus of other people. You might even come to resent the extra time you can supposedly spend with the children because it distracts you from your work.

To some extent these problems are related to the architecture of the home. Future home designs may include features that will resolve some of these difficulties – for example, a purpose-built office in a quiet part of the house. If layout is part of the problem, many homeworkers themselves seem to be undecided as to the best arrangement. Although many set aside a particular room for working, they

▲ **A vision of the future?** The interior of a submarine leaves little room for leisure activities. As communities become more crowded, compactness may be a key feature of tomorrow's high-tech home.

THE INNER LIMITS

■ *The problems of combining the working and living environments are nothing new to offshore oil-rig workers, submarine crews or astronauts. At the extreme, the crews of space stations may have to spend as much as three months in the company of three or four other people, cooped up in four tin-can shaped modules, each measuring no more than 14 by 35 feet, and with the added problem of weightlessness. Moreover, they will be required to maintain peak physical fitness throughout as the work is vitally important, vast sums of money have been invested in it, and it involves a high degree of judgmental decision-making. Yet, the absence of gravity causes muscle fatigue, and even to communicate with other crew members becomes much harder than on earth. Your face puffs up, so that it loses some of its expression and your vocal pitch changes so that you have to speak louder to make yourself heard.*

Research into human resources in confined spaces, such as remote weather stations or underground military bunkers, has so far failed to find the best solution to problems of stress posed by such environments. Indeed, the crew of Skylab-3 once staged a one-day strike because they felt they were being overworked.

often disagree on where that room should be: whether within easy access of kitchen or living room or somewhere more remote. They have also found that even if you do designate a specific room as a workroom, your work can still easily spread through the house. Clearly, the problems of living and working at home are as much psychological – how accessible you want to be to others at different times of the day – as they are architectural.

The "graying of the population"

Not only are we changing in the way we live, we are also living longer. Advances in health care, coupled with the sharp increases in the population of many Western countries during the 1940s and 1950s, will dramatically increase the numbers of older people in society in the coming decades. How will existing housing cope with this change? Research findings in the United States show that only 10 percent of those above the age of 65 live in institu-

tions or retirement communities specially designed for the old. The rest go on living in their houses, managing by themselves for as long as they can.

Staying put does have its advantages. Above all, it saves an elderly person the disruption of breaking with the familiar and having to adapt to new surroundings (see *Ch2*). On the downside, maintaining a family-sized home may prove difficult for a single person or couple incapacitated by advancing years. Nearly one half of the elderly questioned in the American survey who lived at home reported health problems that limited their activities. Some also experienced loneliness.

Some old people who live at home try to preserve their independence by "shrinking" their surroundings to match their reduced physical capabilities. For example, elderly people who had difficulty in moving around might confine themselves largely to a living room, equipped with such essentials as a comfortable chair, a telephone and a televi-

33%
With relatives

57%
In own home

10%

Retirement home
or institution

■ A new home in old age? *For this couple planning their future living arrangements, a retirement community may be an attractive option. Living in a purpose-built apartment would mean freedom from the responsibility for maintaining a home,* *but no loss of independence. LEFT In the United States only a small fraction of people over 65 move into retirement homes or institutions. Living with relatives is a more popular option, but most older people choose to stay in their own home.*

sion. The telephone could stand on a nearby table, within easy reach, along with any essential medicines. The chair might even be of the swivel type, so that they could look out of the window to see what was going on in the world outside or turn it round to watch television.

There are also some specific design changes that can help old people to go on living in their own home. Door levers can be fitted: these are easier to operate than door-knobs, especially for arthritic hands. Showers with seats are less physically demanding to use than bathtubs. Amplified telephone receivers for the hard of hearing are another option, while light switches operated by sensors rather than mechanically would save the infirm from having to get up and down so often.

Making room for elderly relations

Currently, about a third of American men aged 65 or over who have been living alone, and a slightly lower proportion of women, eventually give up their independence and move in with relatives. These are usually their children, many of whom by that time are themselves middle-aged. At the turn of the century only 10 percent of middle-aged couples had two or more parents alive; today that proportion is nearly a half. Given the increase in life expectancy, and the fall in the birth rate of younger generations, many more of the middle-aged and "young elderly" can expect to care for their parents in the future. Moreover, that care may last for many years, as the numbers of people over 80 will have risen by a third by the year 2000.

Typically, it is the daughter or daughter-in-law who assumes the major share of responsibility for looking after an elderly parent (or parents) who decides to move in, usually because they can no longer cope by themselves. It is also she who has to bear most of the emotional strain and

127

■ **The decision to change homes** *as you grow older depends partly on how easily you can maintain your present one.* LEFT *Tending a garden that is a joy to look at demands a high level of energy, and an older house is more likely to require expensive structural maintenance. A small, more manageable house and garden might suit a retired person better as they grow older,* though being uprooted involves an emotional upheaval. TOP LEFT *New designs and materials have produced houses that present even an elderly person with few problems. Caring for a low-maintenance home costs less as owners rarely need to seek expert advice. Low-maintenance homes are also likely to last longer than those built in the traditional way.*

possibly sacrifices, such as foregoing social visits and sometimes even holidays, to make the arrangement work. Not surprisingly, tensions can sometimes arise between generations. Old people often resent losing their independence, while almost invariably the couple looking after them set up home together when they were quite young and have no experience of living with old people. Moreover, their houses were probably not built to accommodate an extended family of different generations with different needs.

The couple may, for instance, feel that their privacy has been invaded, that their routines have been upset, and possibly that relations between them are suffering as a consequence. Likewise some old people who are too weak or ill to feed or bathe themselves may be bitter about their own loss of privacy and uncooperative with their children. Such an atmosphere in the home can be physically and mentally exhausting, particularly for those who are doing their best – or what they perceive to be their duty – to look after their parents.

If, however, the old person is not too disabled, their feeling of independence might be partly restored by giving them their own kitchen and bathroom facilities in a separate part of the house – if it is a large house – or, even better, an adjoining apartment. Then, as they become older and more frail, they can gradually exchange their independence for better care within the main household. Some communities are exploring the possibilities of several elderly people living in one home where they can give help and support to each other. Medical care could be supplied by regular visits from nurses.

▲ **Environmentally friendly changes**. *Igloo-like in appearance, this house in New Mexico has its own independent energy sources. Solar panels heat water in drums, and a windmill on the roof* *pumps heated water around the house. The windmill also supplies electricity for lights and domestic appliances.*

▲ **Increasingly conspicuous forms of consumption** *are one side of technological change in the home. The latest in bathroom technology is a bathtub that controls itself. By means of a console on the wall, you can choose the temperature, pressure and level of the bath water, or adjust the lighting in the room. The console also has a telephone and telescreen for video surveillance of the front door. The bathtub can be controlled through a telephone link, so if you are at the office and decide you want a bath when you arrive home, you can program it to fill in your absence.*

▲ **Earth insulation** *is the key to temperature control in this underground house. Like the sod houses of pioneers on the Great Plains, it stays cool in summer but is warm in winter. Inside, the circular layout*

The home of the future

New technology – such as computer controlled humidity and temperature sensors, automatic lights and electronic keypads – need not change the traditional home beyond recognition. In many cases it can be incorporated into existing houses without major changes in design. In fact, the home of tomorrow may still have the same basic layout as today. Nevertheless, housing forms affect the way we live. Changing our homes, whether architecturally or by the introduction of new technology, to conform with new patterns of social and family life, will in turn inevitably affect those patterns. **BBB, PBH, CW, IA**

129

consists of a central dais surrounded by 10 rooms. Above the dais, a Perspex dome gives maximum light. The house is not only energy-efficient, it is environmentally friendly. The small-scale model *on the table shows that the dome is the only outside sign of the roof – the rest has been completely turfed so that no unsightly concrete spoils the countryside.*

▲ **The environmentally friendly house**. *Solar panels in the roof of this house are the only sign that it differs from the traditional home. In the future, however, as people become increasingly concerned by the shortage of energy sources and want to become independent of national grids, or as they become more aware of environmental issues, house design will have to meet these new demands. Possible features of the house of tomorrow might include the following:*

■ *Careful siting of windows to allow greater use of solar power.*
■ *Facilities for wind energy – homes may have their own wind turbine.*
■ *Greater use of natural building materials – wood, stone and brick, which do not give off harmful chemicals in the home or during manufacture.*
■ *Built-in units for recycling water and household waste.*

2

THE WIDER
ENVIRONMENT

PART TWO

A Sense of Place

A PLACE – a city, a neighborhood, a familiar shopping center or the building where you work – is much more than something you simply look at: it is something you are actively involved with. Places affect us, and – either deliberately or without thinking about it – we affect them. A key factor determining how they affect us and how we react to them is our sense of what each place means to us: people do not drop litter in parks that they cherish and they do not scrawl abusive graffiti except on walls they think little of.

This sense of place is never dictated wholly to us by other people, but it is very dependent on them: belonging to a group for which a place has particular meanings is bound to affect the meaning it has for you. In your own home it is the family group that dominates your ideas and feelings about the place where you find yourself, and because the family is small, and you are an important member of it, you are especially active in giving your surroundings personal meaning. In the wider environment your influence is probably more limited. To a larger degree it is your community that creates the associations that exist in your mind between places and the ideas and images they evoke; and the community judges the value of places and interprets how we should behave in them. However, understanding our own part in creating the sense of place that guides our reactions to a particular location can be a step toward making it a more rewarding or at least a more acceptable one to be in.

Three ways in which places have meaning

Think of a particular place that you regard as ideal – the place you would like to be right now. Why do you like this place so much? You could group your reasons under three

▲ **Celebrating the hundredth anniversary of the Brooklyn Bridge** with a spectacular fireworks display, New Yorkers show that a familiar part of their environment means something special to them. We may feel attached to the places that are significant to us, awestruck by them, or hostile to them – we never feel neutral about the places we remember – for these are the ones that make a difference to our lives and to our communities.

Places that make up the environment we notice and care about have special meanings for us ■ The parts of the world around us that make any impression on us at all stir associations with places and things that we have already experienced ■ We understand and distinguish places through what is likely to happen there.

same time as knowing that outside it is freezing cold. These ideas and images can be thought of as the meaning that the physical features of the place have for you. In general, any place that we are conscious of as a particular place will have associations for us, although not always positive.

A second heading concerns what you see yourself and others doing there. If the place is ideal, then it is ideal for a purpose or activity. Your choice of an ideal spot will be affected by your notion of an ideal activity: you may think of the course where you played your best-ever round of golf; you might yearn for a place to sit arm in arm with your partner; you might think of an excellent place you know of to host a party.

Then, as a third heading, there is your evaluation of the place. We feel that a place is attractive or unattractive, suitable for our purposes or unsuitable, wholesome or

headings, and there would be similar headings for reasons why you react as you do to any other place you can think of.

The first heading is your sensory memory of the physical features of the place: how it looks, sounds, smells and feels. Associated with these physical features are the ideas and images that they evoke in you. You might find the idea of a certain sea-sprayed clifftop exhilarating because it brings to mind the power of the sea; another person might prefer the contentment of sitting in their own home in front of a cozy log fire in the middle of winter, feeling the warmth at the

WHAT DOES THIS PLACE MEAN TO YOU?

What associations does the **physical appearance** of the place bring to your mind – for example, do you think of peace, stability, isolation, poverty? Some-place similar where you have been? Someone you know who comes from a village like this?

What **activities** come to your mind – for example, is this a place where foreign people live and work in foreign ways? Where people you understand live and work? Where tourists visit? Where you might retreat from the world to find a perfect retirement?

What is your **evaluation** of this place? Is it attractive, historically significant, appealing for sentimental reasons, uninteresting? Would it be a stimulating and refreshing environ-ment, or one that confines people – cutting them off from 20th-century life?

133

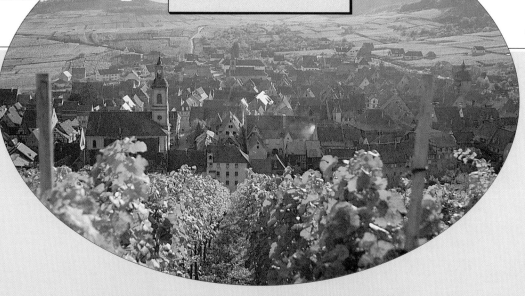

■ You may never have visited the part of Alsace in France where the residents of this village live out their lives, but even from a photograph you are bound to develop a preliminary sense of the place that is uniquely your own, arising from your own past experiences, knowledge and preferences.

unwholesome. These evaluations color our perceptions of places when we are in them and our memories of them later – so that we see and remember the best in what we like and admire; the worst in what we do not.

These three aspects of our sense of place – physical features, activities and evaluation – are not separate but interdependent. For example, the meanings which the physical aspects of the place evoke in us will affect our evaluation of it. Likewise, the activities we think of performing in a place may depend on its physical features. Nevertheless, it can be useful to examine them one by one.

What is the scale of a place?

One of the place's physical aspects is its scale. For example, you may think of a particular room, or of the building which contains it – is that the same place or a different one for you? Or you can think of a larger scale place – a town or even an entire country?

Places belong to hierarchies. Each one is partly defined by what it consists of and what it is part of. For example, a particular building may have a special significance for you because inside it is an even more important place – the first apartment you had after leaving home. Or a building may derive its sense of place from being part of something bigger – for example, from being the tower that gives a square in your city its particular character. The places that have the most significance for you often serve as starting points for locating others.

Finding your way around

When we are finding our way around the physical features of a place, and finding a place by its relation to others, we have a sort of mental map to guide us, but it is not like a street map. It is usually much less complete, with great

WHERE AM I NOW?

In this galaxy?

In this solar system?

On this planet?

In this country?

In this region?

In this city?

In this neighborhood?

In this street?

In this building?

In this room?

■ **Hierarchies of place.** *The penthouse where you live fits inside a building, which is in a street, in a city, in a country, on a continent, on a planet. Our sense of different levels in the hierarchy often reflects their relation to others. A certain building may matter because of what it contains – my apartment. Or it may matter because of what it is a part of – it is a distinctive landmark in the neighborhood. When asked where you are, you are likely to focus on some particular level in the hierarchy, depending on the associations, activities and goals that preoccupy you now.*

detail in some areas and little or none in others. Furthermore, the proportions are distorted in curious ways by physical barriers (such as rivers), social barriers (such as ghettos or areas where the more prosperous inhabitants rarely go), and by transport routes. For example, imagine a city divided into two halves by a river. If people are asked to estimate the distance between two pairs of points, one set in a line parallel to the river, they will overestimate the distance between the points that are not parallel to the river, even when the two distances are in fact the same. Similarly, people sometimes overestimate distances between places on different subway lines, but not distances between places on the same line. This generally holds true when the places are more than 2.4km (1.5mi) apart.

This asymmetry shows that the mental map is not purely visual – a deduction confirmed by the fact that blind people, too, seem to develop mental maps. Instead, the maps involve the meanings places have for us and reflect the fact that one area may be more important in our minds than another for reasons that are not immediately obvious. What is fairly certain is that, although we do develop these maps as a result of gradually accumulating knowledge of an area, this is a very uneven process. The maps seem to focus initially on particular features of the environment, like landmarks and roads, and then expand around these points.

The power of association

A physical location may acquire special significance through the ideas and images it gives rise to, and these are not the same for everyone.

When thinking of your recent tour of Europe, for example, you might find your mental map dominated by the classic tourist sights such as the Parthenon in Athens or the great cathedrals. For some people it is almost impossible to separate physical features of these places from the feelings of awe and the sense of history that they evoke.

But for others these sights may look like little more than collections of old stones, and their memories of the same tour will probably give prominence to other locations – perhaps places where they found markets and bazaars – or they remember, more than anything else, particular people – a helpful tour guide or a friendly taxi driver.

Associations reveal a lot about our relationship to our surroundings. They can help to explain, for example, why some people love cities (eg people who think of them in terms of opportunity and excitement) and others (eg those who think of them in terms of insoluble urban problems) loathe them, or why some people long for an ultramodern apartment and others for an ivy-covered cottage.

We do not see places as a camera does, passively recording the physical presence of this feature or that. Instead, our mental map is active – the meaning that a place has for us is built up and changed over time. When you visit a city for the first time you bring to it your own expectations – if you have heard that it has a wonderful cathedral, you will be more alert to this feature than to others. After living in the city for some time, however, other features will probably become more important for you.

Also memories associated with a particular place can give it, and places like it, a special personal meaning: if you once spent a holiday in a pink-painted hotel, pink-painted decor might ever after remind you of that place.

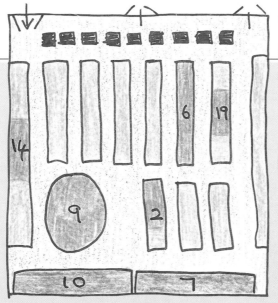

TWO RECOLLECTIONS OF THE SAME PLACE

■ *No two people remember the same place in quite the same way.* RIGHT *A woman, choosing from a list of 20 possible displays in a supermarket she has just visited, locates on a sketch map the seven she remembers best.* FAR RIGHT *Choosing from the same list of 20, her husband locates the seven displays that made the biggest impression on him. Even when giving prominence to the same displays, husband and wife tend to have slightly different ideas of where the displays are.*

1 Dairy products, eggs	6 Kitchenware	11 Car maintenance	16 Coffee, tea
2 Home baking	7 Bakery	12 Gardening	17 Toiletries, babycare
3 Frozen foods	8 Beans, pasta, rice	13 Canned foods	18 Alcoholic beverages
4 Cakes and cookies	9 Fruit, vegetables	14 Books, magazines	19 Clothes
5 Chocolate	10 Delicatessen	15 TV dinners	20 Detergents, soap

Interestingly, the meaning a place has for us can sometimes change if we group it with a town or area that is near it. Real estate agents often capitalize on this. For example, Battersea in London, England is a fashionable address today, but this was not the case in the days before its massive coal-powered electricity generating station was converted to an amusement center. Real estate agents, hoping to promote sales in that area, used always to disguise Battersea's unattractive associations by referring to it as South Chelsea, borrowing the name of the fashionable district to the north.

A mismatch of meanings

The images and ideas associated with particular features of places are often exploited by architects, planners and others. A developer may try to make an ordinary building more impressive by adding a mock portico and columns at the entrance, or an architect may design a modern church with pointed Gothic-style windows to make it look more churchy.

For architects to use associations successfully, however, the associations must be shared by the people who will use the places that architects create, and this is not always the case. We learn many of the associations that we make from the social groups we belong to, and architects constitute a group in their own right, with a shared specialist training that other people have not experienced. The result can be that buildings have a rich meaning for architects and none for the rest of us, to whom they simply look strange.

For example, the designers of a public square in one English university built during the 1960s had in mind the throngs, leisureliness and style of St Mark's Square, Venice. Unfortunately, the vast majority of the students, not sharing this vision, see it as a stark, featureless and windswept space, devoid of any pleasurable associations, and they treat it accordingly.

Do we naturally prefer some places?

It is very difficult to test this suggestion scientifically, but there is evidence that at least some of the meanings that physical aspects of our environment have for us are innate rather than learned. For example, very young babies tend to avoid places where there appears to be a sharp drop in floor level; that is, they are aware that such a place might be dangerous.

One researcher has claimed that we have a genetically determined preference for places that allow a clear view of our surroundings while at the same time providing us with a hiding place or refuge. Another theory proposes that we instinctively prefer places that, on the one hand, offer complexity and mystery (qualities which are appealing to our sense of curiosity) and, on the other, are also coherent so that we can make sense of them.

How activity gives meaning to a place

Examples of how our sense of place is affected by activity can be found all around us. In a bank, for instance, the activities of the staff and customers determine to a very great degree how the place is laid out – usually customer and staff are carefully separated, though some banks do try to

◀ **Activities and clues about activities** *that would be possible and appropriate help us to understand what kind of place we are in, but the clues are not always clear. Are these young seminarians and their mentor on an outing? Have they paused for a moment to amuse themselves on a hotel terrace where normally it is tourists who choose between admiring the Alps and playing table football? In fact, the terrace is part of the seminary, and table football is one of the seminary's everyday activities.*

136

present a less formal image by mixing the two groups.

To take a rather different example, when the streets, bridges and freeways of a busy city are made available for a marathon race these places take on a remarkably unfamiliar character.

Activities can also be used much more formally to define places. A prime example is ritual: consecration can turn an ordinary building into a holy place, and deconsecration can do exactly the opposite.

Since activities are part of places, places that house similar activities have something in common, whichever culture they belong to. A classroom is recognizably a class-room, whether it is in Harare or Chicago. Similarly, even though space is used much more flexibly in Japanese households than it is in Western households, the activities which are carried out in one place – such as a bedroom in Europe or the United States – are likely to occur in one area in Japanese houses. In other words, whatever the culture, a similar organization of activities gives rise to similar sorts of places.

Since whole patterns of activity are associated with particular places, we can attempt to bring about a radical change in our lifestyle by changing scene – for example, we can find adventure or make it easier to adopt a new role by going somewhere else. On the other hand, our associations with places can be helpful. One study found that students performed better in examination rooms they were used to than in rooms that were unfamiliar.

The rules of a place

Because activities to a great extent define a place, there are usually very effective (although often unspoken) rules about how to behave there. The obvious examples are the explicit rules of behavior that makes us feel inhibited in certain places of worship or in libraries. Noisy or extro-verted behavior will conflict with the activity intended for

▲ **Changing the activity asso-ciated with a place** may trans-form the way we feel about that place. This bridge takes on an unfamiliar air when lines of cars are replaced with runners for the New York City Marathon. Think about the office party, the rock concert in a football sta-dium, the shopping mall on a Sunday – how strongly is your sense of place bound up with activities?

137

■ **Environments that impose themselves on unwilling occupants**. *Residents of this ghetto in Philadelphia* LEFT *do not have the power to influence the decay around them. Planners' visions dominate this development in the suburbs of Paris* ABOVE – *images and ideas that are meaningful to architects and artists are not always shared by the people who later have to live with them.*

▶ **Making an impact on the place where they live**, *a youth group has invested time and energy in designing this piece of graffiti on the fencing surrounding a derelict building in New York. Making a visual impression on your surroundings is probably the most effective way of strengthening your sense of a particular place.*

138

HOW WE AFFECT PLACES

■ *Our neighborhoods, towns and cities are created by us and by other people like us. We may not realize the contribution we make, but think of some of the things we do: we improve or do not improve the outsides of our homes; we personalize or do not personalize the cars we park at the curb; we drop litter or do not drop it – we may even pick up other people's litter – and we vandalize or do not vandalize payphones.*

Some of the things we do will be generally regarded as making a place better, some as making it worse. On occasion, it can be hard to tell which is which: a lovingly, if illegally, executed piece of graffiti can be as pleasant to look at as a specially commissioned mural, while a new office block can seem like an act of corporate vandalism.

Residents of communities affected by change may often have an effect on their environment by participating in planning decisions. Those who volunteer to take part may not represent the local population as a whole. However, their participation often brings about much needed environmental improvements and gives a voice to at least some of the people who will be affected by planners' decisions.

the place. Unwritten rules for places include looking away from others (in order to minimize an unwelcome sense of intimacy with strangers) when standing in a crowded elevator.

Social rules specific to them are one of the main ways in which places affect us. Sometimes the rules of a place can destroy individual identity – for example, if they impose an unwanted and restricting role on us.

At their worse, prisons and mental hospitals can be like this. The enforced wearing of uniform, the standard haircut, the lack of privacy and many other factors combine to destroy the inmates' sense of being distinctive each in their own right.

However, our environment is rarely so coercive: rules based on how people usually act in a particular place may guide our behavior but rarely control it completely. For example, a nightclub may encourage you to behave in an expansive, self-consciously stylish way, but it does not force you to: you can, if you wish, sit quietly in a corner.

The value of a place

We are indifferent to very few of the places that form our mental picture of the world around us. The associations that places have can be positive or negative. Places that enter our lives because of activities we have to perform there – such as the parking structure where you daily leave your car or the street you have to walk down to reach your shopping center – seldom escape evaluation, and the evaluation is colored by what we are trying to do – roads passing through mile after mile of superb countryside can seem infuriating if you are running out of fuel and want to reach the next town as soon as possible.

We often find it difficult to separate our emotional or evaluative reactions from our perceptions of fact. The former often affect the latter by twisting our memories of people, events and places: they dictate what we look for and notice, and therefore what we actually see. To take a simple example, when we look at a beach we can see either the beautiful sands or the litter people have left behind; our memory of the place will be governed by which aspect has dominated our attention.

Because they are so important to us emotionally, places become bound up with our sense of identity. Leaving places forever – as when we first move away from the family home – can be extremely upsetting: you feel as if you are losing part of yourself.

This is even more the case when the place ceases to exist, because of an earthquake or other disaster, or because of urban redevelopment. This is not just a matter of the destruction of communities and their social networks that helped make the neighborhood into a place: we are affected as individuals almost as if we were suffering a bereavement, even if, to an outsider, the place might seem to have had very few redeeming qualities. **DC**

EXAMINING YOUR SENSE OF PLACE

■ *You can probably think of places you like visiting and places you avoid, places you feel at home in and others that seem alien to you. You know that you feel different in different places. Some of the ones you do not feel very good about are ones you cannot avoid. Some of the ones you would most like to be in are inaccessible at the moment. However, by examining your sense of the places you must make do with, you may find ways of managing better in them.*

In order to be more aware of the sense of place that a town, street or building has for you, it is useful to ask questions:

1 Does this place have some essential focus or central meaning for me? Is it a place to pass through quickly, or a good place to wait and meet people? Is it a place to be on my own and get away from the crowds, or a place to be on show in?
2 Do other people, who come here for different reasons, see it the same way I do? Did they in earlier days? Will they in the future? Can I learn from the way other people see this place?
3 What can I do to help the changes that are happening to be as satisfactory as possible? Can I start any changes that will contribute to improvement? Are these changes in a) the physical fabric of the place (moving furniture around the office or putting up pictures), b) the activities that go on, or the rules (should we allow people to use the place who have not in the past, or have informal gatherings where only formal ones have occurred?) or c) by enriching associations, for example, by digging into the history of the building, the neighborhood or the city? How many of these meanings, actions and physical forms are a product of what the place is part of – eg the type of neighborhood it is in – and how many come from what the place itself contains?

139

Neighborhoods

MOST OF US think of ourselves as living in a neighborhood, whether it is a small, close-knit rural community, a few streets in a town or a sprawling city suburb. What constitutes a neighborhood is partly a subjective matter – different people have different ideas about the typical size, population and the services or amenities a neighborhood should provide. The word itself traditionally conjures up images of informality, friendliness and mutual support, but numerous other physical, social and cultural factors help us to recognize a particular community as a separate unit, somehow distinct from its surrounding area. Researchers have been able to isolate the most important of these characteristics and to suggest why it has always been important for people to live in smaller, easily identifiable groups, rather than simply to be part of a city, state or region.

What is a neighborhood?

Until recently, there was an easy answer to this question: a neighborhood consisted of about 10,000 people with, as its focus, a school. In the 1970s city planners used this as a rule of thumb when designing new developments. It was many years before they realized that the formula produced

"NEIGHBORHOOD": WHAT DOES IT MEAN TO YOU?

■ *The word "neighborhood" means different things to different people – and can also mean different things to the same person depending on the context in which it is used. When you talk about your neighborhood you might be thinking of:*

◆ *an area in the vicinity of your home, especially if it represents your social status or in some way acts as a symbol of your personal identity*
◆ *a set of people who (whether or not you like them) represent your immediate social environment*

◆ *a village-like community whose boundaries are generally vague but whose residents are linked by face-to-face contact and intimate relationships or who have in common some sort of ideal*
◆ *a named area, like a city suburb, which inhabitants and out-*

▲ **People make a neighborhood**, *and when circumstances – such as low fences and fine summer weather – encourage positive contacts, the sense of neighborhood grows. The most likely people to become involved with neighbors are long-term residents, people with children and those who stay home during the day – for example, retired people and mothers who do not work outside the home.*

Your choice of neighborhood may be a reflection of your personality ■ *Why do only some people identify strongly with their neighborhoods?* ■ *Do we mold neighborhoods, or do they mold us?*

artificial neighborhoods rather than genuine communities.

The main problem is that it is impossible to predict in advance what will produce a neighborhood; only afterward, once a community is flourishing, can we begin to understand why it is doing so. This is because what matters is not whether an outsider thinks of an area as a neighborhood but whether the people who live there do. Some communities may regard themselves as neighborhoods because they

siders alike accept as a social unit

◆ an area based on public and other services, perhaps on a single network of buses

◆ a distinctive physical area, separated from other areas by clear physical and/or generally accepted boundaries recog-

nized by both outsiders and residents

◆ an area in which most or all of the people are linked by a characteristic – such as race, religious affiliation, lifestyle or ideology – reinforced by social relations and the fact that they accept one another's behavior.

occupy a defined geographical area (for example, the land between two rivers). In others, physical borders may not be as important as the ethnic allegiance of most of the inhabitants. The network of communication can also be a determining factor. Areas that share a network of public transport are more likely to be regarded by their inhabitants as one neighborhood.

In terms of how people see their neighborhood, physical size is usually – perhaps surprisingly – more important than population size. There are variations in different places, however. In the United States the areas people accept as their neighborhoods tend to be much larger than the equivalents in many other countries: the population is more broadly scattered, cars are more frequently used and road networks are more extensive. Generally, different groups of people describe neighborhoods of very different sizes, from a few blocks to many hundreds of acres, from one street to 25 or more. Even so, researchers have found that a neighborhood is typically seen as being about 40-80 hectares (100-200 acres) in size. The range of sizes is partly due to the fact that people may distinguish between their neighborhood as a whole and their "microneighborhood" – that is, their immediate locality, sometimes as small as the area they can see from their front door.

◀ **A child's neighborhood** *is often a rather different place, with a different population, than a parent's. Much of it is created by children and adults whom the parent may never meet.*

▲ **Usually more than a few houses on a street,** *but less than the entire city around you, the boundaries of your neighborhood depend ultimately on you. The local area and the people in it that residents iden-*

tify themselves with is often much smaller than any of the districts named on a city street map or organized into community associations.

A place with a distinctive character?

One of the ideals for a neighborhood seems to be that it should have clear boundaries and a distinctive physical character. This may be communicated by visual cues and symbols (for example, the signs on streets and buildings in a city's Chinatown). A neighborhood is also likely to have a name, image or identity (or all three) that people generally recognize and identify with. Ideal social characteristics of a neighborhood include a sense of unity among the inhabitants (which is probably also recognized by outsiders), and generally accepted rules as to the way streets, parks and other public areas are used (even though some members of the community may disregard them). A few of these characteristics would be sufficient to define a neighborhood, but ideally there should be a surfeit of them, so that each

reinforces the next. The more this occurs, the more we will recognize our own neighborhood as a separate entity. A neighborhood is most clearly defined when its social and physical boundaries coincide: for example, if almost all of the jazz-lovers in a city live within a clearly defined area, there will be a very strong sense of neighborhood among them.

It is possible to list hundreds – if not thousands – of physical and social attributes that encourage people to think of their street, town or area as a neighborhood. The important point is that all of these aspects contribute toward a single quality – ambience. This is often difficult to define, but is evident to anyone who has ever traveled across a large city: the boundaries between one neighborhood and the next are surprisingly clear.

■ **A particular style of residential architecture** *not only gives a neighborhood its visual character but helps to create a community where people of like circumstances, and – when they have a choice about what style of house to live in – similar tastes, come together. Oak Buffs* RIGHT *is on the island of Martha's Vineyard, off the coast of Cape Cod, Massachusetts. St Léger les Domarts* BELOW *is a village in France.*

142

DISTINGUISHING FEATURES

■ *The character of a neighborhood is partly shaped by physical aspects and by the services or facilities that are available. Some of these are straightforward: for example, the entire area may smell unpleasant because of a local factory. Other factors are not so obvious when we look around for somewhere new to live (although they may become all to obvious later). Attributes that help give a neighborhood its character include: the natural landscape – rivers, lakes, green areas; the manmade landscape – buildings, walls, street patterns; transportation and services; the way people keep their houses and gardens. The possibilities are immense – a fact that makes the tasks of planners and designers much easier because they have a great deal of scope. Also, names, especially if they are traditional and well known, can be important.*

Birds of a feather flock together

If we look at the human race as a whole – across cultures and through history – we find countless examples of differences of language, dietary customs, religion, and so on. These differences identify one culture from the next. It has even been suggested that the various cultures are rather like different species or subspecies. On the whole, though, like tends to congregate with like – and sometimes to regard the rest with mistrust or condescension. The people within a certain group are regarded as "us," and anyone else belongs to "them." Tribal societies often call themselves "The People": everyone else is not quite human. In the same way the ancient Chinese and Greeks, among others, referred to outsiders as barbarians.

People have always tended to cluster together, like with like, in specific geographical areas. This is especially true when groups have felt under threat for one reason or another: clustering allows mutual support, and so, provided the culture is not nomadic, a neighborhood develops. The reasons why people consider they have something in common, and so should form a community, differ considerably: among them are religion, class, race, tribe, origin, kinship, caste, language, age, education, community of interests and occupation. Whatever characteristics are shared (and there may be more than one), the people in such a neighborhood see it as being made up of other people like themselves.

To an outsider, this may not seem to be the case. The city of St Louis, Missouri has an area called La Clede Town which contains a group of people who, on the basis of income, race and so on, are totally disparate. Yet, studies have shown that the inhabitants share a desire to live in a central-city, heterogeneous region. Because of this they see themselves as a neighborhood of like-minded people.

In developed countries, lifestyle is becoming a more and more common reason why people cluster in particular neighborhoods. The term lifestyle is a rather loose one: we can understand it best by thinking of decisions about how to allocate resources (money, effort, time and so on), especially as these relate to, for example, child rearing, eating habits, everyday routines and leisure activities. Provided we

▲ **Beneath symbols of a shared belief**, *neighbors in a small street in Venice, Italy, pass a few moments together in the late afternoon, each comfortably assured of understanding the other.*

A NEIGHBORHOOD OF LIKE MINDS

■ *People often cluster together because they want to live near those whose lifestyles are similar to their own. There are a number of reasons why we are happiest in a community which, for one reason or another, we regard as being made up of like minds:*

◆ *events are more predictable – or, at least, less unpredictable – so that stress is reduced.*

◆ *the meanings of nonverbal communication (body language, clothing, behavior, tone of voice) are much more easily recognized. They can be interpreted according to the community's rules for decoding them, and this makes it possible to respond appropriately to them – so that confusion and*

misunderstanding are minimized.

◆ *many psychological, cultural and other defenses can operate much more effectively.*

◆ *there is agreement about environmental quality – including issues such as the mowing of lawns, children's behavior and acceptable noise levels. The same goals are understood and shared by all members of the community.*

◆ *this kind of tightly-knit neighborhood provides people with mutual support at times of stress and rapid cultural change. They help cultural groups (such as immigrant communities) to survive.*

On the other hand, people may choose to ignore questions of neighborhood when they

select the area in which they would like to live. Instead they may focus on: access to transportation; proximity to their workplace or ease of travel to it; access to parks and open spaces; location of doctors, hospitals etc; nearness and variety of shops; choice of schools.

have enough money to select a neighborhood that seems to offer the right atmosphere and the facilities and services we need for our preferred lifestyle.

What makes a successful neighborhood?

It is rarely the case that a mixed community leads to greater interaction between the people living there. We may be willing to mix with people who are quite unlike ourselves, but we also like to be able to retreat to a place that we recognize as home. Like other animals, we interact most if we have a secure, private area that we "own." Mixed neighborhoods may lead to unlikely alliances – between artists and artisans, perhaps – but equally they can lead to avoidance or conflict.

In general, three things are essential if a neighborhood is to be happy and conflict-free. Firstly, the neighborhood must be small enough for the people in it to be aware of the other people in it, and of the identity they share. Secondly, the people in adjoining neighborhoods should not be *too* different. Thirdly, within the neighborhood there should be neutral areas in which neighbors can meet.

It is difficult for planners to design such neutral areas in advance, because their neutrality depends on how the people living in the neighborhood see them. It is often thought, for example, that a park will bring a community together: this can be the case, but very frequently it is not, because for certain groups it ceases to be neutral. Parents with young children may feel driven away by gangs of noisy adolescents, or vice versa. A shared school is even less likely to unite a neighborhood, since different parents have

different expectations of how they want their children to be educated. Sometimes people move to a different neighborhood for the schooling they prefer. However, markets, shopping malls or supermarkets can often bind a community together.

Where we live says a lot about us

Whoever and wherever we are, we use symbols as a way of presenting ourselves. These symbols involve colors, clothing, furnishings and the neighborhood in which we choose to live. In today's large-scale societies, it has become the case that to a great extent "you are where you live" – in other words, that your neighborhood is a symbol of yourself. If a person lives in an untidy, poorly maintained neighborhood, we regard them differently than we would if they lived in an uptown area where graffiti was unheard of. This does not necessarily mean that we disparage people from poor neighborhoods; merely that the area in which someone lives influences our impression of that person.

Our housing, furnishings and so on, communicate our identity, reflecting our values, beliefs and ideals. This is particularly important in large-scale, fluid societies where it is more difficult to categorize individuals reliably in terms of their accent or clothes – their neighborhood becomes an important clue to what they are like.

In cities the importance of the neighborhood as a symbol extends beyond this, affecting the behavior of the people living there. The physical environment expresses and communicates various identities, though this defines situations, and in turn, constrains and guides behavior.

▲ **Local shopping** is one of the few shared facilities that reliably strengthen people's sense of belonging to the same neighborhood. Ironically, a school, so often the central feature of a planned community, may be a focus for divisive controversy about educational methods and policy. Even the ways in which different groups, especially different age-groups, want to use the local park can mean that the park accentuates differences between them.

▶ **Planning a neighborhood** is a difficult challenge, because the sense of community to be created must arise in the end from within the people who will live there. If they are unable to identify with each other and with the services and the physical settings that have been provided, many will avoid participation in the community and may come into conflict with it. Three principles of good planning are to make neighborhoods small, to ensure that they do not adjoin neighborhoods with which they are likely to come into conflict, and to include neutral areas, such as small local shopping centers, where neighbors can meet.

Nonurban Uses

Nonurban
Elementary School
Junior High School
High School
Hiking and Biking Tr
Community Park
Ranch Homesites
Historical Site

DU/GRA'
DU/GRA
DU/GRA
-15.0 DU/GRA

1Planning Area
2Dwelling Unit/Gross Res
3Symbolic Only

Is the neighborhood a thing of the past?

In the 1960s a number of experts claimed that, in cities, neighborhoods no longer existed, and that, even if they did, they were no longer important, particularly as cities grew to become metropolises and then megalopolises. The idea was that increased physical mobility and improved communication – radio, television, telephones, computers – had eroded the importance of the specific locality in which a person lived. The concept of the global village appeared. Communities were no longer defined in geographical terms, but in terms of networks of people who might be widely separated but who were linked by mutual interests of some kind. In reality, however, it seems that people whose links are to a worldwide community rather than to neighbors are in a minority – and a small minority. For most of us the idea of the neighborhood remains very important: we rely on family, friends, neighbors, local institutions, services, and so on.

It is true that in developed (and, indeed, developing) countries, a person's immediate environment is no longer likely to be the only setting for their day-to-day activities. This does not mean that neighborhoods no longer exist, but it does mean that the settings for our activities may be quite divorced from each other, we may have a neighborhood that is in two different sections, and may have little knowledge of the territory between the two. We identify with the two localities almost as if they were one rather complex area, which comprises a "home range" ignoring – perhaps even fearing – the land separating them. Because the city has become too large for us to hope to identify with it, we concentrate on those parts which for one reason or another have become familiar to us, and think of them as being in some way joined.

In fact, even in the most traditional societies, neighbor-

146

WHO CARES ABOUT THE NEIGHBORHOOD?

■ Some people value their neighborhoods much more highly than others do.

Studies in several countries have shown that certain groups of people would rather become unemployed than leave their neighborhood, even if they were guaranteed a better job somewhere else. Others have no such qualms.

Lifestyles have profound implications in terms of the importance with which people regard their neighborhoods.

This has even made attitudes about neighborhood a key factor in market research about consumer behavior (see OPPOSITE). In many Western cities research has shown that the local knowledge of certain groups extends only to four blocks; others, by contrast, know extensive areas in detail. Clearly, the neighborhood has a different value for these groups. The former are often recent immigrants, ethnic minorities and the uneducated. In many third world countries, however, the converse is true: well-educated, prosperous people who have lived in a city all their lives may voluntarily confine their activities to their own neighborhood.

hoods have never supplied the setting for the whole of life: people have always strayed outside their most obvious environments. The change, then, may be one of degree rather than of kind. At the same time, as cities and towns grow bigger, we need to associate ourselves with smaller groups – hundreds or thousands, rather than millions – in order to feel "at home." The neighborhood can act as a buffer between the individual and the city or state at large.

Neighborhoods are unlikely to disappear and will almost certainly continue to have an important role in our lives. The melting pot frequently mentioned in the context of cities is unlikely to melt, much less blend, all the disparate elements. In fact, the neighborhood will probably become even more important than it is today. It is unwise to generalize about this since different cultures may in the future evolve in different ways. What is certain, however, is that a neighborhood cannot be objectively defined – prescribed as a particular area, or drafted on a planner's map. We construct our neighborhood in our minds.

147

■ Contrasts in commitment go with these contrasts in neighborhood character. For a Los Angeles street-gang member, the neighborhood LEFT is an all-absorbing territorial imperative – life takes its meaning from his membership in a group drawn from nearby streets and from conflict with similar groups not far away. For residents of a modern housing development ABOVE LEFT, the neighborhood is mainly a place to come back to after experiencing most out-of-the-home life elsewhere. Fast roads lead to worlds of work, shopping and socialization well outside the community. In an unplanned community ABOVE RIGHT, residents who have concentrated on making their homes distinctive, and on securing each their own access to the shore, have incidentally created a distinctive setting with which all can identify.

LOCALITES, URBANITES AND CONSUMER CHOICE

■ In the early 1970s advertisers commonly spoke of two groups of people – localites and cosmopolites or urbanites) – the former being more dependent on neighborhood. An alternative approach was to identify four groups based on lifestyle: consumption oriented; social-prestige oriented; family oriented; community oriented. People in each group have a very different set of desires and values and make very different residential choices: likewise, their evaluation of the importance of their neighborhood differs. Today advertisers recognize as many as 47 group profiles based on lifestyle. They also identify where such groups live and can predict spending habits.

■ The job of advertisers is to sell dreams. In terms of neighborhoods, this means that they have to sell some sort of image of an ideal life. The sale of houses in new developments is very revealing in this respect. Individual houses are rarely shown or even mentioned. Instead, the accent is on the larger setting – the neighborhood and its people.

Out in the City

TODAY we can move about the world rapidly – flying in supersonic airplanes between world capitals, we can arrive at the same time of day as we left – perhaps even a little before. Our mobility and the pace at which we live, however, mean that we really *know* few, if any, places. Furthermore, everywhere we go we find that the streets, the buildings, the cars, the clothes and the advertisement billboards are becoming increasingly similar – often identical. So how do we find our way around an unfamiliar city? And what can we discover by looking at our own city through the eyes of a visitor?

Visual cues

Before the dawn of the age of steam, most people rarely traveled far from home. They might make a weekly journey to their nearest town on market day or, a few times a year, attend festivals or fairs, but most of the time they used only the familiar highways and byways close to their homes. At such a time, and in such places, everyone understood their world according to their education and social station. In towns, pictorial signs told the illiterate visiting peasants where to buy their bread or beer. We use signs today, both written and representational, to help strangers to navigate our cities. In the United States, the development of the

highway-hugging strip has generated high-speed signage. Floodlit or fluorescent signs – advertising everything from gasoline to peanuts, motels to burgers – are clustered on towers 10 meters high to attract the motorist's attention.

At the most basic level, the general style of buildings in a city can carry easily recognizable messages to observers. The mystery and the heavenward aspiration of the Gothic church, the secure and ancient imperial power of the classical court of justice, the moneyed confidence of the offices of city insurers and risk underwriters, or the cozy domestic architecture of an affluent suburb – all of these supply us with readily identifiable associations. However, reading the city is not nearly as easy as it was a few centuries ago, when the population was essentially split into two sections: the uneducated masses and the educated few. Today, because many of us live in multicultural societies, a good cityplanner or guide must be concerned with a staggering variety of cultural values. So, in fact, it has become much easier to subscribe to the values of an international style to which can be added, if necessary, a longhouse roof in Malaysia or a piece of half-timbering in Germany – just to remind us where we really are.

Our tendency to look back longingly to an apparently secure past means that old symbols are again cherished and

◀ **International anonymity.** *Chinese lettering and a name over the entrance are the only indicators of this building's purpose and location. Whatever the particular comforts or quality of the hotel, from the outside it could belong anywhere from New York to Sydney. Increasingly, hotel chains, chain stores and international companies make one city look very much like another.*

What are the signals that enable us to read the city? ■ *How do we react to the fact that everywhere is beginning to look like everywhere else?* ■ *When we move from place to place we use subconscious techniques to find our way.*

149

READING THE CITY

■ *Even in the most modern city, distinctive buildings and features act as visual signals, helping us to find our way around. An elegant spire overlooking the marketplace in Burlington, Vermont* TOP *would identify this building as a church even to a time traveler from the past. Recognizable perhaps only to the modern eye is a movie theater* LEFT. *Even without the illuminated advertising, the building's façade makes its function clear. If you* look closer at a city, you become aware of other nonverbal signs. Some are standardized, but easily recognized only by locals – fire alarm boxes in Paris, for example* ABOVE LEFT, *are painted red.* ABOVE *This sidewalk sign inviting us into a Parisian café, however, is unique, but easily understood by any visitor to the city.*

copied. But by far the commonest signs of the city, readable by all, are the colors, logos and trademarks of the national and international multiples – banks and burger companies and supermarket chains. In an age of sophisticated merchandising, why should this be? Why should moneylenders, retailers and service industries all want to make everywhere look like everywhere else? The answer is simple: the customer passing by is in a hurry and so must be swiftly captured. As service and merchandise become more and more standardized, advertising and brand loyalty are of paramount importance.

How do we find our way around?

A six-year-old child may be able to cross quite a large and complex area of the city yet, on being questioned, may be quite unable to explain how the operation was performed. Landmarks do not appear to have been consciously used, and the child cannot draw any meaningful map or diagram of the journey. When adults are asked to give directions in a familiar environment, or to draw a mental map of their everyday environment, the results can be very surprising.

Research carried out in the United States in the 1950s identified five primary elements in the urban landscape: paths, landmarks, nodes, districts and edges. The first two terms are self-explanatory. Nodes are usually readily recognizable points of focus where a number of paths meet. Districts are relatively large areas which have some common character: they are both easy and difficult to define. The shapes of districts, even those with well-known names (like New York's Greenwich Village), tend to fluctuate because of shifting urban populations with a wide range of backgrounds and lifestyles. The edges between areas of different character are strongest and most useful when they are visually clear and provide some kind of physical barrier: rivers form some of the clearest edges. It appears that, when constructing mental maps, our minds initially focus on features in the five categories and then expand around these points.

150

■ **Finding our way in the modern city** *is a remarkable achievement.* ABOVE *A pedestrian weaves a path between looming urban shapes.* RIGHT *From the air, Sun City, Arizona has a distinctively maze-like design. Maps that each of us carries in our head help us make sense of the city, but they* *do not resemble street plans. Instead of representing a whole area in accurate proportions, they tend to focus on particular landmarks or districts: the streets or buildings that are most important to you are likely to form the basis for your mental map.*

Designers, accustomed to maps and plans, naturally find mental mapping much the easiest model to use to analyze the way people perceive landmarks in the city. They have therefore largely ignored attempts to develop systems that look at how people move rather than at static representations of the places in which they are moving. Nevertheless, in the 1960s the urban designer and teacher Lawrence Halprin drew on the work of his wife Ann, a dancer and choreographer, to explore the possibilities of using choreographic notation systems to produce "scores" for our patterns of movement through the city.

There are good reasons why urban designers should not rely too heavily on mental-mapping ideas. In the modern world, our perceptions of the five basic features are subject to great diversity of view depending on our individual cultural and socioeconomic status. Also, with city-wide rapid transportation systems, it is often no longer very easy to decide what a node actually is, and these same transpor-

tation systems frequently reduce the use of paths. One reason the technique has survived is that urban designers tend to work at district level (filling the gap between town planners and architects). At this level, the use of mental maps and the categorization of place perception into the five elements remain useful aids to design.

Another reason for its survival is that urban design can be part of a democratizing force in the city environment: any tool that can be used to promote dialogue between interest groups in the community is therefore seized on. Debate about the proposed definition of a district or path helps designers to work in a practical way with more broadly based views than their own.

How modern planning affects us

Though we are not always conscious of it, our reactions to a city are influenced by basic design features – such as how many green areas there are. In the last 150 years town

NAVIGATING THE KNOWN

■ *There is much evidence to suggest that a great deal of our navigation of familiar environments is not primarily based on a mental map but is more to do with the unconscious learning of what one researcher has called tactual kinesthetic patterns. In other words, as with riding a bicycle or climbing stairs, we are able to use learned patterns of coordination that respond to physical experience to enable us to achieve a goal. When climbing a stair for the first time we unconsciously anticipate that the risers will be all the same size, and likewise the treads: if they are not we may trip. But, once we get used to an uneven stair, we seldom have any problem with its irregularity. Similarly, once we become accustomed to routes in a city, we can follow them – and variations of them – without having consciously to think about what we are doing.*

planners have been concerned to open up environments to more light and air. Research has shown that, when we work in buildings that entirely cut us off from contact with the outside world and its daily and seasonal changes, we become anxious and uneasy. We can draw great comfort from signs of daily and seasonal change in the city. For this reason, evergreen trees are less popular than deciduous trees. Because deciduous trees change color with the seasons and drop their leaves during the fall, they seem to give greater reassurance to city-dwellers. Most of us are phototropic – we like to be in the light – and so, at least in cities in temperate latitudes, workers have lunch and visitors pause in areas where there is direct sunshine. The more unending and relentless the concrete and glass of the city streets, the more an area of greenery will be enjoyed.

Similarly, different types of street have a different effect on us. In residential areas where housing is set far back from the street, we have little or no contact with what is happening in the houses: our perception of the place is dominated by other visual cues – the architecture, colors, skyline and so on. If houses border on the street, however, our experience can be enriched by glimpses into a private world. In fact, some householders actually display objects in their street windows for the benefit of the passerby. Whereas we may feel like intruders in the culs-de-sac of residential areas, if we are sauntering on a narrow pavement edged with cafés and restaurants, we will look away from the street into the welcoming interiors which become more important than the street itself.

Seeing your city with new eyes

The city as we once knew it is gradually becoming a place to visit rather than somewhere to live or work, and so the tourist frame of mind offers an increasingly appropriate way of looking at our urban environment. In a city where the cultural melting pot succeeds at the expense of cultural definition, where every main street tries to be more like Las Vegas than Las Vegas is, and where every new housing area seems to be made up of little boxes, we begin to crave not just history but meaning. Despite the usually glitzy packaging, tourist guides are genuinely trying to explain our past to us.

We are generally rather uncritical of our own city: so long as we can do the things we want to do we are likely to be little concerned about such matters as its architecture and planning. However, when we visit other cities – perhaps as tourists – these considerations are often a central interest. Many tourists have a well-informed view of the places they visit and are also curious about what they see. Tourist industries all over the world, therefore, have worked to promote a rich experience for tourists. In many cases this experience is rooted in history, and every attempt is made to enhance the credentials and associations of the place, with information centers, guidebooks and maps specially prepared to cater to the tourist. Sometimes this can lessen the authenticity of the experience, as buildings are heavily restored or new features are added that in fact have no real historic roots. Many beautiful German towns, for example, have been subjected to extensive reconstruction in order to recreate their historic ambience.

As tourists, we may be little concerned about authenticity and the fact that all places are beginning to look the same, but as local residents we may have a very different attitude. What is at stake is our sense of place. In fact, even the presence of tourists can alter the character of a place: in some settings (Disneyland, for example) the crowds add to the pleasure, but in others they can destroy it – for local residents and tourists alike. **RH**

DISCOVERING THE CITY

■ If you have lived in the same city for several years, you have probably become immune to many of its attractions. You may never have made the effort to find out about its history or architecture. One remedy is to try looking at your city with a tourist's eyes. What would strike you most about its buildings and streets?

The spectacular view of Paris from the Eiffel Tower RIGHT is a popular tourist attraction, but even a native Parisian might find it revealing. By looking into their city's history they could learn that Paris as we know it today was largely created by city planner Baron Haussmann (1809-1891). The city's wide, straight streets were not in fact designed primarily for their esthetic effect. On the instructions of Napoleon III, Haussmann created the "grands boulevards" for security reasons – they were useful for deploying troops to quell urban uprisings.

Are you aware of the practical or esthetic reasons behind the layout of your own city? As everywhere begins to resemble everywhere else, awareness of our environments, and a strong sense of place are becoming more and more important to our sense of identity.

Coping with Urban Life

THE AUTHOR and physician Oliver Wendell Holmes, father of the great American jurist of the same name, once remarked: "...the chief worth of civilization is...that it calls for great and combined intellectual efforts, instead of simple, uncoordinated ones...more complex and intense intellectual efforts mean a fuller and richer life. They mean more life." He was referring to the feeling of exhilaration that living in one of society's most complicated structures – the city – can give us. However, daily exposure to certain aspects of urban life can transform exhilaration into stress.

We are perhaps overpreoccupied with stress today – the word is used to describe the effects of even the most transitory hardships. In fact, a certain level of stress is essential if we are to function normally: several studies have shown that the absence of a normal level of stimulation for even a short time can have highly unpleasant effects. Nevertheless, for many people stress is a legitimate and serious problem that can even lead to physiological and psychological illness. It has increased in prominence in recent decades partly because of the hectic lifestyles so many of us now have, but in particular because of the increasing burdens that city life places on us.

What causes stress in the city?

If you want to make your life less stressful, the first step is to identify the sources of stress (stressors). Though there is little you can do about stressful life events like divorce or a death in the family, it is worth trying to deal with environmental stressors. After all, the environment is to a large extent made by people, and so can also be changed by them.

One common cause of environmental stress is crowding. The number of people in a particular space can be regarded as its "density," but many psychologists have suggested that

THE EXCITEMENT OF THE CITY

■ *Studies of the urban environment tend to concentrate on its disadvantages – stress, squalor, pollution, crowding and so on – and to ignore many of the points in its favor. Yet millions of people around the world choose to live in cities, finding benefits there that outweigh other considerations. Often the reasons are practical; for example, wages are generally higher (although the same is true of living costs), and in some countries cities may offer people their only hope of employment.*

However, people seek out the city for other reasons. There are likely to be better amenities in the form of stores, restaurants, delivery services, schools and so on. Also, there are the cultural aspects of cities: theaters, movie theaters, galleries, museums, concert halls, rock-music venues, libraries and many other centers of interest. Some of the elements of city life that can act as stressors have an upside, providing a constant source of stimulation and leading to a more exciting life. Cities offer a variety of experiences that can be found nowhere else. With eventfulness, variety, stimulation and choice, it is no wonder that so many people opt for the city life.

66 ... WHAT PEOPLE SAY

I like living in the city because:
◆ There is so much to see and do – there are museums and art galleries to visit, and the stores are wonderful.
◆ I love the nightlife – I can go to the theater, the movies, or out to a good restaurant whenever I want.
◆ The social life is terrific – I get to meet new people all the time who make stimulating conversation.
◆ My work is here and I can go straight out for the evening without having to worry about getting back.

I would like to move away from the city because:
◆ It is dirty and polluted – I feel I need to go to the country every weekend just to get some fresh air.
◆ It is dangerous – there are too many muggings and you risk your life just crossing the street.
◆ I cannot stand the noise – police and ambulance sirens wailing all day makes me nervous.
◆ I do not like crowds – too many people make me feel claustrophobic.

▶ **Is this for me?** *On Fifth Avenue, New York, shimmering tail lights and skyscrapers studded with light glitter with promise for those who thrive on city life. For those who do not, this scene may bring frightening associations to mind.* INSET ABOVE *All of us have moments when we cannot keep up.* INSET BELOW *Does the city select in favor of a particularly tough personality type?*

Are you exhilarated or stressed by city life? ■ *Crowding, pollution and noise cause mental and physical stress* ■ *How should we cope with stressors like these?* ■ *What can planners do to minimize them in the future?*

a sense of crowding is not simply a matter of a place's actual density but also of the individual's usual experience. For example, farmers are usually accustomed to a very low density and so, when they visit a city, they will be far more stressed than seasoned city-dwellers by a rush-hour subway journey. You are also likely to be more aware of crowding if people are obstructing or delaying you – when, for example, you are in a hurry and have to wait in line to buy a ticket. Crowding is subjective. While large numbers of people willingly gather together for a rock concert or a ballgame, and find the experience exciting, others would be stressed by being in such a crowd. Also, the type of crowd different people prefer varies: some like peaceful crowds, others noisy and active ones.

In some countries – for example, Japan – many people actually prefer the experience of being close to others, so that crowding creates little stress. But there is a lot of evidence – in the form of increased levels of crime, aggression, suicide, infant mortality, juvenile delinquency and so on – to suggest that stress is definitely produced by the densities of Western cities.

There is even some evidence to suggest that density affects the level of affection we show toward each other. One study looked at three African societies (the Logali, the Gusii and the Kipsigis) and found that in the most densely populated group it was normal to avoid holding hands with

155

THE CITY PERSONALITY

■ *Stress affects different people in different ways, depending on their personalities. Researchers into heart disease have distinguished two broad categories of personality, named Type A and Type B. Type A behavior is characterized by intense competitiveness, an impatient urge to do everything as quickly as possible, and especially shortness of temper. Type B behavior is more relaxed and easy-going.*

A high proportion of city-dwellers display Type A behavior. They are likely to be severely affected by some of the city's stressors – waiting in traffic jams, the need to meet tight deadlines, and so on. They are therefore particularly vulnerable to stress-related diseases. In addition, such behavior seems to cause a number of physiological changes (for example, in the levels of blood

fats and sugars) which can affect the risk of coronary heart disease. So Type A people are caught both ways. Moving to the country may be no solution for them, because they are likely to find that the understimulation of the rural environment also causes stress. One way out of the dilemma is to take up some form of deep relaxation, such as meditation so that for at least a few hours each week the body is given some respite.

■ **Stress**. *Long-term exposure to emotional stress can decrease the ability of the body's immune system to cope with infectious disease and there is strong evidence that stress can precipitate a relapse or complications in people who are already ill. Allergies, backache, stomach disorders, and headaches can also be exacerbated by stress.*

friends and to describe other family members in more negative terms. It is probably unwise to place too much weight on this, however, because in other cultures the opposite appears to be true. Glasgow, for example, is one of the most crowded cities in Scotland, yet displays of affection there seem to be much more frequent than in most other Scottish cities.

Breathing polluted air

If we are continually exposed to air pollution and noise our health may suffer, and levels of both are often high in cities. Tall buildings can block off winds that might otherwise clear the air of pollutants. (Though this is not always the case as the skyscrapers of many cities tend instead to funnel the prevailing winds.) More pollutants are released into the air by motor vehicles in cities, not just because there is more traffic, but also because cars stop and start frequently. Also, there is often a concentration of waste-producing factories in urban areas.

The effects of air pollution are well documented. For example, there is thought to be a strong relationship between the number of road vehicles in a given area and the rate of deaths from cancer. Exhaust fumes may also cause

cancer indirectly – for example, by exacerbating sinusitis, which in turn seems to be linked with lung cancer. Lead emissions from car exhausts can cause mental retardation and behavioral difficulties in children. (The growing use of lead-free gasoline will help in this area.) Many other conditions are linked with air pollution, including epilepsy and memory disturbances.

Air pollution also impairs our performance of tasks, affecting reaction times, manual dexterity and attention. One study showed that, within 90 minutes of exposure to a "soup" of polluted air similar to that produced in a city, people showed significantly poorer performance in time-judgment tests. It has been suggested that air pollution on major traffic routes may contribute to the frequency of road accidents by impairing driving ability.

How cities assault our ears

Noise pollution is another potential threat to health – it can cause long-term damage to hearing. A survey carried out in 1972 by the Environmental Protection Agency found that nearly three million Americans suffered noise-induced hearing loss. Another study, of an apartment block built over a highway in New York City, found that children living

156

WHAT CAUSES SMOG?

▶ Smog is fog that contains a high proportion of smoke and, usually, other pollutants and it is almost exclusively associated with large urban areas. This policeman breathing oxygen tries to counteract the effects of smog on a bad day in Tokyo. Most Western cities have taken steps to reduce the problem. Los Angeles, once the smog capital of the world, today has relatively clean air, but smog still plagues cities in the third world, like Kanpur, India.

■ Smog builds up to especially high levels when there is a temperature inversion in the air. Normally, in the lower part of

the atmosphere, an increase in altitude implies a decrease in temperature, but in an inversion the converse is the case. Inversions can result from atmospheric disturbances, like weather fronts, or may be the result of an especially cold night. The trapped cold layer

near ground level cannot escape upward in the normal way, bearing with it its pollutants. Higher and higher levels of pollution build up until the air at ground level is an opaque, choking, toxic "soup."

■ Cities are particularly susceptible to smog because of heavy traffic and industry. Thick smogs can endanger life: in London in December 1952, 3,500 deaths were attributed to smog containing high levels of sulfur dioxide.

on the lower stories were more likely to have difficulty in reading tests. This is because reading depends in part on our ability to discriminate between the different sounds of language, an ability impaired in the children by the noise from the highway beneath their homes.

Noise can cause other problems, too. There seems to be a link between infant mortality and the exposure of pregnant women to aircraft noise. The incidence of cardiovascular disorders, allergies, sore throats and digestive problems – all physical symptoms often associated with stress – has also been shown to be related to noise. Furthermore, noise affects us psychologically. A study of psychiatric hospital admissions around one major airport, found that people from the noisiest parts of the area were more likely to require psychiatric help. Of course, this result is not conclusive (the stressors could have been the additional cars,

people, airplanes and so on), but people who live in such areas frequently do report that noise adds to their own personal level of stress.

Like air pollution, noise pollution can make you less efficient, though the relationship between noise and performance is not straightforward. Certain people may be distracted by it and have accidents (there are high accident rates in noisy workplaces – particularly when the noise is unpredictable). On the other hand, someone whose performance is flagging may well be alerted by noise and so become more efficient.

Noise, heat and aggression

Our behavior can be affected by noise in other ways. In a noisy environment people seem to be more aggressive and less likely to help each other (crowding can have the same effect). In one test a researcher repeatedly dropped a pile of books both when there was a lawnmower operating in the background and when there was not. Significantly more people offered to help pick the books up when the noise level was lower. Sometimes the experimenter wore an armcast to signal even more clearly that assistance would be welcomed. This increased the number of offers of help when the lawn mower was off but had no effect when it was running.

As well as being noisier, cities are typically 5-10°C hotter than surrounding rural areas. This is partly because there are more sources of heat – factories, domestic heating and so on – and partly because air pollution tends to trap heat. A hot environment is generally a stressful one, and can lead to raised levels of aggression, particularly when people are already angry. The situation is not as straightforward is it might seem, however. For example, although riots are more likely to occur in hot

157

◀ **Other people's tragedies** are inescapable in a big city. Here police gather round the body of a traffic accident victim as local residents look on. Accidents happen in the country too – with farm machinery, for example – but country dwellers are not so keenly aware of each of them as they happen. The constant wail of police and ambulance sirens is an integral feature of city life. There is a danger of our becoming desensitized to disaster – we shut it out in order to cope with the stress it causes.

weather (or just afterward) than in cooler weather, they are less frequent when temperatures rise to particularly high levels above about 30°C (86°F).

Reactions to urban stress

City-dwellers, consciously or unconsciously, adopt various strategies in order to cope with the stresses they are subject to. These coping mechanisms are not always successful – sometimes they go wrong and only lead to further stress.

If you live in a city one problem you are likely to face is an excess of sensory stimuli – noise, bright lights, social contacts and so on. You may find, for example, that you have more social contacts than you can handle. One strategy is to devote as little time as possible to each encounter, but this often leads to brusque behavior. Alternatively, you could reduce the number of contacts, perhaps by transferring them onto others; at work you might use a secretary as a barrier. Other strategies include having an unlisted telephone number and, at a more basic level, adopting an unfriendly expression, stance or way of speaking. Overall, as research has consistently shown, the greater the density of people around us, the more inclined we become to detach ourselves – to withdraw socially from others. The main problem with using a strategy like detachment is that it can go too far, finally resulting in alienation and loneliness.

In his book *Behavior in Public Places*, written in 1963, Erving Goffman described another strategy for coping with

DO CITIES MAKE US INSENSITIVE?

■ *The effects that places have on us are very important. For example, one common opinion is that living in cities makes people behave in an unfriendly and less helpful way, and that cities are violent and dangerous places. This opinion is not necessarily correct, but stereotypes about cities are powerful and hard to overcome.*

Research has in fact shown that people who live in cities are generally less likely to help one another than people who live in smaller communities; this is known as "bystander apathy." The reasons for bystander apathy are not clear. One popular theory is that the pace of urban living, the overcrowding and the bustle combine to overload our senses; as a result, we mentally shut out much of what happens. Another theory is that the presence of other people makes us feel less personally obliged to assist: we look to the others to assess a situation for us and, if no one else is doing anything, we assume that the problem is not really serious. A third idea is that people help one another within their own neighborhood if they feel a sense of belonging to it, and therefore some personal interest in that responsibility for what happens there. **DC CW**

▲ **Private lives in public places**. *Cities offer opportunities for privacy that are often not found in smaller, less-densely populated communities. To ignore people around you – even a stranger – might* be considered hostile in a small community. It may be virtually impossible to find a quiet moment by yourself if there are other people around.

▲ **Creating a social distance**. *People in crowded places use facial expressions – often unconsciously – to avoid becoming involved with each other. Here a woman in the subway hides behind a mask of heavy makeup and a look that says: "stay away." More often, we simply keep our faces blank* and avoid catching anyone's eye – this signals that we are saving our social energies for more relaxing situations.

social encounters. His "man the actor" model portrays people hiding their true selves behind façades and putting on different "faces" for different social interactions. Most people recognize that they sometimes do this, and the idea that it is a habit in the city rather than the country is not a new one. City-dwellers meet more new people and many of their friends and acquaintances may not know one another. As a result, people in the city have more opportunity for inventive self presentation.

Alone in the crowd

Loneliness is very common in cities, particularly among people who have left home to live there. Such people have cut themselves off from their families and friends, and lack any social support in facing an unfamiliar, and perhaps overwhelming environment. The abundance of people does not necessarily make it easier to find friends, and the design of urban accommodation often discourages social contact. Loneliness in a place where there is so much available company is often portrayed in the media as failure, so that people unhappy about being alone are made to feel worse.

However, many people revel in city life precisely because of its anonymity. They can control their contacts with others, enjoying company some of the time but being alone when they want to be. They can arrange encounters in advance rather than being unable to avoid them. Indeed, they may *have* to arrange meetings: because in the city friends may live at a considerable distance rather than just a block or two away, and people are less likely to drop by casually. On the positive side this gives us more control over our levels of intimacy with others, and allows us to avoid getting involved with people when we do not want to.

The key word is *control*. As research has shown, if we feel in control, an environment is likely to be less stressful. In other words, the degree of contact we have with other people is less important than the extent to which we feel in control of it. This has been shown very clearly in studies of college dormitories: control was associated with high levels of adaptation and seemed to lead to a lack of any sense of loneliness or, conversely, of oppressive overcrowding. The studies also showed that people differ in their ability to cope with particular environments, and in the pleasure they derive from them. Of course, it is easy for the city environment to be uncontrolled and overwhelming: events seem just to happen to us, rather than being under our control. This is the downside of the anonymity of city life.

The nature of friendship in the city also has certain characteristics. What we seem to need are not lots of acquaintances (although we may enjoy these, too) but a few close friends with whom we can discuss our problems or share our triumphs. We all differ in the extent to which we find the company of others either wearing or stimulating. Some people may prefer to have a wide circle of social contacts, but for most of us having too many friends can have low payoffs. In general we value those friends best who show affection only to ourselves and at most a few others: if they seem to be attached to virtually everybody, then we tend to place little value on their apparent affection for us.

159

◀ **Urban isolation**. *If we become too skilled at avoiding social interaction in order to protect our privacy, we may find ourselves isolated, even in the middle of a crowded city. This man walking with a crush of other people probably has no relationship with any of them. Unless he has found ways to meet other people in spite of their resistance, the effect of urban life may be loneliness. There is a fine line between privacy and isolation and realizing where to draw it is part of being in control of your environment and reducing your exposure to stress.*

A concrete jungle?

Cities are sometimes very ugly: they have not been built with any overall esthetic intention (Brasilia, the capital of Brazil, is a rare exception) and their piecemeal planning is often inefficient. The ugliness may be compounded by disorder, dirt, and environmental decay. These, rather than any particular design features, can act as daily stressors, although the degree to which they may do so is uncertain.

Because cities are very complex systems, there are many opportunities for things to go wrong, and in decaying cities things are likely to go wrong more often. The environment is therefore not only ugly but frustrating, so that as citizens, already suffering from an overload of stresses, we may become anxious about the quality of life or even angry about its injustices. The feeling that we are not in control, always a problem in cities, is reinforced by the physical features of the environment: they are large, smelly and unnatural, and often look the worse for wear. In addition, the environment may change frequently and very rapidly,

often not for the better. Some people find the rapid pace of change exhilarating, of course, because they are stimulated by an element of surprise in their environment.

Others enjoy the incongruities they see around them – the juxtaposition of old buildings with new, or merely of large buildings with small. But many of us find these aspects extremely stressful.

Uniformity of the physical environment is no solution: if all a city's buildings were of the same size or in the same style, it would be a very boring place to live in. There is strong evidence that we derive esthetic pleasure from complexity, though too much confuses rather than pleases us, and we need to be able to perceive some kind of order; in other words, order must predominate over complexity – but not by too much.

So a traditional cityscape, whose buildings may be of different sizes yet share something in common, is much more likely to appeal to us than a planned environment which is too uniform, with order being too dominant over

▲ **Feeling in control**. Having conquered the city of Boston for another day these commuters head home. When we believe we have the power to influence what happens to us, we cope well with stresses and challenges. If the city represents interesting and rewarding work, its problems are easier to deal with. The importance of a sense of control has been shown in many experiments on the effects of noise (see Ch 24). In one study, researchers subjected volunteers to a loud barrage of city noises and asked them to perform various tasks. One set of volunteers was supplied with stop buttons so that they could end their participation at any time. Surprisingly, only a few did so.

All of the volunteers performed less well than they would have in peace and quiet. However, those with stop buttons performed considerably better than those without. The mere fact that they were in control of the situation and were themselves deciding to continue with the task despite the distraction, meant that the stressor had a less destructive effect on their performance.

complexity. Tall buildings tend to give a sense of enclosure unless the spaces around them are large enough.

Older cities and neighborhoods have a symbolic quality lacking in modern ones and they are more often visited by tourists. In recent years, there has been a great tide of popular support for those who have spoken out against the excesses of modern architecture. People also seem to prefer natural to urban scenes so the answer may be to introduce more green areas. In recent decades this has increasingly been done in many major cities. The environmental and esthetic benefits are obvious, although it is possible that the intrusion of these natural elements into the urban scene may increase the sense of confusion among at least a few city-dwellers.

The role of the planner

Whether they are improving an existing neighborhood or designing a new one, planners can play a considerable part in reducing the stress a city places on its inhabitants. Ideally they should try to create "responsive environments" where the emphasis is placed less on esthetics and more on the quality of life.

Various steps can be taken to reduce the overall level of noise people experience, without impeding the functions and services that generate it. The positioning of inherently noisy sites, like busy road junctions, can be carefully planned, for example, so that they are not directly outside hospitals. Buildings themselves can be improved to protect against internal or external noise. Motor vehicles can be barred from certain areas.

Design strategies to cope with crowding should be directed toward the enhancement of our sense of personal control. Environments that might create the feeling of high density should be avoided; for example, tall buildings suggest a greater density than lower ones, even if the densities are in fact the same, and so it would seem wise to plan for lower buildings. The proximity of nonresidential spaces – parks, stores and so on – can also serve to create the impression that the density is low, with green areas being particularly useful. Fences, courtyards and compounds help too, and can reduce enforced social contact, another concern which should be at the forefront of the planner's mind.

Above all, it is important for planners to remember that cities and neighborhoods are inhabited by *people*. The requirements of the particular group who will be living in the area should have a profound influence on all decisions. An obvious example is a community designed for the elderly: there should be easy access to stores, a minimum of steps and so on. In other cases the characteristics of the group will be less easily defined, but at the planning stage thought should still be given to tailoring the environment as far as possible to the needs of its users. **TW, RL**

161

◄ **Planners' tricks**. In areas of high population density a major priority is to create the illusion of space. There are various methods that planners can adopt. For example, one way of relieving the oppressive monotony of towering office blocks is to preserve small, period buildings like this one in strategic positions.

Other devices include keeping the number of signs and messages (for example, billboards) under control; designing parts of the area for multi-purpose use; keeping blocks short so that people turn corners more often when they go from one place to another – this makes the journey more interesting and also gives people more opportunity to vary their route without significantly affecting the length of the journey.

Ideally, planners should be working with people in mind – not only improving the appearance of our surroundings but trying to minimize stress by reducing noise and crowding and increasing our sense of personal control.

Scenes of Crime

EVEN IF there is no increase in the number of offenders, crime can grow simply because there is an increase in the number of suitable settings for it. Different locations attract different kinds of crime – dark alleys or secluded paths for mugging, crowds for picking pockets or snatching bags, isolated houses for burglary. In all of these places, victims or goods are within easy reach and this increases a thief or attacker's chances of getting away without being clearly seen or caught.

Our everyday environment plays a large part in determining whether or not we will be a victim of personal attack or whether our property will be damaged or stolen. Some houses and streets are likely to be less crime-ridden than others. At the same time, potential offenders can be strongly influenced by the surroundings – certain places seem almost to invite crime. How have changes in lifestyle made our everyday environments more vulnerable to crime? What steps can we take to make our homes and neighborhoods safer?

New opportunities for crime

In developed countries the incidence of theft has risen because thieves have more opportunity. People tend to own more possessions, so there is more to steal. Apart from this general increase in temptation, however, certain specific changes in lifestyle have increased the opportunities for crime. One significant change came with the invention of the transistor after World War Two. People began to own lighter electronic goods and these were much easier to steal. In fact it is possible to relate the burglary rate for each

year since 1947 to the weight of the smallest television in consumer catalogs for that year. Statistics also show that lightweight durable goods account for a rise in crime of around 400 percent in most developed countries after 1960. Small durable goods, spread over many more unguarded settings, have made the criminal's task much easier.

Another aspect of lifestyle that has affected crime rates has been the change in shopping environments. Since the growth of self-service stores in the 1930s shopping has become much easier (see *Ch 25*). But so has shoplifting. Stealing from the open displays in shops is so easy and tempting that even people who are not established criminals may be drawn to crime. The very processes which make it easy to choose goods, pick them up, pay and walk out, make it easy to pick them up and walk out without paying.

The growth of daytime crime

Since the 1940s there have also been developments in the structure of our everyday lives. More people are living alone and there are far fewer servants. Also, because of economic necessity and the breakdown of traditional gender roles, more women have joined the labor force. All this has had a dramatic effect. In industrialized nations during the 1950s only about one in four houses was empty during the day. By the end of the 1980s, however, only about one in four houses was occupied during the daytime.

These changes have provided ideal settings for crime – empty houses are an obvious temptation to potential burglars. Even if houses are not empty, they may contain fewer

CRIMINALS AND THEIR VICTIMS

■ *The image of the daring or ingenious criminal terrorizing elderly victims or attacking women is exaggerated by the fact that the media prefers to report the unusual and sensational. A truer image, gathered from police records, shows clearly that most crime is very ordinary and rarely sensational. Offenders may well have a lifestyle which is much the same as the rest of us, enjoying the same pastimes and pleasures. Research shows that most burglars operate within two miles of their own homes. With the average burglary lasting about a minute, and shoplifting a few seconds, even offenders with long criminal records can spend most of their time*

doing perfectly legal activities.

We can make some generalizations about typical offenders, however. They are more likely to be drug users and heavy drinkers. They are likely to smoke cigarettes, to do poorly in school, to have trouble holding down a job and to have come from a disadvantaged background. They are very likely to be young males. Even fraud is more likely to be committed by young male employees. In general, involvement with crime accelerates with early adolescence and drops at 20 or even earlier: the most common age of burglary arrest is about 16. Surveys show that the newspaper image of the victim as female or elderly is

equally flawed. Victims tend to be young, and men fall victim more often than women. Single people tend to be more at risk than married people. People living alone are at greater risk than those living with others. These patterns apply to both personal and property crimes. Young people, particularly young single men, are highly subject to theft. Their possessions are more accessible because they often live alone or in accommodation which is empty much of the time; also, they are the people who have possessions other young men want or can easily dispose of. Victims often come from the same social groups as offenders. **MF**

► **A neighborhood that is vulnerable to burglars**. *This attractive housing development offers several open invitations to burglars. The road layout provides easy access and escape routes, the shrubbery gives cover, and the fact that most of the neighbors are out gives intruders confidence that they will not be observed or overheard. A development like this that has been designed with privacy from neighbors in mind is often ideal for burglars.*

How vulnerable is your neighborhood to housebreakers? ■ *Do the roads provide easy access and escape?* ■ *Are your neighbors at home during the day?* ■ *Can they see and hear what is going on?*

people since there are more women living alone and more single parents with no one to help protect them at home. As a result, the most common time for burglaries is no longer nighttime but daytime, especially around 10 in the morning when virtually empty neighborhoods offer easy targets for crime.

After all, it is not only the police who prevent crime but mothers, neighbors, bystanders, car owners, or anybody else whose presence discourages a potential offender from carrying out an illegal act. Many of us act as unwitting guardians against crime on a daily basis simply by being on the street or in a building, especially in sufficient numbers to deter offenders. Empty houses or neighborhoods, then, mean less crime prevention. As the baby boomers of the 1960s reached adolescence, there were more offenders and more targets. In the 1980s, after these children had grown up, crime rates declined, but not significantly.

MORE VULNERABLE HOMES

◆ Low fencing is easy to get over, both when entering the property and when running away.

◆ An empty patio and an empty driveway suggest that no one is at home. Burglars will feel more confident that they can break in without being disturbed.

◆ Neighbors at most nearby homes are away. Several possible points from which burglars might be seen or heard are in fact not covered.

◆ Easy access – all sides of the house can be reached without crossing a neighbor's property.

◆ An open street grid provides burglars with multiple escape routes – making possible an easy getaway by car.

◆ Luxuriant shrubbery provides cover for intruders.

◆ Electrical goods inside – such as videos and music centers – are easy to carry away.

163

How effective are traditional deterrents?

Some features of the environment may actually encourage crime. Easily portable building materials left in accessible spots on building sites can be tempting. Simply covering the materials with a tarpaulin is said to reduce the amount of theft, even though the covering itself does little to impede any would-be thief, because the objects are no longer visible. Fitting security locks may have little real value in deterring a burglar. Locks are generally more easily thwarted than most of us realize. Their main function is to force offenders to make a noise and to allow us a few moments to summon help. If there is no one around to hear the noise, they lose their effectiveness.

Alarms, locks and other conventional crime prevention tactics might help reduce burglary if they are part of a larger crime reduction strategy. However, these devices often fail to prevent crime since their success may depend on the presence of other people. The very lifestyles that have created the need for burglar alarms may make them ineffective since there is no use for alarms if nobody is around to hear them. Offenders can sometimes commit a crime within less than a minute, and in this case; the police can do very little. A further problem is that so many home and car alarms are falsely triggered that we have gradually become desensitized to them. Have you ever ignored an alarm in, say, a parking lot either because you think it has been set off by mistake or because you believe the people you see getting into the car are its owners trying to switch off the alarm?

For thousands of years dogs have been used to warn us of strangers. They can recognize and discriminate between people and, if we are lucky, neighbors will hear them barking at intruders and respond. If the neighborhood is empty, however, guard dogs lose much of their use, though burglars may still be discouraged by their presence.

164

▲ **Guard dog on duty!** *This Alsatian looks fierce enough to deter any burglar but would not be appropriate for everyone. Older people, for example, might find a smaller dog with an insistent bark just as effective and easier to cope with. A determined burglar who knows there is no one at home and no neighbors within earshot might not be deterred, but intruders do not like to have attention drawn to them by noise, and a small dog might very well deter the teenage opportunist.*

KEEPING BURGLARS OUT

◆ *Make sure that doors and windows are double locked.*

◆ *Double glazing is very difficult to break.*

◆ *A solid wood front door is more protective than one that is paneled or partially glass.*

◆ *A barking dog can be an effective deterrent.*

◆ *Leave lights on when you go out, to give the impression that someone is in.*

◆ *Buy a telephone answering machine but do not say that you are out. Say instead that you cannot come to the telephone.*

◆ *Try to vary your routine. Burglars may watch the house to establish when you are likely to be out.*

◆ *Make sure that valuables are locked away or put in a safety deposit box at the bank.*

◆ *Mark your possessions with an ultraviolet marker – if they are stolen they will be easier to recover.*

◆ *A burglar alarm is a very strong deterrent.*

◆ *Lock your car, make sure windows are closed and valuables out of sight, preferably locked in the trunk.*

How can we have safer homes?

The design of our homes, cars, garages and yards can play a large part in deterring crime. Burglars have definite preferences, not only for certain designs but certain locations. Above all, successful burglary requires not only privacy within the house but also good access to and from it.

How should our houses and streets be planned to make access more difficult? One way is to make sure that there are enough people using the streets, so that there is always someone about – for example, by allowing street vendors. Although lighting alone probably does little to prevent crime, it may be useful in certain places such as underground passageways.

The lowest burglary rates of all are found in row houses, or terraces – there are usually no back doors or windows, many windows look out on each entry and people are close enough to hear a door kicked in or a window smashed.

Multifamily dwellings and high density housing can also reduce crime where, for example, neighbors can see anyone breaking into doors or windows, and common space is busy and supervised. On the other hand, if there is the same floor plan in every home, this can make it easy for local offenders to find their way around inside, night or day.

Another design that helps to deter burglars is the four-apartment, two-storey building. There is a good chance that at least one person among the four families will be home and would hear an intruder. By comparison, a single-family home with large yards and bushes to hide behind has a relatively high risk of burglary or break-in. The typical sprawling suburb makes it easy to intrude quietly and remove the television or video unnoticed, especially during the daytime. Efforts to set up a neighborhood watch or other forms of citizen cooperation are largely useless when there is nobody there to watch and no clear view anyway.

▲ **Row housing is more secure**. *This row of houses in Germany is an unlikely target for housebreakers. The houses are built very close together* *and there are no fences or trees to prevent neighbors from seeing that something is wrong next door. There seems to be at least one neighbor at home –* *someone has hung out fresh laundry. In addition, the lake is the only escape route from the rear, and most burglars do not carry dinghies.*

High-rise or low-rise?

In many American and European cities high-rise developments largely replaced old neighborhoods which had a strong sense of community. High-rises may not even have the advantage of housing more people. The developments of the 1960s generally held fewer people than the low-rise neighborhoods which were bulldozed, since a great deal was wasted on hallways, stairwells and open space between buildings. This was not only inefficient but less safe. Walkways and staircases give cover for criminals.

Crime can be reduced if housing is designed in a different way. Low-rise public housing is less crime-ridden, and scattered sites are less likely to produce the concentrations of youths that lead to the formation of gangs. Even concentrated sites can be built better – with fewer apartments per entry, separate stairwells, less public space. The same is true of streets, parking lots and squares.

Shopping centers that become desolate at night are particularly conducive to crime (see Ch25). On the whole, small private areas are better than vast public spaces. Space which belongs to everyone, is supervised by no one. Private ownership of homes and businesses, then, may also help to defeat crime.

Statistics show that the most likely offenders are young males, so where there are concentrations of young people, such as in high-rise areas, the crime rate is often high. On the other hand, high-rise buildings have very low crime rates if they are reserved for older people or for married couples without children. One solution then, is not to tear it down, as has happened in many American cities, but to convert such housing for the elderly and to put controls on entry. Under such circumstances, high-rise buildings have lower rates of property crime than single-family dwellings.

■ **High-rise blocks provide easier targets.** *A strange car parked outside one of these tall apartment buildings* LEFT *will be less quickly noticed than it would be in one of the neighboring streets. Inside, the acceptance of unfamiliar faces is greater than it would be in a four-apartment building. A stairwell* ABOVE *is often where a crime takes place. The crime rate is considerably lower in developments built exclusively for older people: offenders are usually teenage boys who tend to operate near their own territory. Old ladies are often robbed by boys who may not be well known to them but live in the same building.*

"HIGH-RISES, CRIME AND PERSONAL TERRITORY"

■ The design of high-rise apartments has often been criticized for breeding violence and crime. The American architect, Oscar Newman, pointed out that in low-rise apartments levels of crime are much lower than in high-rise ones, even when the population density is the same. He suggested that paying too little attention to the design of entrances can lead to problems.

If your home has a porch or verandah, this will help to mark out your territory. If you live in the kind of housing block where more than four apartments share a single entrance, however, you will probably not feel that the space is yours to defend.

In high-rise blocks containing hundreds of apartments the entrance cannot be seen by the occupants, strangers can come in and out and corridors cannot be surveyed. If territories are not easily identifiable, families will tend to avoid community involvement. As a result, vandalism and violence often go unchallenged. **PM**

Outdoor security

The type of yard we have can also provide an open invitation to theft. From a security point of view, it would be far better to have a neighborhood gardening area, with plots divided among gardeners. This would reduce the size of individual yards and allow houses to be built closer together – giving some view of back doors. Since most of us like to have private patios and yards, however, these should at least be carefully fenced to guard against backdoor intrusion. There should be enough space between the slats in a fence to allow intruders to be seen, but not enough space to make it easy for them to get inside. Yards may be so large that a full fencing of the perimeter is simply too expensive,

and residents choose the worst option – trees and bushes. These provide an attractive sense of privacy but also give complete freedom of entry and screening for intruders.

Many newer cities and suburbs are built in a clear grid pattern, especially where the land is flat. This makes for efficient construction and quick entry and exit by car. But the same conveniences for occupants hold good for offenders – easy access and exit. The crime risk of a particular block is strongly influenced by the number of streets turning into it. Offenders will much more often choose homes located on a block with several streets turning into it where they feel that they can safely escape. The cul-de-sac reduces such chances as there is less certainty of finding a way out.

PRIVACY OR SECURITY?

■ *Everyone values privacy in their home (see Ch 4), but this seclusion may be achieved at the cost of security. The boundaries of suburban houses, often marked by trees, give privacy not only to the residents but also to burglars. Even modern town houses are developed so that windows and entries are private. Owing to the high cost of land, builders pack many houses, with walkways and landscaping, onto one plot. To offset this crowding and give residents a feeling of privacy, planners may design these houses at angles and then add shrubs and bushes. The result is that you cannot see who is entering your neighbor's house and they cannot see who is entering yours. Unfortunately, criminal intrusion is equally unobservable. If you choose to live in an old row house with windows onto the street, you increase your security, but sacrifice some of your privacy.* **MF**

MORE SECURE HOMES

◆ *Access at the back is restricted – a potential housebreaker would have to cross neighbors' property.*

◆ *High fencing provides an obstacle.*

◆ *There is very little shrubbery to give cover to intruders.*

◆ *The houses face inward – a higher number of front doors is visible to each neighbor who is home.*

◆ *There is only one way in for a car and one escape route, which is easily observed.*

167

PLANNING AGAINST CRIME

■ *Once a town or residential area is established, it is very difficult to design away crime. The following points are worth looking out for if you are planning a move to a new area and are concerned about its safety.*

◆ *Heavy traffic flows should ideally pass through the*

least attractive crime targets, lighter traffic through the most attractive areas.

◆ *Curved streets and cul-de-sacs are safer than grid-pattern blocks which offer many ways in and out to an intruder.*

◆ *The safest housing includes multifamily dwellings, row housing, or four apartment two-storey buildings.*

◆ *There should be more than one occupied property on the plot.*

◆ *Communal street gardens are better than large yards.*

◆ *Fences are better deterrents than trees.*

◆ *If schools and shopping centers are kept well apart, this will deter opportunist young offenders.*

◆ *Long narrow parks with easy visibility are better than large secluded ones.* **MF**

Research has shown that a house just off a busy main street or a corner, or a house that has a footpath running alongside it is the ideal target for burglars, as is a detached house with a private yard. Curved streets are less popular with criminals than straight ones. But are we prepared to have the inconvenience? If there is only one entry road this is likely to be congested during the rush hour. Also, curved streets may be safer from burglary, but can be hazardous in other ways; it is harder, for example, for fire engines to enter and exit.

It is impractical to consider rebuilding existing houses and we cannot redesign existing street patterns. Some streets can be blocked off to feed traffic into others, but new problems arise if a street is blocked, and the traffic is routed through adjoining streets: these areas will then have more traffic, noise, risk to children, and risk of criminal attack, while the blocked street benefits. It would be much better if cities could be planned for crime prevention at an early stage, designing traffic flows to be heaviest among the least attractive targets of crime and lightest among the more attractive targets. Busy roads should be routed through junk yards, industrial areas or green-belts and away from homes. **MF**

Why some settings breed crime

Studies suggest that the anonymity of large cities encourages crime since, people who have no sense of individuality, are more likely to engage in antisocial activities. Cities also lack community feeling – people are strangers to one another. This situation has advantages for the criminal: not only is the victim unknown, the bystanders are too. They will be less likely to come to the help of a victim they do not know, and will not recognize an attacker they have never seen before.

■ **Artful dodger**. *The boy snatching this woman's bag in an Italian street is committing a crime which entails close contact with the victim and is quite different from burglary, for example, which requires seclusion and privacy. Studies of the underworld suggest that such criminal activities are often organized as an alternative way of life for whole families. Pickpockets or confidence tricksters often have their own pitches or territories. Most burglaries, by contrast, are committed casually by teenagers.*

In an urban setting the constant presence of desirable goods in shopping displays or in the possessions of wealthier people may be a further incentive to crime. The goods are a temptation and continuously remind the poor that there are many things they cannot afford. There is also a reminder that shops can afford them, which fosters an "us and them" situation between the underprivileged and the wealthy. This also encourages crime – an aggressor may be spurred on to commit a crime by a sense of injustice.

In some cases, such as drug addiction, the need is so great and the breakdown of normal assumptions so advanced, that the offender hardly needs such self-justification. Environments which suggest underprivilege breed hopelessness and crime. However, we may be able to reduce the crime rate in cities by keeping buildings attractive and in good repair. A street which has been vandalized is more likely to attract further crime, whereas a clean, well-kept environment may act as a deterrent. **RL**

AREAS AT RISK FROM YOUNG OFFENDERS

■ *All too often groups of adolescents gather looking for excitement. Also, schools inevitably assemble adolescents and so may be forcing grounds for crime. The proximity to large groups of youths puts areas near the school at risk from vandalism, petty crime, burglary and sometimes more serious crime.*

Since many adolescents live in residential areas and often have the run of them during the day, some of them may very well seize the opportunity to commit an impulsive crime. A burglary from an open house may take only 30 seconds to a minute. Sometimes there is a quick theft from a yard, driveway or garage. Some young burglars may attempt to break into homes, but more often they slip in when a door has been left unlocked.

However, good design of the environment can help keep the young from committing crime. If very large schools cannot be avoided, they can at least be kept away from shopping centers; work opportunities nearby can reduce the length of time it takes parents to get to work and keep them closer to the home; paths from schools to residential areas can be designed to keep youths away from favorite locations for vandalism – such as parking lots; parks can be designed to allow easy visibility.

◄ **Cities create places and attitudes that encourage crime**. *The activity of these boys spraying graffiti on a train in the Paris Metro is met with complete indifference by the occupants of the carriage. The anonymity of large cities contributes towards crime because people who have no clear sense of identity or community with others are more likely to engage in antisocial activities. The inhibitions of offenders are also likely to be lowered by the apathy that seems to descend on city dwellers.*

▼ **Taking the law into their own hands** *these Guardian Angel vigilantes on the New York subway have set out to tackle the problem of public safety. Without their presence, criminals might employ the anonymity of the subway. Onlookers are likely to feel little personal involvement with potential victims and would probably not recognize an attacker in a police line up. The Guardian Angel's very presence is a deterrent, their distinctive red berets signaling their intention to react to trouble.*

Country Living

ARE WE ALL country people at heart? Opinion polls are always asking us what we think about the relative merits of town and country living. In one British poll in 1989, 72 percent of the people asked said they would like to live in the country, while 28 percent preferred an urban lifestyle. Similarly, a United States Bureau of Census survey concluded that people living in cities with more than 3 million inhabitants are up to seven times more likely to be dissatisfied with their lifestyle than people living in towns and rural areas of fewer than 50,000 inhabitants.

There is a growing tendency to identify the countryside with those qualities we consider essential for a fulfilling and civilized life – physical and psychological space. Many people living in urban areas think the country is a healthier

and safer place to live, but how accurate is this view? Are there real benefits to living in the country or does the rural environment generate its own dissatisfactions?

Choosing life in the country

There has always been an ebb and flow of population between city and country. In the Middle Ages the town was seen as a magnet for prosperity; in the 18th century the agrarian revolution brought about a decrease in the number of agricultural jobs. In the 20th century, the agricultural depression of the 1920s and 1930s drove thousands of farmers from their land. In England and Wales, agricultural employment had declined to such an extent by the 1960s that from being the largest occupational group in 1815, it

◄ **Living in the country, working in the city**. *This waterside setting in Londonderry, Vermont, gives an attractive rural home base to a family that earns its keep in the urban economy. In some states more than half the population lives in the country, but only 8 percent of the American workforce works the land.*

Do you long for a home in the country?
■ *Your image of the good life might be out of date* ■ *Commuters are moving in and farmers are moving out* ■ *What is happening to the rural idyll?*

had become the smallest. In France, the number of people in farming fell between the 1950s and the early 1980s from 25 percent of the working population to a mere 7 percent. The situation has been similar in other Western countries – today only 4 percent of people work the land in Britain, only 8 percent in the United States. But although fewer people are working the land the drift to the towns seems to be slowing down and, in some areas, is even being reversed.

Since the 1960s people have been moving away from the cities into the country. These people find housing expensive, the air polluted and life generally too stressful in the city. Faster rail links and improved roads make long-distance commuting an attractive alternative to the ratrace. In North Carolina more than half the population lives outside cities and many commute long distances to work. Everywhere, an increasing number of people commute each weekday between their homes in the country and their jobs in the city. Families seem to be putting quality of rural life above the inconvenience of separation and distance.

WEEKEND RETREATS

■ *Some of us who are drawn to country living can only manage it part-time. We buy a second home in a remote part of the country, where property prices are low. When we visit we like to feel we are a part of the local scene, but in reality we may be the only local scene there is. Areas with tourist potential can create communities that only come alive at weekends and holiday periods. Second-home owners have no need of regular services or stores and in isolated places there are often not enough permanent local residents to justify them. The sorts of business that spring up in their places are craft and gift shops, folk museums and service stations that close out of season.*

There can be a great deal of animosity to second-home owners from the few locals left, partly because second-home owners make housing too expensive for local people. They take housing out of the market but do not occupy it full-time and do not contribute to the daily life of the community. Often, local residents resent the fact that newcomers make little or no attempt to learn about their way of life and may even fear that it is at risk of being diluted or even destroyed by them.

▲ **Living in the country to work the land**. *Montana's fertile, often harsh, open spaces sometimes present a monotonous prospect, but residents of large American cities are up to seven times more likely to be discontented than people who live in country like this.*

▶ **Weekend country living.** *A style of cottage in Devon, England, typically desired by affluent city dwellers as a weekend retreat. Local people may be displaced to unattractive modern housing, while traditional housing stands empty most of the year.*

The shock of the newcomer

This influx of new country dwellers is gradually changing the pattern of community life in rural areas. Communities are no longer based entirely on farming and the various jobs and trades that support it. People no longer have close-knit family ties with the rest of their own or a nearby village. Once traditional rural occupations are now only memories, their passing recorded in the names of newly converted houses – "The Old Forge," "The Old Mill," "The Old Bakehouse." In many countries the situation is particularly well-developed since villages in some areas close to large towns and cities are becoming no more than dormitories for commuters. Few of the newcomers work locally and those that do remain in the village during the day are likely to be retired. House prices have soared in recent years, making it difficult for local people to buy either a traditional cottage or a newly-built "executive" home. In Britain, public housing in many areas has been sold off privately and not replaced. The lack of affordable housing may force local people to move away, so changing the nature of the village even more.

However, newcomers can sometimes help to support the community. They may reinforce the popular belief that the country is secure and friendly, full of people who take a pride in their way of life. Because they want to share in this image, they tend their gardens and restore neglected properties, providing much-needed employment for rural craftsmen in the process. They usually take a strong interest in local affairs and it is often the new inhabitants who work hardest to preserve the innate character of the community. Outsiders can also bring to the area a wide variety of new interests and activities. On the whole, the cultural life of rural communities is more often enhanced by its new residents than impoverished.

Growing up in the country

Families who have just arrived in the country often find they relate more easily with established residents when they have children. Sharing the ferrying of children to and from school or having your child's friends over to play are ways of developing new friendships. Children are often a significant

▲ **Wool does not grow on trees,** as any rural child knows. Growing up in the country means that children are less ignorant of nature. A 1980s survey of 7-year-olds in London, England, revealed that 82 percent were unaware that peas grow in a pod. Greater familiarity with nature, however, does not necessarily mean greater respect for it. Most of the political pressure to limit urbanization of the countryside, and to abandon farming methods that cause pollution, is exerted by people who grew up in cities.

factor in parents' decision to move to or stay in the country – they feel that it is a better place to bring up children. Studies have found that rural children know their immediate neighborhood better than city children. City children have fewer opportunities to explore on their own because parents are worried about the dangers of traffic and crime. They may see more than their country cousins but learn less if they do not actually experience what they see.

Younger children seem to enjoy their country existence and many spend their time in much the same way as urban children – watching television, reading, playing ball and cycling. Only about 10 percent of them spend their time in specifically rural activities. However, children are especially fond of the grassy open spaces and local shopping. A British journalist, brought up in the country recalls the day men walked on the moon as "the day our village shop burned down. A giant leap for mankind and a devastating blow to the village." When children are asked at school to write about their village they invariably refer to its "friendliness." The friendships of young children in the country may be more likely to cross social and occupational boundaries and barriers. If this is the case, the child growing up in the country may develop a more rounded view of society.

A sense of isolation

When children get older and they move from the local junior school to the high school, however, they seem to lose their positive attitude to the rural environment; unless they live in a fairly large rural town there is no coffee bar, no movie theater, nowhere to meet. Surveys have shown that this is not so much a dislike of the country as a need to have access to leisure facilities. Most of the schools for these older children are in a local town that draws pupils from a wide area. The children are transported in and out by bus and may make friendships at school with young people who live far away from them and whom they will not be able to meet outside school. It is also difficult for these children to take part in extracurricular activities after school unless they have parents willing and able to drive the long distance to pick them up afterward. The independence they enjoyed as young children, when all their social needs were met in their immediate environment, changes to an increased dependence on their parents for transport. This is often completely at odds with their emotional development and a desire to spread their wings. Not surprisingly, teenagers in the country may feel frustrated, isolated and trapped.

Happy childhood memories

Also, as children grow up, how they feel about staying in the country will depend on their individual circumstances. The expectations and behavior of a youth who will one day take over the running of the family farm, for example, are likely to be very different from those of a child with no roots in the country or with no means to future prosperity there. Many will have to leave – either to get an education or just to find employment. However, many – especially young children – do show a sense of nostalgia and even a resentment of change. They appear to appreciate that they once lived in a rural environment and most look back on their country childhood with affection. As a young waitress from Pamlico,

173

▶ **Social life for rural children.** *These children playing ice hockey have a guaranteed social life because they live fairly close to one another in a small rural town. Very young children often enjoy the country because most of their social needs can be met within their immediate surroundings. Older children who attend large schools in distant locations may experience a sense of isolation during out-of-school hours.*

North Carolina put it: "Out here is like livin' in a poem." There is a vast array of literature – from such writers as Sherwood Anderson, Flora Thompson, Marcel Pagnol, Laurie Lee and Mark Twain – that is based on memories of growing up in the country. Although their memories are often fond ones, they do also reflect the harsher aspects of country life.

What has happened to the village school?

In many rural areas the number of school-age children is declining. When numbers fall below a certain level the local school closes and the village loses a central part of its life. The problem can be caused in part by a housing crisis in small communities. Demand for houses in the country makes them more expensive and, in the end, the only people who can afford to buy them are wealthy people, usually from the towns. These people often do not send their children to the local school, so there are not enough children to keep the school going and it closes. The remaining few children may have to be taken by bus to a new school, which is likely to be some distance away. A village school is a focal point for the community – it brings people into the village. Closure of the school only takes people away.

The bus comes on Tuesdays

The loss of the village school is not the only disappearing local facility. A major problem across Europe and the United States is the demise of the local store (see box feature). Increasingly, people in rural communities are forced to travel to the nearest town to buy food and other items or even to visit the bank or use a post office. Because such local services as do still exist are not usually on their doorstep, rural people often need transport more than people in cities: they have to travel greater distances, and also the population is scattered over a wider area. If they do not have a car then life in the country can be particularly difficult. For example, in Britain one in five people needs public transport to go anywhere, but public transport is fast becoming a thing of the past in many rural areas. There are fewer services, and the services that do exist tend to be concentrated in the early morning and in the evening. There are few services during the day or on Sundays.

SAVE YOUR SERVICES

■ *What can you do to save an important public service in your rural area? Individual action is usually not enough – really effective force can only come from harnessing the skills, abilities and time of the whole community. Most important, do not wait until something has disappeared before you complain. It is never too soon to start to think how you might protect your local store, school, bus service or environment.*

◆ *Keep informed about long-term plans of proprietors and local authorities.*

◆ *Inform other people in the area about what is happening – leaflet them, make house calls, stick up posters.*

◆ *Organize public meetings.*

◆ *Mount a campaign.*

◆ *Organize fund-raising events.*

◆ *Make friends with the local press and get publicity.*

◆ *Most important of all – persuade people to use the threatened service.*

"Use it or lose it" is an effective slogan. Direct community action works; local pressure groups have in the past stopped the building of airports and nuclear power stations in areas of outstanding natural beauty, and persuaded the authorities to revitalize rural transport services.

◀ **This village post office** on the island of Harris in Scotland is guaranteed to survive so long as migration to the mainland does not completely depopulate the community. In less isolated rural areas, residents who do not own cars are disadvantaged by the tendency for services to become concentrated in a few large towns.

The loss of public transport means isolation and hardship for many – those who are too old to drive, those who cannot afford a car, young people, mothers at home with children. Lack of transport becomes particularly noticeable when you need to get somewhere in a hurry. If you become ill or if you have to visit the doctor on a regular basis, not being mobile can make life very difficult.

Community health services

Not many villages have their own doctor. In rural areas you will probably have to travel many miles if you need medical attention, to the nearest large community where there is a local health center. The advantage of the center is that it can offer a complete range of medical care from a team of doctors, nurses and paramedics. The disadvantage is that without a car it is difficult to get there easily. Other medical services such as hospitals are almost always in the regional center possibly even further away. There are fewer and fewer local hospitals or clinics. The old and the chronically sick often find that this is just one practical burden too many.

The erosion of these basic services at a local level underlines the fact that more affluent inhabitants can obtain goods and services elsewhere because they are mobile. The problems arise for those whose access to the facilities they need may be severely curtailed because they do not have either cars or public transport.

New jobs, new people?

The removal of local services encourages movement away from rural areas and as people move away so the demand for services declines. The spiral continues with

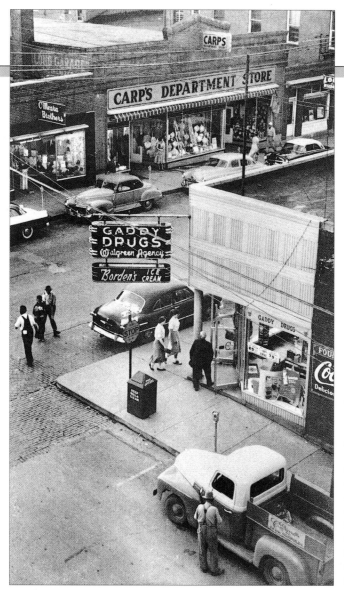

SMALL-TOWN AMERICA

■ *Small towns have a declining place in the culture of the United States. They are remembered with nostalgic affection as places of contentment and stability where people had a shared sense of purpose and values. But the character of these local communities is changing under the influence of large chain stores, interstate highways and the diminishing role of the family farm.*

In 1910, when small urban

▶ **A day in Rolla, Missouri,** *in 1955, captures the essence of an aspect of small town life that has more or less disappeared. Carp's department store and Gaddy Drugs have now been replaced by huge discount stores. A big reduction in the number of family farms, which were once the main reason for the existence of the small town, together with technological changes and improved roads have completely changed the character of small-town America.*

living was at its height 17 percent of Americans lived in towns with populations under 10,000. Between then and 1980 this had fallen to 11.2 percent. Small towns existed largely because of farms and were usually located close enough for any farmer to get there and back in a day in his horse-drawn wagon.

A million farms were lost between 1960 and 1970 and with them went the rural population. Changes in technology and economics have robbed the small town of its purpose. The automobile and the highway took away the historic reason for the town – the day's ride in the wagon – and freed the farmer, and the townsfolk, to take advantage of the lower prices in the city.

The small towns that have managed to survive are those that can attract retired people, those near enough to large urban centers to attract commuters and those that can attract new industries. As for the rest and the way of life they symbolized, the future is unpredictable.

175

facilities shutting down and the towns becoming more attractive. If the country is to exist in its own right and not just as a dormitory area for cities it has to have jobs. Recently, however, both in the United States and in Europe, there has been a steadily growing trend for new information-based businesses and services, using computers, to move into rural areas. These have the capacity to provide alternative forms of employment for local residents, showing that the countryside is still a place where people can live and work.

For example, the concept of the "tele-cottage" was launched in 1985 in a small village in a remote area near Sweden's Norwegian border. Vemdalen is a winter ski resort and forestry area, but it had only limited employment opportunities and a falling population. The tele-cottage, devised by a Swedish businessman, has changed all this. The tele-cottage is equipped with 15 personal computers and wordprocessors, telex, fax and teletext equipment and satellite television receivers, all financed by local and central government and locally raised funds.

In it, children and adults have opportunities to learn new technologies. Formal education and self-study in computer uses relevant to business and private needs can take place, so saving people the effort of traveling to distant colleges. Local merchants can try out computer programs and be trained in skills such as bookkeeping, and they can use telex, fax and electronic mail service facilities. There is access to international data bases, broadcasts and other users of electronic communications. People have a new social meeting place since the cottage is equipped with a lounge and kitchen. Local people can work for employers many miles away using the computer technology, without travel costs or wasted time.

Good ideas like this spread fast: 35 tele-cottages now

exist in Sweden and others are being set up in Norway, Finland and Austria. Now 75 countries have joined an international association, Tele-cottages International. The president of this association describes the tele-cottage or the "electronic village hall" as a place of training, discovery and sociable work using computers. Alternative electronic technology seems to offer small village communities a real future.

Other national and local initiatives are also emerging, aimed at regenerating the rural economy and indeed the whole fabric of rural life. In France groups of communes are encouraged to work together and combine resources. Rural development schemes have also been established in

WOMEN'S WORK IN THE COUNTRY

■ Work for women in rural areas is usually badly paid, with poor working conditions. There are seldom extra benefits and it is often seasonal or unskilled work. Agricultural work such as fruit picking, harvesting, or working in a poultry factory or meat-packing plant is often classified as casual labor and the employers take no responsibility for sickness or holidays. The employment is insecure, the women are seldom members of a union and they have little bargaining power against unfair conditions.

Women with preschool chil-dren are the fastest growing group in the work force, yet not all countries have the sort of child-care facilities that are available in the United States. Britain probably has the worst provision in Europe for this sort of facility, particularly in rural areas. Women in the country may also be severely restricted by the lack of public transport. This not only stops them getting to and from work but, because it makes domestic tasks such as shopping more time-consuming, it reduces the number of hours available for work outside the home.

► **Air pollution** is not something you would normally associate with living in the country. Before you buy your country retreat, check that crop-spraying will not be a problem for you, and that behind the next hill there is not a factory. This village community in Germany lives in the shadow of a power station.

Britain, the Netherlands, Italy and Austria. Although tourism, which is a growth industry in many countries, can bring some jobs to rural areas, few of these are permanent or well-paid.

The good life

Living in the country can be largely a matter of attitude. Of course, there are hardships and isolation, but these can also exist in towns. Rural life is not intrinsically more or less glamorous than urban life – people have the same concerns for the well-being of individuals, employment, social organizations and friendship.

On the other hand, some people consciously seek out what to others would be intolerable. They want to live in isolation, away from the mass of humanity and the trappings of civilization. Others prefer to live in a small but intimate community where everybody knows everybody's business. People who have *chosen* to live in the country, either in solitary splendor or as part of a close-knit community, have done so because of what it offers *them* and they are happy to turn their backs on the city. In a world of rapid change, these people feel the need to live at a slower pace. They want space, fresh air and room to grow: "I don't live in the country because I think you get a nicer sort of person there but because I can grow things and I like the look of it. And the sound of it." **JB**

◄ **Traditional country crafts** *still survive in small isolated pockets of many rural communities. They are not a good source of income, and most nonagricultural rural employment is in factories. This man is demonstrating wicker basket-making.*

177

LIFE IN THE COUNTRY – IS IT FOR YOU?

■ *You have had enough of city streets, muggings and exhaust fumes, so you decide it is time to find some green space. You remember the pretty little town where you spent a holiday in the heart of some spectacular scenery, so decide to set off in search of your dream house. But there are several important questions to consider before you make your move to the country.*

Are you sure that the village you liked so much during your vacations will be the same during the rest of the year? There *are villages that seem very lively in the summer, but lose many of their services when the vacationers leave.*

Will you miss the culture – the art gallery round the corner, the bistro for morning coffee and a gossip with friends?

 WHAT PEOPLE SAY

I would like to move to the country because:
◆ It is so much easier to make friends.
◆ I love peace and quiet and feeling close to nature.
◆ It would be healthy for the children to have so much space and fresh air.

I would like to move away from the country because:
◆ I have to travel so far to shop and visit the doctor.
◆ I have nothing in common with the other people here.
◆ My partner works in the city and takes the car, leaving me without transport.

What about the children's education? Evidence suggests that country schools offer a less diverse and less stimulating education than their urban equivalents. And smaller schools mean fewer teachers. Do you see yourself as your children's taxi driver, taking them to all those activities they insist on doing?

As long as you think hard before taking the final step, you will probably make a successful move. The country has a lot to offer those who are prepared to make a few sacrifices.

WORKING THE LAND

■ Farmers and their families are part of the traditional fabric of rural life. In most countries they do not live in the settlements but in the countryside around them. They vary from the marginal farmer on a low income to the new breed of "agribusinessman" who has a lifestyle comparable to that of the president of a large corporation. Somewhere in between come family partnerships. It is these that own the majority of agricultural holdings.

For them the daily round is more than just another job – it is a way of life. There is no end or beginning to the work because it is inextricably linked to the natural cycle. The demands are heavy but the emotional rewards are great.

Personal fulfillment ranges from the pleasure of being close to nature, to the assurance that the land will be passed on in good heart to the next generation. In farming, more than in any other way of life, there is a real sense of continuity and tradition. Even if methods change and the pursuit of profit becomes more important than survival, the most common characteristic of the farmer is a strong concern with the satisfaction to be derived from the farming process itself.

KEEPING IT IN THE FAMILY

Farming is one of the few occupations that keep a family together with most of its members working as a team. Children usually help on the farm from an early age, thus experiencing a rare form of apprenticeship. Rapidly changing agricultural technology and the need to incorporate business management procedures have generally meant a degree of specialization within the farm family. Children who once sought to better themselves through education and employment outside now find that their education is not only useful but essential in the family business.

Many women are also finding that their role is improving. The farmer's wife is frequently less an unpaid extra laborer and more an entrepreneur in her own right. In most developed countries, farm diversification is seen as a way of boosting the farm income, so wives are taking the lead and developing new sources of income. They run bed and breakfast businesses,

farmhouse inns, or open farm shops to sell their produce direct and supply city supermarkets with high-quality foodstuffs. By doing this, they can increase their own sense of self-esteem and their satisfaction with their life.

In a well-run family farm the various members are to some extent cushioned from the problems facing the rest of us. Housing is not usually a problem, unemployment is rare, worries about what the children will do for a living will not arise if they join the farm partnership. When it comes to retirement, the older members of the family are not cut off from their families like so many other people in society and they usually continue to live either on the farm or very close by. Of all the people in the countryside it is probably on the family farms that we find the highest level of satisfaction. The farm lifestyle is unique in involving the entire family in a basic process that everyone depends on, that of producing food.

ALTERNATIVES

Reductions in government price support for agricultural commodities in surplus has encouraged some farmers to consider alternative methods of production. It is no longer odd to farm in an organic way, using no artificial chemicals. Farmers who use these methods are finding that they can continue to be economically successful if they go organic because of the excellent prices they can obtain from the health-conscious public. They will probably never make huge fortunes but they have the satisfaction of knowing that they are following a more ecologically sound way of farming and preserving their soil.

Other farmers, concerned that the number of breeds of animals was being reduced to a handful of cross-breeds, have turned to rare-breeds farming. They breed only traditional, rare breeds of animal, which they produce for meat, milk, wool and eggs in the same way that the conventional farmer does. It may seem strange to produce a rare animal in order to sell it for meat but, in fact, this is the best way of keeping the breed alive. If people are prepared to buy the product the animal is economically viable.

▲ **Scanning the skies to gauge the weather,** *Sheila Erickson works a hayfield in North Dakota in exchange for two-thirds of the harvest. She* will use her share to feed the cattle that are her livelihood. Women, traditionally the plant-gatherers in hunter-gather societies, were probably the first farmers. It is they who plant and tend the crops that form a supplementary source of food in many herding societies and among some hunter-gathers.

Color Outside the Home

IMAGINE a world without color. How would you tell a ripe orange from an unripe one? How could you do a litmus test or know if the traffic signals were saying "Stop" or "Go"? Would you be able to tell the Dutch flag from the German flag or the Irish flag from the Italian? Color identifies things – it can even change their apparent shape and structure. Living in a colorless world would be like living in a black and white movie – the only visual distinctions would come from shadow and form. Countless aspects of our daily life depend on the innate ability that we have to distinguish one color from another.

We also use color for decoration, but very often the color we are exposed to is chosen for us by architects and planners. They devise color schemes for everything from housing developments, factories and office blocks to museums. Think about the color on the buildings around you or at work. How do you react to this color? Does it make you feel part of the surroundings or do you find it intrusive or irritating? You may feel that there is not enough color in your environment.

Architects and designers often have different ideas about the use of color from the people who have to live with their choices. The most popular buildings are usually those where the residents or employees have participated in choosing the colors and deciding where they are applied. But why do we use color on buildings? Is it just a question of personal taste or are biological and psychological factors coming into play as well when we choose one color or set of colors over another?

A natural response to color

One theory about why we respond to color, proposed by the British zoologist Nicholas Humphrey, links the evolution of color vision to the evolution of color in nature – in a world without color, we would have had no need for color vision. In the natural world, the most striking colors act as visual signals that attract, repel and warn. Although humans respond to these signals, the only way we are able to make similar ones is by applying color artificially to objects or to ourselves. In fact, the only color we can reproduce naturally in order to communicate signals is red – when we blush or redden with anger. The part of the brain that responds to bright, strong color is called the "paleo cortex" – the center of emotional and unconscious behavior. Subtle colors appeal more to the higher brain – the "neo cortex" – which is the center of language and logical deduction.

When architects are deciding which color to use on a building they have a choice whether to build on our natural tendency to treat color as a signal or whether to use color in an arbitrary way. Some people criticize modern architects for refusing to acknowledge our primitive need to externalize emotion through the use of strong color. They complain that too much subtle color – or even no color at all – is used on contemporary buildings.

Creating a more colorful environment

Buildings that lack color are a relatively new phenomenon. In most cultures – from the Ancient Greeks and Aztecs to the Victorians – buildings have been colored.

THE SIGNIFICANCE OF RED

■ According to popular belief red has a special significance. There is a deep-rooted association of red with blood and fire, and we respond to red with the emotional part of our brain rather than with the logical part. It is often the first color that comes to mind when we are asked to list color words. Preschool children almost always give red as their favorite color.

But the meaning we give to red varies according to the cultural associations we learn about it. The Chokwe people of Angola associate red with sickness, sun, men and death, while the Lavale associate it with life, blood and fertility. The Russian word for red is the same as the word for beautiful. The significance also depends on the context. Red often acts as a signal but we have to learn how to interpret that signal. A red light is a warning to stop, whereas a red carpet symbolizes ritual welcome.

Our liking for red may alter according to where we see it. You may love red cars but dislike wearing red; red in a corridor where you spend a short time may be more tolerable than red in a windowless office where you spend a great deal of time.

▲ A striking color for a striking shape. The visual impact of this unusual sculpture in La Défense near Paris, is reinforced with vivid red paint.

Color is all around you ■ *Do you like what you see?* ■ *Would you like to see more?* ■ *The more we take part in decisions about how our surroundings will be colored, the better we feel about the result.*

▲ **Colorful buildings** are important to Friedensreich Hundertwasser, the painter who became an architect. His "gingerbread house" in Vienna is a fantastical, undulating, labyrinthine apartment building full of vivid colors and unexpected shapes. Strong colors act on the part of our brain that governs emotional and unconscious behavior, whereas softer colors appeal to the brain's center of language and logic. Other architects have often been criticized for not recognizing our emotional need for strong color in our surroundings.

However, younger architects are now beginning to revive the tradition of creating strongly colored buildings and there is a more positive attitude to color in the environment. One reason for the change in style is the availability of permanent color in building materials such as metals and plastics. Color was previously restricted to paints that soon deteriorated and had to be renewed, or to glazed tiles and bricks that were time-consuming to apply.

Of course, color is not a cure for bad architecture but it can transform otherwise drab neighborhoods into attractive environments. It is also a way of achieving much-needed variety, especially in city areas that are remote from the natural variety of a rural landscape. Studies have shown that people do not like monotonous buildings. One experiment asked the residents of a modern housing estate with no exterior color to evaluate their feelings about it. They were asked first to consider it as it was and then to imagine that there were trees planted between the buildings. The results showed that, even when the trees had been added, the residents disliked the gray, monochromatic environment.

The Byker housing project in Newcastle upon Tyne, England shows how architects can use color to create an environment full of variety and complexity. They used renewable materials and colored brick and invited the residents to paint parts of the buildings themselves. The result is a varied environment that allows the residents to have some control over, and involvement in, their living space. Being able to choose color in this way is important both for our sense of identity and the need to define our territory. Identity is vital to our self-esteem and one of the ways we can express it is with color. People who live in row housing often paint the fronts of their houses in different colors so that their territory is clearly defined.

Studies in sensory perception show that people welcome a change of color in their environment because color has an uplifting effect – it makes us feel better. Color also makes buildings seem less anonymous by introducing a human element into their design. Buildings with color are no longer faceless – they show that someone has thought about them and about why they are there.

▲ **Color participation** was a privilege of the residents of Höchst in Germany when Gerhard Schweizer undertook his color restoration experiment. Using a color wheel, he consulted the inhabitants of each building. They were then able to make a choice based on full knowledge of the colors chosen by their neighbors so that they could harmonize with them. The experiment was a success and it is interesting that the colors chosen were not neutral ones that would be "safe," but strong ones that made a bold statement.

Choosing colors with care

It is not enough to splash color around indiscriminately, however. The same color can have different effects depending on the material used and the light in which it is seen (see *Chs 7, 8*). Architects use color on the outside of buildings to highlight or to disguise certain features and to produce particular visual effects. By using pale colors on undulating or indented surfaces, for example, the architect can reveal shadows that might have been concealed by darker colors. In the same way, saturated colors used next to subdued colors may alter the shape of the building or

show up important details. Colors are always modified by the way they blend or contrast with surrounding colors. Building materials, too, have their own color, so every change in material provides its own color variation. A red brick will not look the same as a red pipe because its shape, texture and reflective properties are different.

Architects can use these principles to help blend new buildings into their environment or to soften the harsh raw concrete of modern structures. They can also use the apparent weight of color to give a building balance, using the darker, heavier colors at the bottom and lighter ones at the top. However, these principles are themselves subject to modification depending on where a building is situated. Colors seen under a combination of direct and indirect, or reflected, sunlight tend to be more intense. In drier latitudes, then, where lighter ground surfaces mean there is more reflected light, colors seem brighter. This effect is also produced when there is snow on the ground on a bright winter's day. Colors that contrast strongly in direct sunlight often lose their effect in countries where there is cloudy or gray northern light and dark ground surfaces. In the same way, a color that looks good in a clear coastal or mountain light may look quite wrong in the industrial haze of a city. In dull light, colors must be chosen carefully so that they contrast well.

If you move from a sunny climate to a more cloudy one you will probably not be aware of the difference this will make to your appreciation of color. If you paint your new home in the bright colors you are used to, instead of giving a vivid effect, these will now tend to look tawdry. Nevertheless, in Europe and North America the influence of the strong colors preferred by immigrants from the Caribbean, South America and India is noticeably changing the way color is used on buildings.

183

■ **Reflected color** can sometimes produce exciting visual effects and architects often take advantage of this. The façade of this building in Honolulu ABOVE LEFT might well have been chosen for its magnificent ability to capture the setting sun. Smooth, clear glass gives the Elf Building in Paris FAR LEFT both color and an extra dimension, reflecting soft, gray and white clouds against a storm-blue sky. Street lamps lend this cobbled street LEFT a special texture — very different, perhaps, from the one it will have during the day or even in the rain.

Familiarity breeds tradition

It is possible that we get used to colors with time. In one study, residents of a new, blue-painted apartment block were asked if they would like living in a blue building. When they were asked in the laboratory they said they disliked the idea, but when they actually came to live in the block, they expressed a liking for it. In another experiment, students were asked to evaluate their main lecture theater. This was painted predominantly in green. At the beginning of their course they described the space as green, then gave it various attributes such as serious, formal, ordinary, comfortable. Three years later they described the room as boring, dismal, monotonous, ordinary, heavy – hardly mentioning the color at all. With the passage of time they had ceased to notice the color and concentrated instead on the association they had with the room. It seems that although color has an initial impact, we may well learn to live with it over a period of time so that it adds to the atmosphere of an environment rather than dominating it. On the other hand, there are some colors that never seem right. A violet-painted corridor in one building was consistently unpopular over a six-year period and eventually had to be repainted.

Familiarity may account for the fact that some regions and cultures use certain colors more than others. People originally made their colors from locally obtained pigments in plants and the earth and so were restricted in their color choice according to what materials were available in their area. These practical reasons for using particular colors eventually became part of a cultural tradition and the same locally used colors persist today, even though there is no longer any difficulty in obtaining different pigments.

The strength of colors used, again, often depends on the quality of light. In Mexico, for example, there is a very free use of strong, bright colors, whereas in the Baltic area buildings are commonly painted in pastel shades. People may instinctively choose appropriate colors to use in conjunction with their neighbors because they have been exposed to a traditional color scheme. French architect Jean-Philippe Lenclos believes strongly in regional color. Before he designs the colors for new building developments he takes samples of all the available pigments in the surrounding earth and existing local buildings so that he can devise a scheme that fits in with local tradition. Similarly, German designer Gerhard Schweizer created a color wheel of traditional colors when he came to restore the medieval houses in two cities and allowed residents to choose their own combinations.

Getting a message across

Our traditional associations of color are not restricted to the colors we use on buildings, however. We are exposed to many colors in the environment and we may react differently to them when we see them in different contexts. Color

184

COLOR AND CULTURE

■ *The meaning of particular colors can vary from culture to culture. For example, Western brides marry in white to signify their purity while a Japanese bride will often marry in white to symbolize her "death" to her family. Also, honoring the dead in the West is symbolized by a funereal black, whereas the Chinese mourn their departed in white or undyed clothing to show humility and sorrow. Other colors, owing to their rarity as metals or pigments, have maintained their symbolism throughout time and across cultures – the rarer the color, the greater its symbolic power. For instance, gold has always*

symbolized opulence, divinity and the sun, and purple has always been a sign of the highest rank. The modern association of purple with royalty and religious hierarchy goes back to ancient Greece when thousands of murex seashells had to be crushed in order to obtain a small quantity of the dye. Consequently, its use was confined to the clothing of kings, priests and emperors.

◆ *Many of these symbolic colors came to be applied to buildings. For instance, the layered stages of Babylonian ziggurats were coded in the hues of the planets and applied*

by an astrologically motivated culture. The ancient Egyptians worshipped colored gods; they painted the Sphinx's face in a life-giving red and decorated their temples in the fertility-giving colors of the Nile. The ancient Greeks painted the Parthenon in strong colors. It is a misconception that this building was painted white.

◆ *Stripped of their original meanings, the colors of many cultures – or what we take to be their colors – have entered our*

own. A "Parthenon white" still exists – it can be found in the late 18th century interiors by the English architect Robert Adam, on Nash terraces in London and on the countless white-painted churches dotted across America. The greens, yellows and blues of ancient Egypt were resurrected – together with Indian and Chinese color symbolism – in the Odeon-style movie theaters of the 1920s and 1930s Art Deco period. **TP** can be used to direct us – for example, the color-coded direction symbols on highways. It can also be used to warn us. In some situations color can be the symbol of political or religious allegiance – we tend to associate red with communism, blue with conservatism and green with environmental issues. Buddhist monks wear saffron, and in the Catholic church cardinals wear red.

The European Community has issued a directive that all

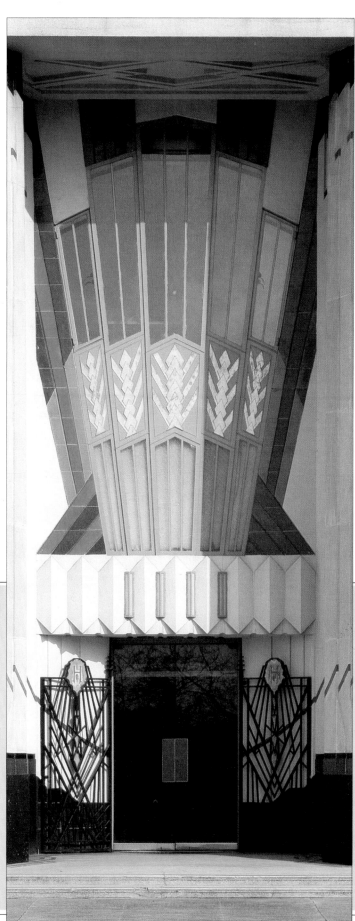

◄ **Color in the ancient world.** *Most archaeological ruins give us the false impression of an ancient world dominated by the color of natural stone. In fact, many of the stone surfaces were painted with scenes of the time, often in striking colors, such as these on the reconstructed Palace of the Minotaur at Knossos in Crete. The Parthenon on the Acropolis in Athens was very colorful in its original appearance.*

▲ **Local conditions create local color schemes.** *In New Mexico, Indians have for centuries embellished their earthen-colored buildings with turquoise trim, derived from the same mineral with which they fashion jewelry. Plentiful bright sunlight ensures that it stands out strikingly against pale walls.*

► **Borrowing from the Old World and the New,** *this detail from the Hoover Building in London – one of the finest examples of 1930s Art Deco – shows a cultural cocktail of ancient Egyptian and American Indian color themes.*

safety signposting must comply with a standard color system. In this system, red means prohibition, yellow means caution, green is for information, brown is for fire equipment and blue is for safety. Black is reserved for general notices. Our color associations are usually much the same as those in neighboring countries so a standard system like this should not cause any problems. Occasionally, though, there are differences that can be confusing. An American visitor with a letter to mail in France will not find the familiar blue mail box – it is yellow; in Spain it will be silver with a yellow and red stripe, in Britain red all over. The association of color with a mechanical activity such as mailing a letter can make it very disorienting when the color changes.

Camouflage and exhibitionism

Whatever our reaction to specific colors, the use of color in general can modify our reaction to an object or building. Most countries are faced with the problem of needing to build more and more large buildings for industrial or residential use and there is a great deal of public concern about

▲ **Hide it or flaunt it?** *Camouflaged as part of the skyscape, the exterior decor of these huge apartment buildings* TOP LEFT *in La Défense near Paris, attempts to make their bulk less noticeable. Camouflage here fails in its aim to make large,* ugly buildings more acceptable to the public eye, and merely accentuates the loss of identity people suffer when they have to live in them. This oil refinery TOP RIGHT off Long Beach, California, makes a cheerful gesture toward disguising itself as a block of apartment buildings. The Pacific Design Center in Los Angeles BOTTOM RIGHT makes no attempt at concealing its presence – it asserts itself with an imposing, undiluted blue. The Klinikon hospital outside Aachen in Germany BOTTOM LEFT shouts about its existence – bright panels of juxtaposed colors help to make the building a center of attention.

the impact these will have on the landscape. There are two solutions – make the buildings blend in or make them exciting, colorful additions to the scene.

Large strategic buildings and equipment are usually painted in a mottled greenish-brown pattern. From the ground it is hard to see how this could possibly conceal anything, but from the air the paint makes objects very difficult to identify. The matt finish reduces reflection and the strong contrasts between light and dark areas disrupt the shape and form. It is possible for architects to exploit these properties of color to blur the outline of a building so that it merges better with its surroundings. Another way of softening the visual impact of a structure is to use the colors that predominate in its location and to match these to the background against which the building will be seen. When the Golden Gate bridge in San Francisco was first built, the plan was to paint it gold as a tribute to the Gold Rush. In the end, though, the bridge was painted with red oxide so that it blended in with the surrounding earth. On this occasion, the planners favored discretion rather than flamboyancy.

■ **The writing on the wall.** There is a theory that murals and graphics deter graffiti writers. To test this out, an underpass was painted with vertical colored stripes and the amount of graffiti before and after the painting was recorded. After two months, despite the fact that the local football ground was only 300 yards away, there was no graffiti. However, graffiti gradually appeared as the paintwork deteriorated. It is possible that people react destructively to poorly maintained places and that graffiti is more the result of a lack of respect than a way of personalizing a space.

When six identical cubicles in a library were painted in primary colors and one was left white, they all received the same amount of graffiti. Color clearly does not cure vandalism, but signs that the authorities care about an area and take the trouble to paint it or to organize murals, may trigger a greater respect from younger residents.

187

THE IMPORTANCE OF WALL DECORATION

■ *Murals have been used to decorate walls from prehistoric times. The images we use today to decorate public buildings and walls are part of a tradition stretching back to Roman mosaics and the Lascaux cave paintings. Although some people think they are expensive irrelevancies, others consider that color graphics help people* know and understand the environment they live in, especially if they are able to take part in creating them.

We often use murals as landmarks – they are novel and have a high originality value. As the number of murals in a particular area increases, however, their impact lessens and we begin to develop preferences for some rather than others. One study tried to discover if local residents could correctly identify where a number of murals were located. They were also asked which murals they liked. The results showed that the most popular ones were also the ones people placed correctly – if we like something, we remember it. Occasionally,

▲ **Graffiti upon graffiti.** "Bicycles don't smell" is the original message, but a later artist has added an exhaust pipe to this drawing.

the mural is of such exceptional quality – for example, the wall of windows in Soho, New York – that it becomes a tourist attraction.

However, color can be used more freely to turn buildings into modern sculptures. Color can help them proclaim their individuality and difference from their surroundings. It can draw attention to a building and create visual interest where there might otherwise have been just an intrusive mass. Visitors are attracted to Frank Lloyd Wright's performing arts center in Sarasota, Florida because it is painted purple, and the multicolored Centre Beaubourg in Paris similarly acts as a visual magnet.

Color at work

Many employers know that color encourages interest and have experimented for years with the use of color to motivate their workers. The aim has usually been to increase productivity and efficiency at the same time as reducing absenteeism (see *Ch 24*). It is generally believed that color in the workplace plays an important role in increasing both the safety and satisfaction of workers, especially if the workers are allowed to participate in the choice of colors used. At the beginning of the 20th century the engines in Jewell's Mills, Brooklyn were painted with coach black and real gold leaf so that the engineer felt he was in charge of a noble machine. The ironwork of the McCormick Harvester works in Chicago was painted in bright colors that changed from room to room with the intention that stimulation would improve efficiency.

At the Renault car company in France, an artist was employed to decorate the factory. The employees were encouraged to discuss his ideas with him so that they were happy with the finished result. The company recognized that many of the workshops were anonymous and that workers did not identify with their workplace. To rectify this the artist used color to pick out particular features and so give them personality. He also used color to identify function – tables, chairs, desks, offices, cabinets and enclosures were all painted in different colors. Red was used for workshops, blue for control, yellow for handling and green for maintenance. Monotonous, single-colored corridors were broken up using color panels interrupted by door frames in different colors. Access areas such as corridors and staircases were painted in bright colors to encourage people to pass through them quickly and work areas were painted in more muted colors because it was believed this would aid concentration.

Sometimes, though, we would prefer not to be reminded of the function of a building. Hospitals and dentists' waiting rooms, for example, often have reception areas decorated in a warm, comfortable color that contrasts with the clinical activity of the building. Similarly, seating at John F Kennedy airport in New York is a cozy red that counteracts the impersonal, transitory function of the place. The governor of

Alcatraz prison, anxious to take the prisoners' minds off their incarceration, had the walls of the canteen painted light green believing it would have a calming effect on their violent emotions.

Getting it right

Public buildings, factories, houses and apartment blocks are meant for people to use, so the success of any color scheme depends, ultimately, on whether we, the public, like it. Many architects are now testing people's reactions to colors before actually using them. One way of doing this is to paint hardboard in the colors to be used and then attach this to the building so that they can be seen in the exact position and under the actual light conditions. This exposure allows local residents to experience the colors before their final application and gives the people who will have to live with the color scheme a chance to participate in choosing it.

If you live in a dull, gray, monotonous area, you could try organizing your neighbors into an action group to get things changed. Consult your local planners' and architects' departments and experiment with color on the outside of your buildings. If your workplace is dreary and uninspiring, ask your employers if you can use color to brighten it up. We have the ability to enjoy and benefit from color, so why should we live in a monochrome world? **BM**

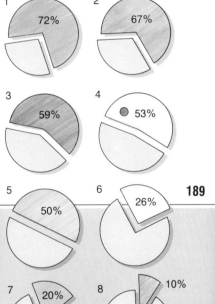

OFFICE WORKERS' COLOR PREFERENCES

1 — 72%
2 — 67%
3 — 59%
4 — 53%
5 — 50%
6 — 26%
7 — 20%
8 — 10%

■ **Making color work for you.** *In some working environments, color is used in a creative way to make people feel better about their surroundings. Parts of the Stockholm subway in Sweden FAR LEFT were deliberately painted a cool blue to combat perception of the close warmth generated by a subterranean environment. Color was also used constructively in the interior of the Abteiberg Museum in Mönchengladbach, Germany, LEFT designed by the Austrian architect Hans*

Hollein – people passing from the neutral cream of the corridor are stimulated by the warm, deep tones of the room they are about to enter. The explosion of color in this Gobelin tapestry by Jean Lurcat transforms the reception desk of a Zurich bank ABOVE from a practical store of useful information into an Aladdin's Cave of possibilities.

▶ **Working with color.** *Most color preferences based on judgments of small patches of color fall into the order blue, red, green, violet, orange, yellow. This survey of 1,000 office workers (percentage in favor of each color scheme) revealed that at work, however, we dislike strong, saturated colors like red and green. This could be because these colors reflect little light and make rooms appear less open.*

1 Cool colors (blue/green)
2 Pastel colors (light blue/pale yellow)   3 Warm colors (yellow/red)   4 Subdued colors with intense color accents
5 Neutral colors (beige, putty, tan)   6 White   7 Intense colors (bright red, bright green)   8 Gray

The Workplace

SOME OF US find work more satisfying than others. Sometimes this is because the work itself is more interesting, more challenging or better paid. But our physical work environment also plays an important part in determining how we feel. We spend about half our waking hours at work and the surroundings affect us as much as our home environment. Noise, air pollution, crowding and the amount of privacy all contribute to our mental attitude and to how efficiently we do our work.

Productivity is something managers value highly and one way employers can increase it is by ensuring that their employees are happy in their working environment. If you are physically comfortable you are more likely to work well and to experience greater job satisfaction. Office design, in particular, should reflect job status and personal preferences as well as the type of work done and the need to maximize efficiency. However, studies on the effects of the physical environment in offices have found that our performance may well be more affected by our attitude to our working conditions than by the conditions themselves.

Working in an open space

Do planners and senior managers always make the right choices when it comes to designing our workplaces? In the pursuit of more efficient and socially interactive working environments, employers have made more and more offices open-plan. These are not always popular with those who have to work in them but despite increasing evidence of employee dissatisfaction they are still on the increase. In the United States, the percentage of office furniture destined for open-plan offices rose from 40 percent in 1978 to 50 percent in 1980.

But why do many people dislike the open-plan office? An important concern among many employees is the issue of privacy. Human beings, like other animals, have territories. We mark these symbolically and regulate their use so that other people know who we are and what our status is (see *Ch 8*). In a traditional office, usually with its own window and door, you can control access according to whether or not you want to be available to others. If you leave your office door open, it tells your colleagues that you are willing to be consulted or interrupted. If you sit with your back to a colleague, you are indicating that you do not want to be disturbed. On the door of the traditional office we usually see the occupant's name and their title or position.

Open-plan offices sometimes fail to display this information and tend to create both uncertainty about role and status in the eyes of visitors and a reduced sense of personal identity in the minds of the occupants. In addition, the loss of the ability to regulate our privacy can often cause discomfort and stress.

A study that examined office workers' feelings about how much privacy they had before and after changing from a traditional to an open-plan office found that workers who were already sharing space reported no additional loss of privacy; those who had shared with just one other person reported slightly reduced privacy, but those who had moved from their own office experienced a severe loss of privacy. Another study showed that this loss of privacy, together with a loss of perceived status, also caused them to feel that their jobs had become less important.

A PROBLEM OF SPACE

■ *A stock analyst* LEFT *spreads his work across the available work surfaces. Office workers* RIGHT *finish another day, adapting to the division of space that their company has arrived at after years of planning and tinkering. How successfully their surroundings have served them and their organizations will depend on how well the balance has been struck between conflicting needs. If all points worth considering are reflected in the design of your own workplace, you are very fortunate. These points may include the need to locate you in the only available building – one with less than ideal facilities. Like anyone else, you are highly adaptable and will learn to cope. However, there is a price (in diverted energy and lost efficiency) to pay for this, and both you and your organization may benefit from initiatives to customize your personal space to the aims and the methods of the work that you do, and to ensure that the lighting, heating and ventilation are right.*

Did you have a good day at the office? ■ If you do not feel happy at work, your company may not be making the most of your potential ■ Employees who have enough space and like their environment enjoy greater job satisfaction.

Are you afraid of being overheard?

Workers in an open-plan office are usually unable to escape from visual and verbal interruption; most of them find that overhearing snatches of conversation is much more distracting than background noise generated by equipment. The inconvenience of other people's conversation is often called the "cocktail party phenomenon" because of the way we suddenly pick out an interesting comment from general background chat, often without even realizing that we were listening.

Sometimes employers raise the background level of noise above intruding speech levels to provide more privacy – or try to block noise with office furniture. Although filing cabinets, screens and plants can provide visual barriers, many office workers still complain that their auditory privacy is less than desirable. They feel that they are unable to have a private conversation either with other colleagues or on the telephone. This has the effect of inhibiting normal interaction and can severely affect the way they handle their job.

If you have to make delicate or confidential telephone calls in your work, you may easily feel embarrassed if you think other people can overhear what you are saying, or you may be forced into having superficial conversations that do not involve serious or confidential issues. Managers might feel that the open-plan office discourages nonproductive chit-chat, but a certain level of chatting among colleagues is necessary for good working relations.

Supportive colleagues often help workers to deal with stress at work or at home, but the fear of being overheard may inhibit this kind of exchange. In addition, open-plan offices may also discourage serious discussion about work, especially when it involves referring to individual colleagues, and may prevent staff from tackling work-related problems. So, although open-plan offices do increase the opportunity for communication, in practice it may not be the sort of communication that benefits productivity.

The need for peace and quiet

Increased communication can present another problem in the open-plan office. Some tasks *are* done better in this environment – if you are working in a team on the same problem then it can be helpful to discuss things across the room without having to visit another office. Equally, some processing tasks that involve liaison between various departments can be done more efficiently when all the staff are in the same work area. However, other tasks, such as writing reports or detailed strategy planning, require quiet and concentration.

■ **Why an open plan?** *Work that constantly requires short bursts of communication thrives in an open plan. Typical open-plan offices include newspaper editorial rooms, police stations, stock exchanges, drawing offices, and this foreign exchange trading room RIGHT in Geneva, Switzerland. However, work that requires concentration and privacy demands individual spaces. If these are provided as a compromise ABOVE that simply partitions large areas that reach deep into a building, distracting noise and unnatural lighting can undermine morale. The root cause may be architectural – in many large office buildings of the 1970s a square, undivided deep-plan arrangement was needed to make special heat-recovery systems work (these reuse energy from lights, office equipment and bodies to reduce power demands).*

Some firms get round this problem by providing separate rooms where you can make confidential phone calls, work alone, entertain visitors and hold interviews. But these rooms are usually anonymous and impersonal – simple things like not having your own desk or having to carry files and papers from your work area can be irritating and time wasting.

The types of noise people find distracting vary according to the job they are doing. If you are operating a machine or monitoring a process, you are more likely to be distracted by occasional bursts of high-frequency sound, such as a telephone bell, than by a constant buzz of low-frequency noise. During routine or simple tasks, music may be an effective block against other sounds and can even aid concentration. In these cases music is not just a way of blocking other noise, it may raise the level of mental stimulation during repetitive tasks and may encourage a faster pace. It is quite common to see people at work listening to personal stereos and some companies provide background music in certain work areas.

On the other hand, if your work involves concentrating on intellectual tasks such as accounting, proofreading or report writing, you are much more likely to be distracted by

your colleagues' conversations than by sudden noises. However, no matter what kind of noise interference you have, you will find it less of a problem if you know you can control it. In a number of American experiments, people were asked to perform difficult tasks while listening to loud bursts of noise. Some of them were shown a switch and

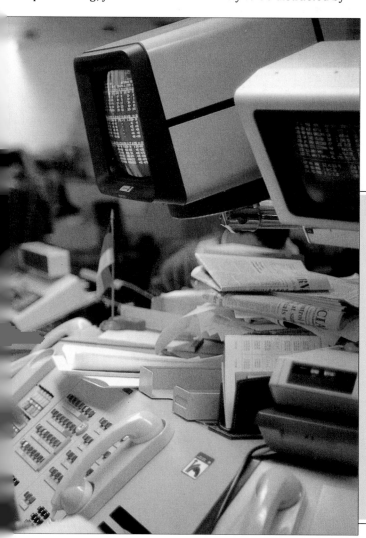

LIVING WITH NEW TECHNOLOGY

■ *Personal computers and visual display units are now part of the everyday scene in offices, revolutionizing the workplace and the way we do our jobs. For employers, this new technology is very often a viable and advantageous economic alternative to traditional working methods. There are both pros and cons for employees.*

ADVANTAGES

The careful introduction of new systems into your organization can provide a good opportunity for the company to create psychologically more rewarding jobs. New technology takes the load off purely mechanical mental operations and makes decision-making and communication faster and more stimulating. Very often the scope of a job goes beyond the tasks done by the machine and workers can be asked to take on new responsibilities and develop new skills. It makes sense for both employers and employees alike to see technology as an opportunity for job enrichment.

DISADVANTAGES

The benefit to the employer of needing fewer employees is one of the greatest drawbacks of new technology for those of us who work. Many people worry that technology will make them redundant. If the public can get money from a cash dispenser, why employ a bank clerk? If a typist using a new design keyboard can type up to 80 percent faster than someone using the traditional board, will employers need fewer typists?

Another drawback to electronic systems, from the

employee's point of view, is that they reduce contact between people, making workers feel isolated. Because so much information is given to and extracted from a machine, there is less opportunity for employees to work together and develop rapport.

An employee's sense of esteem can be reduced even further if managers use information technology to centralize decision-making rather than to develop a free flow of communication.

HEALTH HAZARDS

Do visual display terminals affect the health of office workers? Carefully controlled studies show that people using these terminals suffer from more eye strain, aches in the neck and shoulder and blurred vision than other employees. Suggestions on how to relieve some symptoms by improving the design of equipment and offices include a recommendation that no one spend more than five hours per day in front of a screen and that they have hourly rest breaks and regular eye tests at their employer's expense.

Pregnant women have been particularly concerned about risks to their babies from spending too long in front of the screen. Several studies have suggested that this might be hazardous and although nothing has yet been proved, the potential threat is worrying for many women. They find themselves trapped in a situation where they risk losing their job if they refuse to work at the screens and risk damaging their baby if they do not express concern.

193

were told that they could cut off the noise if they wanted, although it would be preferable if they left it on. None of them did, in fact, turn off the switch. It seems that just knowing they *could* if they wanted to made the noise less disturbing. They all performed better on a proofreading task than those who had not been shown the switch and who, therefore, had no control over the noise.

Noise distraction does not seem to reduce the speed it takes to do a job, but it does interfere with concentration and can cause errors.

194

PROBLEMS OF LIGHT AND AIR

▲ **Natural lighting**, over and above any illumination it provides, is an important factor in how satisfied office workers are with where they sit. A high-status job usually guarantees more window space and a better view. In one experiment clerical workers were asked to estimate what proportion of illumination came to their work station from daylight through windows. Those who were some distance from the windows markedly overestimated the light from that source.

■ Many modern office blocks combine uncomfortable overcrowding, inappropriate construction, artificial light and recycled air. Such combinations have been blamed for the fact that so many office workers suffer from what has been called the Sick Building Syndrome – offices are blamed for causing Legionnaires' Disease, asthma, tiredness, headaches, dry eyes and sore throats. The culprits include:
◆ airconditioning in general – there is widespread concern about the general low levels of air ions in airconditioned

offices. People react differently to the balance of positive and negative ions – many display faster reaction times and better motor coordination when there is a high concentration of negative ions.
◆ poorly designed or badly fitted and maintained airconditioning systems that spread bad air (see main text).
◆ tobacco smoke – it can be hazardous to health even if you do not smoke yourself.
◆ basement garages and the intake of carbon monoxide. Carbon monoxide is poisonous and odor-free. We are not

aware we are breathing it, but in excessive amounts it can restrict the oxygen-carrying capacity of the blood.
◆ synthetic building and furnishing materials. Research has isolated 62 known volatile organic compounds in office carpets and furnishings. There is now a trend to "burn off" harmful gases from new buildings by running the heating at high temperature for a short time before companies move in.
◆ electrical irritants such as fluorescent lighting and computer screens.

Shedding light on the problem

Next to irritation with noise levels at work, we are most likely to be concerned with the quality of the light we have to work in. Offices and other workplaces often lack sufficient natural daylight so they have to be lit by artificial light. It is no easy task to design a lighting system that suits everyone. The two main types of lighting system are the filament lamp and the fluorescent lamp. Overhead fluorescent tubing is both economical and efficient and studies have shown that people perform manipulative tasks faster and more accurately under it than under filament lamps. However, it is generally believed that most people do not like working under fluorescent light. They complain that it distorts colors and causes eye strain because of the glare from white surfaces. Other types of light are available – tungsten desk lamps create a pool of light that illuminates just the work area and gives a relaxing light to work by; electric arc lights using zenon gas are especially useful for replacing natural daylight and faithfully reproducing colors. These tend to be favored by designers and artists who spend a lot of time matching colors.

Not everyone has the same need for light when they are working. You may find that you work quite happily in low light levels, especially if you do not move between differently lit areas. Older colleagues, though, will probably need much brighter conditions to work comfortably. If you have your own office, this is not a problem because you can regulate your own light. In an open-plan office, however, there is often no choice about whether the lights are on or off – usually they are on.

If every employee is able to control their light source, there is less chance that they will be discontent about it. Overhead lighting can be arranged so that it can be turned on or off in sections and if each employee also has their own desk lamp, no one need be inconvenienced. A rational use of different types of lighting reduces eye strain and so makes the work less tiring, while at the same time improving productivity by eliminating a source of discomfort.

Bad air – the invisible enemy

Disruption from noise and light are irritating but in time you become aware of them and can sometimes control your exposure to them. Air, on the other hand, is invisible and unavoidable. Many recently designed buildings replace opening windows with airconditioning systems that filter and recirculate air. The consequence is usually less-than-clean air.

The level of carbon monoxide, air ions and foul odors in the air we breathe at work may all affect our well-being and our performance. If you work in an airconditioned building, have you noticed that you occasionally suffer from sore eyes, inexplicable allergies, dry skin and headaches? All of these can be caused by impurities in the air.

Airconditioning is now known to be responsible for

■ **Two approaches to lighting**. *An illuminated ceiling* BELOW *allows personnel in a computer room to move freely from one machine to another* *without having to adjust the lighting. Office workers with more stationary tasks usually express strong dislike for high levels of artificial light, even* *when its artificiality is offset by windows that look out onto gardens and other outdoor scenes. Desk lamps* ABOVE *for* *individual lighting allow designers working at computer screens to reduce glare and avoid onscreen reflections that tire the eyes. Lighting technology in the sixties and seventies aimed for higher and higher levels of illumination, on the assumption that this would increase efficiency. However, many offices designed in the eighties reflect research findings that workers are more comfortable and work more efficiently with lower intensities of light.*

spreading a great number of respiratory infections among the people working in a building. Infectious microorganisms may breed in the cooling towers and ducts. The most dramatic of these infections is the deadly Legionnaires' Disease – a type of pneumonia. Foul air containing smoke, fumes and microorganisms may also be sucked out of one office and passed to another.

Diseases like this are such a hazard that architects and planners are having to rethink the whole design of air-conditioning in public buildings. Employees are starting to complain about being exposed to the risk of disease and feeling constantly unwell.

An ideal working temperature?

While it is fairly easy for employers to provide individual light for employees, it is more difficult for them to provide individual temperature control, especially in an open-plan office. So how do you keep everyone happy? In determining the ideal working temperature in an office, engineers refer to "comfort envelopes."

These specify a range of temperature best suited to both personal comfort and efficiency according to the type of clothing worn and the activity engaged in. The convention-

ally accepted norm for an office worker wearing light clothing in 45 percent humidity is between 24° and 27°C (75° and 80°F).

But how often do you and your colleagues wear exactiy the same weight of clothing? You are probably going to feel comfortable in different temperatures and unless you have your own office you will have to compromise and put up with someone else's "ideal" temperature.

Curiously, performance is actually better if you are slightly too warm or too cold than if the temperature is just right – but this depends on the type of work you are doing. Even so, prolonged exposure to the wrong temperature will impair your performance, especially on complex tasks.

It has been found that productivity falls off under very warm conditions, especially for manual work, but cognitive tasks, such as office work, are only affected after a period of time. You can work unaffected for about 30 minutes in temperatures up to 38°C (100°F), but if you are working for three hours on a task your performance will deteriorate if the temperature rises above 30°C (86°F). Excessively cold temperatures affect jobs requiring sensitive manual dexterity and if the temperature of the skin drops below 14°C (57°F) there is a marked drop in performance.

THE IMPORTANCE OF WHERE YOU SIT

■ *The location of your office is a good indicator of your status in the company. The most desirable locations are those nearest to the decision-maker, so senior managers will have offices close to the chief executive and the mail room will usually be tucked away at the bottom of the building. In landscaped open-plan offices corner positions are considered to indicate high status and are generally* occupied by senior staff. Vertical position is of particular importance to American companies – generally, the higher the floor, the greater your status, and there are also likely to be fewer people occupying the same floorspace.

Another test of importance is your accessibility. Junior typists are usually grouped together in pools that are open to anyone needing typing at any time.

Senior executives shield themselves from intrusion with secretaries, personal assistants and junior managers. The size of your office is an obvious clue to your status. Office space is a symbolic way of rewarding performance and companies wishing to motivate promising staff will use the carrot of a bigger and better office to increase their productivity.

HOW DISTANCE AFFECTS SHARED SPACE

■ *Normally, no one needs to accept intrusions into the intimate 45cm (18in) closest to them in order to do their job. This is a space that we share only in close relationships or in hand-to-hand combat. However, finding space for everyone in an office can mean asking some staff to allow overlaps between a wider space, the personal 1.2m (4ft) around them that most people like to control exclusively. This kind of sharing can be stressful. It* makes us feel crowded: other people seem to be imposing their presence upon us. More frequently, the social zone (up to 3.7m – 12ft) is shared. This can make it easier to communicate with other people about work, but it can also expose you to distracting interruptions.

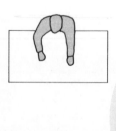

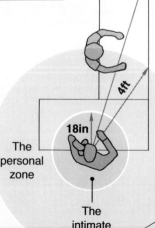

The public zone

The social zone

The personal zone

The intimate zone

12ft

4ft

18in

Do you control your own space?

Fundamentally, having your own space is very much a matter of being able to control your working environment. Decorating your office space with possessions is often one way of setting up a territorial zone. Furniture or other items often act as barricades in an open space, but solutions such as this do not really answer the problem of controlling your environment.

Because the walls in a traditional office give us the illusion of being physically distant from others, people who work in an open-plan office need more space around them, to make them feel "distant" enough to be comfortable. One study found that the amount of space an employee has is the single best predictor of their satisfaction with the office. However, the study also found that if people have the choice between the *same* space in either a traditional or an open-plan office, they will prefer the traditional office.

The personal touch

It is possible to create the illusion that you are on your own territory even in an open-plan office. If you look around any workplace you will find some evidence of that person's taste and interests. It might be photographs of the family, art posters, postcards, exotic plants, curios or ornaments – most of us do something to make our working area more personal. It is another way of establishing our boundaries

and of saying "this is my space." If you feel that your office is in some way an extension of yourself, then you are more likely to work better and be more productive.

How much you can personalize your space depends on how public your work is and the function of your job. Certain areas may simply be inappropriate places to have personal photographs or distracting objects. But, even if your managers discourage you from displaying personal objects, they can still involve you in the choice of furnishings, plants, pictures, colors and the detailed specification of equipment.

Esthetic objects and plants are very important – they make us feel more comfortable. So does tidiness. Some people try so hard to make their work area a home from home that they clutter up all the available space with personal objects, reducing the area of worksurface and making

■ **The way you personalize your workspace** *sends messages to others about your work.* RIGHT *A gold-plated oil derrick and a swooping bird of prey (a bald-headed eagle) symbolize the occupant's exercise of power. Artistic clutter* LEFT *advertises that the work done here is creative. Because of their status both occupants are free to send extreme signals. If she were not the owner of her company, too much tidiness at the desk of the one might be interpreted as meaning she does not have enough work to do: a reason-able amount of mess is an indication that you are busy and committed. However, if he were not an independently success-ful, sought-after science fiction writer, the other might feel more pressure to display well-organized papers and surfaces as a sign that he is on top of his job and feels confident about what he is doing. When you are arranging and maintaining your own workspace, you may have to balance the degree to which you impress people with order and the degree to which you impress them with activity.*

197

THE ADVANTAGES OF FLEXIBLE ARCHITECTURE

■ *When Centraal Beheer – a large Dutch insurance company – decided to move its offices from Amsterdam to Apeldoorn, little more than a country town, the management considered it important to offer encouragement to the staff who would be asked to relocate.*

One incentive was to involve them in plans for an attractive and flexible working environment.

The company's new building was designed by the architect Herman Hertzberger. He met the employees during project briefing – so that he could hear from them directly what kinds of surroundings would help them to work effectively and comfortably. These office workers also helped to monitor Hertzberger's plans as they developed.

The architect's solution to the broad range of predictably conflicting needs and priorities put before him was to plan a building that can make flexible use of standardized units of space.

The building is organized as a series of linked square boxes, arranged around interior courtyards that bring natural lighting deep into the interior.

Each box can be divided by a crossed-shaped corridor into four partitioned or partially partitioned office spaces, each 2.8m (9ft) square.

These spaces provide either individual or shared offices, and when the need arises, unpartitioned boxes or half boxes provide open-plan offices. The same 2.8m spaces provide conference rooms and informal lounges, while larger segments of boxes accommodate restaurants.

The use of muted materials and colors gives the building an unfinished appearance as an encouragement to occupants to personalize individual workspaces.

At the same time, the open framework of the building is aimed at keeping people more in contact with each other, breaking down barriers between colleagues and visitors. A generous allotment of easily accessible areas reserved for chatting and relaxing is a key element in this strategy. **RH**

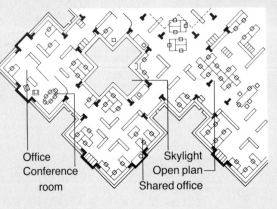

Office
Conference
room

Skylight
Open plan
Shared office

▲ **Natural light and a sense of open space** *set the mood inside the Centraal Beheer offices in Apeldoorn, Holland, yet many of the workspaces benefiting from the structure's ample windows and skylights are located deep within the building, and they are well enough demarcated from each other to allow a sense of privacy and personal control.*

things harder to find. Instead of creating a comfortable, welcoming workspace, they end up with an untidy office that is unlikely to impress others with their efficiency.

But too much tidiness may be interpreted by others as meaning that you do not have enough work to do. A reasonable amount of mess is an indication that the occupant is busy and heavily involved in their work.

How to arrange the furniture

Another way you stamp your own personality on your workspace is in the arrangement of the furniture. Although many offices are laid out to suit the type of work done, most of us have some choice in the exact positioning of the furniture. A study of offices belonging to university professors revealed a marked difference between the way reserved faculty members organized their space and the way more extroverted ones arranged their furniture. Extroverted professors tended to have their desk against a wall so that visitors were immediately in direct contact with them. Reserved professors placed their desks so that they formed a barrier between themselves and any visitors.

If you have a choice as to how to arrange your office, where do you prefer to sit? We use the position of our desk and chairs in many ways to show what level of interaction we are experiencing with visitors. If you are reprimanding a junior member of staff or if you have a grievance with your manager, you will probably sit across the desk from that person. You are more likely to sit side by side with someone if you are cooperating with them on a task or supervising their work.

If your job involves you in meeting visitors from outside, or from other departments within the company, it is important that you feel able to maintain control.

You can often do this by carefully positioning the furniture so that your office has "public" areas – perhaps with chairs for visitors – and "personal" areas – behind the desk, for example. In many organizations junior members of staff have little or no control over where they sit – only high status confers this privilege; low status brings with it a low level of control which may result in a poor sense of self-worth.

Most people have to manage several different kinds of encounter in their workspace – some purely cooperative, some in which difference of rank is important – and it is not always possible to establish an office layout that is ideal for all of your needs. **MHB**

▲ **Arrangement 6**: the occupant, often an academic, maintains accessibility by sitting side-on to the door.

HOW HAVE YOU ARRANGED YOUR DESK?

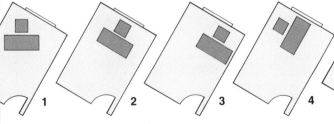

1   2   3   4   5   6

■ A study of business, government and academic office layouts found that six main ways of positioning a desk have a marked effect on how people interact with the occupant. Types 1-4 enable more formal interactions: the occupant maintains a private zone; discussions take place over the desk; visitors are seated some distance from the occupant.

1 Desk arranged as a diagonal barrier across the corner of the room opposite the door. This is most common in government and business offices.
2 Desk as a barrier open at both ends and opposite the door.
3 Desk as a barrier open at one end and opposite the door – common in business.

4 Desk arranged as a barrier within the room but open on the door end – common in business offices.
 Types 5 and 6 are less formal: the private zone is less well defined, there being no clear physical barrier between occupant and visitor. Academics are likely to opt for these arrangements to make themselves easily approachable by

students. They do not sit with a full, commanding view of their office entrance.
5 Desk against wall or window at opposite end of the room from the door. Occupant has back to door.
6 Desk against side wall, not as a barrier – the occupant sits with one side of body to the door.

THE EVOLVING WORKPLACE

200

■ Wherever you work, whether it is in a service or a manufacturing industry, you may feel that your working environment is less than perfect. Perhaps there is not enough light or it is too hot, cold or noisy. Factories in particular have still not completely lost the reputation they had during the industrial revolution for bad working conditions.

THE CUSTOMER COMES FIRST

About two-thirds of workers in Western Europe and North America are employed in service industries – including banks, stores, restaurants, libraries, leisure centers, hotels and hospitals – as opposed to one-third in manufacturing industries. This means that often the workplace has not been designed primarily with the needs of the employees in minds,

but as a place for serving customers or clients. In many cases, employees can control few aspects of their working environment and have little choice as far as color schemes, noise levels or temperature are concerned. In stores and restaurants, music is often a constant background noise. Employees have to wear a company uniform and colors are those of the company logo or are strictly functional. Furthermore, in most service industries there is little chance for privacy – it is part of the employee's job to make contact with the public.

PRODUCTIVITY OR COMFORT?

When we think of factories, we usually think of noise and dust, with long hours of work that is often dangerous and repetitive. In the 20th century, the tyranny of the

◀ **Rest periods help to break up the monotony** *of production-line work in the Kommunal Automobile Plant. Founded in 1863, it is one of the oldest in Zaporozhye, Ukraine. Modern factory design concentrates on bringing comfort and natural light into the workplace, creating a pleasant environment for the employees.*

▼ **Pride in the workplace**. *When working conditions in factories began to improve in the 19th century, considerations for the appearance of the building sometimes exceeded concern for the workers. The façade of this modern industrial park in Swindon, England, however, not only creates a favorable impression on visitors but gives employees a feeling of pride and pleasure in their place of work.*

production line has taken over from the tyranny of the overseer. Employers have become much more interested in the well-being of their workers, though generally with the aim of making them more efficient rather than from any sense of altruism. Even the most enlightened employers have tended to spend more time and thought on the development of leisure facilities and holidays than on enhancing working conditions.

In the 19th century, factory conditions improved mainly as a result of concern for the health and safety of employees. But there was often more concern for the appearance of a factory than the working environment it provided. Factory buildings were designed to impress the passerby or the influential visitor.

Today, the establishment of the production line has led in many cases to the product being more important promotionally than the place of production — Henry Ford wanted each of his employees to own a Model "T." However, some architects have tried to give employees a sense of pride and pleasure in their place of work by imaginatively designing the factory façade. The huge dome of the Union Tank Car Company in Baton Rouge, Louisiana, and the AEG building in Berlin, Germany, were both designed to make workers feel part of the new era.

THE NEW WORKPLACE

Modern factory and workplace designers are increasingly concerned to bring style, comfort and natural light into the work area instead of simply concentrating on the exterior. Many companies are beginning to realize that it is important to create a clean and stimulating environment for employees. Ecological awareness is creeping into corporate thinking too — if you want the public to buy your product and use your services, you have to present a caring image. Examples of this new breed of industrial workplace have many elements in common, especially the importance given to natural light and the fact that workers are allowed more contact with the outside world. Some promote the employers' reputations through their sophisticated high-tech constructions, others are more traditional and blend with their surroundings. The David Mellor cutlery and kitchenware factory in Derbyshire, England, looks like a converted railway roundhouse from the outside but inside the space is full of light. There is a central roof light and a continuous band of glass between the roof and walls. The roof, designed like a spoked wheel, echoes the craftsmanship of the factory's products. The workshop has views out onto trees and sky, and the light is primarily natural.

In contrast, the Inmos computer factory in Wales is a modern scientific building with a structure designed to give a working area completely free of unnecessary walls and columns. It has a main circulation corridor housing the heating and ventilation systems that keep the internal environment accurately modulated, dust-free and clinically clean. The center of the workspace is opened up to rectangular courts so that workers have natural light and are in contact with the outside world.

Companies are also becoming increasingly aware that they are part of the outside world. The Renault warehouse in Swindon, England, has been planned in such a way that its exhibition hall can be used for local community events. From the outside, the building looks like an elegant, brightly colored steel marquee and serves as a stockroom, warehouse, showroom and staff-training center. **RSH**

201

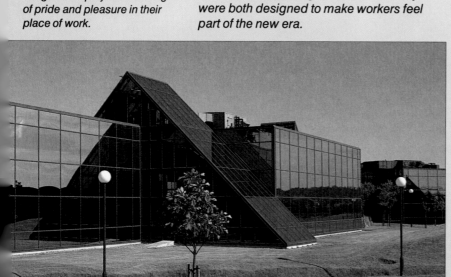

Places for Learning

FROM THE TIME we are born we start learning. As infants, we learn from our surroundings and from watching parents, neighbors, anyone we have contact with. We become aware, at first subconsciously, how adults set about their work, and we copy them.

For many centuries, places of learning existed where a small minority of boys were trained to be priests or scribes, learning the mysteries of religion or literacy. The idea that everyone should have the opportunity to learn everything is relatively modern. Once work moved out of the home and into the factory, the unconscious learning of the home environment was replaced by deliberate teaching. In not much more than a century, schools grew from simple classrooms to complex institutions which have a profound influence on our lives.

Most people would agree that the quality of teaching, the relationship between teacher and pupil and the wider educational aims of a school are of primary importance. But what about the effect on both pupils and teacher of the physical environment? What do school buildings and their surroundings teach us?

Early learning

We have all been children, and even if we have forgotten, our parents always remember the day we first crawled across the room, the day we walked unaided or our first sight of the sea. But ask children themselves what their first memories are, and they will recall best small physical details and sensations: the coldness of metal, the mystery of glass, the feel of the surface of the stairs laboriously climbed up and down, the texture of wool or silk, the fur of an animal. As children grow, their world expands to include streets and their stores and services, new sights, sounds and smells. Whether this is in a city, suburb or a small town, it is a vivid sensory experience, a learning situation.

Obviously the younger children are, the closer their eyes are to the ground, and this is one of the reasons why the *floorscape* is so significant. This is the texture and subdivisions of flooring and surfacing, as well as changes of level in steps and slopes (small enough to walk up for an adult, big enough to sit on for a child). When urban geographers asked adults what they remembered from their early childhood, they named particularly the floor of their environment, the tactile rather than the visual qualities of their surroundings.

As soon as children start walking, they observe avidly objects in the street – the garbage truck, the ambulance, the fire engine. When they learn to talk, they name vehicles and

◀ **Eyes down, hands on.**
The learning environment for a toddler may include wide vistas, but it is usually the floor or the ground that excites their curiosity. Adults who try to remember their earliest surroundings mention especially a floor or a lawn, and they remember how things felt more than how they looked. Some educators create special floor effects in order to capitalize on the particular proximity to young children of this part of the environment (see p204).

HOW SCHOOLROOMS HAVE CHANGED

■ *When boys grew up to be clerks or clerics, the environment for teaching was simple. A classical education required nothing more than books and writing materials, a teacher and a class and could be conducted anywhere. When places were specially built to serve as schools, they were bleak and bare with no concessions to childhood or the comfort of pupils. The idea may conjure up pictures of ancient buildings with rows of dusty benches in which generations of boys have carved their initials; of dreary mechanical learning and of stern punishments.*

■ *In the last 100 years, ideas about school design have been through many changes. An elderly person attending a concert or drama in a modern junior school might remark that "Schools weren't like this when I was young!" They may remember high railings around*

What does it matter where a child is taught? ■ *The most important variable in education is the teacher's skill, but the physical environment can help to make it easier for teachers to teach and for students to learn.*

letters on street signs and stores, endlessly asking their meaning and eager to learn. By this time the most fortunate children are already attending a day nursery or a play group, interacting with other children and familiarizing themselves with a new environment. Good pre-school education will feed the child's zest for new discoveries and learning opportunities. Children may be given a chance, for example, to experiment with building materials: bricks, wood, water and sand. Few of these groups are organized in purpose-built premises. Most are run, often by parents themselves, in private houses, church halls or in schools with a room to spare. Apart from strong tables and chairs of the right size, the essentials are objects and the space to use them, including outside areas for games, for digging and for using cycles, scooters and push-along toys.

Jug, clay or flower?

The idea of child-centered education and the need to encourage the child to explore its world and experiment with the physical environment, were the most significant of the changes that slowly crept into our attitudes toward schooling. There are three main approaches to the education of children: in the first, the child is seen as an empty jug to be filled. This is the traditional view, the notion that there is a body of learning and basic skills of language and arithmetic that has to be poured into the jug. These are called subjects, and the school curriculum in the 20th century has broadened to include an ever-widening range of human knowledge. When a new public issue arises, like road safety, sexual hygiene or computer literacy, it is the task of the school to pour this too into the jug. The jug theory implies that children are lined up in rows to receive wisdom, so this is the traditional classroom design.

In the second approach the child is a lump of clay to be molded by a skilled potter – the teacher. Society wants

the schoolyard and notices: "Parents Are Not Allowed Beyond This Point."

■ They are certain to remember that window ledges used to be high enough to prevent children from looking out and notice that today they are low enough to ensure that children can. They remember the rows of benches and desks all facing the teacher. Today children often work in small groups with the teacher circulating among them.

■ If the aged visitor was taught at a one-room school where all ages were taught together, they may be surprised by the number of specialist rooms in the modern school – for arts, crafts, sciences and language teaching. Many architects like to think of a school as a learning laboratory.

▲ **A century apart**. *ABOVE LEFT Children learn computing in a modern vocational school that accommodates 2,000 adolescents in highly specialized classrooms. ABOVE RIGHT The entire school, with an age-range from 5 to 18, turns out for a photograph in the town of Alma, Wisconsin, sometime in the 1890s.*

203

good citizens, so the child must be shaped into citizenship; religions want believers, so the child must be formed by religious belief; employers need workers, so it must be disciplined into reliable working habits. This model, too, implies that the classroom is deliberately isolated from outside influences which might impede the potter's work.

Third, the child can be seen as a flower to be lovingly nurtured, given the right growing conditions and allowed to develop in its own way. This child-centered approach implies that the school environment should be designed for the needs of the child. There should be child-sized furniture, a welcoming color scheme, small groups instead of rows of desks. The teacher is a helper and stimulator, not a formidable instructor.

The problem is that we tend to hold all three of these attitudes at the same time. We want a child to be jug, clay and flower, and when it fails to live up to this we blame the child, or ourselves or, most frequently, the school.

Small is best?

Today, schools, particularly high schools, often have many pupils. The head of one rural school pointed out that a child from his school, with 31 pupils, would transfer to the local high school some distance away, with 2,750. The size of schools is a hotly-contended area of educational politics. Parents tend to favor small schools, which they see as a more intimate, friendly institution. Administrators favor the large school, claiming both the economies of scale that apply in other industries and the possibility of a wider range of subject expertise. Small size is seen as an advantage in the private sector of education and as an anachronism in the public sector. It is only publicly funded schools that are closed because of their small size.

Research into the relationship between school size and educational performance is hard to conduct, partly because we are not all agreed on what we expect of schools and partly because of differences in the social class and home

USING THE FLOORSCAPE

■ *Some teachers seize the learning opportunities provided by the fact that children's eyes are closer to the ground. Here, a creative use of carpeting in the open-plan kindergarten of Chicago Lakes Primary School in Minnesota keeps children in close touch with numbers and the alphabet.*

In an inner city district of Worcester, Massachusetts, in the 1970s, geographer Roger Hart and his class of seven and eight-year-olds built up a map of the city on the classroom floor using aerial photographs. Hart asked the children to bring in their matchbox-toy model cars, made on an appropriate scale for the maps. Everyone then set out to find the way to the city center on the floor-map. This led them into problems of traffic congestion and of finding a place to park. It also resulted in crashes and the need to get an ambulance through the traffic and back to the hospital.

Other primary schools use an outsize ruler printed on a plastic groundsheet for teaching basic arithmetic. The distance between the numbers is about the length of a child's stride. Children can learn to add and subtract in a way that naturally appeals to them, by walking up and down the ruler.

ARE YOU SITTING COMFORTABLY?

■ *In the earliest schools the pupils sat in a ring around the teacher (1). When teaching became routine pupils were arranged in rows in front of the teacher (2). In the modern primary school the teacher wanders among pupils working* *in groups (3). In the modern secondary school the class may be arranged like a board-room (4), with the teacher in the chair. In a seminar (5), a student reports to the class, with the teacher as one member of the group.*

background of pupils. One of the most significant pieces of experimental research on the effect of school size on children was carried out in the United States and repeated in Canada, and on a smaller scale in Cheshire, England. Results showed that in large schools there was a wider range of activities and that the best pupils achieved higher results than pupils in small schools. The advantage of small schools, however, was that their pupils took part in more activities – both academic and extracurricular. Pupils were generally more motivated and scored higher in versatility and performance.

The almighty wall

The school is the daily environment of children for only a few years, but those years are vital and their effects last for a lifetime. For teachers, the school is the environment for their whole working lifetime. In the 19th century, Edward Thring, a famous head teacher in Britain, described the classroom as the "Almighty Wall," pointing out that "no living power in the world can overcome the dead, unfeeling, everlasting pressure of the permanent structures, of the permanent conditions, under which work has to be done." He was referring to the fact that the physical fabric of any institution can depersonalize those who work in it and restrict their activities.

Most people at work, even in the most computerized office environment or factory work-station on an assembly line, instinctively personalize their workspace. Railwaymen have their own shacks by the trackside, truck drivers decorate their cabs. Teachers, too, stamp their style on their sur-

roundings, if only by filling a cupboard with the books that are important to them and having the materials they use around them. Language teachers, for example, often surround the room with posters, printed matter and objects evoking the culture of another country. This reminds pupils that real people speak the language in a real context and that it is worth knowing. Art and craft teachers may enjoy filling their workshop with things that provide a justification for the skills they try to pass on.

To counteract the possible negative effects of bricks and mortar, schools and colleges in different countries and with different ages of children operate in a variety of ways. The movement around the school building, or complex, is the first thing any visitor notices. Sometimes the pupils move to the home-bases of particular teachers; sometimes the teachers move with their personal equipment from room to room; and sometimes the rooms themselves (workshops, art rooms, laboratories, gymnasia) are filled with the equipment for a specialist field of learning.

Do open-plan designs work?

Over the last 30 years there has been a trend toward doing away with the almighty wall wherever possible. The desire for a more free-flowing school design led first to the

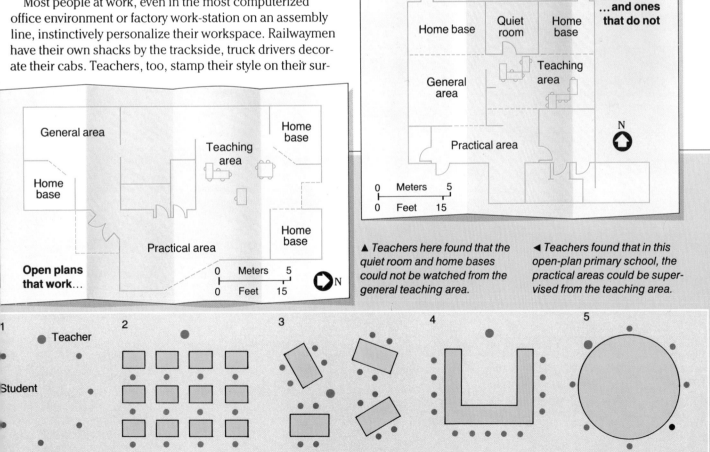

Open plans that work...

▲ Teachers here found that the quiet room and home bases could not be watched from the general teaching area.

◀ Teachers found that in this open-plan primary school, the practical areas could be supervised from the teaching area.

205

development of open-plan primary schools. Besides being less expensive, the new plans cut out the wasted space of corridors. They are arranged to give each teacher and class a home base separated only by furniture and cupboards from a series of activity areas through which the children move from one lesson to another.

Researchers have studied whether the open-plan layout works, and whether children and teachers like it. One group of British researchers looked at classes of five to seven-year-olds in open-plan schools and found that teachers there spent less time actually talking to pupils and more time on the routine of school management. They also found that the children spent less time talking to one another, and spent more time than children in ordinary classrooms in taking an interest in what the teacher was doing, and in the work and the activities of other pupils. The open plan made no difference to their progress in basic skills.

Another study found that only a third of teachers in open-plan schools actually like them; that they are more stressful to work in; and also that pupils in open-plan primary schools could spend one-quarter of their day tidying up, moving from one activity to another, or waiting around. Perhaps the popularity of the open plan depends on each individual's personal psychology, just as it does in offices (see Ch 24). It is possible that extroverts enjoy continual interaction with others, while introverts prefer and need a secure enclosed "nest."

Both studies found that there are good and bad designs for open-plan primary schools, and that their effectiveness depended on the extent to which the general working area could be supervised from the home base. This is a natural response from teachers, who are paid to supervise what happens in schools, but who are not usually consulted about their design.

206

▲ **Playground space** is essential to school design, because children have short attention spans and plenty of physical energy. If they are required to sit in one place for 45 minutes concentrating on one topic, they must have time afterward to shout and talk. Those who want to chat quietly or read a book need a lounge or library to relax in.

Schools or prisons?

However sensitively and imaginatively schools are designed, many children still hate them. One reason for this is that, because we are there under compulsion, schools are different from any other human environment except one – prisons. Even in the wealthiest countries there is always a proportion of children who evade school as much as they can, and do their best to disrupt its workings and destroy its premises. School vandalism and school arson, as well as endless theft of salable equipment from schools, present a difficult and very expensive problem for the education authorities.

Ironically, in poorer countries, with an acute lack of buildings, books or equipment, or the money to pay teachers, education is often seen as something precious to be striven for at any cost. When Kenya was struggling for independence from British rule in the 1950s there was a period known as the Mau-Mau Emergency, when the British army rounded up huge numbers of men and boys as sus-

DESIGNED TO MAKE LEARNING ATTRACTIVE

■ *While school buildings cannot overcome all the obstacles that may prevent school being enjoyable and appreciated, they can certainly play a part. There should, for example, be enough space for children to pursue different activities at different times.*

Color can play an important part in stimulating or calming pupils. Buildings painted in dull colors are more likely to be disliked by both teachers and pupils. Stimulation can be overdone, however, and a vibrant environment may hinder rather than help the learning process. Warm colors and elaborate decor should be reserved for rooms that need to be stimulating, such as those where the subjects taught are repetitive and do not demand concentrated effort. Cooler colors can be used where the subjects taught require concentration or are themselves highly stimulating.

Furniture affects attitudes toward school and a child's ability to study. An office worker is rarely expected to sit uncomfortably and still keep alert, so why should we expect children to be able to perform well in run-down schools with uncom- *fortable furniture? Environments like this can only exacerbate the poor image some children have of school.*

It also helps if the surroundings are pleasant. Many schools now have large windows that look out onto a natural environment with grass and trees.

Children make a lot of noise, and schoolrooms and corridors often magnify and the sounds of scraping chairs, feet, and high-pitched voices. With careful design of furniture and floor coverings they do not need to.

Crowding is another problem in corridors. They must be wide enough to take the flow without crush, but research on crowding shows that, generally, smaller corridors do not feel as crowded as larger ones.

Children are impressionable and easily led into imitation of behavioral models. Since schools presumably try to present them with standards to which they should conform, it is important that a school provides children with a decent environment. By its very existence, a well-designed school can teach that surroundings can be desirable, attractive, soothing and even elegant. **RL**

pects and put them in camps surrounded by barbed wire. To occupy their time, an army captain organized them into houses and classes according to age, and appointed his soldiers and the older boys to be teachers of reading, writing and arithmetic. Fortunately, his solution worked too well: beyond the barbed wire crowds of parents and children demanded that they too should be given this marvelous privilege – he had turned his prison into a school.

In the wealthier countries the tendency is to turn city schools into prisons. Vandal-proof buildings are designed, with no windows or destructible surfaces and furniture, reversing the trends of the last hundred years. Policemen stalk the corridors. But often it is all in vain – those who

want to can still destroy the school and many more can find ingenious ways of staying away.

What the pupils want

Would children reject school less often if they were consulted more? Schoolchildren are not often asked for their ideas about the design of school buildings. When they are, the most frequent comment they make is on the *squareness* of schools – they object to the fact that almost all schools are simply an assemblage of rectangular blocks. Instead, they ask for round schools, domes, or irregular and irrational buildings. They want unexpected corners and more color and excitement in their surroundings. They also

◄ **Study-hall policeman.** *For generations, the "pion," who has no teaching duties, has been a fixture of the French schoolchild's learning environment. Every school has several, to supervise the study hall, corridors, the lunch room, playgrounds and, in boarding schools, the dormitories.*

▲ **Schools are prison-like.** *Like convicts, schoolchildren are compelled to be where they are. This basic fact spawns negative associations in their minds – a fence erected to prevent playing children from running into a busy street can appear enclosing. The school-bus, with its routines and its inevitable destination, can seem regimenting.*

ask, reasonably enough, for basic comforts: moderate temperatures, sound proofing, adequate furniture and common rooms where they can be at ease. When school surroundings were discussed, several explorations of the opinions of children in Britain and the United States showed a universal desire for trees. One child wrote, "There should be places of darkness and light, of grass and of earth."

Alternative solutions

Policing or punitive attempts to keep children in school are negative responses to the problem. But, on the other hand, there have been attempts to create alternatives to schools. Some dedicated teachers have turned the "Sin Bin" or truant center into a place of learning for people who have rejected school. The examples that have actually worked share several characteristics. The first is that they are small and not like school. They may be a club set up in a private house or a lock-up store. The second is that they are built around the needs of an individual child, not around a school subject transmitting a body of learning. The third is that they depend on a direct, person-to-person relationship between the teacher and the pupil. In many cases, the small, personal environment has been successful where the impersonality of the large school has failed.

Schools without walls

In the 19th century, the novelist Leo Tolstoy decided to start a school in his Russian village, so he toured around schools in Germany, France and Britain. His conclusion was that "Education is an attempt to control what goes on spontaneously in culture: it is culture under restraint." In the French city of Marseilles he went to every school and talked to children and parents. He found that schools were prison-like buildings with children mechanically learning the con-

tents of their books without being able to read, spell or add up anything else.

How then did people become educated? Tolstoy found the answer after school, wandering around the city itself, its cafés, museums, workshops, quays and bookstalls. He found that real education came from the environment.

He eventually contributed to education by teaching on his estate and by starting 12 schools.

More than a century later, Western educators rediscovered this message. Known as the "Deschoolers," they included Ivan Illich in Mexico, John Holt, Paul Goodman and Everett Reimer in the United States. They set up "storefront schools" using vacant shops as teaching places, or they developed "learning networks" through which people seeking some particular knowledge could acquire it from a practitioner. They also invented the "School Without Walls," using the city itself as the means of teaching children. In the 1960s the Parkway Education Program in Philadelphia set up a home base, with office space for staff and lockers for pupils, and then sent art students to the Art Museum, biologists to the Zoo, mechanics to a garage and business students aged between 14 and 18 to offices and newspapers. In Chicago, in the Metro High School, pupils were similarly sent by bus and the subway and elevated railways to the places where they could learn from the city itself. Métro Education Montréal exploited the city's underground railway to give rapid access to a variety of under-used facilities throughout the city center: empty cinemas, vacant office space, unexploited computer centers, parks, restaurants, libraries, clinics and laboratories.

All the resources for learning were there already, but these activities contradicted a century of increased special-

---

A PLACE THAT IS VALUED

■ In their infant years, many children look forward to going to school. Many adolescents, however, yearn to leave it – they want to be streetwise. In the poorer countries where children gain their street wisdom at an early age, they usually value schooling – for them it ends all too soon.

■ In the 1970s the United Nations funded a project, which attempted to evaluate the relationship between children and their urban surroundings. Children aged 11 to 14 were studied. Researchers found that the children in the richest group, from an Australian

suburb, lived in an environment where they were suffering from "experiential starvation"– they were starved of experiences. They attended an architect-designed school with the usual range of specialist rooms and equipment but had no love for it, and would have preferred to be somewhere else.

■ The poorest group in the survey were the children of a squatter settlement outside Mexico City whose environment seemed to be harsh, bleak and monotonous. But the investigators found that these children, whose school had been built by the efforts of their

own community, lovingly referred to it as their favorite place. The researchers concluded that this must be a tribute to the public education system in that unofficial settlement. However, it is more likely

◄ One of the most valued buildings in the community, this simple cement-block construction represents opportunity to Eritrean refugees in the Sudan. In affluent countries, children often reject schools that are architect-designed and expensively equipped.

---

to be an indication that the schoolrooms, crudely built of concrete blocks, were appreciated because of the citizens' own labor and belief in education. Because educational opportunities were limited and the school existed as a result of their involvement, they put a high value on education.

ization in school design and demanded a high degree of organization and stage-management beyond the normal expectations of teachers. Education authorities, with huge budgets to consider, and the expectations of parents, could not cope with the experiments in deschooling.

Community education

Is it possible to make some kind of compromise between the radical ideas of the deschoolers and our own expectations of education? A variety of educational thinkers have seen schools as part of the learning or leisure resources for the whole community. As schools become bigger and more expensively equipped, it seems absurd to reserve them for the use of only one section of the population for only part of the day, part of the week and part of the year. This view is supported by authorities on vandalism who urge that school buildings should be kept open as long as possible out of school hours, so that people are there continually.

This approach sees the school no longer as an isolated building surrounded by playground and fences, but as a community facility, set among stores and public buildings. There is no school hall: a hall used for every purpose by the public is also used by the school. There is no dining hall: the children use a café open to the public and behave accordingly. There is no gymnasium: the school uses the sports hall open to all. And there is no school library: the public library has a far greater stock. Classrooms and laboratories are scattered among the stores and offices and shared with other organizations. As a result, the daily lives of the community and its children are inextricably mixed, just as they were in previous centuries.

In such a plan, the traditional distinctions between the different stages of schooling are equally blurred: day nursery, infant and junior school, high school, college and adult education centers all use the same environment.

However, integrating a school into the community in this way requires an immense effort. One scheme which has succeeded is the Abraham Moss Centre in Manchester, England. Here the difficulties are not due to design, since teaching and learning can occur in any kind of environment. Problems arise because of compartmentalization and the different pay-scales of the public and private bodies involved. But the idea that a school is not a special place, but simply a particular user of public space, is gaining support in several countries. Its advantages include an improvement in children's attitudes toward the community and in the attitude of the community toward its children. It provides a model for education in the 21st century. **CW**

■ **Places that teach us**. *Our environment is richly supplied with places and things worth learning about. Many of them have been specially designed or adapted to serve us in this way, such as the goat farm* RIGHT *that doubles as a tourist attraction.* LEFT *Visitors admire old and new feats of architecture at the Louvre Museum in Paris. Increasingly, schools themselves are seen as inadequate – the school trip has become an essential technique for putting children in direct contact with the world they are learning about. It also teaches them about opportunities for learning that can be exploited throughout life.*

Going Shopping

SHOPPING is a pleasure for some, a chore for others, but for most people it is necessary. Whether we enjoy it or not depends partly on our personality and on what we are shopping for – the weekly visit to the food store can soon lose its appeal. However, it also depends on the kind of places we shop in. Markets, shopping centers, local stores all have their own advantages and drawbacks. Most of us are aware of how advertising and packaging can affect our choices of goods, but are probably less aware of the extent to which the shopping environments themselves – their location, arrangement and design – can shape our behavior.

The self-service revolution

In the first half of the 20th century shopping was part of a communal lifestyle. Although those who could afford it still tended to have goods delivered, stores were within walking distance of the home. Shopping meant seeing and being seen by neighbors, and talking to friends. The storekeepers themselves were often friends.

Since most people did not have the means to transport large quantities of goods, and since food could not be stored for long periods, it was necessary to shop frequently. As a result, daily life was in some respects more public, sociable and community-oriented than it is now. These social advantages were accompanied by disadvantages – limited choice, drudgery, lack of privacy – but there was no alternative to local shopping (except for the very rich).

It was not until the Depression of the 1930s that self-service food stores began to appear in the United States. These could keep prices low by allowing the public to do the work formerly done by storekeepers or their staff. In order to have lower prices than a local store, a self-service store with the same number of staff has to be considerably larger. A pattern began to emerge whereby stores were fewer, larger and further apart. Shopping became less sociable as it became more convenient for people to shop by car, buying more per trip, and to shop less frequently.

Once the pattern of shopping for food more infrequently by car was established, the scene was set for the introduction of the shopping center – a group of stores under the same roof or in the same location, sometimes serving an entire region containing thousands of people. In the United States these developed out of town. They were able to offer their customers better parking facilities and easier access. Once the food store made a location attractive, the opportunity was there to incorporate a variety of other stores and customers were offered more choice and, thanks to shared overheads, lower prices.

The planned shopping center – whether in town or outside – differs greatly from the group of stores that may have evolved over many years. In the first place, in order to encourage and to facilitate the maximum amount of spending it will have been designed to control the flow of people – ensuring that they move in particular directions. The food

UNDERSTANDING CONSUMERS

■ *Retailers and producers took an early interest in trying to explain our shopping choices for sound commercial reasons. It was in their interests to try to find out, for example, why we bought one product or brand rather than another. Knowing this would enable them to persuade us to choose their goods rather than a competitor's, or to use their shops rather than the others.*

In 1957 Vance Packard's book "The Hidden Persuaders" described how the findings of psychology were being used and developed to sell not just products, but also ideas and attitudes. Both producers and retailers were investing heavily in what was called motivational research, or simply MR, in an attempt to gain insights into people's desires and drives,

and so to enable product designers and advertisers to appeal directly to our hidden needs and desires.

But this psychological explanation cannot fully account for the way shoppers actually behave. It does not, for instance, tell us why different cultures shop for different goods in different ways. Nor can it explain major changes that have occurred in our shopping habits since the 1930s.

A different approach was suggested by Mary Douglas and Baron Isherwood in their book "The World of Goods." Looking at products in the context of social life, they argued that we use them to build a world which makes sense to us; in other words, we use them to construct and represent a particular lifestyle. Sometimes this

will mean making ourselves distinctive through what we buy: we use purchases to set up fences between ourselves and others. Sometimes it might mean conforming to the expectations of others: we use purchases to build social bridges.

To some extent we behave in an automatic way – rather like bees in a beehive. But, in addition, we are individuals, family groups, classes, subcultures, cultures and so on. Some societies are still relatively stable and unchanging. Others allow individuals to act as a motor for change in concert with an economic system which feeds on these changes. So, when we go shopping we behave both as part of a society that determines some of our attitudes and also as individuals, free to make choices. **AA**

The places where you shop can shape your behavior and affect your lifestyle ■ *Are you being manipulated by well-planned stores and shopping centers?* ■ *Or are you exercising your own choice?*

"WHY I LIKE TO SHOP AT THE CORNER"

◆ Shopping every day gives me fresh food every day
◆ Personal contact with the storekeeper makes the atmosphere more friendly
◆ You can save money on fuel by walking
◆ It is easier to find or ask for what you want
◆ It is more conveniently located if you run out of anything

211

"WHY I SHOP AT THE SUPERMARKET"

◆ There is a wider choice
◆ It is a one-stop shopping trip
◆ It is cheaper to shop in bulk
◆ Shopping less often gives you more free time
◆ Parking facilities close by mean it is easy to load the car afterward
◆ You can browse, linger and change your mind

■ **Convenient shopping, or personal contact?** *This super-market in San Diego* LEFT *is an extreme example of the larger-scale, cheaper, more efficient way of shopping that has emerged since the 1930s. Huge bags of popcorn and soap can be purchased on the same bill as a tree for the garden, a spare tire and a life-size toy sheep. This sort of choice is not available in a street market in France* ABOVE *but the market has the advantages of a more friendly, intimate atmosphere.*

store – the main purpose for the center – is usually placed nearest the parking lot, and as you arrive you often bypass it, buying a shopping cart full of food last of all so that you can easily push it back to the car. You are likely to start with the various smaller stores selling speciality goods. Even if you are not already planning to buy something at one of these, you may be tempted to do so as you pass by.

Flows and magnets

At the far end from the parking lot there may be a department store – a shopping center within a shopping center – which will sell many of the items on an average shopping list. The department store is an example of what psychologists call a magnet. These magnets are placed so as to draw shoppers from the parking area past smaller stores. Magnets may also be branches of larger chain stores or they may be an existing town-center shopping area. They all act as attractions – either because of the range of goods they sell or because they are well-established and familiar. Without realizing it, we are being manipulated: by positioning these magnets in a sequence, each 200-250m (660-820ft) apart, developers aim to maximize the pedestrian flows past storefronts on each side. We are encouraged to keep to a straight and narrow path. Too much choice of route would dilute the pedestrian flow.

A typical shopping center might consist of stores facing onto a mall, with a glazed roof to protect shoppers from rain and heat. Above the stores are offices and perhaps a public service center; below are service and storage areas. Tenants are usually responsible for installing storefronts and store fittings. In commercial terms these centers are often successful. There is seldom difficulty in renting or leasing shops and they are usually busy. And yet, despite the care which has gone into the design, some people find this kind of modern shopping center soulless.

Has shopping become more impersonal?

If we do not have much time, the convenience of a shopping center is an advantage – the pedestrian flows from parking lot to magnets help to keep us to our tasks. If we have plenty of time, however, we may choose an older shopping area – perhaps with narrow curved streets and a more haphazard design – or a market. Here people tend to eddy untidily from store to store or stall to stall. In a covered market there are many stalls attracting our attention. There

212

■ **Shopping centers control the flow of traffic.** *ABOVE RIGHT A typical floor plan for a shopping center: the parking structure, a starting point for much of the pedestrian traffic that will pass through the center, is positioned at one end. Shoppers are channeled toward magnets at the other end –* *such as department stores and the town center. They pass all the smaller shops, making it worthwhile for these outlets to rent the space. ABOVE LEFT An example of a multi-story center, in which this directed flow is repeated on several floors, ensuring a more economical use of expensive land.*

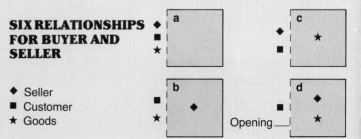

SIX RELATIONSHIPS FOR BUYER AND SELLER

◆ Seller
■ Customer
★ Goods

THE APPEAL OF A COVERED MARKET

■ *Covered markets are found in many of the older towns in Europe and are also common in South East Asia. The narrow passages and small stores – most of them open-fronted – create a more traditional setting where personal contact is important. While some of the market shops have sophisticated displays, others are more amateurish, with untidy arrangements of goods and hand-lettered labels; all of this may make us feel that shopping here is a more personal experience.*

An older covered market is also likely to be more stimulating to the senses. Flowers and fresh, or freshly cooked, food provide a range of appealing smells. Because the shops are small, there appears to be a greater variety of goods and of color, shape and texture. Interestingly, when people were asked to compare the shoes on sale in a British shopping center with shoes in a nearby town market, they felt that the market offered a greater range, though this was not in fact the case. Displays may add to the sense of variety in a covered market – there may be meat hanging from hooks, bunches of bags or baskets suspended from a ceiling or hanging flower baskets. While price and the freshness of local produce are strong attractions, shopping in a covered market is, for many people, as much an enjoyable experience as a necessity. **AA**

are many ways in and out, and there are many diversions.

The way that modern, large-scale stores are managed tends to make shopping a more impersonal experience. Department stores, chain stores and supermarkets are owned and managed quite differently from a small local store. It is less common, for example, for the owner and the storekeeper or manager to be the same person, and we are less likely to know store managers personally. We do not meet the butcher or the grocer, we meet assistants – often young people who are not well paid. Staff in large stores have less reason, and perhaps less opportunity, than the owner of a small store to take a personal interest in their customers. Also, because there is usually a high turnover of staff, we rarely get to know the people who serve us and it is less common to stop and exchange pleasantries with them.

■ **Traditional markets are less regimented.** *The floor plan of the covered market in Oxford, England* BELOW *established in the 1880s, shows how this type of arrangement allows the flow of shoppers to eddy undirected from stall to stall. At any given intersection shoppers have a choice of avenues.* RIGHT *Shoppers in the Oxford covered market at one of the intersections.*

◄ **How buyer and seller meet.** *Some relationships between buyer and seller are more equal than others. Here are six examples, listed in order from most to least equal. All six are common in markets, but in many shopping centers only* **e** *and* **f** *are common. In situation* **a** *the customer, the goods and* the seller are all in a public space, on equal ground – eg at a sidewalk fruit stand. In **b** the buyer and the goods (eg a rack of toys) are on the outside of the store or stall and the seller is inside. In **c**, the seller is outside with the customer, who might be pointing out goods inside an open booth, which only the seller enters. A sandwich bar might be an example of **d**, in which the customer is on the outside and the seller and goods are inside an opening. In **e** the customer is outside, windowshopping. In **f** customer, goods and seller are all inside the seller's territory.*

The relationship between the retailers and their goods has also changed. Compared to the modern store manager, owners of small stores are usually more closely involved with the goods they sell, in most cases being personally responsible for choosing, buying and displaying them. Many stallholders on markets still have this kind of close involvement with their stock.

Finally, the degree of personal contact between retailer and shopper can be minimized or maximized by the store-fronts. These are the interfaces between a seller (whether a storekeeper, manager or assistant) and a buyer, as well as between a buyer and the goods for sale. Shopping centers are more likely to have glazed storefronts. This arrangement favors the seller as the transaction occurs within his domain. Small, open-fronted stores and market stalls seem less intimidating and more welcoming since contact between buyer and seller and between buyer and goods is more immediate.

Shopping centers change neighborhoods

As our lifestyles have changed – for example, with the advent of the car, the effort to save time, the boom in con-sumer spending – so the shopping center has become a standard feature in many countries. The growth of these centers has affected our environment in various ways. The first concern of developers is to locate shopping centers in relation to potential demand and the costs of development. A less expensive site, for example, will take priority over one that elderly people or children can easily reach on foot.

In some cases planning constraints have limited shopping-center developments to an existing town center. This can produce complex consequences. One of the most direct is the arrival in the town center of its largest single building in terms of ground space. Because the designers are aiming to create the right flow of pedestrians, storefronts face inward onto a mall. All that passersby see are the huge, blank backs of the buildings – making the surrounding streets desolate and even unsafe places to be.

During shopping hours the spaces lined with stores are crowded with pedestrians and cars are probably excluded, but the rest of the town center is empty of pedestrians and full of cars. The neighborly contacts of traditional shopping and the varied design of the old-fashioned market are exchanged for cars and crowds. Since the shops are closed at night and on Sundays, and there are often no other uses for the center, it becomes bleak and lifeless, an inviting scene for crime (see *Ch 21*). A common solution is to close off these areas outside opening hours. This means that part of the city center becomes controlled access and there may even be security guards in evidence.

Because shopping centers have developed mainly on out-of-town sites, trade and thus social life have been drawn away from surrounding downtown areas. In some towns, attempts are being made to revive these traditional areas but what usually results is a kind of stage-set environment where stores are artificially traditional in every way – except in their prices.

Whether the shopping center is in or out of town, how-

◄ **Turning their backs on their surroundings**, *most shopping centers face inward, and save their attractions for those who enter. Neighbors are left with an unappealing townscape on their doorsteps – featureless rear walls and acres of parking lot. When centers close at night and on Sundays they become bleak and deserted, and so may encourage crime. Shopping centers developed on out-of-town sites may draw business and social life away from downtown areas, working a negative effect on these more distant areas of the city in turn.*

ever, the consequences are similar. The concentration of shopping means that other areas lack stores; residential areas and working areas become more segregated and this in turn affects our behavior. If a residential area has nothing but houses, then apart from visiting the homes of nearby friends, there are few reasons to go out on foot and so the majority of journeys are made by car. As a result, public space is dominated by cars. Measures to slow traffic down and make roads safer become necessary. Quite often the solution is to separate vehicles and pedestrians – footpaths take shortcuts which can be isolated and dangerous at night.

The relationship between our lifestyles and the places we shop is a circular one. Changes in the development of shopping facilities which have met our needs and preferences have in turn affected our social and community lifestyles. Perhaps the reintroduction of small food stores that open for longer hours seven days a week and serve local needs, is a reaction against the dominance of large shopping centers. **AA**

THE ENTERTAINMENT VALUE OF SHOPPING CENTERS

■ Increasingly, modern shopping centers are being planned with entertainment in mind. This shopping mall in Edmonton, Canada, doubles as a fun park, with central areas given over to elaborate amusements. Stores are located around the edges. Other entertainment in shopping centers includes libraries, theaters, health studios, restaurants and cafés, bars and discotheques, even ice rinks.

There are three main advantages to having such facilities. From the point of view of the store owners, they attract more shoppers to the center and encourage them to spend more time there – and probably more money as well. They make shopping a family affair as parents are more likely to take their children shopping with them. A shopping center with leisure activities may also open in the evenings or on Sundays, rather than becoming a deserted and useless place whenever its stores are closed.

We are more likely to associate shopping with fun in shopping centers that have interesting decorative features such as fountains, musical clocks, floral displays, play areas for children, or glass-sided elevators which are not only useful but also provide a fun ride. At Christmas, particularly, the range of decorative possibilities in a shopping center may be considerable.

DRAWING CUSTOMERS INSIDE

■ Although the overall design of a shopping center may lack the personal contact and the variety provided by a market, the interior of a well-planned store – whether or not it is part of such a center – will attract us in a number of subtle ways and encourage us to spend money. Heating and lighting, for example, can make a store a pleasant or unpleasant place to be. On cold days, a well-heated entrance is welcoming, giving us a positive feeling about the store from the moment we enter it. Lighting should not be so bright or glaring that it is uncomfortable and should be arranged so that it makes the products look as attractive as possible. Special lighting toward the rear of a store can help to draw us in further. Store designers are often careful to light mirrors in a way that is flattering to customers.

The layout of a store is equally important. Many department stores try to avoid the "gridiron" pattern that is often used in traditional markets. With a freer, less regimented layout we move around the store without having to make conscious decisions about whether to turn right or left – the idea is that we will be more relaxed and so more receptive to displays.

Decisions about where to display which goods may also be influenced by psychological considerations. In general, the most attractive, luxury items – the "impulse" goods that we probably do not visit the store specifically to buy – are placed where we cannot avoid seeing them – usually toward the front of the store so that we have to walk past them to reach the more commonplace "demand" items. The way that the goods are displayed may also encourage us to spend. Larger stores often use the comparatively modern idea of thematic displays or displays that show the goods in context.

For example, rather than there just being a collection of kitchen furniture and accessories, complete kitchens are set up. Many people then buy the whole thing, saving themselves the trouble of deciding which items to combine. This kind of display also encourages us to buy items we might otherwise overlook or get along without. The display of items according to

their separate categories tends to break down our associations. Displaying them in their proper context, however, shows them as we are used to seeing them. It may also make the store seem more relaxing since, like our homes, it is divided into "rooms."

Often, tricks of display persuade us to buy more than we originally intended. The behaviorist psychologist John Watson was the first to suggest the idea of putting candy and other small items near the checkout in supermarkets. This is a perfect example of the right product being displayed at the right point in the store. Because they are inexpensive, we may be tempted by them as we wait. The novelty of this technique has now worn off to some extent, although many stores continue to use it. One major supermarket chain found that there was a certain amount of customer resistance, partly because the customers recognized that they were being manipulated.

IS A CHANGE AS GOOD AS A REST?

Above all, stores need to arouse our interest in what they are selling. Regularly changing displays and the layout of the store is one way of doing this because it encourages us to look around shelves that contain items we were not actually trying to find. However, it is counterproductive if we are frustrated by our inability to find what we did come to buy.

Whether novelty pays off generally depends on the type of products being sold and the type of customers using the store: in a store where the customers are usually rushing in to get something and have no desire to linger, the value of changing everything around will be lower than if the customer has time to browse.

Special seasonal displays – particularly for Christmas – are effective because they provide both novelty and familiarity.

The same thing happens every year and stores can even use the same or similar displays year after year – they maintain a degree of novelty because we have not seen them for some time.

Christmas displays also have a thematic content, so there is no need to create a special one, although some stores do build on particular aspects, such as food and drink. **RL**

▲ **Personal attention** *at Bloomingdales' cosmetics counter in New York. Large stores can sometimes offer more intimacy than small ones – for example, when they are able to employ a specialist cosmetician who, free of other duties, can spend time with a customer.*

◄ **Interiors are designed to draw us inside,** *creating an atmosphere in which we will want to buy. In Macy's in New York, shopping islands call to mind the informality of a market, creating a relaxed atmosphere which allows us to be more receptive to the goods on display.*

CREATING THE RIGHT INTERIOR ATMOSPHERE

■ *Stores that are aiming at a particular section of the market often have interiors that create an appropriate atmosphere. For example, a supermarket that is aiming at a high turnover with low profit margins and low overheads may be presented in the style of a warehouse. As well as cutting costs, a basic, functional interior gives shoppers the message that they are getting very good value for money precisely because the store has no frills. In contrast, someone who sets out to sell expensive evening dresses may be aiming at a low turnover but high profit per item. They may not have many customers but will need to persuade those*

they do have that they are getting a high quality product and are being given the attention and personal service that their spending potential entitles them to. In this kind of small, exclusive store the atmosphere of privilege and expense is all part of the package, because it underlines both the value of the goods for sale and the value of the customer.

Stores that emphasize value for money will have in-store advertisements giving details of discount items or credit terms. The exclusive store, on the other hand, will display prices in a discreet way – if at all – and will imply that customers are putting quality first. If we are

buying a refrigerator or washing machine we are looking for economy and reliability, not glamor or originality. If we are buying an expensive item of clothing, we are involved in an exercise of self-projection. Comfortable surroundings and a friendly atmosphere may almost make us forget that we are not obliged to choose any of the items on offer in this particular shop. Extreme deference may be paid to the customer and this will be reflected in plush decor and muted lighting. The items on display are carefully placed and it appears that everything is designed to enhance the customer's comfort. **RL**

Eating Out

WHY DO WE eat out when eating at home is certainly less expensive and probably more nutritious than a meal in a restaurant? The cooking is not always better than home cooking either. It is true that there will be no shopping, preparation, or washing up to do. But that is seldom the only or even the most important reason for going out.

A special occasion

Unless we are away from home on holiday or on a business trip, few of us eat out from necessity; dinner at a restaurant is usually a special occasion, a break from our everyday routine. All meals, to a greater or lesser extent may be seen as ceremonial events, but going out requires far more ceremony than staying in. Even if we do not go to an expensive restaurant, dining out is still an event that we spend money on, not so much for the sake of the food, as for the entertainment value. It is different enough from routine to be stimulating and refreshing. Children often seem to be aware of this and may be more easily persuaded to eat their food when they are out than when they are at home.

Eating at a restaurant requires a special effort. We have to get ready to go out, and the occasion is often marked by different behavior as well as different dress. An informal meal out may depart little from dinner at home – a visit to the local cafe or burger bar for a quick meal, for example. But even in these places, the experience of eating in public is likely to affect our behavior to some extent. Also, before we go out we have to make various decisions about where to go – what kind of food we want to eat and, depending on our mood and the nature of the occasion, the type of setting we prefer – this can matter just as much as the menu.

One major difference between eating out and eating in is that in a restaurant there is more choice. Even the humblest eating place has a choice of dishes on the menu, and this alone can provide interest that the home meal lacks. Also, however informal the restaurant is, behavior that may be tolerated at home will not be tolerated in public. A certain degree of restraint is required, particularly from the young, and this again serves to mark the occasion out as special. Many parents find that eating out is a useful socializing experience for young children.

Eating and role playing

One of the reasons we so enjoy eating out is that it gives us the chance to assume roles that are different from our normal ones. For example, we may enjoy indulging in junk

▲ **A quick snack lunch in an informal setting** *is the commonest type of meal eaten outside the home. We are unlikely to regard it as an occasion, since such a meal is eaten for convenience and is probably a part of the day's routine. Even in* the bitter cold of a Moscow winter these women are eating next to a fast food stall rather than in the comfort of a restaurant.

Are you dining out tonight? ■ *Do you do so often?* ■ *Why do people choose to dress up and leave their home comforts to go out in possibly inclement weather for a meal that may be no better than they could prepare themselves?*

food that we would normally condemn as unhealthy. Settings sometimes dictate the kind of food we permit ourselves to eat – hot dogs at a ball game or ice cream at the beach are more or less compulsory. Junk food may seem more acceptable if we indulge in it as part of a nostalgia for childhood – the time we were allowed treats. So giant sundaes and milk shakes or sloppy joes and hot dogs with all the trimmings are all right to eat so long as they are treated as fun food. The settings in which we can eat this kind of food vary from outdoor hot-dog stands to elaborate ice-cream parlors with bright plastic furniture and a battery of machines to produce the required combination of flavors. These are ostensibly for children but adults can eat there with no self-consciousness and without the excuse of accompanying children.

It is also fashionable deliberately to eat downmarket (see *Ch11*) – for example, eating the peasant or working-class food from many countries: the French bistro (once a working-class venue before it became a chic haunt for the middle classes) with its wonderful casseroles and biftek avec pommes frites; the Italian trattoria with cheap seafood, again gentrified in foreign settings; the incomparable diner in the United States; the grand fish and chip restaurant in the north of England; the beer and sausage halls in Germany; and the open-air food markets in many hot countries.

Conversely, eating "upmarket" allows us to assume a role above our normal station. If we dine away from our mundane environment, one of the reasons we may feel special is because we are being waited on. Waiting was once, and at its best still is, a profession requiring training and expertise. The tradition once found in the great eating establishments has been passed down to a large number of restaurants, and many waiters and waitresses are justly proud of their skills.

The attention we receive from good service matters because it allows us to feel spoiled, pampered and above all, important. After a day of working hard, having someone to attend to our needs in attractive, relaxing surroundings is a welcome indulgence. Generally, the more removed from eating at home we feel, the better we like it. It is pleasant to feel unique, and dining out is one way of achieving this. We have romantic dinners, birthday dinners, anniversary dinners, retirement dinners and they almost always take place outside our home or workplace, in the arena of public ritual.

THE TRADITION OF EATING OUT

■ *Throughout history most food has been made and consumed at home. Food was provided in inns and taverns for travelers who were served basically what would have been on the domestic table anyway.*

Regular eating out, and eating out for the sake of status with special foods reserved for the occasion is a West European and predominantly French custom that developed during the Industrial Revolution. The size of the cities that grew up in the 19th century presumably encouraged staying out for lunch. But why was it a French custom in the first place? The French upper classes had previously made a great public show of attending court or church. When both these institutions declined in importance after the revolution, attendance at great restaurants became a substitute. These were almost like renaissance palaces with vast, hierarchically organized kitchens and rigid and elaborate rules. It was here that restaurant waiting as a profession started and waiters were trained to the high standards of the great establishments.

Predictably, the habits of the upper classes came to be imitated by the bourgeoisie, and eating out became more commonplace in France and later spread to all other Western countries.

◄ **Celebrating an occasion** – such as a birthday or a promotion – by means of a meal out occurs only seldom and because it is unusual it helps us to commemorate the special event. We temporarily raise our status by surrounding ourselves with gourmet food, glamor, and personal attention – all of which are offered by the New York restaurant where these women begin a meal with smoked salmon.

It is not uncommon for a restaurant to provide a cake and singing waiters for their birthday client. Eating out to mark a special occasion makes a public announcement regarding your status – "I have a new girlfriend," "We have been married ten years," "I have finished working."

What am I paying for?

When we choose a special place to celebrate a promotion or take someone out for an intimate evening, it is not merely the food we consider. Of course the food has to be good, but the type of food is probably less important than the atmosphere of the place. The effect of setting is brought home by the example of two adjacent Indian restaurants in

A TASTE OF FOREIGN LANDS

■ *In the many migrations from country to country during the 20th century, dining out became a way for immigrants to keep their own culture. What started as cooking for each other has become a substantial industry of various ethnic eating places with a clientele far wider than the immigrants themselves. The Chinese led the way, usually in ports and bigger cities. Chinatowns were exotic and especially from the 1950s on, it became fashionable for non-Chinese to eat there in San Francisco and New York. The variety of Chinese cooking and its unusual use of ingredients made it highly popular. The fashion for dining out on Chinese cooking spread to other cities where "Chinese restaurant" had previously meant a place to get an inexpensive plate of meat and potatoes followed by apple pie, while in the kitchen, the proprietor and his family ate rice from bowls. The fashion spread to other countries, and Chinese families took the opportunity to open cafés in the most remote places.*

Why did they become so popular? In the first place, the food was comparatively cheap, which may account for it becoming the first "foreign" food to capture both the gourmet and popular market at the same time. Also, status distinctions can easily be made

between gourmet and mass taste so that food connoisseurs can pursue Hunan and Szechwan cooking and leave chow mein to the populace. But it cannot simply be cost or a concern for status that makes a person choose Mongolian beef over American charred steak. Perhaps eating foreign food is a form of armchair traveling, offering the excitement of an exotic land without the effort of actually visiting it.

What started with the Chinese has spread to a wide variety of immigrant cuisines. Even small towns in Europe and the United States now have many ethnic establishments where you can eat and drink. The way we eat now reflects the internationalizing trends in fashion generally. It gives us all a chance to display our cosmopolitanism in a world that values it more and more. We may order food in languages as different as Urdu, Thai, Cantonese, Italian, Arabic, Armenian and Hungarian, even if we speak none of them.

It is not surprising that the restaurant industry has created a subindustry of critics and restaurant writers who are attentively read and followed. Knowing a wonderful undiscovered Portuguese bistro is one way of persuading others that we are able to cope with our complex cosmopolitan civilization.

▲ **A taste of another nation's culture** *is provided by exotic food, at home or abroad.* MAIN PICTURE *This Japanese restaurant in Tianjin, China, is enjoyed both by the Chinese and by Western visitors.* INSET *In* Kuşadasi, Turkey, Turkish carpets and crockery and the Middle Eastern practice of sitting on cushions are probably more important than the food itself at this tea party for touris

London where the same kitchen served both and the food was identical. In the first clients clustered around communal long tables covered with oilcloth. The food was cheap and casually served, and music, recorded from local Indian movies, was loud.

In the other, there were curtains and carpets, a liquor license and good wine served by attentive, uniformed waiters. Quiet sitar music played in the background and the tables had immaculate white linen. The food – exactly the same as in the other restaurant – was four times the price, yet many diners at the less expensive restaurant longed to eat here. If they had had the money they would have been prepared to pay for the more luxurious ambience.

▲ **The East adopts Western tastes** *just as readily as the West has taken to oriental food. American sundaes are served amid American decor – only the Asian faces of the assistants (in* American uniforms plus face-masks for hygiene) give us a clue to this ice-cream parlor's real location: Singapore.

BURGERS IN TOKYO

■ The fast-food restaurant has been remarkably successful. One American burger chain has the fastest growing franchise in Japan, and has extended its operations to China. When it first opened in Tokyo it sold so many burgers so fast that the cash registers burned out from excess use. A fried chicken chain is having similar success in Peking, and in Berlin it is the chic place to eat among the young. The meals that fast-food chains sell are simple and predictable: hamburgers, hot dogs, pizza and fried chicken are found almost anywhere. Nevertheless, fast-food restaurants have changed eating habits in many parts of the world. Why are they so popular, particularly among the young? Certainly prices are reasonably low and meals are available almost instantly, both obvious attractions. But the ambience, too, probably accounts for a large part of their popularity. The surroundings are imper- sonal – you could equally well be in Singapore, Paris, or Vancouver. In complete contrast to expensive restaurants which attract customers by making them feel specially privileged, fast-food restaurants are neutral ground – places where everyone is treated equally.

Why decor matters

Different settings are suitable for different occasions. If you are taking a client out for a business lunch, the best choice will be a small quiet restaurant with well spaced tables so that no one can be overheard, whereas a large noisy café with large tables and unfussy table settings would be a more obvious choice for teenagers meeting before a movie. Secluded seating and spacing are also more suitable for a romantic dinner, as opposed to a bar, for instance, that is designed for sociability and interaction. If you have young children, however, the most suitable table plan may be one where tables are divided from each other by benched seating so that the children's manners and loud voices will not intrude on other diners. To be avoided are carefully set tables with lots of glass and cutlery on crisp white damask tablecloths.

The type of lighting used in a restaurant attracts particular clients. If you are having a business lunch you will need bright but not garish light. You may need to look at papers and you should be able to see the other person's face so that you can read their moods and intentions. On the other hand, a dim candlelit atmosphere conducive to quiet, intimate conversation would more likely be your choice for a romantic dinner. Lighting also affects how long we stay in a place. Generally, the brighter the light in a restaurant, the more noisy the clients become and the quicker people leave. A restaurateur who wants people to come in, spend their money and go, will use bright lights and not concern himself too much with soundproofing. But if the idea is that clients stay all evening, dim lights and sound-absorbing surfaces are best. The low lights encourage greater intimacy between couples and so the seating capacity can be increased. This type of restaurant is unlikely to attract people who want a meal before going to the theater as service will no doubt be slow and leisurely.

The furniture used in a restaurant will also dictate the type of client it attracts. Wicker furniture with ferns and plants creates an informal setting that suggests a casual lunch with a friend, for example. But thick carpets, heavy drapes and brocade furniture – somewhat reminiscent of a bedroom – are designed for romance. Such decor is also sound-absorbing and therefore likely to keep clients there longer.

One of the greatest determinants of the average age of patrons is the type of music played. Music is largely responsible for creating a mood and the manager of a restaurant with dim lighting, intimate tables and thick carpets would never indulge their own personal taste for rock music or Heavy Metal. There is more likely to be a pianist playing Cole Porter or Gershwin. Conversely, the muzak emanating from fast-food restaurants fits in well with the ambience of anonymity. It evokes no emotion and creates no mood. Ethnic restaurants do the opposite. They usually promote their own culture's music so that clients may almost feel they are in Portugal as they listen to Fado, or in Indonesia as they listen to the Legong.

Keeping the customers moving

The kind of people who go to a particular restaurant is also influenced by where it is situated and what it looks like from the outside. However, there are many subtleties that restaurateurs use to bring us in, keep us there or hurry us

■ **Neon lights and juke box** and even period advertising posters ABOVE contribute to this restaurant's self-conscious image: the 1950s recreated. Nostalgia? Unlikely, since the people eating here are too young to remember the fifties. Like eating foreign foods, visiting a period restaurant gives us a glimpse of a lifestyle different from our own. Austerity is another option for chic restaurateurs RIGHT, with just the abstract drawings to remind us that starkness is here dictated by taste not just economy.

out. When Danish café owners approached a furniture designer to help them cope with the problem of customers lingering over their coffee, the designer created a chair which puts unpleasant pressure on the spine if occupied for more than a few minutes. The chair is now marketed in the United States. And hoteliers have also realized that when planning new hotels they must not make their lobbies too inviting. When Conrad Hilton took over the Waldorf Hotel he noticed well-dressed and polite people were sitting on the comfortable divans day after day but not spending any money, so he moved the couches out of the lobby into a part of the hotel which served food and drink. Hotel policy is usually small lounges, big cafés and the same strategy is used in airport terminals. Chairs in waiting areas are uncomfortable and buckled side by side, which does not invite interaction with other people. As a result, people are drawn into areas where they will spend money, such as cafés and bars.

Picking up the tab

If you are choosing a restaurant in which to entertain other people the setting you prefer will depend on your reasons for entertaining them. You may want to show friendship by being with friends on neutral ground; you may want to make an impression on a visitor or business associate; or you may merely want to give someone a change. At home we do this by departing from the normal routine in dress, setting and cuisine. When we go out, we have much more

choice as far as style, setting and expense are concerned. The intimacy of the occasion varies with your relationship to the people you are taking out. Entertaining grandparents or in-laws is often done at home, so a meal at an impressive restaurant would be a real treat and would probably be reserved for a special occasion. Conversely, it is more normal to go out to eat with the boss and his wife first, and then, once intimacy has been established, to invite them to your house. As far as dating is concerned, there is again a tendency to move from public to private eating. Dates may begin in a crowded public place such as a bar or disco, then a later meeting may be in a restaurant. An invitation to eat at home may follow.

223

■ **Bold colors and bright lights** *draw customers into fast-food restaurants — but also discourage them from slowing down the fast-food business by lingering. Seats that are attractively stylish, but uncomfortable after 20 minutes, can also contribute to a fast turnover. By contrast, this exclusive Mexico City restaurant ABOVE offers privacy, discreet decor and individual service. The higher prices on the menu are in effect the rent-money for a pleasant place to spend the evening.*

Eating for business and pleasure

Other traditions of eating in public serve a different purpose. The English tradition of the Inns of Court (originally real inns where lawyers stayed because the main courts of law were in London) is that a certain number of dinners must be taken "in hall" in order to become a barrister. Eating here is a form of initiation. Similarly, communal dining requirements apply in colleges at Oxford and Cambridge to those who want to qualify for a master's degree.

"Doing lunch" is regarded in some countries as a kind of sacred operation, where – we are led to believe – the most important deals are made. When President Carter tried to curtail spending on the "three-martini lunch" by excluding it from tax-deductible expenses, the tax deduction was defended passionately by businessmen, and the best the government could do was to reduce its value by 20 percent. Would business really have suffered if he had had his way or was it all to do with status? Just to be having business lunches at all marks you as a success in the world of business, for usually only executives have them.

The lunch that the business man or woman has had during the day may well be basically the same as the food served in the evening. While, in many Western countries, it is usual to serve more elaborate meals at night, these are often not very different from the lunch menus except in size and number of courses. In fact there are restaurants that serve the same food at dinner as at lunch, but at night they light the candles, dress up the waiters, have live entertainment and charge more. In the end, we usually eat out for entertainment, and we are as willing to pay for it as we are for any other entertainment.

Going out for a drink

Drinking habits vary greatly from country to country, governed largely by the laws and administrative rules that different societies make about alcohol. For instance, until about 25 years ago, Australians had the most infamous drinking habits. Bars closed at 6 pm and stories of the "six o'clock swill" – a mad dash to drink as much as possible between finishing work and closing time – were legendary. The bars were, naturally, male-only establishments. Though women are now allowed in, the bars are still on the whole uninviting to women, and wine bars are a more popular choice for mixed parties.

Canada has a tradition of highly regulated beer parlors, where the Liquor Control Act of each different province lays

▲ **Social interaction** *of a particular kind is often the motivation for visiting one restaurant rather than another. The relaxed atmosphere of a restaurant like this one can be an ideal place to introduce children to behavior in public. Here they may get* *a sense of a special occasion without excessive formality which they might find intimidating.*

down rules even about the shape and size of the table at which drinkers will sit. In some provinces only beer can be served in a beer parlor, in others beer and whiskey – other drinks are available only in the much more expensive "licensed lounges." In the 1950s in Calgary and Edmonton, the two main cities of Alberta, men and women were segregated into separate parlors. "Drink and drive" (out to country towns) was essential for mixed drinking until the "ladies only" parlors were replaced with "ladies and escorts" in the 1960s. Later all sex segregation was abandoned. Hot food and games such as shuffleboard were further liberalizations. To enable patrons to move freely to the games, an old rule designed to prevent disorder was dropped: it was no longer an offense to get up from your table and carry a glass of beer to another part of the room. Previously, you had to ask a waiter to do it for you.

In Britain, on the other hand, pubs have long been a focal point in the community. They are places to meet with friends for a sociable evening's drinking (not necessarily alcohol) and/or eating. Games such as darts are often played. Nearly every small village has a pub and, increasingly, children are catered for as family rooms or gardens become available – some pubs even have adventure playgrounds.

In the 17th century one writer recorded over 1,000 ale-houses and eating-houses in London, and by the 18th century that number was even larger (one estimate suggests that one in six houses in London had a drink-license in the early 18th century). Many of these houses were primarily for eating. Dinners were inexpensive and a matter of convenience, not dining out as we know it. Peacham (1647) described the use of taverns as "necessary" because "if a man meets with his friend...whither should they go. . . especially in rainy or foul weather, but to a tavern?" He tells us that both food and drink were available in these places and complains about the prices in some of them.

For the French, drinking has never been a cause for restrictive laws. A man on his way to work may stop off somewhere and take his first brandy with his first cup of coffee – opening hours will depend on the owner. **RF**

◄ **A midday rendezvous** *in a café which is informal enough for a relaxed conversation, but sufficiently chic to allow a sense of occasion. Meeting for a meal or even just a drink together can be one of many marking-points in a developing personal relationship.*

▲ **A lunchtime meeting** *allows two businessmen to strike a deal on neutral territory – neither has the psychological advantage of being in his own office. A meal with business associates also provides a chance to catch up on the latest company news, whether or not you have a specific transaction in mind. Having the meeting in the middle of the working day rather than in the evening keeps the conversation on the matter at hand, and the choice of a quiet restaurant with plenty of privacy encourages serious talk.*

Vacationing

EXPERTS predict that tourism will be the world's biggest industry in the year 2000. Technological advances and computerization are making more and more time available for leisure, and increasing numbers of people are finding they have opportunities for travel. Why do we travel about so much when we could probably relax just as well at home? We might distinguish "push" factors (the need to escape from the monotony and routine of work and everyday life and from unattractive urban environments), and "pull" factors (our attraction to a particular holiday destination). Ideally, going away on vacation is a safety valve, an opportunity to recharge our batteries so that we return to our work refreshed. Unfortunately, not all vacations live up to this ideal: sometimes we make the wrong choices about locations or traveling companions. Sometimes going away seems to involve almost as much effort as a day at the office. Deciding what you want from a vacation is a first step toward making the most of it.

Why vacations are important

Everyone has a different reason for vacationing, each of us being motivated by a different combination of factors. But we can identity some main trends concerning why we travel for pleasure. One is that vacations are a chance to switch off, opt out of a work routine and recuperate in a different environment. Although we may be attracted by beautiful scenery or the prospect of enjoying some sun, we are traveling away from something negative rather than toward something positive. In this sense, which destination we choose does not matter so long as it is different from our usual environment.

Another important motive is the stimulus of being in new places. Since the early seventies, there has been a growing preference for "active" vacationing – increasingly, people want the fun of trying something new and go on explorations and safaris to ever more remote corners of the world. This quest for novelty knows no bounds. Even dog-sledding in the Antarctic may be popular soon, as tourists have already begun to go there.

Although people often cite the mind-broadening aspect of travel – that is, using our experience of other cultures to enrich our perception of ourselves – as being among its main attractions, it actually comes quite low on the list of reasons for traveling. Research proves that we regard vacations as a time for taking rather than giving. Exercising the mind is something that only appeals to an enterprising minority. Most people believe that, having worked hard to earn their vacation, they are entitled to be spoiled and pampered while it lasts. They do what they want to do because that is what they have paid for. Self-indulgence comes first.

What kind of vacationer are you?

In general, the level of satisfaction you derive from vacations depends on the sort of person you are in everyday life. If you are fulfilled and happy in your work, leisure and

◄ **The most spectacular vacation sites** *are usually those that are hardest to get to, easy access can cause a beautiful location to become overrun by commercial development which could be just what you are trying to get away from. So a hiking vacation can be doubly rewarding, giving you access to unspoilt natural beauty and providing a sense of achievement at having got somewhere on your own initiative. But you might equally well find the physical effort and lack of home comforts stressful rather than relaxing.*

What is the right vacation spot for you?
■ *The choice of places to go is immense, but we often overlook sound basic principles when deciding between them* ■ *Have you matched your destination with your expectations?*

relationships and have a positive outlook, then on vacation you will probably be outgoing, responsive, ready to learn and make new friends. People who are bored and frustrated because they feel they have not realized their full potential, will find that being away from it all for a few weeks will not work a miracle, despite what the brochures say.

Vacations are an opportunity for self-discovery, a chance to measure your capabilities against those of other people. Self-aware people use vacations as a source of emotional and intellectual regeneration by exploring new environments in depth, meeting people from different cultures, and using their freedom creatively. While still a minority group, they are increasing fast and have a new approach to travel.

▲ **Do you take your vacation lying down?** *Sunshine and a spectacular view are the simple pleasures of this resort at Portofino in Italy, which you can enjoy without even standing up. While time spent in this way fulfills a basic need to relax away from the stresses of our everyday lives, a completely passive vacation is seldom the most rewarding way of using your free time. Cut off from the people and cultural heritage of the country you are visiting, you may find yourself going home having missed the chance to enrich your view of the world.*

▶ **Exploring art, culture and history** *are highly esteemed as vacation activities, yet few people actually use their vacation time in this way. Some tourist centers such as Florence, Italy, owe their popularity largely to their art treasures, but there is art waiting to be discovered in many lessknown places – as this visitor to Stanford University in California has found. Intellectual stimulation is a benefit that lasts long after your vacation has finished.*

Not for them the role of uncritical consumer in the seller's market of package-tour operators. "New-wave" travelers want to be independent and treated as individuals. Their tastes are sophisticated and instead of a concern for basic material needs, they appreciate quality. They think of fitness, health and the possible effect their vacations might have on the environment or the local community they are visiting. They are prepared to give, want to learn and are very discerning and critical when it comes to choosing the kind of vacation that suits their needs.

Different people, different needs

The American psychologist Abraham H Maslow used the device of a pyramid with five steps to show the process by which we achieve full realization of our potential as human beings. The principle is that each step represents a category of needs which we have to satisfy before we can progress to the next one. This could be applied equally well to the similar process of developing and perfecting ourselves as travelers.

The first step represents purely physiological needs. If we

◄ **Who are you trying to please?** *Over-ambitious vacation plans can lead to definite displeasure, as the faces of these tourists show. Having traveled across the world to see the Great Wall of China they feel compelled to see as much of it as possible, even if this means enough exertion to make them wish they were back home. To enjoy a vacation you need to go with a clear idea of what you are and are not going to do, and not let the expectations of others get in the way of your enjoyment.*

THE STRESS FACTOR

■ *Although vacations are a time of self-fulfillment and renewal, they can also be extremely stressful. Before setting out, we may have to work more intensively to meet deadlines. We also need to ensure that any developments at work during our absence can be dealt with effectively by others. Once we are on our way, the hassles of everyday life may take their toll. Being stuck in traffic, braving strikes and delays, pacifying fractious children and even minor worries like leaving our sunglasses behind can irritate us out of all proportion because they are part of the routine that we thought we had abandoned.*

If we travel abroad, we expose ourselves to an unfamiliar, even alien, environment where people look different and behave in unfamiliar ways and perhaps speak another language. We may well suffer in consequence – perhaps falling easy prey to muggers, for example. The pace many people set for their vacation is unnecessarily hectic. They rush headlong to their destination even if it is thousands of kilometers away and immediately start trying to acquire a tan, see the sights, socialize and taste the local cuisine. It is small wonder therefore that so many of us wish we could have an-

other vacation to recover from the exertions of our first one.

Doctors and psychologists now recognize the existence of "holiday syndrome." The symptoms are insomnia, exhaustion and anxiety. To combat it, they recommend either that people take breaks of three successive weeks or that they return about four days before going back to work. Experts say that we need three days to rest, relax and fully recuperate. Returning from a vacation at the weekend and going to work on Monday morning when we are in the middle of our recovery period is likely to make us tense and irritable and can produce more

serious psychological disturbances. "Cushion time," in which we overcome travel-induced stress and recover our normal form, also helps at the start of a vacation. A study of people on six-day package holidays on the islands of Australia's Great Barrier Reef showed that halfway through their vacation they were suffering minor physical ailments. These ranged from the effects of jet-lag and change of latitude to upset stomachs, and sunburn. By relaxing for a three-day period, we allow our bodies to adapt to different conditions, becoming fully aware of our new environment.

are at this stage, our basic concern is to have enough food, drink and sleep while we are on vacation. The second step represents a need for safety and security. Most people, even though they have deliberately broken with everyday routine to take a vacation, are disconcerted at the prospect of total freedom and a lack of structure in their lives for the next few weeks, so they turn to the leisure industry for a substitute holiday routine. With transport and accommodation booked and car-hire arranged, they plan as much as possible in advance in order to ensure the predictability of everything until they return home again. The third step represents a need to feel affection and belong socially during a vacation, either as half of a couple or as a member of a family or group. We are reassured if we can merge easily with the anonymous hordes of vacationers around us. The fourth step represents a need for self-esteem. Dealing effectively with the challenges of daily life in a foreign environment, taking risks and surviving setbacks all help us cultivate a

sense of our own worth. After this comes the top step of the pyramid: our need for self-actualization, which brings a feeling of inner harmony and a sense that we are at one with the world. If we have developed this far, the places and people we visit on vacation are no longer just a means of satisfying our physical and recreational needs; instead, we want to relate to them in a meaningful way that will enrich us emotionally.

The step of the pyramid a person starts on often reflects their family background and educational level, but their vacation choices thereafter reflect their development as a traveler. Not many travelers reach the top step. In many cases, a person's age, finances, family responsibilities or poor health keep them to the lower steps, despite the frustration they probably feel at not being able to fulfill all their needs.

Others decide that all they want from their vacations is good food and drink, sunshine and new relationships.

▲ **Personal preference alone** *has determined this man's choice of location and mode of transport. He can make up his itinerary as he goes along and discover new points of interest – and enjoy moments of solitude and contemplation that would be impossible on a more conventional vacation.*

TRAVELER'S TALES

■ *Part of our enjoyment of vacations lies in sharing our experiences when we return. But although we are willing to talk about some things, we are more reticent about others. In a recent study, a selection of travel stories was presented to a group of people who were asked whether they would tell them to everyone, selected*

friends only or no one.
The results were that they would tell:
Everyone
◆ *Tales of universal holiday disasters, eg loss of luggage, stomach upsets, accommodation problems.*
◆ *Tales where they appeared to advantage in a foreign setting.*

Selected friends only
◆ *Tales of feeling deeply moved eg by war graves.*
◆ *Tales where friendship and casual relationships suffered.*
No one
◆ *Tales where they looked ridiculous or naive.*
◆ *Tales where close relationships suffered.*

Getting what you want

Once you have decided which interests and activities you want to pursue on your vacation, your next task is to choose the vacation that suits you best. One way of doing this is to start by making a list of your needs, then to analyze and compare what the brochures offer. You can then make another list of which of your interests are catered for at each of the places that appeal to you and choose the one that is closest to your original list. One advantage of this method is that it can prevent you from being unduly influenced by

▲ **Building family relationships** *can be an important side-effect of vacationing, especially when the routine of work and school does not allow families time together at home. Spending leisure time together in an environment free from pressure and distractions can give parents an opportunity to witness their children's emotional and intellectual development.*

▶ **A group tour**, *can give you access to places off the usual tourist route – such as these rock-tombs in Indonesia – which would be unknown or prohibited to casual tourists. However, a badly chosen tour can herd you along a well-trodden path through monuments and souvenir shops and force you into the company of disagreeable traveling companions.*

clever advertising. It is generally better to pay slightly more than risk choosing a holiday that does not quite fit the profile you have drawn up.

However carefully you select your vacation, you could still find yourself somewhere you do not want to be. A study of the diaries of tourists in Singapore showed that although 48 percent were interested in modern shopping centers, 83 percent visited them. There were also discrepancies in the level of interest and numbers of tourists in the case of Tiger Balm Gardens (28 percent were interested, though 38 percent went). The explanation for this is that tourist organizations were arranging guided tours of these places in return for commission on purchases the visitor made.

Doing what you want to do can also be difficult. The same study showed that although 49 percent of the tourists wanted to visit rural Indonesian communities, only 23 percent actually did so. Only 32 percent saw puppet shows and dancing displays, whereas 53 percent wanted to, and only 9 percent visited the Southern islands although 29 percent wanted to. Here, the problem was that there were not enough facilities for this kind of sightseeing.

To counter such frustrations, it is a good idea to take time before you leave home to find out about the country and people you intend to visit and to learn a few key words and phrases of their language. You could note down the particular areas, buildings and local activities that interest you – being well-informed will help you to plan your time to suit yourself and you will be less likely to miss hidden gems. Your preparation will also give you a measure of independence and the confidence to leave your fellow vacationers and explore on your own. Seeing the sights that you want to see and controlling your own program will enhance the satisfaction you gain from your vacation. Research shows that captive vacationers, such as those in an isolated island resort, also feel more fulfilled when they depart from the list of planned group activities and devise their own. Looking for shells, if that is what you want to do, will give you more pleasure than joining in the beach barbecue. Holiday satisfaction means knowing what you want, being prepared to exert yourself to get it and cultivating your independence.

Traveling companions

Traveling with your partner, your family or a group means that you have others to share your experiences with. However, there are also disadvantages. For example, vacationing successfully as a couple can be difficult. Apart from the initial problem of agreeing on where to go and what kind of vacation to have, research shows that domestic roles are often a cause of friction. In self-catering accommodation, some women who would welcome their partner's help with the daily round of chores find that it is not forthcoming – on vacation, just as when at home housework is often seen as a woman's responsibility. On the other hand, in some cases, the sense of freedom and novelty associated with being on vacation may encourage couples to abandon their usual roles and even to establish new routines to try out at home.

Couples who spend a significant amount of their working day apart face another problem – that of adapting to a period of intensive togetherness. Many welcome the opportunity, but others may have difficulty coping with their partner full-time. Whether a vacation can rebuild a relationship that is breaking down depends on the reasons for its collapse. If the difficulties are due to major conflicts, time spent together on vacation will only make these differences emerge more clearly.

Vacationing with the family is a chance to strengthen ties, especially for working parents. Studies of the behavior of families visiting museums, theme parks and zoos show that

▶ **A child's curiosity** often gives parents an opportunity to take an interest in things they would otherwise pass by. Whether enjoying the amusements of a theme park or, like here, answering questions about the animals during a country vacation, adults may find their travels enriched by the company of children – provided, of course, that there is enough variety to prevent them becoming bored and irritable.

parents enjoy and participate in activities by involving their children. On their own, they might be reluctant to ride on the scream machine or try the computer exhibit for fear of looking silly. With a child in their charge, such inhibitions vanish. Sociologists call this behavior "role-distancing" – adults are enjoying themselves by doing something childish but their conduct is acceptable because it is child-directed. Moreover, as the evidence suggests that the more activities people pursue on vacation the greater their satisfaction, children help by permitting parents a range of amusement from which they would otherwise have felt excluded.

Many people find that group tours meet their vacation needs perfectly. Being with a group means tolerating other people, even those you would not naturally get on well with, but it also has many advantages. As a group member, you can enjoy special trips, lectures and experiences that you could not as an individual. Your personal safety is not an issue, and board, lodging and travel arrangements are made for you. Your social – and perhaps even romantic – needs are supplied by fellow group members.

Whether you join an expensive cultural cruise or a low-budget camping tour, you will become part of a unique group dynamic, which is carefully orchestrated by the group leader. Most of us need encouragement to overcome our inhibitions and part of the leader's task is to help us do this so that we can pursue our interests by ourselves. Research shows that all tour groups need initiators to deal with outsiders and make suggestions; comedians to relieve tension and provide amusement; scapegoats to be blamed for difficulties and be the butt of good-humored fun, and willing followers to be the audience. You will also notice couples who only relate peripherally to the group, and perhaps some fiercely independent individuals who give the impression that they could manage by themselves. Experienced group leaders encourage this role-playing because it helps the group dynamic to function properly. However, before the roles become filled, petty power struggles can occur, which may make what is happening inside the coach a more immediate concern for you than what is happening outside.

Experiencing a new environment

Many vacationers make the mistake of hurrying from one tourist landmark to the next in the belief that knowing a place means seeing everything in it. As a result, their impressions are often muddled and confused. It is not how many sights you see that counts, but how you see them.

One way of increasing your awareness of your new surroundings is to practice what researchers call "mindfulness." This means that instead of mentally processing the world around us in a routine and unselective way, which makes ordinary everyday events hard to remember, we process it actively by concentrating on

232

▶ **Shopping with the inhabitants** *is one way to get closer to the everyday life of the place you are visiting, since purchasing habits vary widely from one culture to another. In the Mediterranean countries, for example, people regularly buy provisions at open-air markets like this one in Crete. But beware that the market you choose is indeed the genuine article and not just a collection of "traditional" stalls designed to bait tourists.*

certain aspects of our behavior, the environment and other people. If, when we receive new information, we make a conscious effort to link it to our existing information networks, we can recall it much more easily. Even in the 18th century, the Scottish economist, Adam Smith, advised those going on the Grand Tour to ask questions continually and keep a notebook of the answers. Studies show that vacationers who make an effort to find out why the country they are visiting is the way it is, will derive more satisfaction from their time there. It is important, too, to stay for as long as possible in the places you visit, to give yourself time to absorb new impressions. Why not make a point of returning to places you have visited before, perhaps at a different time of year? In this way, you will stop being just another tourist. The locals will see that you care about and have a commitment to where they live and this will help you establish a relationship with them. It is easier to develop this kind of contact in a place that is not too far away. In 1987, a forecast of the major trends in European travel predicted that we would be taking many more short-haul trips.

Crossing the great divide

If you are vacationing abroad, especially in a country with a different cultural background, you may feel confused, alienated and disoriented. In third-world countries, you will also be a "have" in the land of "have-nots." "They" are very

different from you and you may be unsure how to relate to them and their way of life, but they are probably just as disconcerted by you. Research shows that a superficial level of contact between traveler and host often reinforces existing prejudices.

Package tourists returning from an adventure holiday in Morocco reported finding the locals even more grasping, mercenary and excitable than they had expected. To a local resident, on the other hand, tourists may be people who are so rich they never have to work, or may represent a corrupting force bringing with them drugs and outlandish customs. Each side has a distorted view of the other, and while this persists any contact between them cannot be meaningful.

Because it is difficult to disguise the fact that you are a tourist, there is little hope of the locals treating you in the same way they treat one another. What you can do, though, is to avoid behaving like a tourist. If you approximate your behavior and lifestyle as much as possible to theirs, the differences between you will be less obvious.

When in Rome…

If you familiarize yourself with the culture of your host country before going away, this will prevent confusion and frustration when you deal with the locals, and enhance your enjoyment by ensuring that your contact with them is positive

233

◄ **Taking the local bus** – *or indeed any other means of public transport – is another means by which tourists can see something of local life, especially in third-world countries where private vehicles are rare and buses and trains a way of life. Here you might try out some snatches of the local language that you may have learned, which will show that you are genuinely interested in the country, not merely imposing yourself as an alien.*

rather than negative. Dress is one sensitive area. Although topless bathing (and even nude bathing on certain beaches) is broadly acceptable in Europe, it is disapproved of in the United States and Asia. Women in the Middle East should wear long sleeves and high necks, while men should not wear shorts.

It is also important to show respect for places of worship in any culture. When visiting churches women should have their arms, shoulders, and head covered, and you should always remove your shoes in mosques. In Sri Lanka, tourists have offended the inhabitants by climbing over shrines and monuments to take pictures where they are forbidden to do so and even scratching graffiti on statues of Buddha, and as a result, the Minister for Tourism has called for them to be

punished. It is generally wise to be careful when taking pictures, especially of people. Do it covertly if you must, or use a zoom lens, but do not intrude on the privacy of others, and never photograph military installations.

Find out, too, about social conventions in your host country. If you are vacationing in Asia, for example, you should avoid asking personal questions or volunteering too much information about yourself. In certain circles, you should never ask what a man's occupation is or inquire if he has a wife and children, but in India and Pakistan it is polite to show an interest in family matters. Western men, invited to a Muslim family gathering, should not expect to be introduced to female members of the household who will remain in another room. It would even be bad manners

TOURISM – VICTIM OF ITS OWN SUCCESS

■ We all deserve and benefit from vacations abroad. But the fact that millions of us take them at the same time of year and go to the same places can have a very negative effect on the destinations we visit, especially in the long term. Little by little, we transfer to our coastal playgrounds the very urban development we are trying to escape from. Massive hotels appear on the Greek Islands and holiday and retirement homes mushroom along the Spanish coasts. It is not just the environment that is at risk. Especially in third-world countries, tourists can "infect" the local population with their own social ills. Their legacy is a higher crime rate and cost of living, drug abuse, child begging, delinquency and prostitution. One situation is to keep tourists in colonies sited well away from local population centers. Perhaps worst of all is the fact that the locals will have little say in the future of their area once the leisure magnates win financial control. Countries such as Libya and Albania, conscious of the power of tourism to engender social

change, have decided to keep their doors closed to tourists.

In European resort areas, the leisure industry should encourage diversification so that tourism is not the only source of income. Promoting local skills, crafts, architecture and cuisine would help keep the traditions and character of each place intact. Besides increasing individual tourist-appeal, this would also keep the economic benefits and therefore the planning of future development where they should be – under local control.

The arguments of ecologists and conservationists are leading to a growing awareness of environmental issues. Vacationers attracted by alternative travel and adventure holidays may feel guilty about exploring pockets of disappearing rainforest or observing Amazon Indian settlements. Controlled tourist visiting of environmentally endangered areas, however, encourages local populations to manage them effectively for conservation purposes. If they do not do so, no tourists will come and valuable income will disappear.

to ask after them. In many countries, it is impolite to decline food offered as a gesture of friendship.

Although it is possible to offend in these areas, there are others where you may feel at a disadvantage because your hosts interpret a concept differently. Time is a case in point: "Be there at seven" can mean "Be there at five to seven" in Japan, or "Be there at seven thirty" in the United States. "Leave it until next week" can mean "It needs thinking about" in Anglo-Saxon communities or "Let's forget it" in Latin American ones. By actively trying to blend in with the foreign culture, you can turn culture shock into cultural euphoria. Finally, traveling with only a few companions will make you less intimidating to your hosts and may encourage them to respond positively to you.

Souvenirs: the Japanese approach

The purchase of objects as a way of symbolizing a vacation is a fascinating behavior. The idea of the souvenir – the word is French for "memory" – is extended in Japanese culture to that of souvenir-gifts. The Japanese do not just purchase objects to remind themselves of the holiday, but also to communicate the success and attraction of their vacation to members of a large social group. The custom is termed "omiyage" and is regarded as essential to a satisfying holiday. Of importance to local economies is the Japanese preference for "meibutsu" – or locally produced goods which are unique to the destination. In an Australian study, Japanese tourists bought gifts for an average of 15 friends or relatives and 75 percent of them bought soft toys as a part of their purchases, invariably examples of the local fauna such as koalas and kangaroos. Other popular purchases included opals (48 percent) and wool products (36 percent). It is clear from the range, number and style of gifts bought by Japanese visitors that much thought and attention is given to the question of what to give to each person in one's group. In terms of expense, taste and social subtlety omiyage is far removed from the Anglo-American custom of buying a tea towel or T-shirt for the folks at home. **PLP**

▲ **When tourists outnumber the local people,** *it is time to start asking what the vacation industry is leading to. Here the Qinghai people of Western China and their traditional costumes have become another sight to be seen and photographed. Unless we exercise extreme sensitivity, our travels to discover unfamiliar cultures can be the beginning of the end of those very cultures.*

235

Places for Recreation

HOWEVER MUCH we enjoy being in our homes and taking advantage of the opportunities for leisure there, almost all of us pursue other leisure activities away from home. For some pastimes – most sports and games, for example – we go out because we have to; others we could just as easily do at home, but choose not to. Sometimes, the very fact that the activity is taking place away from home gives it a special appeal. Or, we take up a leisure activity for no other reason than to get out of the house. The additional pleasure we gain from going out during our leisure time probably accounts in some part for the continued popularity of the theater, the movies, spectator sports, concerts, opera and ballet. Substitutes are more cheaply available at home in the form of videos, television and so on, yet these substitutes do not completely satisfy us. The excitement of going out is an important part of the experience.

How do we choose our leisure activities?

You probably feel that you choose your leisure activities freely, but in reality various factors limit and to some degree control what you do in your free time. In the first place, your choices will depend on which facilities are available locally. Social factors can also play a part – short-term crazes for particular games, for example. Those responsible for providing leisure facilities both follow trends and, by playing upon our tastes, try to create them.

The nature and development of leisure activities differs from country to country, but despite these differences there are three principal agents involved, either together or separately: government (national or local), the commercial or private sector, and the voluntary sector. The focus of government is usually on leisure as a way of contributing to social or individual welfare; the commercial sector's main motive is profit (and the vast majority of its enterprises are concerned with passive forms of leisure); in voluntary endeavors people help themselves and others, often by means of clubs and charities (and they are concerned mainly with active pursuits, ranging from sports to amateur theater).

A few out-of-home leisure activities are so popular that they enjoy the support of a majority of the population. These are mainly passive and social pursuits, like eating in restaurants (see *Ch 27*). Each of the active pursuits, in contrast, has a much more limited following but, taken together, they are increasing in popularity as we become more health conscious. For example, figures suggest that more than half the adult population of the United States now claim to take regular exercise, in contrast to less than a quarter in 1961.

Despite the widespread concern for sexual equality, a person's sex in some cases still influences which leisure pursuits they choose. Most sports participants are men – indeed, in some sports a female player is such a rarity that she may find her photograph in the newspapers, just for participating. In some sports – tennis and sailing, for example – there tend to be about as many female partici-

A ROMAN VILLA IN CALIFORNIA

■ *The American oil multimillionaire J Paul Getty (1892-1976) lived in Europe from 1951 until the end of his life, and so never saw the museum he endowed in Malibu, California. In the late 1960s, while entertaining guests at his home in Sutton Place, a Tudor manor house in Surrey, he announced that he had decided to construct a new building in the United States to house his collection. It was to be an accurate replica of one of the largest villas built during the Roman Empire, the Villa dei Papiri, uncovered during the excavations at Herculaneum, the Roman town buried along with Pompeii in AD 79 after the eruption of Vesuvius. He later wrote that*

the main reason for his choice "concerns the collection of Greek and Roman art which the museum has managed to acquire...and what could be more logical than to display it in a classical building where it might originally have been seen?" The building welcomed its first visitors in 1974.

A visit to the Getty Museum involves far more than merely looking at objects. This is because of the considerable care that has been taken to create the delusion that the building as a whole, despite its modern facilities, is somehow not of this time.

The most immediately striking feature is the Main Peristyle Garden, a long rectangular

area surrounded by a colonnade. Much of the space is occupied by an artificial pond, also long and approximately rectangular; around it are walkways, seating, plots of shrubs and other plants, and a few small sculptures on pedestals. Beyond the peristyle on one side, there are further gardens, again very formally arranged, with plants chosen not only for their beauty or interest but also for their scent. The Roman theme is continued rigorously within the main structure

housing the exhibits: Norman Neuerburg, Getty's historical consultant for the project, concerned himself as much with fine detail as major considerations, such as the choice of appropriate construction materials.

The environment and the exhibits intermingle in such a way that it is difficult for the visitor to distinguish the two elements. Here design is tailored to a leisure activity so skillfully that it has become an inseparable part of that activity.

We get out of the house for 40 percent of our leisure ■ *Where we go and how well we like it depend in part on available facilities and the success of their design* ■ *The environment both suffers and benefits from our drive for recreation.*

pants as there are male, and in a few – such as yoga, keep-fit and riding – women are more numerous than men. In aerobics, dance and keep-fit classes, women may outnumber men ten to one.

Age, money and mobility

Age is another factor governing who does what. Involvement in outdoor sport is about 13 times greater among those aged 16-19 than among those aged 70 or over. The reasons for this fall-off are not nearly as obvious as you might think. Team sports are generally the first to be abandoned, usually for social reasons: it can be hard to organize a team outside the framework of a school or college. Games involving two people, like badminton, golf and squash, are easier to arrange and so are likely to be pursued for longer, while sports that can be practiced individually, like swimming and angling, persist longest of all. Although physical decline gradually curtails the activities of older people, many elderly

people of today have not simply abandoned sports activities, they have never taken part in them. Young people, who have been introduced to a wide range of leisure opportunities, are in this respect better prepared for later life.

In fact, our choice of leisure activities relates not just to age in years, but to stages in our individual life cycle. During late adolescence, socializing, excitement and partner-seeking are particularly important, and as a result young people make much use of movie theaters, discos, amusement arcades and fun fairs. Courtship and marriage increase the likelihood that leisure activities will be done as a pair, so eating out, evenings in town and weekends away become more frequent. Parenthood brings constraints of time as well as money, since a couple must make arrangements for child care, take the children along or do fewer out-of-home activities together.

Two important influences are linked, money and personal mobility. Wealthier people can spend more on leisure, and can use private transport to reach leisure centers. Surveys carried out in Britain found over 50 percent of people in professional occupations taking part in outdoor sport com-

237

▲ **The activity is what chiefly matters** *when we look for a place to go for entertainment, but the place itself can have an important impact on our choice, and so can our access to it. Events that we might otherwise be little concerned with can become attractions when they occur on our doorstep, allowing us to enjoy the fun without going out of our way. The consequence may be the discovery of a new interest which we can share with friends and family.*

This French grandmother has invited her grandson to share a perfect view of the Tour de France in the street outside her house.

pared with only 20 percent of unskilled manual workers. Furthermore, different social classes favor different sports: middle-class people often play squash, badminton or tennis, whereas working-class people prefer weight training, bodybuilding and cycling.

Why leisure environments matter

When places where people are to take part in active leisure are being designed, three main factors need to be taken into account – safety, function and ambience.

The designer of a gymnasium, for example, has to consider many safety aspects: there should be few if any objects protruding from the walls – ideally not even light switches; the color of the walls should contrast with that of balls; lighting should be bright and even, and the fixtures should be protected by wire netting or plastic; windows and viewing panels, even the smallest, must be made of shatterproof glass or shielded by wire netting. The equipment for all the different activities needs to be laid out in such a way that there is adequate room for the exercise and pieces of equipment do not protrude dangerously into other areas. Once these factors have been taken into account, the designer can determine whether they are reconcilable with a pleasing ambience that will encourage people to participate.

Similar considerations apply to outdoor sports. However, in some the ambience assumes much greater importance. In a game such as golf, for example, the countryside surrounding the playing area can contribute greatly to the pleasure of playing.

Places for watching

For every person who plays a particular sport there are countless others whose involvement is restricted to watching. Most of this is done through television, because sports arenas can cater to only a certain number of spectators. Also, television viewing has distinct advantages – it costs less and involves less effort to watch a game at home, and on television we can view the very best games featuring star players. Close-ups, and slow-motion replays ensure that we do not miss important events.

▲ **Designed to enhance the excitement of watching.** *The unique roof of the Olympic stadium in Munich has practical, structural advantages, but none is as important to the stadium's function as the sense this roof generates in spectators of being in a special, exciting place.*

▶ **Designed as a setting for grand entertainment,** *La Scala in Milan is the archetype of an opera house. It achieves its successful ambience partly through association – originally, with the private royal-court theaters that it copied on a large scale; today, with its own glorious history.*

It might seem surprising, then, that some people prefer to attend in person. That so many thousands of people do is testimony to the fact that there is more to watching a sporting contest than simply seeing what is happening. Mixed in with the thrills of the game are other satisfactions generated by the fact that you are there, that the drama is unfolding directly in front of you. Then there is the atmosphere of large sports arenas, particularly when they have a capacity audience. People who might never otherwise have met sit shoulder-to-shoulder, sharing the same triumphs and disappointments and talking to each other, often with unusual openness.

There is also the excitement of being one of the crowd, taking part in applause, singing or chanting with hundreds or thousands of other people. In recent decades architects have begun to pay keen attention to the design of major

sports arenas in an attempt to increase the excitement of the occasion. Even the exterior of a modern athletics stadium, like those used for the Los Angeles Olympics in 1984, is tailored to quicken spectators' pulses and footsteps as they approach the site.

Older sports arenas often have a strong sense of history about them because of the famous successes and feats of skill that have been performed there in the past. Pre-game displays – military bands, cheerleaders and so on – can be used to increase the feeling of spectacle and participation among the audience. Unfortunately, certain design features are necessary to protect players and the peaceful majority of spectators from the very raucous and sometimes violent minority. More and more design effort today is being dedicated to ensuring that spectators can enjoy watching their favorite sport in safety.

THE SHOPPING MALL: AN UNPLANNED LEISURE CENTER

■ *After World War II, the creation of suburbs on a vast scale created a new kind of community in the United States – one without a center. There was no plaza or piazza, no tribal dancing ground, no market or fair ground, no ceremonial center that was common to all the inhabitants, and no common area for shopping, gossiping and just hanging out. Enterprising businessmen soon began to build mammoth shopping malls with acres of parking in the still unclaimed wilderness areas near the suburbs (see Ch 26).*

What started out as a purely commercial venture, however, rapidly took on social uses that had little to do with trading. The encouragement of family shopping – the whole family spending the better part of the day there – turned the malls into family meeting places. It became the weekend thing to do to spend the day in the mall – whether shopping or not. Often, little shopping was done.

People window shopped, tried the different eateries, bought from a choice of literally hundreds of kinds of ice cream, sent the children to a movie while they had a meal by

themselves, wheeled babies around the wide arcades and let their toddlers play around the benches and tubs. Soon the mall began to look very like the fair on the village green.

▶ **Hanging around** *with friends is the chief recreation of adolescents who make a leisure center of their local shopping mall. This shopping mall is in Hong Kong.*

More significantly, adolescents, tired of playing around the suburban streets or the schoolyard, began to take over the mall. Teenagers need somewhere to hang out, and the suburbs were notoriously lacking in the equivalent of the main street drug store. There was no main street in the suburbs. The mall replaced it, becoming the new town center. It could be used in all weathers, there was no entrance fee and no harassment. It was all very public and safe for girls.

Malls are colorful and exciting social places. The bustle and the movement, the food teenagers love, and even movies – but most of all, just loitering about, meeting friends, making friends, drinking coke, gossiping, joking, making dates. Social contacts, parade and display are all important. The participants are mainly between 11 and 16. They have created a whole lifestyle around the mall, with customs and clothing peculiar to its environment. They create "looks" and styles in mixing and matching clothing items that have the originality of haute couture and certainly as much care and concern. Older teenagers tend to regard "malling" as a phase to be grown out of for more sophisticated activities. **RF**

How leisure affects our surroundings

Many leisure activities leave their mark on the environment. This is especially true of country and water-based recreations, but even indoor activities can have an effect if buildings have to be constructed to house them. First, there is the direct physical impact of leisure activities – for example, the pitting of rockfaces by climbing equipment and the erosion of river banks by the wash of passing boats. Then there is disturbance to wildlife – depletion of stocks through an excess of anglers and hunters during the wildlife season, for example. Sometimes the disturbance is inadvertent – swans can be poisoned if they eat the lead weights used by anglers. Obviously, many leisure activities bring with them the risk of pollution: fuel spillage from motorboats, exhaust fumes from cars and motorbikes, sewage dumping from pleasure boats, and so on. Even environmentally friendly pursuits can bring pollution to remote sites if large numbers of participants travel there by car.

People are part of the environment and they, too, can be adversely affected by outdoor leisure pursuits. Large-scale, environmentally insensitive sites and/or badly designed leisure activity developments can esthetically damage beautiful locations; vast luxury hotels are notable offenders, but thoughtlessly positioned trailer parks and camping areas can have just as bad an effect.

Growing public awareness of the need for conservation is helping to limit the damage that recreation causes. Sometimes a particular activity has to be temporarily banned to allow natural resources to recover. The impact of leisure activities can be positive, however. Inner urban areas have much to gain from outdoor leisure. These areas are often

RECREATING BALTIMORE HARBOR

■ Unused, and unattractive resources can, with imagination, be developed to provide leisure facilities and at the same time help regenerate areas that have gone to seed. A fine example of this is the Inner Harbor at Baltimore, Maryland. An area of about 10,000 square meters surrounding the harbor basin has become a home for recreational, educational and cultural facilities including

◆ the National Aquarium with over 5,000 marine creatures and a rainforest section.

◆ the Harborplace, an indoor market with more than 130 shops and restaurants.

◆ a marina capable of berthing more than 150 craft.

◆ the Pier Six Concert Pavilion, a 2,000 seat outdoor concert venue.

◆ the Maryland Science Center, with exhibition space, conference rooms, a science museum, a planetarium.

◆ the Power Plant, a center for evening entertainment based in a former generating plant.

◆ the Promenade, a wide area where people can sit at their ease, stroll by the water's edge, look at sculptures or enjoy the small parks.

The development also features apartments for the elderly, luxury hotels, upmarket retail stores, a convention center and the World Trade Center and Observation Deck – a 32-story pentagonal office tower with a visitor center and an observation deck on the 27th story. The development is planned as a venue for fairs and water festivals.

■ **Leisure at odds with the environment?** Motorized sports LEFT in the countryside destroy vegetation and disrupt natural habitat for animals. Dune buggy tracks may persist in desert landscapes for many decades. However, leisure interests can also stimulate environmental improvement, as in the Baltimore Inner Harbor Development ABOVE.

marked by unused buildings, and derelict and despoiled land. They may also have high unemployment, a lack of community life and poor housing and social conditions. Leisure developments cannot provide a complete solution to these problems, but in certain cases they can make an important contribution. Among the possible advantages are visual improvements to the environment – the upgrading and reuse of derelict land, and the redevelopment of redundant buildings; job creation; the growth of a new community spirit; new income from tourists and other visitors; and, last but not least, the provision of local recreational opportunities for the residents themselves. **SG**

THE HERITAGE INDUSTRY

■ Most nations preserve parts of their cultural heritage for the benefit of future generations. Trust funds, government grants and admission charges pay the bills. The heirs of some of Britain's ancestral homes have realized that, because the public is so willing to pay to view historic houses and their contents, the enterprise can be put on a solely commercial footing. Visitors to one of the many stately homes now open to the public can see works of art, antique furniture and so on in a more realistic context rather than in a museum. The gardens of the stately homes, too, are often very beautiful. RIGHT A tourist explores the grounds of Blenheim Palace in Oxfordshire, England.

Some owners have even turned their homes into family fun centers. For example, the

grounds of Longleat, the Elizabethan stately home in Wiltshire, England, owned by the Marquis of Bath, although originally designed by 18th-century landscape architect Capability Brown for people to stroll through, are now used as a lion safari park.

241

CLIMBING WALLS FOR A CHANGE

■ Rock climbers who live in cities may have to travel long distances to find suitable faces, and so for many decades the more dedicated of them have practiced their sport on the walls of buildings and bridges (in some countries including the United States this is illegal). During the 1980s more and more leisure complexes installed specially designed indoor climbingwalls ABOVE.

■ **The urge for something different** from our normal routine motivates how we spend our leisure time, according to the "compensatory theory" of leisure. So, for example, city-dwellers go to the country in their leisure time and country-dwellers to the city. There is some evidence to support the theory: those in sedentary jobs do deliberately exercise in their leisure time (for example, a

1984 survey found Swedish managers to be enthusiastic joggers). Although more American white-collar workers exercise regularly than blue-collar workers, the difference is not very marked. In one survey 52 percent of professionals said they exercised daily, while 48 percent of blue-collar workers made the same claim. In another survey of leisure activities more country-dwellers than

town-dwellers reported hunting and fishing as recreations. In this case, opportunity obviously plays a part. However, other typical recreations cited by town-dwellers in the same survey included skiing, sailing, picnics, hiking and nature walks. All these are probably more available to country-dwellers on a day-to-day basis, but in general they leave them to their urban neighbors. **RL**

LEISURE IN A NATURAL SETTING

■ From about the 18th century on, planners began to make an effort to introduce or preserve open spaces within the expanding cities. These spaces took the form of parks, in the design of which skilled landscape architects demonstrated considerable ingenuity. The movement reached a peak in the latter part of the 19th century. Of particular note were the parklands created in 1875 for Boston by Frederick Law Olmsted (1822-1903) – two concentric rings around the city center, linked by the broad – nearly 75m (246 ft) – tree-lined Commonwealth Avenue. A more recent concept is the "green wedge," a stretch of greenery running from a city center to the surrounding countryside.

◀ **Urban greenery**, City parks such as Central Park in New York create an apparently natural setting for recreation. Providing relief from city noise and a visual contrast with the gray of buildings and streets, they are an important means of reducing urban stress.

▶ **Wilderness reserve**. Leigh Lake and Mount Moran in Wyoming are an example of a protected area in which visitors can appreciate flora and fauna in their natural habitat. Protection means limiting the facilities available to visitors.

PLACES FOR URBAN RECREATION

Green areas such as parks are important leisure facilities. They are places where we can take exercise to become physically fit which, in turn, helps us cope with stress and its physical consequences (such as the risk of heart failure). Nearby parks also provide a safe environment for children's leisure, for example, parents need not worry that their offspring may be playing near traffic or are traveling long distances to reach recreational facilities. Moreover, though they do not always help to unite a community (see Ch18), parks

PATTERNS OF CROWDING ON A SUNDAY AFTERNOON

■ Most of us do not visit a natural recreation area to be surrounded by other people. We vary, however, in our need of privacy, and one person's reactions may even differ from one time to the next. In some moods we might feel that a wild area was insufferably crowded if there was another human being in sight, but in a different mood our isolation might make us feel uncomfortably lonely, even scared. The locale plays a part, too: an empty, unspoilt beach is a delight, but an empty beach at a fashionable resort like Cannes might be unsettling, since this is a beach on which we expect a crowd.

The maps RIGHT illustrate our tendency to bunch together even when we have gone out to the country to enjoy some open space. They show the distribution of people at four different

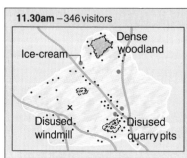

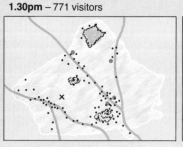

times during a typical summer Sunday at The Westwood, an area of common land in Humberside, Britain. The area is crossed by four roads, and there are no restrictions on access. It contains undulating grassland, a clump of dense, ancient woodland, and two small knoll-like areas created by former quarrying. There are few specific recreational facilities aside from seating at a number of vantage points and mobile ice-cream and snack bars. Cars may not be parked more than 15 yards away from any road, but nothing prohibits people from leaving their cars and distributing themselves evenly across the terrain.

Even from the first map we can see that they do not. People are dispersed, but have clustered together in certain places; 51 percent of them remain within the permitted parking zones. Most others have been drawn either to the edges of The Westwood's sub-areas or to self-contained enclosures within them; we can see the first effect clearly around the woodland in the west and the second in the disused quarry pits in the east. Landmarks, vantage points and facilities (like the refreshment vans) are other magnets.

We might expect the pattern to change during the day as new visitors arrived and sought

long ago as 1864, Congress gave Yosemite to the State of California to keep as a park.) A multitude of acts passed in the 1960s testify to the concern to preserve the wilderness. For example, the "Multiple Use – Sustained Yield Act" of 1960 which directed the United States Forest Service to combine environmental objectives with its economic concerns, and the "Natural Environment Policy Act" of 1969 which provided for the "management, protection, enhancement or creation of areas of natural beauty and human enjoyment."

Not everyone chooses to "get back to nature" in their leisure time. Even among those who do, the desire to escape human contact is not equally strong. Large numbers of city-dwellers get back to nature by driving into the wilderness and camping in large car-borne tents or campers on a crowded campsite.

KEEPING A "GREEN LUNG"

The availability of green recreational facilities influences our leisure choices and attitudes. This is obviously true for those who live 1,000 miles from the sea – they are less likely to be interested in maritime pastimes than those who live in sea-board fishing villages. But legal as well as practical restrictions can play a part.

There is considerable use of reservoirs for recreational purposes. The opening of a large new reservoir in Oklahoma in the 1960s affected the leisure activities of 15 percent of people who lived within a 100 mile radius of it. However, recreational use of reservoirs has been forbidden in various parts of the country. The prohibitions led neither to protests nor illicit use. This could have been because of the plentiful supply of alternative leisure facilities or because residents were not aware that the right to recreational use of reservoirs was taken for granted in other areas.

At the beginning of the 20th century there were protest rallies in Britain's Peak District when landowners attempted to stop people from going walking there. This area is a natural "lung" for large industrial cities. The protesters eventually won and the area is now a National Park. **RL**

0pm – 1,094 visitors

ut less crowded areas but this oes not happen: there are few igns of people wanting to pread out and create more pace for themselves. The con- ast between the intensive use f some areas and no use at all f others becomes progres- ively more striking: at 11.30am e visitors are occupying a ere 21 percent of space vailable to them, but at 4.30pm e figure is even lower – as tle as 15 percent.

and play areas do give people opportunities to meet while they are engaged in leisure activities that they enjoy, and this can help and improve social contact: it has been shown that, if you meet people in surroundings that you find pleasant, you are more likely to form friendships with them. In general, parks and other green areas are not vandalized as much as other parts of cities.

LEISURE IN THE GREAT OUTDOORS

In more recent years, however, partly in response to pressure from environmental groups, planners all over the world have realized that what people in the cities really need in addition to parks, tree-lined streets and so on, to help them retain "green lungs," are areas of untamed nature where plants and wildlife can flourish. Though the health benefits and the esthetic value of nature have been recognized for a long time, the provision or control of areas of outstanding natural beauty is primarily a 20th-century phenomenon. (Though as

A Green Environment?

THE STANDARD of living that has been achieved by the developed countries in the 20th century is at an all-time high – if we measure it in purely material terms. Never before have we had access to such a range of products – video recorders and microwave ovens, for instance – designed to make our lives easier and more fun. Yet more and more people are questioning the *quality* of life we have achieved.

Unfortunately, many of the technological advances that have given us an easier and more stimulating life have had unwelcome side effects. The way we live – our lifestyle – has brought the natural world to the point of near collapse. Our health is more at risk than ever from polluting chemicals, and the stress of modern living may also undermine it. Human interference has already begun to attack the planet's natural protective systems – for example, through the "greenhouse effect" and depletion of the ozone layer. Recently, more and more political leaders and voters are coming to believe that changing our way of life in a number of ways is a cost worth paying for government policies that could help to arrest these trends. Also, without waiting for political solutions, more people are looking for ways to adjust their personal lifestyle to make it easier on the planet. What are the environmental problems that they should be aware of, and how can they avoid contributing to them?

Hiding away from nature

One of the features of modern urban life is a lack of contact with the outside world (see *Ch19*). We spend most of our time indoors. Instead of traveling on foot we get from place to place in cars. We are surrounded by fabrics, household furnishings and goods made from artificial materials. Even the food that we eat is often highly processed. The pace of our days is determined by man-made factors like tax days and work weeks. In general, our

WASTE NOT WANT NOT

■ *Because there are so many more people today and we have become more skilled at exploiting nature, the 20th century has been an age of waste. But we can start to erode the rubbish mountain today. Here are some practical steps you can take.*

Reduce your consumption. *Buy only what you need or genuinely want. Many purchases are made on the spur of the moment, as a response to advertising pressure or an attractive display. Many of our purchases are compulsive, an attempt to satisfy emotional needs through instant gratification, and this fills our homes with things we do not need.*

Resist unnecessary consumption. *Look out for over-packaging. Roughly one-tenth of the money we spend every week goes on packaging. Count the number of layers that surround goods you buy – few products need more than two.*

Reuse what you buy. *In some countries, bottles can be returned and reused, which is more efficient than resmelting the glass. Many things which now go to waste could be used by someone. Sell useful items, or donate them to charities.*

Recycling waste. *Separate the contents of your garbage so that different materials can be recycled. The home of the future may have a variety of containers in the kitchen or garage, for paper, glass, metal and recyclable plastic.*

CONTROLLING YOUR CONSUMER STYLE

What do you consume?

How much do you consume?

The planet benefits environmentally and the individual benefits psychologically from a consumer style which is governed not by impulse but by personal control. Ask yourself questions about particular purchases and about your style of consumption.

How efficiently do you use it?

What happens to it afterward?

▲ **Testing for acid rain**. *Created by emissions from cars, factories and power-stations reacting with moisture in the air, acid rain has a* destructive effect on trees and freshwater lakes and rivers. The health of our natural environment is vital to the quality of our lives.

Your present lifestyle could pose a threat to the quality of your life ■ *How does the way you live now affect the natural environment?* ■ *What can you do to make a more positive contribution to sustaining a healthy planet?*

lifestyle tends to make us feel independent of the natural environment, which we often ignore or undervalue.

The natural pattern of production and consumption is a cyclic one, where waste becomes a resource – dead trees rot and enrich the soil to encourage a continuation of plant life, for example. Modern agriculture, dependent on insecticides and chemical fertilizers, has broken this cycle of natural renewal. In the 1950s people welcomed the advent of what has come to be known as the "throwaway society," and we rely increasingly on the convenience of products that are thrown away. It is easier to transfer a processed meal from freezer to microwave than to cook dinner, and it is easier to throw away your baby's disposable diaper than to deal with piles of dirty washing each week. But microwave meals are the height of overpackaging and waste, and the raw materials needed to make paper-and-plastic disposable diapers drain the earth's limited petroleum reserves and timber stocks (in the United States 100,000 tons of plastic and 800,000 tons of woodpulp every year). Furthermore, the disposal problem that disposable diapers present is so great that some state legislatures are considering a ban.

The poisoned planet

In some cases a hasty and ill-judged use of chemicals has had unforeseen repercussions. A group of chemicals known as PCBs, used in the manufacture of electrical transformers, are a case in point. Once these chemicals are released into the open environment they poison plant life and accumulate in the body tissues of animals. Through agricultural produce, the PCB poison is passed on to human beings –

babies have been known to suffer debilitating illness as a result of PCB poisoning in their mothers' milk. Recent media attention has focused on another group of chemicals – CFCs (chlorofluorocarbons). Once thought to be the ideal propellant for use in aerosol cans, this group of chemicals has become the main cause of the breakdown of the ozone layer, the portion of the atmosphere that protects the earth from harmful solar radiation.

Why the earth is overheating

Today, we consume natural oil, gas and coal – fossil fuels which were laid down millions of years ago – at such a rate that they may be gone within the 21st century. The nuclear energy which was heralded as a viable alternative power

245

MOBILITY OR POLLUTION

■ Cars have a profound influence on our lifestyle – in fact, they have become so much a part of our lives that it is difficult to get a clear view of exactly how they affect our lives, our health and the health of society. Each of us wants to be as individually mobile as possible, but recently people have become aware that our reliance on this one means of transport is hampering rather than advancing society.

More efficient, less polluting cars may help, but only in the short term. Cars with catalytic converters emit far fewer pollutants, but produce slightly more carbon dioxide than ordinary

engines – and motorized transport, already contributing 40 percent of the global carbon dioxide release, is a major contributor to the greenhouse effect. Even if we could produce a nonpolluting solar- or ethanol-powered car, problems would still remain. In towns cars take up a great deal of space – 30 percent or more – and road-building has caused the loss of a great deal of beautiful countryside.

The mobility offered by private cars was once equated with freedom but today it is becoming clear that complete independence does not lead to a healthy society – without any

interdependence we cease to be truly social beings. Nobody finds an area clogged with traffic a pleasant place to be, and cars have driven us from many areas – such as the street – where people once found meeting places outside the home.

▲ **Car pollution.** *A thick pall of smog hangs over the Los Angeles freeway, caused by cars pumping nitrogen oxides and other gases into the atmosphere. Freedom of movement needs to be weighed against the harm to ourselves and our environment.*

source has been shown to create enormous disposal problems with its radioactive waste materials. A dramatic indication that we have been overusing energy is global warming – the greenhouse effect. When factories or engines burn fossil fuels, carbon dioxide (CO_2) is released. Although this is transparent to incoming radiation from the sun, it impedes the escape of heat from the earth. The effect is amplified by the build-up of other gases which include CFCs (from aerosols and refrigerators), methane (from agriculture and landfill) and nitrous oxide (from cars).

The amount of carbon dioxide in the atmosphere is now more than 15 percent higher than in preindustrial times and could easily double during the 21st century. This increase could cause temperatures to rise by anything between 1°C (1.8°F) and 5°C (9°F), which may in turn bring about disastrous changes in weather patterns, and widespread flooding as the polar icecaps melt and sea levels rise.

Preserving the earth's "lungs"

Some scientists think that the destruction of the rainforests is our worst environmental problem. The rainforests of the tropical zones are little known to Westerners, yet they play a vital role in maintaining the ecological balance of our entire planet. They have been described as the planet's lungs, as the vast areas of dense vegetation consume carbon dioxide and replenish the oxygen in the atmosphere. The forests have for millions of years been the habitat of countless plant and animal species and home to thousands of people, and they are irreplaceable. Yet, an area of forest the size of West Germany is cleared each year and turned into grazing land partly to give people in the developing countries enough to live on, and partly in response to a world demand for cheap timber and beef.

A lifestyle for the future?

What can we hope for in the future? While we can gain some useful insights by looking to the past, the society of the future will not be the safe, rural idyll that we often imagine the past to have been and which often looks so much more attractive than the world we live in. The real challenge is to learn to live in a healthy, sustainable way.

KEEPING IN TOUCH WITH THE NATURAL WORLD

■ *Knowing and appreciating the natural world is an essential step in learning to care for it. Some ways of keeping close to nature in the modern world:*

◆ *Your neighborhood. While wilderness holidays are one way of getting to know nature, do not overlook your local environment. There may be environmental problems close to home which you can act on – a polluted stream, or open countryside threatened by urban development.*

◆ *Outdoor recreation. Do as much as you can out-of-doors, by walking or cycling to the grocery store or to work. Play football or take a walk in the park. Revel in the seasons, in the rain and snow, instead of* viewing weather as something to be avoided.

Try to make some of your sports outdoor ones: running or orienteering instead of squash, for example. Whenever you can, get away from roads, towns and other people so you can enjoy the sounds and smells of the woods or shore.

◆ *Bringing nature into your home. Tree branches or flower buds will swell and open in a warm room, and table centerpieces can be a pile of seashells, a bowl of mosses or autumn leaves and cones.*

By living more closely with the world outside, we can increase our knowledge and awareness of it, and add a vital dimension to our lives.

This means making informed and practical choices about everyday things – what detergents to use for the laundry, what to feed the dog, where to go on vacation.

We cannot and should not turn our backs on technology, but we can insist that it will not repeat the mistakes already made – such as the use of CFCs or the destruction of rainforests. We also need to find new ways to measure progress.

A dictionary definition of progress is "advancing or developing toward a better state." One way that we can do this is to stop environmental damage and start the process of restoration. We are faced with an unprecedented and unavoidable challenge, which requires that we rethink the ways in which we live, but which promises us a healthier future. **KC**

READERS may want information about other aspects of a subject, or detail on particular topics that have aroused their interest. Some generally available books and periodicals suggested for further reading are listed below. The main published sources consulted by the contributors to this book follow the further reading suggestions.

1 The Home as Territory
Altman, I and Werner, C (eds) 1985 *Home Environments* Plenum, New York; Altman, I and Wandersman, A (eds) 1987 "Human Behavior and Environment: Advances in Theory and Research" *Neighborhood and Community Environments*, Vol 9, Plenum, New York; Csikszentmihalyi, M and Rochberg-Halton, E 1981 *The Meaning of Things* Cambridge University Press, Cambridge; Rapoport, A 1977 *Human Aspects of Urban Form* Pergamon, New York.

2 Needing a Home
Altman, I and Chemers, M 1980 *Culture and Environment* Cambridge University Press, New York; Erikson, K T 1976 *Everything in its Path: Destruction of Community in the Buffalo Creek Flood* Simon and Schuster, New York; Hombs, M E and Snyder, M 1982 *Homelessness in America: A Forced March to Nowhere* The Community for Creative Non-Violence, Washington, DC; Rapoport, A 1969 *House Form and Culture* Prentice-Hall, Englewood Cliffs, NJ.

3 Choosing a Home
Forty, A 1986 *Objects of Desire* Thames and Hudson, London; Rapoport, A 1969 *House Form and Culture* Prentice-Hall, Englewood Cliffs, NJ.

4 Managing Privacy
Altman, I 1975 *Environment and Social Behavior: Privacy, Personal Space, Territory, and Crowding* Brooks/Cole, Monterey, CA; Altman, I and Chemers, M M 1980 *Culture and Environment* Brooks/Cole, Monterey, CA; Kron, J 1983 *Home-Psych: The Social Psychology of Home and Decoration* Clarkson N Potter, New York.

5 Personal Home Style
Csikszentmihalyi, M and Rochberg-Halton, E 1981 *The Meaning of Things: Domestic Symbols and the Self* University of Chicago Press, Chicago, IL; Kron, J 1983 *Home-Psych: The Social Psychology of Home and Decoration* Clarkson N Potter, New York.

6 Objects on Display
Csikszentmihalyi, M and Rochberg-Halton, E 1981 *The Meaning of Things: Domestic Symbols and the Self* University of Chicago Press, Chicago, IL; Sudjic, D 1985 *Cult Objects* Paladin, London.

7 Color in the Home
Birren, F 1978 *Light, Color and Environment* Van Nostrand Reinhold, New York; Mahnke, F H and Mahnke, R H 1987 *Color and Light in Man-Made Environments* Van Nostrand Reinhold, New York; Porter, T and Mikellides, B 1973 *Color for Architecture* Van Nostrand Reinhold, New York.

8 The Effects of Light
Porter, T 1982 *Colour Outside* The Architectural Press, London; Whitney Library of Design, New York 1988 Editorial Trillas, Mexico; Rowntree, D 1964 *Interior Design* Penguin, Harmondsworth.

9 Touch, Sound and Smell
New Scientist and *Scientific American*.

10 Design for Leisure
Cherry, G E 1982 *Leisure in the Home* Sports Council/Social Science Research Council Joint Panel on Leisure and Recreation Research, London; Chubb, M and Chubb, H R 1981 *One Third of Our Time? An Introduction to Recreation Behaviour and Resources* John Wiley, New York.

11 Eating and Entertaining
Mennell, S 1985 *All Manners of Food*, Blackwell, Oxford; Tannahill, R 1988 (rev edn) *Food in History* Penguin, Harmondsworth.

12 Cars
Marsh, P and Collett, P 1986 *Driving Passion: The Psychology of the Car* Cape, London/Faber, Winchester, MA; Pettifer, J 1984 *Automania* Collins, London.

13 The Role of Pets
Fox, M W 1978 *The Dog: Its Domestication and Behavior* Garland STPM, New York; Katcher, A H and Beck, A M 1983 *New Perspectives on our Lives with Companion Animals* University of Pennsylvania Press, Philadelphia, PA; Serpell, J 1986 *In the Company of Animals* Blackwell, Oxford; Trumler, E 1973 *Understanding Your Dog* Faber, London; Turner, D C and Bateson, P 1988 *The Domestic Cat: The Biology of its Behaviour* Cambridge University Press, Cambridge.

14 Garden Effects
Berall, J S 1978 *The Garden: An Illustrated History* Penguin, New York; Harris, J 1979 *The Artist and the Country House* Sotheby Park Burnett, London; Stuart, D 1988 *The Garden Triumphant: A Victorian Legacy* Viking, London.

15 Living Together
Alexander, C et al 1977 *A Pattern Language* Oxford University Press, New York; Hayden, D 1984 *Redesigning the American Dream: The Future of Housing, Work, and Family Life* Norton, New York; McCamant, K and Durrett, C 1988 *Cohousing: A Contemporary Approach to Housing Ourselves* Ten Speed Press, Berkeley, CA.

16 The Changing Home
Franck, K A and Ahrentzen, S (eds) 1989 *New Households: New Housing* Van Nostrand Reinhold, New York; Hayden, D 1984 *Redesigning the American Dream: The Future of Housing, Work, and Family Life* Norton, New York.

17 A Sense of Place
Canter, D 1977 *The Psychology of Place* Architectural Press, London; Canter, D, Krampen, M and Stea, D (eds) 1988 *Environmental Perspectives* Avebury, Aldershot, UK; Canter, D, Krampen, M and Stea, D (eds) 1988 *Environmental Policy, Assessment and Communication* Avebury, Aldershot, UK; Canter, D, Krampen, M and Stea, D (eds) 1988 *New Directions in Environmental Participation* Avebury, Aldershot, UK.

18 Neighborhoods
Hayden, D 1984 *Redesigning the American Dream* Norton, New York; Rapoport, A 1977 *The Human Aspects of Urban Form* Pergamon, New York; Rapoport, A 1982 *The Meaning of the Built Environment: A Non-Verbal Communication Approach* Sage, Beverly Hills, CA.

19 Out in the City
Cullen, G 1971 *The Concise Townscape* Architectural Press, London; Lynch, K 1960 *The Image of the City* MIT Press, Cambridge, MA and London.

20 Coping With Urban Life
Baum, A and Epstein, Y M 1978 *Human Response to Crowding* Erlbaum, Hillsdale, NJ; Hall, E T 1966 *The Hidden Dimension* Doubleday, New York.

21 Scenes of Crime
Brantingham, P J and Brantingham, P L 1984 *Patterns in Crime* Macmillan, New York.

22 Country Living
Blunden, J and Curry, N 1985 *The Changing Countryside* Croom Helm, London; Carlson, J E, Lassey, M L and Lassey, W R 1981 *Rural Society and Environment in America* McGraw Hill, New York; Newby, H 1985 2nd edn *Green and Pleasant Land?* Wildwood House, London.

23 Color Outside the Home
Baer, M, Pomada, E and Larsen, M 1978 *Painted Ladies: San Francisco's Resplendent Victorians* Dutton, New York; Bayes, K 1967 *The Therapeutic Effect of Environment on Emotionally Disturbed and Mentally Subnormal Children* Unwin, London; Porter, T and Mikellides, B 1976 *Colour for Architecture* Studio Vista, London; Porter, T 1982 *Colour Outside* Architectural Press, London.

24 The Workplace
Gifford, R 1987 *Environmental Psychology: Principles and Practice* Allyn and Bacon, Boston, MA; Salvendy, G (ed) 1987 *Handbook of Human Factors* Wiley, New York.

25 Places for Learning
Moore, R C 1986 *Childhood's Domain: Play and Place in Child Development* Croom Helm, London; Ward, C 1979 *The Child in the City* Pantheon, New York, 2nd edn (in press) Bedford Square Press, London.

26 Going Shopping
Campbell, C 1987 *The Romantic Ethic and the Spirit of Modern Consumerism* Blackwell, Oxford and New York; Douglas, M and Isherwood, B 1978 *The World of Goods* Basic Books, New York; Scott, N K 1989 *Shopping Centre Design* Van Nostrand Reinhold, New York.

27 Eating Out
Mennell, S 1985 *All Manners of Food* Blackwell, Oxford; Tannahill, R 1988 (rev edn) *Food in History* Penguin, Harmondsworth.

28 Vacationing
Furnham, A and Bochner, S 1986 *Culture Shock* Methuen, London; Krippendorf, J 1984 *The Holiday Makers – Understanding the Impact of Leisure and Travel* Orell Füssli Verlag, Zürich and Schwäbisch Hall, translated by Andrassy, V 1987 Heinemann, London; Langer, E 1989 *Mindfulness*

Addison-Wesley, New York; Pearce, P L 1988 *The Ulysses Factor: Evaluating Visitors in Tourist Settings* Springer-Verlag, New York.

29 Places for Recreation

Goodale, T L and Witt, P A 1985 *Recreation and Leisure: Issues in an Era of Change* Venture Publishing, PA; MacEwen, A and MacEwen, M 1987 *Greenprints for the Countryside?* Allen and Unwin, London.

30 A Green Environment?

Christensen, K 1989 *Home Ecology: Making Your World a Better Place* Arlington London, Fulcrum, Boulder, CO; Seymour, J and Giradet, H 1987 *Blueprint for a Green Planet* Dorling Kindersley, London/Prentice-Hall, New York.

Kate Fox Kibby played a major role in assisting Peter Marsh with the development and editing of this volume. Her efforts are gratefully acknowledged.

CONTRIBUTORS' SOURCES

1 The Home as Territory Altman, I 1975 *The Environment and Social Behavior* Brooks/Cole, Monterey, CA; Altman, I and Chemers, M 1980 *Culture and Environment* Brooks/Cole, Monterey, CA; Brower, S 1965 "The Signs We Learn to Read" *Landscape*, Vol 15, 1, pp9-12; Cooper, C 1974 "The House as a Symbol of the Self" in Lang, J, Burnette, C, Moleski, W and Vachon, D (eds): *Designing for Human Behavior* Dowden, Hutchinson and Ross, Stroudsburg, PA; Lorenz, K 1966 *On Aggression* Harcourt, Brace and Jovanovich, New York; Mead, M 1966 *Male and Female* William Morrow, New York; Rapoport, A 1969 *House, Form and Culture* Prentice-Hall, Englewood Cliffs, NJ; Sebba, R and Churchman, A 1983 "Territories and Territoriality in the Home" *Environment and Behavior*, Vol 15, 2, pp191-210; Sebba, R and Churchman, A 1986 "The Uniqueness of the Home" *Architecture and Behavior*, Vol 3, 1, pp7-24; Sommer, R and Becker, F 1969 "Territorial Defence and the Good Neighbor" *Journal of Personality and Social Psychology*, Vol 11, pp85-92; Stea, D 1965 "Space, Territory and Human Movements" *Landscape*, Vol 15, 1, pp13-16.

2 Needing a Home Altman, I and Chemers, M 1980 *Culture and Environment* Cambridge University Press, New York; Altman, I and Rogoff, B 1987 "World Views in Psychology: Trait, Interactionist, Organismic, and Transactional Approaches" in Stokols, D and Altman, I (eds): *Handbook of Environmental Psychology*, Vol 1, Wiley, New York; Baum, A, Fleming, R and Singer, J E 1982 "Stress at Three Mile Island: Applying Social Psychological Impact Analysis" in Bickman, L (ed): *Applied Social Psychology Annual* Sage, Beverly Hills, CA; Brown, B B and Harris, P (in press) "Residential Burglary Victimization: Reactions to the Invasion of a Primary Territory" *Journal of Environmental Psychology*; Cooper, M C 1978 "Remembrances of Landscapes Past" *Landscape*, Vol 22, 3, pp34-43; Erikson, K T 1976 *Everything in its Path: Destruction of Community in the Buffalo Creek Flood* Simon and Schuster, New York; Fried, M 1963 "Grieving for a Lost Home" in Duhl, L J (ed): *The Urban Condition* Basic Books, New York; Gauvain, M, Altman, I and Fahim, H 1983 "Homes and Social Change: A Cross-Cultural Analysis" in Feimer, N R and Geller, E S (eds): *Environmental Psychology: Directions and Perspectives* Praeger, New York, pp180-218; Hombs, M E and Snyder, M 1982 *Homelessness in America: A Forced March to Nowhere* The Community for Creative Non-Violence, Washington, DC; Proshansky, H, Fabian, A and Kaminoff, R 1983 "Place Identity: Physical World and Socialization of the Self" *Journal of Environmental Psychology*, 3, pp57-83; Rapoport, A 1969 *House Form and Culture* Prentice-Hall, Englewood Cliffs, NJ; Stone, R A and Levine, A G 1985 "Reactions to Collective Stress: Correlates of Active Citizen Participation at Love Canal" in Wandersman, A and Hess, R (eds): *Beyond the Individual: Environmental Approaches and Prevention* Haworth, New York, pp153ff.

3 Choosing a Home Birchall, J 1988 *Building Communities* Routledge and Kegan Paul, London; Bishop, J and Davison, I 1989 *Good Product: Could the Service be Better?* Housing Research Foundation, National Housebuilding Council, London; Bishop, J 1986 *Milton Keynes: The Best of Both Worlds?* Occasional Paper 24, School for Advanced Urban Studies, University of Bristol; Cooper, C 1974 "The House as a Symbol of the Self" in Lang, J et al (eds): *Designing for Human Behavior* Dowden Hutchinson and Ross, Stroudsburg, PA; Cooper, C and Sarkissian, W 1986 *Housing as if People Mattered* University of California Press, Berkeley, CA; Forty, A 1986 *Objects of Desire* Thames and Hudson, London; Gans, H 1962 *The Urban Villagers* Free Press, New York; Oliver, P 1971 *Shelter and Society* Barrie and Jenkins, London/Praeger, New York; Rapoport, A 1969 *House Form and Culture* Prentice-Hall, Englewood Cliffs, NJ.

4 Managing Privacy Altman, I 1975 *Environment and Social Behavior: Privacy, Personal Space, Territory, and Crowding* Brooks/Cole, Monterey, CA; Altman, I and Chemers, M M 1980 *Culture and Environment* Brooks/Cole, Monterey, CA; Altman, I, Nelson, P A and Lett, E E 1972 "The Ecology of Home Environments" *Catalog of Selected Documents in Psychology* American Psychological Association, Washington, DC; Altman, I, Vinsel, A and Brown, B B 1981 "Dialectic Conceptions in Social Psychology: An Application to Social Penetration and Privacy Regulation" in Berkowitz, L (ed): *Advances in Experimental Social Psychology, 14* Academic Press, New York, pp107-160; Brown, B B and Altman, I 1981 "Territoriality and Residential Crime: A Conceptual Framework" in Brantingham, P S and Brantingham, P L (eds): *Environmental Criminology* Sage, Beverly Hills, CA, pp55-76; Marshall, N J 1974 "Dimensions of Privacy Preferences" *Multivariate Behavioral Research, 9*, pp255-71; Mehrabian, A and Diamond, S G 1971 "Effects of Furniture Arrangement, Props, and Personality on Social Interaction" *Journal of Social and Personality Psychology*, 20, pp18-30; Osmond, H 1957 "Function as the Basis of Psychiatric Ward Design" *Mental Hospitals*, 8, pp23-30; Parke, R D and Sawin, D B 1979 "Children's Privacy in the Home: Developmental, Ecological, and Child-Rearing Determinants" *Environment and Behavior*, 11, pp87-104; Rosenblatt, P C and Budd, L G 1975 "Territoriality and Privacy in Married and Unmarried Cohabiting Couples" *Journal of Social Psychology*, 97, pp67-76; Scheflen, A E 1971 "Living Space in an Urban Ghetto" *Family Process*, 10, pp429-50; Sommer, R 1967 "Sociofugal Space" *American Journal of Sociology*, 72, pp654-9; Taylor, R B 1988 *Human Territorial Functioning* Cambridge University Press, New York; Vinsel, A, Brown, B B, Altman, I and Foss, C 1980 "Privacy Regulation, Territorial Displays, and Effectiveness of Individual Functioning" *Journal of Personality and Social Psychology*, 39, pp1104-15.

5 Personal Home Style Altman, I and Chemers, M M 1980 *Culture and Environment* Cambridge University Press, New York; Altman, I and Gauvain, M 1981 "A Cross-Cultural and Dialectic Analysis of Homes" in Liben, L, Patterson, A and Newcombe, N (eds): *Spatial Representation and Behavior Across the Life Span: Theory and Application* Academic Press, New York, pp283-319; Brown, B B 1987 "Territoriality" in Stokols, D and Altman, I (eds): *Handbook of Environmental Psychology*, Vol 1, Wiley, New York, pp505-31; Csikszentmihalyi, M and Rochberg-Halton, E 1981 *The Meaning of Things: Domestic Symbols and the Self* University of Chicago Press, Chicago IL; Werner, C M, Altman, I and Oxley, D 1985 "Temporal Aspects of Homes: A Transactional Perspective" in Altman, I and Werner, C M (eds): *Home Environments: Human Behavior and the Environment*, Vol 8, Plenum, New York, pp1-32.

6 Objects on Display Caplow, T 1984 "Rule Enforcement Without Visible Means: Christmas Gift Giving in Middletown" *American Journal of Sociology*, 89, pp1306-23; Csikszentmihalyi, M and Rochberg-Halton, E 1981 *The Meaning of Things: Domestic Symbols and the Self* University of Chicago Press, Chicago IL; Furby, L 1978 "Possessions: Toward a Theory of Their Meaning and Function throughout the Life Cycle" in Baltes, P B (ed): *Life-span Development and Behavior*, Vol 1, Academic Press, New York, pp297-336; Korosec-Serfaty, P 1984 "The House from Attic to Cellar" *Journal of Environmental Psychology*, 4, pp303-21; Werner, C M, Altman, I and Oxley, D 1985 "Temporal Aspects of Homes: a Transactional Perspective" in Altman, I and Werner, C M (eds): *Home Environments: Human Behavior and the Environment*, Vol 8, Plenum, New York, pp1-32.

7 Color in the Home Acking, C A and Küller, R 1972 "The Perception of an Interior as a Function of its Colour" *Ergonomics*, Vol 15, 6, pp645-54; Birren, F 1961 *Color Psychology and Color Therapy* Citadel Press, Secaucus,

CONTRIBUTORS' SOURCES CONTINUED

NJ; Birren, F 1978 *Light, Color and Environment* Van Nostrand Reinhold, New York; Mahnke, F H and Mahnke, R H 1987 *Color and Light in Man-Made Environments* Van Nostrand Reinhold, New York; Porter, T and Mikellides, B 1973 *Color for Architecture* Van Nostrand Reinhold, New York; Sharpe, D T 1974 *The Psychology of Color and Design* Nelson-Hall, Chicago, IL; Varley, H (ed) 1980 *Color* Knapp, Los Angeles, CA; Zöld, B, Toth, T and Tolna, J 1986 "Colour Preference: A New Approach" *Perceptual and Motor Skills*, 62, pp739-52.

8 The Effects of Light Birren, F 1982 *Light, Color and Environment* Van Nostrand Reinhold, New York; Munsell, A H 1981 *A Color Notation* Munsell Color, Macbeth, A Division of Kollmorgen Corporation, Baltimore, MD; Porter, T 1982 *Colour Outside* The Architectural Press, London Whitney Library of Design, New York 1988 Editorial Trillas (Mexico); Porter, T and Mikellides, B 1976 *Colour for Architecture* Studio Vista, London, 1976 Van Nostrand Reinhold, New York; Taylor, F A 1962 *Colour Technology* Oxford University Press, London; Varley, H (ed) 1983 *Colour* Marshall Editions, London.

9 Touch, Sound and Smell This chapter was based on the author's analysis of a wide range of sources, including articles in various issues of *New Scientist* and *Scientific American*.

10 Design for Leisure Cherry, G E 1982 *Leisure in the Home* Sports Council/Social Science Research Council Joint Panel on Leisure and Recreation Research, London; Clarke, J and Critcher, C 1985 *The Devil Makes Work* Macmillan, Basingstoke and London; Coleman, A 1985 *Utopia on Trial* Hilary Shipman, London; Glyptis, S A, McInnes, H A and Patmore, J A 1987 *Leisure and the Home* Sports Council/Economic and Social Research Council Joint Panel on Leisure and Recreation Research, London; Goodale, T L and Witt, P A 1985 *Recreation and Leisure: Issues in an Era of Change* Venture Publishing, PA; Institute of Housing and Royal Institute of British Architects 1983 *Homes for the Future* The Institutes, London; Kelly, J R 1982 *Leisure* Prentice-Hall, Englewood Cliffs, NJ; Parker, S 1985 *Leisure and Work* Allen and Unwin, London; Patmore, J A 1983 *Recreation and Resources* Blackwell, Oxford; Torkildsen, G 1983 *Leisure and Recreation Management* E and F N Spon, London.

11 Eating and Entertaining Boyd Eaton, S, Shostak, M and Konner, M 1988 *The Paleolithic Prescription: A Program of Diet and Exercise and a Design for Living* Harper and Row, New York; Fussell, B 1983 *Masters of American Cookery* Times Books, New York; Levi-Strauss, C 1969 *The Elementary Structures of Kinship* Beacon Press, Boston MA; Luard, E 1987 *The Old World Kitchen* Bantam Books, New York; Mennell, S 1985 *All Manners of Food* Blackwell, Oxford; Remoff, H 1984 *Female Sexual Choice* Dutton, New York; Sommer, R 1969 *Personal Space. The Behavioral Basis of Design* Prentice Hall, Englewood Cliffs, NJ; Tannahill, R 1988 (rev edn) *Food in History* Penguin, Harmondsworth; Wolf, R and Tiger, L 1976 *China's Food* Friendly Press, New York.

12 Cars Basham, F, Ughetti, B and Rambali, P 1984 *Car Culture* Plexus, London; Knapper, C K and Cropley, A J 1981 "Social and Interpersonal Factors in Driving" in Stephenson, J-H and Davis, M J (eds): *Progress in Applied Social Psychology* Wiley, New York; Mandel, L 1977 *Driven: The American Four-Wheel Love Affair* Stein and Day, New York; Marsh, P and Collett, P 1986 *Driving Passion: The Psychology of the Car* Cape, London, Faber Winchester, MA; Parry, M H 1968 *Aggression on the Road* Tavistock, London; Pettifer, J 1984 *Automania* Collins, London; Sears, S W 1977 *The Automobile in America* American Heritage Publishing Company, New York; Silk, G 1984 *Automobile and Culture* Abrams, New York.

13 The Role of Pets Cooper, J E, Hutchinson, M F, Jackson, O F and Maurice, R J 1985 *Manual of Exotic Pets* BSAVA, Cheltenham; Fox, M W 1978 *The Dog: Its Domestication and Behavior* Garland STPM, New York; Gittleman, J L 1989 *Carnivore Behavior, Ecology and Evolution* Chapman and Hall, London; Hart, B and Hart, L A 1985 *Canine and Feline Behavioral Therapy* Lea and Febiger, Philadelphia, PA; Katcher, A H and Beck, A M 1983 *New Perspectives on our Lives with Companion Animals* University of Pennsylvania Press, Philadelphia, PA; Lorenz, K 1954 *Man Meets Dog* Methuen, London; Mech, D 1970 *The Wolf* Doubleday, New York; Serpell, J 1986 *In the Company of Animals* Blackwell, Oxford; Trumler, E 1973 *Understanding Your Dog* Faber, London; Turner, D C and Bateson, P 1988 *The Domestic Cat: The Biology of its Behaviour* Cambridge University Press, Cambridge; Willis, M 1989 *Genetics of the Dog* Witherby, London.

14 Garden Effects Austen, R 1665 *The Spiritual Use of an Orchard, or Garden of Fruit Trees* London; Blomfield, R 1892 *The Formal Garden in England* London; Burke, E 1757 *A Philosophical Enquiry into the Origins of our Ideas of the Sublime and the Beautiful* London; Downing, A J 1849 *A Treatise on the Theory and Practice of Landscape Gardening* Boston MA; Ellwanger, G H 1896 *The Garden's Story* New York; Lawson, W 1618 *A New Orchard and Garden* London; Loudon, J C 1838 *The Villa Gardener* London; Price, U 1810 *Essays on the Picturesque* London; Robinson, W 1881 *The English Flower Garden* London; Stuart, D 1979 *Georgian Gardens*, Robert Hall, London; Stuart, D 1984 *The Kitchen Garden: An Historical Guide to Traditional Crops* Sutton, London; Stuart, D and Sutherland, J 1987 *Plants from the Past* Viking, London; Stuart, D 1988 *The Garden Triumphant: A Victorian Legacy* Viking, London.

15 Living Together Alexander, C et al 1977 *A Pattern Language* Oxford University Press, New York; Alexander, C et al 1979 *The Timeless Way of Building* Oxford University Press, New York; *Diggers and Dreamers: The 1990-1 Guide to Communal Living* Communes Network, Lifespan Community, Townhead, Dunford Bridge, Sheffield, UK; *Gimme Shelter: Even Middle-class Americans Now Feel the Housing Crisis* Rolling Stone Magazine, 1 December 1988; Hayden, D 1984 *Redesigning the American Dream: The Future of Housing, Work, and Family Life* Norton, New York; *Interested in Joining a Community...?* (private publication) Birchwood Hall Community, Birchwood Hall, Malvern, UK; McCamant, K and Durrett, C 1988 *Cohousing: A Contemporary Approach to Housing Ourselves* Ten Speed Press, Berkeley, CA; McLaughlin, C and Davidson, G 1985 *Builders of the Dawn* Stillpoint Publishing, Walpole, NH.

16 The Changing Home Alexander, C 1967 "The City as a Mechanism for Sustaining Human Contact" in Gutman, R (ed): *People and Buildings* Basic Books, New York, pp422-31; Alexander, C et al 1977 *A Pattern Language* Oxford University Press, New York; Brown, L R and Shaw, P 1982 *Six Steps to a Sustainable Society* Worldwatch Papers, 48, Worldwatch Institute, Washington, DC; Chandler, W U 1983 *Materials Recycling: The Virtue of Necessity* Worldwatch Papers, 56, Worldwatch Institute, Washington, DC; Christensen, K 1989 *Home Ecology: Making Your World a Better Place* Arlington, London and 1990 Fulcrum, Boulder, CO; Connors, M M, Harrison, A A and Akins, F R 1986 "Psychology and the Resurgent Space Program" *American Psychologist*, 41, pp906-13; Flavin, C and Durning, A B 1988 *Building on Success: The Age of Energy Efficiency* Worldwatch Papers, 82, Worldwatch Institute, Washington, DC; Franck, K A and Ahrentzen, S (eds) 1989 *New Households: New Housing* Van Nostrand Reinhold, New York; Gabe, F 1983 "The Gabe Self-Cleaning House" in Zimmerman, J (ed): *The Technological Woman: Interfacing with Tomorrow* Praeger, New York, pp75-82; Harrison, A A and Connors, M M 1984 "Groups in Exotic Environments" in Berkowitz, L (ed): *Advances in Experimental Social Psychology*, Vol 18, Academic Press, New York, pp49-87; Hayden, D 1984 *Redesigning the American Dream: The Future of Housing, Work, and Family Life* Norton, New York; Lawton, M P 1985 "The Elderly in Context" *Environment and Behavior*, 17, pp501-19; Mindel, C H 1986 "Multigenerational Family Households: Recent Trends and Implications for the Future" in Troll, L E (ed): *Family Issues in Current Gerontology* Springer, New York, pp269-83; Pearson, D 1989 *The Natural House Book* Conran Octopus, London; Poulshock, S W and Deimling, G T 1986 "Families Caring for Elders in Residence: Issues in the Measurement of Burden" in Troll, L E (ed): *Family Issues in Current Gerontology* Springer, New York, pp226-45; Renner, M 1989 *Rethinking the Role of the Automobile* Worldwatch Papers, 84, Worldwatch Institute, Washington, DC; Rousseau, D 1988 *Your Home, Your Health, and Well-Being* Ten Speed Press, Berkeley, CA; Sherman, H and Spring, E 1984 *A New American House: Architectural Design Competition 1984: Catalog of Winning and Select Designs* Minneapolis College of Art and Design, Minneapolis, MN; Venolia, C 1988 *Healing Environments* Celestial Arts, Berkeley, CA.

17 A Sense of Place Barker, R G 1965 "Explorations in Ecological Psychology" *American Psychologist*, 20, pp1-14; Canter, D 1972 "A Psychological Analysis of The Royal Hospital for Sick Children: Yorkhill, Glasgow" *Architects' Journal*, 6 September, pp525-64; Canter, D 1974 *Psychology for Architects* Applied Science Publishers, London; Canter, D 1977 *The Psychology of Place* Architectural Press, London; Canter, D 1986 "Putting Situations in Their Place" in Furnham, A (ed): *Social Behaviour in Context* Allyn and Bacon, Boston MA, pp208-39; Canter, D and Canter, S (eds) 1979 *Designing for Therapeutic Environments* Wiley, Chichester; Canter, D, Krampen, M and Stea, D (eds) 1988 *Environmental Perspectives* Avebury, Aldershot, UK; Canter, D and Stringer, P 1975 *Environmental Interaction* International Universities Press, New York.

18 Neighborhoods Campbell, A, Converse, P and Rodgers, W L 1976 *The Quality of American Life* Sage, (Beverly Hills, CA; Hayden, D 1984 *Redesigning the American Dream* Norton, New York; Rapoport, A 1977 *The Human Aspects of Urban Form* Pergamon, New York; Rapoport, A 1982 *The Meaning of the Built Environment: A Non-Verbal Communication Approach* Sage, Beverly Hills, CA; Rapoport, A "Environmental Preference, Habit Selection and Urban Housing" *Journal of Social Issues*, 36, 3, p118-34; Wats, N and Knevitt, C 1987 *Community Architecture* Penguin, Harmondsworth.

19 Out in the City Alexander, C et al 1977 *A Pattern Language* Oxford University Press, New York; Cullen, G 1971 *The Concise Townscape* Architectural Press, London; Gold, J R 1980 *An Introduction to Behavioural Geography* Oxford University Press, Oxford; Halprin, L 1969 *The RSVP Cycles: Creative Processes in the Human Environment* George Braziller, New York; Harvey, D 1989 *The Condition of Postmodernity* Blackwell, Oxford; Harvey, D 1989 *The Urban Experience* Blackwell, Oxford; Jacobs, J 1961 *The Death and Life of Great American Cities* Random House, New York; Lynch, K 1960 *The Image of the City* MIT Press, Cambridge, MA and London; Raban, J 1974 *Soft City* Collins Harvill, London; Smith, P F 1977 *The Syntax of Cities* Hutchinson, London; Tuan, Y-F 1977 *Space and Place: The Perspective of Experience* Edward Arnold, London.

20 Coping With Urban Life Aiello, J R, Baum, A and Gormley, F P 1981 "Social Determinants of Residential Crowding Stress" *Personality and Social Psychology Bulletin*, 7, pp643-9; Baum, A and Epstein, Y M 1978 *Human Response to Crowding* Erlbaum, Hillsdale, NJ; Cohen, S et al 1986 *Behavior, Health and Environmental Stress* Plenum, New York; Hall, E T 1966 *The Hidden Dimension* Doubleday, New York; Jain, V 1987 *The Psychological Consequences of Crowding* Sage, Beverly Hills, CA; Sargent, S 1980 "Crowding and Cognitive Limits" in Harvey, J H (ed): *Cognition, Social Behavior and the Environment* Erlbaum, Hillsdale NJ; Stockols, D and Altman, I (eds) 1987 *Handbook of Environmental Psychology* Wiley, New York; Walmsley, D J 1988 *Urban Living: the Individual and the City* Longman, UK.

21 Scenes of Crime Brantingham, P J and Brantingham, P L 1984 *Patterns in Crime* Macmillan, New York; Clarke, R V G 1983 "Situational Crime Prevention: Its Theoretical Basis and Practical Scope" *Crime and Justice, an Annual Review of Research* Vol 4, University of Chicago Press, Chicago, IL; Felson, M 1987 "Routine Activities and Crime Prevention in the Developing Metropolis" *Criminology*, November.

22 Country Living Blunden, J and Curry, N 1985 *The Changing Countryside* Croom Helm, London; Blunden, J and Curry, N 1988 *A Future for our Countryside* Blackwell, Oxford; Blunden, J and Turner, G 1985 *Critical Countryside* BBC Publications, London; Bryant, C R, Russwurm, L H and McLellan, A G 1982 *The City's Countryside* Longman, London; Browne, W and Hadwiger, D 1983 *Rural Policy Problems* Lexington Books, Lexington, MA; Carlson, J E, Lassey, M L and Lassey, W R 1981 *Rural Society and Environment in America* McGraw Hill, New York; Cloke, P and Park, C 1985 *Rural Resource Management* Croom Helm, London; Coulmin, P 1986 *La Décentralisation – la dynamique du développement local* Syros Adels, Paris; Gilg, A (ed) 1988 *The International Yearbook of Rural Planning* Elsevier-Geo, Barking; Newby, H 1985 2nd edn *Green and Pleasant Land?* Wildwood House, London; Pacione, M 1984 *Rural Geography* Harper and Row, London.

23 Color Outside the Home Baer, M, Pomada, E and Larsen, M 1978 *Painted Ladies: San Francisco's Resplendent Victorians* Dutton, New York; BOSTI 1981 *The Impact of Office Environment on Productivity and Quality of Working Life: Comprehensive Findings* Buffalo Organization for Social and Technological Innovation, Buffalo, New York; Hård, A 1969 *The NCS Colour Order and Scaling System* Swedish Colour Centre, Stockholm; Humphrey, N K 1971 "Colour and Brightness Preferences in Monkeys" *Nature*, 229, 615, pp615-17; Humphrey, N K 1976 "The Colour Currency of Nature" in Porter, T and Mikellides, B (eds): *Colour for Architecture* Studio Vista, London; Küller, R 1973 *A Semantic Model for Describing Perceived Environment* Document D12, National Swedish Institute for Building Research, Stockholm; Lenclos, J P 1976 "Living in Colour" in Porter, T and Mikellides, B (eds): *Colour for Architecture* Studio Vista, London; Mikellides, B 1979 "Conflicting Experiences of Colour Space" in Simon, J D (ed): *Conflicting Experiences of Space* Proceedings of the 4th IAPS, Tome II, Catholic University of Louvain, pp679-703; Newman, O 1976 "The Use of Colour and Texture at Clason Point" in Porter, T and Mikellides, B (eds): *Colour for Architecture* Studio Vista, London, pp47-55; Sivik, L 1974 "A Study of Exterior Colours" *Göteborg Psychological Reports*, 4, (ii), University of Göteborg, Sweden; Smith, P 1987 *Architecture and the Principle of Harmony* RIBA, London.

24 The Workplace Gifford, R 1987 *Environmental Psychology: Principles and Practice* Allyn and Bacon, Boston, MS; Landy, F J and Trumbo, D A 1980 *Psychology of Work Behaviour* Dorsey Press, Homewood, IL; Piercy, N (ed) 1984 *The Management Implications of New Information Technology* Croom Helm, London; Proshansky, H M, Ihelson, W H and Rivlin, L G (eds) 1976 *Environmental Psychology: People and Their Physical Settings* Holt, Rinehart and Winston, New York; Salvendy, G (ed) 1987 *Handbook of Human Factors* Wiley, New York; Warr, P (ed) 1987 *Psychology at Work* Penguin, Harmondsworth.

25 Places for Learning Blishen, E (ed) 1969 *The School That I'd Like* Penguin, Harmondsworth; Bremer, J and von Moschzisker, M 1971 *The School Without Walls* Holt, Rinehart and Winston, New York; Canter, D (ed) 1974 *Psychology and the Built Environment* Architectural Press, London; Lynch, K 1978 *Growing up in Cities: Studies of the Spatial Environment of Adolescence* MIT Press, Cambridge, MA; Saint, A 1987 *Towards a Social Architecture: The Role of School Buildings in Post-War England* Yale University Press, London; Sutton, S 1985 *Learning Through the Built Environment: An Ecological Approach to Child Development* Irvington, New York; Tizard, B et al 1988 *Young Children at School in the Inner City* Erlbaum, London; Tuan, Y-F 1974 *Topophilia: A Study of Environmental Perception, Attitudes and Values* Prentice-Hall, NJ; Ward, C (ed) 1977 *British School Buildings: Designs and Appraisals* Architectural Press, London; Ward, C 1988 *The Child in the Country* Robert Hale, London.

26 Going Shopping Beddington, N 1982 *Design for Shopping Centres* Butterworth, London; Douglas, M and Isherwood, B 1978 *The World of Goods: Towards an Anthropology of Consumption* Penguin, Harmondsworth; Jacobs, J 1961, 1965 *The Death and Life of Great American Cities* Pelican, Harmondsworth; Kirby, D 1988 *Shopping in the Eighties: A Guide to Sources of Information* The British Library, London; Packard, V 1960 *The Hidden Persuaders* Penguin, Harmondsworth.

27 Eating Out Boyd Eaton, S, Shostak, M and Konner, M 1988 *The Paleolithic Prescription: A Program of Diet and Exercise and a Design for Living* Harper and Row, New York; Fussell, B 1983 *Masters of American Cookery* Times Books, New York; Levi-Strauss, C 1969 *The Elementary Structures of Kinship* Beacon Press, Boston MA; Luard, E 1987 *The Old World Kitchen* Bantam Books, New York; Mennell, S 1985 *All Manners of Food* Blackwell, Oxford; Remoff, H 1984 *Female Sexual Choice* Dutton, New York; Tannahill, R 1988 (rev edn) *Food in History* Penguin, Harmondsworth; Wolf, R and Tiger, L 1976 *China's Food* Friendly Press, New York.

28 Vacationing Csikszentmihalyi, M 1977 *Beyond Boredom and Anxiety* Jossey-Bass, San Francisco, CA; Furnham, A and Bochner, S 1986 *Culture Shock* Methuen, London; Krippendorf, J 1984 *The Holiday Makers: Understanding the Impact of Leisure and Travel* Orell Füssli Verlag, Zürich and Schwäbisch Hall, translated by Andrassy, V 1987, Heinemann, London; Langer, E 1989 *Mindfulness* Addison-Wesley, New York; Lew, A 1987 "English-speaking Tourists and the Attractions of Singapore" *Singapore Journal of Tropical Geography*, 8, pp44-59; MacCannell, D 1976 *The Tourist* Schocken, New York; Pearce, D 1988 "Tourist Time-Budgets" *Annals of Tourism Research*, 15, pp106-21; Pearce, P L 1982 *The Social Psychology of Tourist Behaviour* Pergamon, Oxford; Pearce, P L 1988 *The Ulysses Factor. Evaluating Visitors in Tourist Settings* Springer-Verlag, New York; Pearce, P L and Moscardo, G 1985 "Visitor Evaluation" *Evaluation Review*, 9, pp281-306; Smith, V (ed) 1978 *Hosts and Guests* Blackwell, Oxford.

29 Places for Recreation Chubb, M and Chubb, H R 1981 *One Third of our Time? An Introduction to Recreation Behaviour and Resources* Wiley, New York; Fairbrother, N 1977 *New Lives, New Landscapes* Pelican, Harmondsworth; Kelly, J R 1982 *Leisure* Prentice-Hall, Englewood Cliff, NJ; MacEwen, A and MacEwen M 1982 *National Parks: Conservation or Cosmetics?* Allen and Unwin, London; Newby, H 1988 *The Countryside in Question* Hutchinson, London; Pack, C M and Glyptis, S A 1989 *Developing Sport and Leisure. Good Practice in Urban Regeneration* Her Majesty's Stationery Office, London; Patmore, J A 1983 *Recreation and Resources* Blackwell, Oxford; Shoard, M 1980 *The Theft of the Countryside* Temple Smith, London; Shoard, M 1987 *This Land is Our Land* Paladin, London; Torkildsen, G 1983 *Leisure and Recreation Management* E and F N Spon, London.

30 A Green Environment? Bunyard, P and Morgan-Grenville, F (eds) 1987 *The Green Alternative Guide to Good Living* Methuen, London; Button, J 1989 *How to be Green* Century, London; Capra, F 1982 *The Turning Point* Wildwood House, Aldershot, UK; Christensen, K 1989 *Home Ecology: Making Your World a Better Place* Arlington, London (in press) Fulcrum, Boulder, CO; Hardyment, C 1987 *From Mangle to Microwave* Polity, Cambridge; Lappe, F M 1982 *Diet for a Small Planet* 10th anniversary edition, Ballantine, New York; Odent, M 1984 *Entering the World* Marion Boyars, New York; Seymour, J and Giradet, H 1987 *Blueprint for a Green Planet* Dorling Kindersley, London/Prentice-Hall, New York.

ACKNOWLEDGMENTS

PICTURE AGENCIES/SOURCES

A Allsport UK Ltd.
AC Arcaid.
A-Z A-Z Botanical Collection.
B/C Blackstar/Colorific.
C Colorific Photo Library Ltd, London, New York.
C/D Colorific/DOT.
C/PG Colorific/Picture Group.
EW Elizabeth Whiting.
FSP Frank Spooner Pictures, London.
G/FSP Gamma/Frank Spooner Pictures, London.
H The Hutchison Library, London.
HHi Colorphoto Hans Hinz.
I Impact Photos.
JS Jessica Strang.
L/FSP Liaison/Frank Spooner Pictures.
ME Mary Evans Picture Library, London.
MG Magnum Photos Ltd, London, Paris, New York.
N Network Photographers, London.
OSF Oxford Scientific Films.
R Rex Features Ltd.
RHPL Robert Harding Picture Library Ltd, London.
R/S Rex/Sipa, London.
SRG Sally and Richard Greenhill, London.
T Topham Picture Library, Kent.
TIB The Image Bank, London.
V Viewfinder Colour Photo Library, Bristol.
Vi/C Visions/Colorific.
WP/C Wheeler Pictures/Colorific, London.
Z Zefa, London.
Z/S Zefa/Stockmarket.

PICTURE LIST

Page number in **bold** type. Photographer's initials in parenthesis.

Frontmatter
2 Family at lunch, Z. **6** Doorway into house, EW. **7** Skyscrapers, Z. **8** Yellow car (MMe) C. **9** Cat-shaped hedge, EW. **11** Man on fire escape (SW) TIB. **12-13** Log cabin (SSm) C. **14-15** Glassbottom boat (ECh) Z.

Part One At Home
16-17 Conservatory, Z/S.

1 The Home as Territory
18-19 Treehouse, L/FSP. **20** Barbeque, Germany, Z. **21** Canal scene (AI) TIB. **22** Family watching TV (RK) MG. **23** Couple moving in (TBi) TIB.

2 Needing a Home
24 Man building igloo (EB) FSP. **25** Girl reading at window (NK) Z. **26** Family on porch (PFu) MG. **27** Family Christmas (JH) C. **28** Home robbery (CMu). **28-29** San Francisco earthquake Oct 18, 1989 (MN) MG. **29** Sinkhole (RFe) L/FSP. **30** Homeless, Tent City (GPe) MG. **31** Berlin Wall camp (PPi) G/FSP.

3 Choosing a Home
32 Building new home (BPl) TIB. **33** Rotterdam (CHi) FSP. **35** House in Arizona (CTH) TIB. **36** Couple in empty room (JFr) TIB. **36** Couple decorating, Z. **37** Moving furniture in (JFr) TIB.

4 Managing Privacy
38 Hallway of plants. EW. **39** Man relaxing in apartment (AFo) TIB. **40** Family in bath (MMe) C. **40** Family relaxing (NDMcK) H. **41** George Bush and family, B/C. **42** Child reading (JAz) C. **43** Woman at desk (LJ) JS. **43** Watching TV in

greenhouse, V. **44** Mother and son at computer (MW) C. **45** Garden room, EW. **45** Deck overlooking beach, EW.

5 Personal Home Style
46 Mohammed Ali (MSe) C. **47** Susan Colyer, T. **48** Taste for fantasy, California (ESa) FSP. **48** House & cacti, Arizona (DHr) MG. **48** Wood cabin, Alaska, Z. **49** White cottage, Cornwall, England, Z. **49** Plywood flowers, Arizona, EW. **49** House and garden, Germany, EW. **50** House, Z. **51** Chequered bathroom (TH) MG. **51** In bath (JMcN) C. **52** Terrace houses, England (BL) N. **52** Child's bedroom (KJ) C. **54** Living room in cave, Sardinia (RK) MG. **55** Town housing, San Francisco, H.

6 Objects on Display
56 Walter & Leonore Annenberg (EF) C. **56** Curtis Sharpe Jnr with self portrait (TH) MG. **57** 1950s-dominated room, T. **58** Kaffe Fassett, T. **58** Woman with doll collection (ESa) L/FSP. **59** Plants in bathroom, EW.

7 Color in the Home
61 Blue bedroom, EW. **61** Red bedroom (MCr) EW. **62** Black room, EW. **62** White lounge, EW. **63** Round window (ESa) L/FSP. **64** Black/white room (JKy) TIB. **65** Indian decor, EW. **66** Green bedroom, EW. **67** Blue kitchen, EW. **68** Yellow living room (MDo) V. **69** Blue bathroom, EW. **69** Brown kitchen, EW. **68-69** Child's room, EW.

8 The Effects of Light
70 Natural light, TIB. **70-71** Lighting for evening's entertaining (SPl) EW. **73** Anglepoise lamp, EW. **73** Table lamp, R.

9 Touch, Sound and Smell
74 Family relaxing (BD) MG. **75** "Fallingwater," USA, R. **76** Girl climbing stairs, Z. **77** 10 details, various textures, Andromeda.

KEY TO PHOTOGRAPHERS

AFo A Foerster. **AI** Alberto Incrocci. **AL** Andy Lewin. **AMo** Alain Morvan. **ANo** Albert Normandin. **AR** Alon Reininger. **ASa** Anne Sarcten. **ASc** A Schumacher. **AVe** Alan Veldenger. **AVDV** Anne van der Vaeren. **AWe** Alex Webb. **BB** Bruno Barbey. **BD** Bruce Davidson. **BDe** Bernard Derenne. **BGi** Bernard Giani. **BGl** Burt Glinn. **BHe** B Hermann. **BL** Barry Lewis. **BMi** Dr Byron Mikellides. **BPl** Butch Powell. **BRy** Brian Rybolt. **CBe** Carl Berquist. **CBo** Cesarel Bonazza. **CCp** Cornell Capa. **CFi** Chuck Fishman. **CFe** Charles Feil. **CHi** Chip Hires. **CHo** Chris Honeywell. **CM** Costa Manos. **CMo** Colin Molyneux. **CMu** Chris Munday. **CPe** Christine Pemberton. **CS** Christopher Springmann. **CSP** Chris Steele-Perkins. **CTh** C Thomson. **DBe** David Beatty. **DBw** Derek Berwin. **DCo** Dann Coffey. **DD** Donald Dietz. **DHr** David Hurn. **DHu** Don Hunstein. **DK** Don Klumpp. **DMo** David Moore. **EB** Eric Bouvet. **ECh** Erwin Christian. **EF** Enrico Ferorelli. **EH** Erich Hartmann. **EL** Elyse

Lewin. **ELe** Elisa Leonelli. **EM** Eric Meola. **ESa** Eric Sander. **FF** Frank Fournier. **FS** F Scianna. **GdeL** G de Laubier. **GAR** Guido Alberto Rossi. **GCo** Guiliano Colliva. **GFa** G Faint. **GGl** Gerhard Gesell. **GK & VH** GK & Vikki Hart. **GM** Gideon Mendel. **GPe** Gilles Peress. **GW** George Wright. **GZ** George Zimbel. **HMa** Hiroyuki Matsumoto. **IB** Ian Berry. **IL** Ian Lloyd. **JAz** Jose Azel. **JBe** J Becker. **JBu** J Budge. **JCoo** J Coolidge. **JDe** Joseph Devenney. **JDn** John Downman. **JFr** Jay Freis. **JH** Jim Howard. **JHo** Jeremy Homer. **JJB** J J Bernier. **JKy** John P Kelly. **JLu** Jim Lukaski. **JLG** James L Grant. **JMcN** Joe McNally. **JPg** John Paling. **JR** Joseph Rodrigues. **JRa** Jake Rajs. **JSu** James Sugar. **JWe** Jeff Werner. **K** Kermani. **KC** Kay Chernush. **KG** Kurt Goebel. **KJ** Kenneth Jarecke. **KL** Katherine Lambert. **KW** Kafael Wullmann. **LB** Lee E Battaglia. **LD** Larry Dale Gordon. **LJ** Lynn Johnson. **LM** Laurent Maous. **LT** Liba Taylor. **MA** Mike Abrahams. **MAl** Murray Alcosser. **MCr** Michael Crockett. **MDo** Martin Dohrn. **MMe** Michael Melford. **MN** Michael Nichols.

MPo Mike Powell. **MS** Michael Salas. **MSe** Mark Sennet. **MRi** Marc Romanelli. **MW** Mark Wexler. **MWP** Margaret W Peterson. **MY** Mike Yamashita. **NDMcK** Nancy Durrell-McKenna. **NK** Neville Kenton. **P** Pillitz. **PCr** Philip Craven. **PF** Paul Freestone. **PFu** Paul Fusco. **PJG** Philip Jones Griffiths. **PMi** P Miller. **PPi** P Piel. **PWo** Philip Wolmuth. **Ro** Rosenfeld. **RB** René Burri. **RBl** Ron Blakeley. **RBr** Richard Bryant. **RD** Raymond Depardon. **RFe** Ric Ferro. **RHJ** R H Jarosch. **RI** Robert Isear. **RJa** Ronny Jaques. **RK** Richard Kalvar. **RPh** Robert Phillips. **RSt** Richard Steedman. **RWa** Robert Wallis. **St-Po** Street-Porter. **SD** Steve Dunwell. **SEP** Sarah Errington Porlock. **SKz** Shelly Katz. **SN** Steve Niedorf. **SPl** Spike Powell. **SSa** Sebastiao Salgado Jr. **SSh** Shepard Shebell. **SSm** Steve Smith. **SW** Stephen Wilkes. **SWo** Steve Wolt. **TBi** Tim Bieber. **TH** Thomas Hoepker. **TMcH** Tom McHugh. **UK** Urve Kuunik. **WB** Werner Bokelberg. **WBi** Walter Bibikow. **WLo** William Logan. **WM** Wayne Miller. **Y** Youlgarojoulos.

10 Design for Leisure
78 Green pool, EW. 79 Aerial view, California (CCp) MG. 79 Indoor pool, Hearst Castle, California (UK) C. 80 Attic, G/FSP. 80 Bedroom, EW. 80 Kitchen, EW. 82 Family room (CFi) C. 83 Living room (EL) TIB.

11 Eating and Entertaining
84-85 Jane Asher, T. 85 Eating outdoors (RHJ) Z. 86 Couple in kitchen (SD) TIB. 86-87 Food and flowers, EW. 87 Family eating, H. 88 Couple at barbecue (MS) TIB. 89 Circular table (EB) FSP.

12 Cars
90 Garage doors, EW. 90-91 Cruising, Las Vegas (MN) MG. 92 Executive travel (GK & VH) TIB. 93 New York City (HMa) C. 93 Lombard Street, San Francisco (FS) MG. 94 Teenagers in car (RWa) C. 95 Convertible car (ASc) TIB. 96 License plate, California (GFa) TIB. 96 Four-wheel drive (SKz) B/C. 96-97 Vintage cars (MN) MG. 97 Cadillac fins, 1959 (MN) MG. 97 Chevy van (RB) MG.

13 The Pets People Choose
98 Man and lizards on bicycle (JBu) L/FSP. 98 Count Basie & boxer (CFi) C. 99 Squirrel on picture (JPg) OSF. 99 Tiger in car (CBe) FSP. 100 Boy and rabbit, V. 100-101 Dog wash (DK) TIB. 102 Hounds (CM) MG. 103 Couple with dog (CFi) C. 103 Lady with pekinese (WM) MG. 103 Four Afghans (K) FSP. 104 Man with cat (K) FSP. 105 Cat on shoulders (JCoo) TIB. 105 Siamese cats (EH) MG. 106 Shar Pei (WM) MG. 106 Paris dog logo (BL) N. 106 Walking dogs (KW) FSP. 107 Cat and bell, SRG.

14 Garden Effects
108 Lawn & hedges, EW. 108 Man watering garden (Ro) Z. 108 Garden with pond. EW. 108 Digging compost, EW. 109 Garden path, EW. 109 Jacuzzi (RBi) C. 110 Vegetable garden (GW). 111 Maze, Z. 111 Pond, EW. 113 Man working in garden, Z. 114 Children playing, EW. 115 Window box, EW. 115 Conservatory, EW. 116 Bonsai, A-Z. 116 Japanese garden (CMu). 117 Moorish courtyard, Z.

15 Living Together
118 Graduate students, California (CS) C. 119 Mailboxes, R/S.

16 The Changing Home
122 Modern house (JJB) FSP. 123 Family in kitchen (SSh) C. 124 Man on home computer (GK & VH) TIB. 124 Mother and daughter (WB) TIB. 125 Boy in bedroom, JS. 125 Submarine crew, FSP. 126 Elderly couple at table (JH) C. 127 Woman cleaning gutter (DD) C. 127 Woman in garden, N. 128 Solar home (TMcH) SPL. 128 High-technology bathroom (LM) FSP. 128 Underground house, T. 129 Solar house (RPh) TIB.

Part Two The Wider Environment
130-131 Shipdeck, FSP.

17 A Sense of Place
132-133 Fireworks (EM) C. 133 Alsace, France (RJa) C. 134 Penthouse, New York (JRa) TIB. 136 Table football (AMo) FSP. 137 Marathon, New York (EF) C. 138 Ghetto, Philadelphia (P) N.

138 Painted works of art, France (BDe) G/FSP. 138-139 Mural, West Harlem (JR) C.

18 Neighborhoods
140 Backgardens, T. 140-141 Children crossing road, Canada (GZ) C. 141 City at night (BHe) C. 142 Martha's vineyard, Cape Cod, USA (BD) MG. 142 Street, France (CSP) MG. 143 Street scene, Venice (BB) MG. 144 Market scene, England (MA) N. 145 Planners, Z/S. 146-147 Silicon valley (LB) C. 146 Boy with gun, L/FSP. 147 Houses on shore (WBi) TIB.

19 Out in the City
148 Hotel, Beijing, China (SN) TIB. 148-149 Cinema (CBo) R. 149 Market place and church steeple (PMi) TIB. 149 Fire alarm box, Paris, R. 149 Café sign, Paris (ASa) R/S. 150 Sculpture, New York City (AWe) MG. 150-151 Sun City, Arizona (AR) C. 152 Croissant, coins and subway ticket (CHo). 153 View from Eiffel Tower, Paris, R.

20 Coping with Urban Life
154-155 5th Avenue at night (MRi) TIB. 155 Girl and cello, H. 155 Girl on car phone (GAR) TIB. 156 Policeman, Japan (IB) MG. 157 Street accident (RD) MG. 158 Public benches (AWe) MG. 158 Women in subway (BD) MG. 159 Crowd (AL) B/C. 160 Commuter Ferry, Boston (MMe) C. 161 Buildings, Manhattan (PWo) H.

21 Scenes of Crime
163 Aerial view, California (EH) MG. 164 Family pet, Johannesburg (GM) MG. 165 Terrace houses, Germany (JBe) Z. 166 High-rise blocks, Z. 166 Woman going up stairs (AVe) WP/C. 167 Houses (BGl) MG. 168 Graffiti, Paris subway (Y) FSP. 168 Bag snatcher, R/S. 169 Guardian Angels (JLu) Vi/C.

22 Country Living
170-171 Farm, Montana, USA, Z. 170 House, Vermont, USA (GCo) TIB. 171 Thatched cottages, Devon, England, Z. 172 Boy with pigs, SRG. 173 Ice hockey (DHu) C. 174 Post Office, Outer Hebrides (CPe) H. 175 Town of Rolla (JLG). 176 Pollution, A-Z. 177 Basket maker (AVDV) TIB. 179 Woman on tractor, North Dakota, USA (PJG) MG.

23 Color Outside the Home
180 Red Sculpture (BMi). 181 Multicolored buildings (BMi). 182 German Houses (BMi). 183 Downtown Honolulu (PFu) MG. 183 Elf building, Paris, FSP. 183 Cobblestones and manhole (ANo) TIB. 184 Greek Temple (BMi). 185 House, New Mexico (BMi). 185 Hoover building, England (RBr) Ac. 186 La Défense, Paris, N. 186 Oil wells, California (JH) MG. 186 Pacific Design Center, Los Angeles (ELe) MG. 186 Klinikon hospital, Aachen, Germany (BMi). 187 Graffitti (BMi). 188 Subway, Sweden (BMi). 188 Museum, Germany (BMi). 189 Bank reception desk, Zürich (EH) MG.

24 The Workplace
190 Man at desk (JFr) TIB. 191 Office block at night, London, England, Z. 192 Cubicle offices (CFe) C. 192-193 Foreign exchange, Geneva (EH) MG. 194 Computer by window (SW) TIB.

195 Computer room, Z. 195 Office with desk lamps (KC) TIB. 196-197 Man and dinosaur (TH) MG. 197 Texan billionairess (G de L) FSP. 198 Centraal Beheer, Insurance Company, Apeldoorn, The Netherlands, Foto Starke by kind permission. 199 Houghton Library, Cambridge, Massachusetts (SD) TIB. 200 Soviet Industrial Complex, Ukraine (SSa) MG. 200-201 Windmill Hill Industrial Park, England (PCr) RHPL.

25 Places for Learning
202 Baby crawling on pier (JDe) TIB. 203 Computer class (SD) TIB. 203 School, Alma, Wisconsin, c. 1897 (GGi) State Historical Society of Wisconsin. 204 Kindergarten class, USA (JDn) H. 206 Playtime (JDn) H. 207 School bus (BL) N. 207 Supervision during study time, ME. 208 School, Sudan (SEP) H. 209 Le Louvre, Paris, R/S. 209 Boy feeding goat, SRG.

26 Going Shopping
211 Open market, France (TLG) C. 210-211 Supermarket, California (BL) N. 212 Shopping arcade, Sydney, Australia (RBi) C. 213 Covered market, Oxford, England (PF) 214 Aerial view, Edmonton, Canada (JWe) C/PG. 215 Shopping center, Canada (EF) C/D. 216-217 Bloomingdales cosmetics counter, USA (JMcN) C. 216 Macy's, New York (MAl) TIB.

27 Eating Out
218 Snack lunch, Moscow (LT) H. 218-219 Gourmet restaurant, New York, C. 220-221 Japanese restaurant, Tianjin, China (LD) TIB. 220 Refreshment time, Turkey (DBe) TIB. 221 Serving ice-cream, Singapore (IL) H. 222 Family in booth (St-Po) FSP. 222 Gorky café (ELe) C. 223 Open air restaurant, Los Angeles (FF) C. 223 Couple dining at "Delmonico's" (RPh) TIB. 224 Family in hamburger restaurant (CFe) TIB. 224-225 Young couple in café (JHo) H. 225 Business lunch (KL) C.

28 Vacationing
226 Alaska, USA (RSt) Z. 227 Portofino, Italy (EF) C/D. 227 Looking at sculpture (MWP) TIB. 228 Great wall, China, Z. 229 Canyon, Utah (DCo) TIB. 230 Coastline, Norfolk, England (CMu). 230 Indonesia, Z. 231 Family and horses, Dartmoor, England (CMo) TIB. 232 Market, Crete (BRy) I. 233 Bus travel, Pakistan, Z. 234 Street, Germany (Ro) Z. 235 Tourists with Qinghai herdsmen, Z.

29 Places for Recreation
236 Getty Museum, Z/S. 237 "Tour de France" (JMcN) C. 238 Olympic Stadium, Munich (KG) Z. 238 Opera House, Milan (FS) MG. 239 Shopping mall, Hong Kong, SRG. 240 Desert biking (MPo) A. 240 Baltimore Harbour (JH) C. 241 Climbing wall (BGi) A. 241 Looking at guide map, Blenheim Palace, England (CMo) TIB. 242 Central Park (DMo) C. 243 Family by lake (WLo) TIB.

30 A Green Environment?
244 Man by lake (SWo) C. 244 Litter on beach (DHu) C. 245 Cars on freeway (MN) MG. 246-247 Boy drinking (MY) C.

253

INDEX

Bold numbers indicate fuller information. Where information continues over more than one page, the number of the beginning page only is given.

accidents 157
adolescents
  in the country 173
  and home 25
  involved in crime 169
  and shopping malls 239
aggression, and heat in cities 157
"agribusinessmen" 178
agriculture, and environmental
  issues 245
  see also farming
air pollution
  in cities 156
  in the country 176
airconditioning 194, 195
animal behavior therapists 107
animals
  domestic **98**
  territorial behavior 20
architecture
  advantages of 198
  exploitation of associations 136
  and gender 122
  and materials 77
  "motorcentric" 91
  residential and character of
    neighborhood 142
  and use of color 180, 183
  of the workplace 201
associations
  with place 133, 135
  of possessions 56, 58

bathrooms, and personality 51
birds, cage 100
Bonsai gardening 116
boundaries
  and gardens 114
  social and physical of
    neighborhoods 142
buildings
  harmful materials in 194
  use of color on 180
burglary
  defense against 164
  and dogs as deterrents 102
  psychological effects 28
business entertaining 224

car cults 93
  and car accessories 96
carbon dioxide 246
carbon monoxide 194
cars **90**
  company 92
  number of privately owned 90
  and pollution 245
  reveal personality 92
  and sex 94
  as territory 90
cats
  pedigree 105
  as pets 98, 104
CFCs 245
change of scene 137
child-centered education 203

children
  color preferences 68
  in a community 121
  early learning environments 202
  and gardens 114
  growing up in the country 172
  home and development 25
  ideas on school design 207
  and pets 100
  tactile sensations 76
  and vacations 231
Christmas, at home 27
chroma of color 60
cities
  anonymity of life in 21, 148, 159
  apathy in 158, 169
  esthetics 160
  friendly 156
  growth of 146
  pets in 105
  planning for crime prevention 168
  pollution in 156
  stress in 158
city
  mental maps of the 150
  opinions on the 154
  personality 155
  seeing it as a tourist does 152
  visual cues in the **148**
clustering 143
"Co-housing" schemes 118, 120
"Cocktail party phenomenon" 192
collectors 58
color
  camouflage or exhibitionism 186
  for children 68
  choosing with care 183
  constancy 72
  and culture 184
  in different lights 60, 70
  different shades 68
  effect on other colors 65
  and emotional needs 181
  features of 60
  in the home 58, **60**, 62
  and judgment of weight 62
  and mood 66, 110
  outside the home **180**
  and personality 66
  preferences 67
  preferences of office workers 189
  private 61
  reflected 183
  in schools 206
  and taste 66
  traditional associations 184
  used to mark out territory 21
color schemes 62, 64, 67
  local 185
color wheel 60
colorlessness 180
colors
  differences between 61
comfort, and the home 22
commitment, and neighborhood
  character 147
communal living **118**
communication, network of 141
community
  designing a 120
  elderly people in a 121
  raising children in a 121

sense of 144
  see also neighborhood
community education 209
community health services, rural 175
community life, in rural areas **172**
commuting 171
  avoiding problems of 125
computers, personal 22, 193
Confucianism 116
conservation, public awareness of 240
consumers
  behavior and neighborhoods 147
  control of style 244
  understanding 210
consumption, conspicuous forms
  of 128
control
  and the home **18**, 24
  sense of in the city 160
  and stress level of environment 159
cooking
  interest in 123
  for other people 86
  outdoors 88
corporate hierarchy, and car type 92
country living **170**
  attitudes to 177
creativity, and your garden 108, 112
crime
  new opportunities for 162
  and personal territory 166
  planning against 167
  scenes of 162
  settings that breed 168
  victims of 162
crime prevention 163
crowding 154
  patterns of 242
cuisines, immigrant 220
cult objects 57, 93
cultural groups 143
culture
  color and 184
  and possessions 56
  and vacations 227, 233
cultures
  "contact" 74
  sensitivity to different 233

dating, and eating out 223
decor
  in the home 46, 60
  in restaurants 222
decoration
  color in 180
  wall 25, 187
  see also interior decoration
department stores, as magnets 212
"deschoolers" 208
design 57
  for leisure **78**
desk arrangement 199
developed countries, lifestyle in 143
diets 87
dining out, *see* eating out
display of objects **56**
dogs
  breeding 102
  choosing a pet 102
  as pets 98, 100
  problems of ownership 106

Douglas, M
  The World of Goods 210
drinking habits 224
drive-ins 94
drug addiction 169

eating
  outdoors 85
  place for 84
  and role playing 218
eating habits **84**
  culture-bound 88
  healthy 87
eating out **218**
  ethnic 220
  and socializing for young
    children 218, 224
ecological awareness 59
  and gardening 110
  and the workplace 201
ecological balance 246
education
  approaches to 203
  community 209
  environment for 202
  pre-school 203
  value put on 208
elderly people
  in a community 121
  numbers of 126
  and pets 104
elderly relations, coping at home
  with 127
electrical irritants 194
electronic media, and the home 22
"electronic village hall" 176
emotional needs, and color 182
employment, rural 176
entertaining
  and eating habits **84**
  reasons for 223
environment **244**
environmental issues
  and house design 128
  and tourism 234
Environmental Protection Agency 156
eye strain, and visual display
  units 193

façades 47, 48, 201
factories, changes in 200
families
  and farming 178
  privacy rules 40
  and television rules 82
  and vacations 231
family
  extended system 119
  meals 84
  nuclear 118
  relations inside and out 41
farming **178**
  alternative methods 178
  family 178
  number of people in 171
  organic 178
  rare-breeds 178
  women in 178
father, relationship with child 40
floorscapes 202, 204
flowers
  from the East 117

growing wild 111
and the table 86
use of 112
food
and fashion 87
foreign 220
food etiquette 88
food smells, attitudes to 75
freedom
and car 94
and privacy 39
friendship, in the city 159
furniture
arrangement in the workplace 199
in restaurants 222
in schools 206

garages 90
garden societies 115
gardening **108**
Bonsai 116
personality types 108
as therapy 112
gardens
ecological 111
formal 111
Moorish 117
Oriental 116
secret 113
for socializing 114
sounds and scents 112
as source of spiritual
satisfaction 112
use of 81, 114
gender, and architecture 122
gifts
ideal 59
souvenir 235
global village 146
Goffman, E
Behavior in Public Places 158
Goodman, P 208
government policies, on the
environment 244
graffiti 138, 169, 186
green areas, in the city 151
"Green lung" idea 243
"greenhouse effect" 244
group decision-making 120
group identity, and home style 54
group profiles, based on lifestyle 147
group vacations 230, 232

Halprin, L 151
heating, in the home 82
herbs, use of 112
heritage industry 241
"holiday syndrome" 228
holidays, *see* vacations
Holmes, O W
on complexity 154
Holt, J 208
home
attitudes to 26
changes in the functions of **122**
choosing a **32**
color in the **60**
definition of 24
disruption in the 28
importance of 24
as indicator of personality 56
leisure time at 78, 83

moving into a new 23, 32
new technology in the 122, 129
office at 124
privacy in the 38
psychological benefits of **24**
sensual stimuli and 75
social value of 31
as territory **18**
uniqueness 21
home owners, second 171
home style, personal **46**, 50, 52, 54
homelessness 118
coping with 31
trauma of 29
urban 30
homeliness 36
homes
safer 165
vulnerable to crime 163
horticultural therapy 112
house
building a new 32
choosing a 32, 36
moving, *see* moving house
smell 74
house names 52
house style
exterior 34
personalized interiors 35
housebreaking, psychological
effects 28
houseplants 59
houses
environmentally friendly
changes 128
grouping of 35
housing
commodification of 37
and increase in numbers of the
elderly 126
private schemes 33
public 33
housing community
privacy in 118
setting up a 121
hue 60
Humphrey, N
evolution of color vision 180
hygiene, and pets 107

identity
and cars 93
and home 24
and personal home style 46
and place 139
sense of and color 182
Illich, I 208
image, creating an 57
insulation, earth 128
intentions, signaling 43
interior decoration 46
and color 60
and lighting 70
redecoration 50
seasonal 54
intimacy 39
Isherwood, B
The World of Goods 210
isolation
in the countryside 173
urban 159

Japan
gardens 116
privacy in 44
job enrichment, and new
technology 193

kitchen, changes in the use of the 123

land, working the,
see farming
landmarks 150
landscape architecture 242
learning
early **202**
networks 208
places for 202
Legionnaire's Disease 196
leisure
access to facilities 173
design for **78**
inventory 81
time at home 83
leisure activities
age and 237
choosing 236
"compensation theory" 241
and the environment 240
mobility and 237
money and 237
leisure developments 241
leisure environments **236**
less developed societies, tactile
sensations in 77
light
effect of on color 183
effects of **70**
lighting
in different rooms 64, 82
domestic **70**
for domestic work 72
effective home 71
office 194
in restaurants 222
types of 72, 195
limbic system 84
living, standard of 244
living together **118**
localities 147
location, in house selection 34
loneliness 39
in cities 159

markets, covered 213
Maslow, A H
realization of potential steps 228
meals
in restaurants **218**
sharing 120
mealtimes 43, 89
mental disorder, and
homelessness 30
mental maps 134
of the city 150
methane 246
mood
and color 66, 110
and gardening 110
mother, privacy from children 41
motivational research 210
moving house 23, **32**
"choice" moves 32
"forced" moves 32

see also relocation
frequency of 37
and growing old 127
"Multiple Use – Sustained Yield Act"
(1960) 243
murals 187
music, in restaurants 222

"Natural Environment Policy Act"
(1969) 243
natural resources, use of 240
nature
contact with 243, 244, 246
and leisure activities 242
needs, and vacations 228
neighborhoods 138, **140**
ambience 142
children's 141
of like minds 143
as mental constructs 147
planning 138, 144
sense of belonging 140, 158
size of 141
successful 144
value of 146
vulnerability to crime 162
neighbors
and boundary disputes 115
increasing social contact with 123
neo-cortex 180
nitrous oxide 246
noise
and concentration 194
and the open-plan office 192
responding to 75
see also sound
and a sense of control 160, 193
noise pollution, in cities 156
nuclear energy 245

objects on display **56**
offenders, young 169
office design 190
offices
location and status 196
open-plan 190
"omiyage" 235
openness 38, 43
optical illusions, with color 62
Oriental gardens 116
ornaments, importance of 58
overheating, of the earth,
see "greenhouse effect"
ozone layer, depletion of 244

Packard, V
The Hidden Persuaders 210
paleo-cortex 180
parenting styles, and children's
privacy needs 42
parks 242
Parkway Education Program,
Philadelphia 208
PCBs 245
personality
and possessions 56
Type A 155
Type B 155
and your car 92
pets
choice of **98**
and the environment 107

future trends in ownership 107
problems of keeping 104
and psychological comfort 100
resemblances to 102
urban planning for 105
pheromones 74
phototropism 152
pictures
importance of 58
preferences 56
place
defined by activities 136
with distinctive character 142
for eating 84
hierarchies of 134
preferences 136
rules of a 137
scale of 134
sense of **132**, 152
value of a 139, 208
your ideal 132
places
for learning **202**
for recreation **236**
planning, urban 151, 161
playground design 206
pollution 244
by chemicals 245
in cities 156
from cars 245
and leisure activities 240
in offices 194
population, "graying" of the 126
possessions 56
pregnancy, and visual display
units 193
primary schools, open-plan 205
privacy 38
children's need for 42
in the city 158
degree of 39
in the family 38
and gardens 113
in a housing community 118
regulation equation 38
societies without 41
versus open-plan offices 190
versus security 167
property
crime and 162
to suit your lifestyle 114
protection, and the home 22
psychological withdrawal 44

quality of life 244
in cities 161

rainforests, destruction of 246
recreation
places for **236**
urban 242
red, significance of 180
redundancy, and new technology 193
Reimer, E 208
relocation, voluntary and
involuntary 31
respiratory infections, and
airconditioning 196
"responsive environments" 161
restaurants
decor in 222
eating in **218**

fast-food 221
lighting in 222
retirement community 126
revolutions
agricultural 20
industrial 20
information 20
ritual, and place 137
"role-distancing" 232
rooms, use of 81
rural development schemes 176
rural life, *see* country living

safety, standard color system 186
salesdogs 103
saturation (chroma) of color 60
scents, in the garden 112
school buildings
design 206
psychological effects of 206
"School Without Walls" 208
schools
alternatives to 208
open-plan design 205
optimum size of 204
rural 174, 177
"storefront" 208
seating, in the classroom 204
security
and the home 22, 24, 28, 165
outdoor 167
privacy of 167
self-discovery, and vacations 227
self-expression
and cars 90, 92
and the home 22
and your garden 108
self-presentation, in cities 159
sensory memory 133
sensory overload 158
sensual stimuli
and the home **74**
and your garden 110
service industries 200
services, saving rural public 174
sex
cars and 94
privacy for 44
sexuality, eating and 84
shared activities, in the home 122
sharing resources, Danish-style 120
shoplifting 162
shopping
consumer psychology 216
impersonal styles 212
local 144, 211
and personal contact 211, 213
practices **210**
self-service 210
self-service and crime 162
supermarket 211
on vacation 232
shopping centers 210
and crime 166, 214
effect on neighborhoods 214
entertainment value 215, 239
Sick Building Syndrome 194
signals, outward and inner
meanings 43, 52
smell, sense of **74**
Smith, A 233
smog 156

sociability 39
social change, and home design 123
social conventions, on holiday 234
social ritual, eating and
entertaining 85
social status
and home style 50
and possessions 56
and your garden 108
social support networks 119
solitude 38, 119
sound **74**
sounds
acceptable and unacceptable 75
in the garden 112
souvenirs 235
space
personal 38, 45
personalizing your 197
physical and psychological 170
shared and distance 196
use of personal in offices 190, 197
use within the home 45, 78
speed, appeal of 95
sports 238
passive participation 238
stores, displays and atmosphere 216
stress
and confined spaces 125
diseases related to 155
levels 154, 244
and noise 157
urban 154, 158
on vacation 228
stressors 154
symbols
cars as 93
gardens as 116
homes as 46, 56
of neighborhood 144

table
flowers on the 86
sitting at 88
tactual kinesthetic patterns 151
technology
advantages and disadvantages
of new 193
new in the home 59, 122, 129
"tele-cottage" 176
telefax machines 23
telephone answering machines 23
television 23
siting of set 82
"teleworking" 124
temperature
and color 62
ideal working 196
territorial behavior 18, 44
aggression on the road 94
territory
car as extension of 90
color to define 182
garden as 115
home as **18**
office as 190
personal and crime 166
primary and secondary 20
and sensual stimuli 74
textures 77
theft, incidence of 162
see also burglary

Third World countries
neighborhoods in 146
vacations in 233
Thring, E
classroom as "Almighty wall" 205
togetherness 38, 231
Tolstoy, L 208
touch **74**, 151
and memory 77
tourism, and the environment 234
transport
local public on vacation 233
public 174
travelers
"new-wave" 228
tales 229

United Nations, "Experiential
starvation" study 208
urban design 151
urban landscape, primary
elements 150
urban life, coping with **154**
see also cities
urban planning 151, 161
urban recreation 242
urbanities 147

vacations **226**
active 226
activities on 227
behavior on 233
choosing 230
company on 231
passive 227
personality types and 226
stress factor 228
victims of crime 162
vigilantes 169
visual cues, in the city 148
visual display units, health
hazards 193

waiting at table 219
waste
radioactive 246
recycling of 244
Watson, J
behaviorism 216
weekend retreats 171
wildlife, and leisure activities 240
women
position in society and
architecture 122
work in the country 176, 178
workplace **190**
color in the 188
the evolving 200
home as 124
productivity or comfort 200
workspace, personalization of 205
"workstations," domestic 125

Zen Buddhism 116